Social Networks in Youth and Adolescence

2nd edition

This thoroughly revised new edition looks at the nature of social networks, their changing configurations, and the forces of influence they unleash in shaping the life experiences of young people between the ages of 12 and 25 years.

The author draws on both social and psychological research to apply network thinking to the social relations of youth across the domains of school, work and society. Network thinking examines the pattern and nature of social ties, and analyses how networks channel information, influence and support with effects on a wide range of life experiences. The book comprises eleven chapters, which contain discussion on key topics, such as youth transitions, network analysis, friendship, romantic ties, peer victimization, antisocial behaviour, youth risk-taking, school motivation, career influence, youth citizenship, and community organizations for young people. Chapters contain discussions of practical ways in which schools can provide support, and suggestions for youth organizations on how to assist young people to become effective citizens.

John Cotterell has worked with young people for most of his adult life, as a high school teacher, youth worker, and university teacher and researcher. He has published many journal articles and book chapters in the fields of adolescence, child development, youth leisure, education, psychology, counselling, and environmental psychology.

Adolescence and Society

Series editor: John C. Coleman

The Trust for the Study of Adolescence

The general aim of the series is to make accessible to a wide readership the growing evidence relating to adolescent development. Much of this material is published in relatively inaccessible professional journals, and the goals of the books in this series will be to summarize, review and place in context current work in the field so as to interest and engage both an undergraduate and a professional audience.

The intention of the authors is to raise the profile of adolescent studies among professionals and in institutions of higher education. By publishing relatively short, readable books on interesting topics to do with youth and society, the series will make people more aware of the relevance of the subject of adolescence to a wide range of social concerns.

The books will not put forward any one theoretical viewpoint. The authors will outline the most prominent theories in the field and will include a balanced and critical assessment of each of these. Whilst some of the books may have a clinical or applied slant, the majority will concentrate on normal development.

The readership will rest primarily in two major areas: the undergraduate market, particularly in the fields of psychology, sociology and education; and the professional training market, with particular emphasis on social work, clinical and educational psychology, counselling, youth work, nursing and teacher training.

Also available in this series:

Adolescent Health
Patrick C.L. Heaven

The Adolescent in the Family
Patricia Noller and Victor Callan

Young People's Understanding of Society
Adrian Furnham and Barrie Stacey

Growing up with Unemployment
Anthony H. Winefield, Marika Tiggermann, Helen R. Winefield and Robert D. Goldney

Young People's Leisure and Lifestyles
Leo B. Hendry, Janey Shucksmith, John G. Love and Anthony Glendinning

Sexuality in Adolescence
Susan Moore and Doreen Rosenthal

Adolescent Gambling
Mark Griffiths

Youth, AIDS and Sexually Transmitted Diseases
Susan Moore, Doreen Rosenthal and Anne Mitchell

Fathers and Adolescents
Shmuel Shulman and Inge Seiffge Krenke

Adolescent Coping
Erica Frydenberg

Young People's Involvement in Sport
Edited by John Kremer, Karen Trew and Shaun Ogle

The Nature of Adolescence (3rd edition)
John C. Coleman and Leo B. Hendry

Social Networks and Social Influences in Adolescence
John Cotterell

Identity in Adolescence (3rd edition)
Jane Kroger

Social Networks in Youth and Adolescence

2nd edition

John Cotterell

Routledge
Taylor & Francis Group

LONDON AND NEW YORK

First published 2007 by Routledge
27 Church Road, Hove, East Sussex BN3 2FA
Simultaneously published in the USA and Canada
by Routledge
270 Madison Avenue, New York NY 10016

Routledge is an imprint of the Taylor & Francis Group, an Informa business

© 2007 Routledge

Typeset in Times by Regent Typesetting, London
Printed and bound in Great Britain by MPG Books Ltd, Bodmin, Cornwall
Paperback cover design by Hybert Design

This publication has been produced with paper manufactured to strict
environmental standards and with pulp derived from sustainable forests.

British Library Cataloguing in Publication Data
A catalogue record for this book is available from the British Library

Library of Congress Cataloging-in-Publication Data
Cotterell, John, 1941-
    Social networks in youth and adolescence / John Cotterell. -- 2nd ed.
      p. cm.
    Rev. ed. of: Social networks and social influences in adolescence.
London ; New York : Routledge, 1996.
    Includes bibliographical references and index.
    ISBN-13: 978-0-415-35949-8 (hardback)
    ISBN-10: 0-415-35949-X (hardback)
    ISBN-13: 978-0-415-35950-4 (soft cover)
    ISBN-10: 0-415-35950-3 (soft cover)
    1. Teenagers--Social networks. 2. Group identity. 3. Peer pressure.
4. Friendship in adolescence. 5. Adolescent psychology. I. Cotterell,
John, 1941- Social networks and social influences in adolescence. II.
Title.
    HQ796.C8218 2007
    305.235--dc22
                                    2006039170

ISBN 978-0-415-35949-8 (hbk)
ISBN 978-0-415-35950-4 (pbk)

Contents

Figures

Boxes and tables

Boxes

Table

Preface

This book is written for researchers and practitioners in education, health, and youth work. The title captures the subject matter of interest between two bookends: social networks on the one hand, and young people's behaviour on the other. Networks occupy greater prominence in the current edition than previously, in order to demonstrate the utility of network thinking for the topics discussed in the following chapters. The expansion of network research in many scientific fields, from engineering to geography and national security, is a reminder of the widespread appeal of network concepts to areas of human activity. The time is ripe for incorporation of these recent advances into the study of youth relationships and youth experiences in education, work and leisure.

The population of interest in this new edition is young people 12 to 25 years of age, a period of life marked by extensive changes in crucial components of the lifecourse, as lifestyle choices are made and qualifications are acquired that together expand or constrain the individual's social opportunities. My decision to focus on the years from young adolescence to young adulthood is deliberate. It acknowledges that the time period for young people to attain adulthood in modern society extends well into the third decade. My experience of seeing my own children deal with the issues of young adulthood has also increased my awareness of the continuing transition.

The contents of this edition are markedly different from the previous edition. They reflect my attempt to explore issues that have always been important to youth, as well as some that have gained importance in the past decade. There are discussions of romantic relationships, volunteerism, interethnic conflict, school shootings, anger and assault. At other times, familiar topics (like school motivation and youth reliance on adults) have been studied from a fresh perspective, and young people's lifepaths beyond high school are explored.

The book seeks to bridge the divide between sociological and psychological research on young people, while providing a scholarly treatment of topics that are important to all. My approach is deliberately eclectic, and readers will find citations of research from health, psychology, education, sociology, counselling, social work, and management. The landscape traversed in this book is admittedly a wide one, but hopefully the writing is not as dry as the continent in which the author resides. Social networks supply a broad frame to the topics, within which social and psychological processes are more closely examined. The trails followed are my selections, and it is my hope that although the journey is a demanding one, it will prove interesting, without leaving the reader exhausted. Sometimes the stories of young people I have taught over the years or worked with in youth work or in academic life have intruded into the discussions. They are there as a reminder that the issues in these pages directly affect the lives of real people, and that they are ultimately my justification for writing. The success of this book will be judged by its ability to encourage the reader first to reflect on the issues it explores, and second to consult it as a guide to research and practice. Whatever faults and shortcomings remain in content or style, are mine.

John L. Cotterell
Brisbane, September 2006

Acknowledgements

I gratefully acknowledge the kind permission of the following publishers for the right to reproduce figures that were published in various journal publications.

Thanks to Springer Science and Business Media for permission to use Figure 1 which appears on page 200 of an article by M. Weeks *et al.*, 'Social networks of drug users in high-risk sites: finding the connections', in *AIDS and Behaviour*, 6, 2002, pp. 193–206. Thanks to Elsevier Ltd for permission to use Figure 2 (Theatre network) from an article titled 'The ties that bind: the effect of clustering on dyadic relationships', by L. L. Salzinger in *Social Networks, 4*, 1982, pp. 117–145, and Figure 8 ('Strong component of the Gagnon-MacRea prison network') on p. 277 of an article titled 'Peer influence groups: Dense clusters in large networks', by James Moody, in *Social Networks, 23*, 2001, pp. 261–283. Also thanks for permission to use Figure 3 on p. 1865 of the article, 'Girls, pecking order, and smoking', by L. Mitchell and A. Amos, in *Social Science and Medicine, 44*, 1997, pp. 1861–1897.

Thanks also to the publishers Taylor & Francis Ltd, for permission to use Figures 1 and 2, from an article by G. Abel *et al.*, 'Peers, networks or relationships: strategies for understanding social dynamics as determinants of smoking behaviour', in *Drugs, Education, Prevention and Policy, 9*(4), 2002, pp. 325–338.

I would also like to acknowledge permission to quote from the following text sources:

W. W. Norton & Company, Inc., for permission to quote from *Nexus – Small Worlds and the Groundbreaking Science of Networks*, by M. Buchanan, published in 2002; Blackwell Publishing for permission to quote an extract from 'The strength of weak ties: a network theory revisited', by Mark Granovetter (which was published in *Sociological Theory, 1*, 1983, pp. 201–233); Elsevier Science Publishers, for permission to quote extracts from 'The future of knowledge: increasing prosperity' (2003) by

Verna Allee; and the estates of Michael Flanders and Donald Swann for permission to quote from 'Just Friends' by Michael Flanders and Donald Swann, 1963.

Thanks are also due to the editorial team at Routledge/Psychology Press: Lucy Kennedy, Tara Stebnicky, Imogen Burch, Sarah Pearsall, Becci Waldron and Ruben Hale, and my series editor John Coleman, for their calm counsel and prompt responses to my queries, and helpful direction as the book took shape. Thanks also to the manuscript reviewers, especially Nick Emler and Rainer Silbereisen. There are also many friends to thank, especially Brian Carss, Inge Bø, Jill and Jeff Shepherd, Glyn Davies and Keith Wallace. Thanks to my children, Liz, Dave and Andrew, whose lives and lifepaths have prodded me to think about the issues in this book, and who continue to remain amused as I try to understand them. Above all is the patient longsuffering of my wife Sue, who manages to listen to my gripes as an author while not reading much of my work (a longstanding joke between us).

Introduction and overview

One of the simplest yet most profound truths about human beings is that people are connected to others by a variety of social ties. We live in a networked society. The ties bind us together in many-stranded links that extend out through those known to us to others known only indirectly, in a giant interlocking pattern. The networked nature of our social relations is a source of wonderment: in chance encounters we find that we are linked to an apparent stranger through a shared social contact, and exclaim, 'What a small world!' Communications technology continues to shrink the world further, to the extent that it was claimed that by July 2004 over one billion offices and households had become connected to the internet. The interlinked nature of society cannot be denied. As the extent of the links is recognized and the benefits celebrated, we are also aware of the dangers, as the SARS outbreaks of 2003 and the menace of bird flu in 2006 make clear.

This book employs network thinking to understand the social experiences of young people and the influences on their behaviour as they individually journey on the lifecourse from early adolescence to young adulthood. Network thinking provides a fresh way of investigating and interpreting social phenomena, and it offers richer insights to the researcher and practitioner than the peer group framework that has dominated youth research and writing for many decades. Network thinking is relational; it focuses on the links among units (people, objects, nations) rather than on the specific properties of the units themselves. It involves the adoption of new tools of analysis, but it is more than a method: it provides a way of looking at social structures that extends beyond the immediate group in the local setting to incorporate larger patterns of relationships.

Networks are not a new idea. Network concepts were applied by the Romans and have been employed by scientists for at least several generations, in fields as diverse as electronics, mathematics, geography and sociology. In the social sciences the interconnected nature of society was discussed in the writings of Georg Simmel (Simmel, 1908/1955) and the linked nature of personal relationships was graphed by Moreno (1934); but the value of social networks was not recognized until much later. Leadership came from social anthropologists at Manchester University, who noticed how patterns in the social relations observed in fieldwork explained social problems. They employed the term *social network* to describe 'a set of ties linking members of a social system' (Barnes, 1969, p. 54). Outside Britain, the networks fuse spluttered along slowly for a while, but flared into life in the 1970s with impetus from Harvard scientists under Harrison White, and aided by the establishment of a society for social network research (INSNA). The twenty-first century has seen the networks concept explode in the public consciousness, to the extent that 'network' and its verb form 'networking' are now part of everyday speech. There are natural networks to be found in river systems, tundra permafrost, and heated fluids. Indeed Buchanan (2002) concludes his book by claiming that the small-world network (where clusters are connected by a few common links) 'appears in the architecture of everything from the human brain to the web of relations that bind us unto societies, as well as the languages we use to speak and think' (p. 208).

Astute minds in every generation have known the value of social networks. One of the greatest exploiters of social network ties at the dawn of the modern scientific age was Charles Darwin. Following his return from five years' voyaging around the world on *The Beagle*, Darwin launched into a series of publishing projects on geology, botany and zoology that were a prologue to his great work *On the Origin of Species*. The scientific papers that flowed from Darwin's pen were based on field observations made during the voyage, as well as on detailed examination of the vast number of biological and geological specimens that Darwin had collected. But Darwin was more than an astute and patient observer. Crucial to his achievement was his ability to enlist the leading scientists of his day as research collaborators who would examine his specimens themselves or comment specifically on his observations. Less well known is Darwin's access to key people who could support his writing projects. For example, Darwin obtained a research grant of £1000 from the Admiralty in 1837, by exploiting his Cambridge network of friends. Their personal contacts ensured that testimonials were obtained from the presidents of the three leading scientific societies of the time: the Linnean Society, the Geological Society, and the Zoological Society. Second, Darwin contacted members of his scientific network to obtain scientific specimens from them and so broaden his specimen base. In 1845, after Darwin had written an 'essay' on his theory which ran to well over 200 pages, but had decided not to proceed to publication for fear that public acceptance of the theory would be unfavourable, he undertook a comprehensive zoological investigation of barnacles which proved crucial to supporting key aspects of his theory.

Over the course of the investigation, Darwin contacted scientists, explorers, and ship's captains around the world, to increase his range of specimens. Through a friend at the British Museum, he obtained a loan of the entire museum collection of barnacles; he sought additional specimens from a friend at the Paris Museum; he wrote asking Agassiz in America for barnacles from the Great Lakes; and he penned letters to British naval captains and travellers he knew, asking them to collect barnacles on their voyages. Not content, he corresponded with scientists known to him in France, Denmark, Holland, Germany and Sweden, in order to borrow their collections of fossil barnacles. Thus the author of a theory that was to reverberate around the scientific world utilized a vast social network of scientists and explorers to supply him with specimens and to comment on his ideas, while he himself undertook no travel but remained at Down House, patiently dissecting his barnacles and assembling his theory in the confines of his own study and within earshot of his own children.

Part I: Networks and young people

Part I of the book introduces the two central concerns that shape its content. First of all, the book is concerned with young people's relationships in the major public contexts of school, work and leisure, in their development through adolescence and young adulthood. Second, the nature of their relationships is discussed in terms of the social networks in which their lives are embedded.

Chapter 1 provides an overview of youth development and discusses the changing social contexts in which modern youth negotiate a lifepath. The concepts of transition, agency and biography are signalled as guiding the interpretation of young people's development across the lifespan. One of my purposes in writing this book is to show the relevance of lifespan theories of development for understanding some of the major issues confronting young people during the period of their lives from early adolescence to emerging adulthood. These include experiences of acceptance as well as rejection in their social and personal relationships, the dangers from risky behaviour when 'mixing with the crowd', the pressures of schooling, the benefits of participation in community activities and the value of support in times of difficulty as well as in deciding one's future. The merit of a lifespan approach is that it acknowledges the contextual and dynamic nature of human development. People are creatures of their own time and place, but are also active contributors to their development.

The science of network analysis is discussed in Chapter 2. My advocacy of network concepts and methods is based on my own experience in studying entire communities and finding patterns in the structures of social relations among families and youth that could only be detected by network methods. The merit of network analysis is in revealing the structural patterns and showing who is connected to whom, but other analysis at a more fine-grained level is needed if the nature and quality of relationships is to be understood, including the nature and strength of social influences from peers and adults. Admittedly, network thinking has yet to make a real impact in the youth and adolescence field. Despite the leadership of Robert Cairns, Marvin Krohn, Susan Ennett and Karl Bauman in investigating young people's social networks, network analysis has been ignored by the majority of investigators studying young people. Why have researchers on youth been so reluctant to adopt a networks perspective? Ennett and Bauman (1996) suggested that the primary obstacles to social network analysis in adolescent research were the large number of ties detected and the associated heavy demands of collecting information from all the adolescents in the network. Processing of network data was also formidable with the computer power that was available in the 1990s, but subsequently there have been big improvements in data management and processing. An example is health risk research, where network analysis is widely employed and the advantages of network thinking are clearly recognized. In other fields, such as delinquency research, network thinking and methods of analysis are increasingly being utilized. The time is opportune to apply social network analysis more generally to research and practice in the youth field.

Developmental psychology and sociology are increasingly recognizing the associations between lifecourse concepts and social network thinking (e.g. Levitt, 2005). In this book, network concepts and methods provide valuable insights into 'the geography' of social relations, but beyond this point, an acknowledgement is made of the need for other theoretical tools to explore the qualities of particular relationships. Two psychological theories are enlisted for these duties in this book: attachment theory and social identity theory. The broad task of the later chapters is to provide evidence concerning the merits of network thinking and lifespan development, both for researchers on youth issues and for practitioners working with young people.

Part II: Social networks

Understanding groups and the nature of young people's social relations in different kinds of peer groups and cliques is the concern of Part II of this book. Two aspects are of central interest in these chapters: the range of different social structures that comprise the social network, and the kinds of relationships expressed in these. Different kinds of groups are described, and ties among individual persons are discussed and related to the person's network role, based on their location within the social network.

Through social interactions in various group contexts, adolescents grow in their understanding of the nature of their relationships with others as well as in their understanding of themselves. The social demands made on young people by participation in broader components of a social network are likely to be different from those needed for participation in a clique of friends, where there is greater similarity. Giordano (2003, p. 275) suggests that the broader network constitutes a 'tougher audience' for the adolescent than does the clique, and that interacting with members of these social clusters and loose groups 'can engender feelings of awkwardness and insecurity', because the relationships are more distant. Compared with social relations in the small clique, learning to fit in with the clusters in the wider network of peers may require, she suggests, 'a developmental *stretch* in social skills' of a kind that is not usually activated when one is in the company of one's close friends.

Chapter 3 employs network terminology to describe different kinds of social structures and social relations in face-to-face groups, ranging from small cliques to local networks. Social ties are described and related to the person's network role, based on their location within the network. Examples are given of the application of network analysis to the study of friendships, interethnic group relations, and the identification of people who are key links within a social network.

Group life allows friendships to take root and flower. Chapter 4 examines the nature of friendship relationships, including opposite-sex friendships. Friendship relations grow in importance as young people enter their twenties and turn to their friends and acquaintances not only for companionship but also for guidance and advice. Many of the friendships made in our adolescence endure into our adult lives. The chapter describes the microsocial processes of friend interaction and communication and the kinds of self-disclosure that occur in friendships as they evolve from adolescence into adulthood. Conflict and friendship betrayal are also explored, so as to round out our appreciation of the central importance of close interpersonal relationships for understanding many of the topics that are discussed in subsequent chapters.

The concern of Chapter 5 is young people who are loners and outsiders, the people who are left out of cliques and on the margin of the larger group. Some are loners by choice or temperament, while others find themselves excluded or outsiders because they are different in some way. One area of difference that is discussed is foreignness. The chapter explores the group processes of exclusion and rejection that may be at work, and examines the feelings experienced by those who are isolated or rejected.

Part III: Social influences

This section is concerned with social influences, particularly peer influence or peer pressure. Although peer influence is beneficial to many aspects of social development, peers are generally viewed as exerting a powerful negative force in young people's lives, one which adult society has difficulty in neutralizing. It is important that we develop a realistic appreciation of the extent of peer influence, while accepting that 'delineating the processes of peer influence is very difficult' (Hartup, 1999, p. 179), and has challenged even the best researchers to quantify. As a result, research on peer influence now comprises thousands of studies, and no single theory or approach can explain all the kinds of influence.

Discussions of peer influence remind us that most people are only partly aware of the extent to which their attitudes and behaviour are shaped by social forces. For example, Carter *et al.* (2003) found that their respondents did not see themselves as easily swayed by others, although they themselves used peer influence to explain *other* people's behaviour. If young people are unaware that they are susceptible to influence from others, researchers need to devise theories that are robust enough to withstand the distorting effects of adolescents' exaggerated claims about their independence.

Since publication of the first edition of this book, social network research into peer influence has expanded considerably, both in surveys and as case studies of specific networks at the local level. This research has contributed to advances in our understanding of how peer contexts exert influences on behaviour. For example, Abel *et al.* (2002), Kirke (2004) and James Moody (2001) employ network diagrams to communicate the structural nature of peer influence in substance use. Other researchers, for example Hussong (2002), employ network concepts to 'consider multiple dimensions of adolescents' peer contexts' (p. 219). The chapters examine how peer influence is transmitted within different peer networks, from street crowds to friendship cliques, and across different domains of behaviour in education, leisure and health.

Network analysis is employed here to identify the relational ties between actors, and the chapters harness social identity theory to provide insights into social influences at the group level. From a social identity perspective, influence arises from social categorization processes, where persons assign others, including themselves, to groups based on broad social categories, and then identify with the attitudes and beliefs that they associate with their group. Conformity to group norms is explained as 'an effect of the mutually perceived similarity between self and ingroup others, produced by the formation and salience of shared social category memberships' (Turner, 1991, p. 160).

Chapter 6 examines youth antisocial behaviour in a variety of group contexts, including gangs, street groups, schools and mass crowds, and describes some of the methods used to induce young people to engage in antisocial behaviour. Group processes are discussed both as intragroup forces that bind individuals into the group, and also as intergroup activity, including school bullying and interethnic hostility and victimization.

The subject matter of Chapter 7 is student motivation in school. The topics discussed include class participation, failure, and dropping out. Social identity processes and group attachment are scrutinized, particularly as they apply to stereotyping and the maintenance of image and reputation, in order to shed light on the ways in which adolescents are influenced by their peers in contexts like the classroom.

In Chapter 8 the influences of the loose group of mates as well as the circle of best friends are explored as these affect smoking and drinking among adolescents and emerging adults. The chapter also explores how environments contribute to health risk behaviour, particularly to binge drinking. An additional aspect, relevant to education and prevention, is the effects of image and beliefs both for initiation into smoking and drinking and for maintaining these behaviours as a leisure lifestyle, despite their known health risks.

Part IV: Social support

The focus in this section shifts to intergenerational relations and the support that flows through links between young people and organized groups in schools and in the community. The argument in this section is about youth agency, not deficiency, and interest lies with youth competence, not youth problems. The focus is primary prevention through actions that promote positive youth development, rather than intervention among the distressed, delinquent or disadvantaged. This means that support for the most part is directed at points upstream from where serious youth problems are found. When Humpty Dumpty has had his great fall and needs to be put together, that is the time to turn to the criminologists and psychiatrists. My concern is with strategies to prevent Humpty Dumpty from such shattering experiences, by installing supports that supply him with the confidence and self-control to stay away from dangerous walls.

The epidemiologist Cobb (1976) emphasized that support is *information* communicated to a person by others that s/he is valued and worthwhile. Over the years, the meaning of support became narrowed to that of providing compensation and relief to persons in distress, and its relevance to the broader informational functions of encouragement was neglected, along with the importance of information for guidance in making decisions in everyday situations. The perspective taken in these chapters is one that accepts that several kinds of support exist, and that support may occur in youth work and educational settings not only in emotional and nurturant forms but as information, affirmation, and instructional guidance. Moreover, support may be expressed as environmental provisions, not simply as support from individuals. In some cases, the young person's involvement in a youth club or participation in a soup kitchen may be an affirming experience that promotes positive development. In other cases, social belonging to a group or institution supplies a valued identity.

At the heart of support practices are actual interactions between those offering support and those who are the targets. These include positive helping such as listening, not taking over, accepting the other person, being genuine and interested, and conveying to the person the message that s/he is valued. Support is not a commodity of exchange, although the use of terms like 'resources', 'give', 'provide' and 'offer' would suggest this to be the case. Support is not an electrical current that can be suddenly switched on. It is better to think of support as associated with a certain quality of relationships, whether these derive from friendship or from professional concern. Human interactions themselves are supportive, as they supply a sense of being valued through attachment to others (see Cotterell, 1994; Hobfoll and Stokes, 1988; Rook, 1987). Support is not separate from everyday life: it is 'communicated in the routine conduct of personal relationships' (Gottlieb and Sylvestre, 1994, p. 55).

The function of schools as sources of support is the subject of Chapter 9. It describes support programs and the roles of students as well as teachers as supports, and includes a discussion of the qualities found in effective helpers. It cites support programs to assist adolescents who are victims of bullying and exclusion, and interventions directed at trauma support. These separate activities are seen as expressions of a school environment that in its very essence is supportive, because of the sense of community it establishes for all its people.

Chapter 10 describes youth and community organizations as major sources of structured leisure-time activities for young people. They also serve as major points of contact between youth and adults outside the formal settings of school classrooms. A second beneficial effect of contacts with adults is that adolescents can become connected to, and identified with, adult society. From a social identity perspective, the establishment of ties between participants in an organized group fosters the development of a group consciousness, which strengthens into membership loyalties. The individual becomes 'bonded into' the club or organization.

Conclusion

The concluding chapter gathers the discussions of previous chapters on young people's development and the role of social networks to suggest how knowledge of networks can assist professionals in promoting youth futures. It relates the notion of support to social capital, derived from a person's connection into a network of supportive ties, and explores the potential of network thinking in education and youth work. It proposes the use of network thinking both for youth themselves to apply to their social relations, and for practitioners to adopt in creating settings in the school, workplace and community that connect young people to the wider society and assist them in building a positive future.

Part I

Networks and young people

1 Young people and development

Change is a byword for any book that features adolescents or youth in its title. Young people are not only experiencing change personally, as they grow and develop from a young adolescent of 12 years of age to a young adult in their mid-twenties; they are also living in a society that is changing. Moreover, the forces impelling these changes – the internal processes of maturation, and the social changes associated with a global economy and an interconnected world – cannot be denied. The fact that change is inevitable does not have to mean an obligatory and passive acceptance of change; one may instead adapt, like the surfer, riding the waves of change with confidence and finesse and harnessing their force so as to shape one's own path through the waters. Human beings are not puppets on life's stage: they are agents of their own development; and by charting the broad parameters of youth development outlined in this chapter, we are better placed for understanding the issues that confront young people in the course of their development to adulthood. There is merging of previously different fields of social science as researchers place more value on what they hold in common than on what separates them. In keeping with such a view, literature from both the psychology of adolescence and the sociology of youth has been closely consulted for the topics discussed here. The value of this 'zoom lens' approach is that both the social and the personal can be brought into sharp focus, to benefit the discussions.

Change is viewed through different theoretical frames by writers on adolescence, youth, and young adults. Writers on adolescence customarily focus on intra-individual change – and associate such change with adolescent development. Typically, texts include several chapters describing the physical, cognitive and psychological changes that begin at approximately 10 and 11 years of age and continue for several years after this, so that the young person of 16 years of age looks and acts very differently from how s/he did when just a few years younger. The rapidity of these changes in physical stature and in thinking often evokes surprise. It seems that in a very brief period of time, the girl has become a young woman, and the boy has grown into a man. I recall encountering one of my son's friends, a boy of 15 at the time, who I had not seen for many months. He and my son were hunched over the home computer. As I greeted him, he stood up. He seemed taller than I remembered, so that he seemed to tower over me. Surprised at his sudden change in stature I blurted out, 'Steve, what happened to you?', which attracted his dry response: 'I had my growth spurt.'

In texts on youth, a more collective viewpoint of young people is taken, where youth as a group or category are positioned within societal change, such as labour market changes, rural drift or community marginalization. Writers examine status changes among youth as a consequence of societal change and government policy, for example, the changing nature of skills in a globalized labour market, or the effects of youth training schemes in reducing youth unemployment. Writings on youth have employed concepts like pathways and lifepaths to capture the sense that the individual young person is on a journey which is both common to other young people in the same age cohort as well as having unique characteristics that individualize each young person's biography. The markers on the journey through life are statuses, such as school completion, stable employment, independent living, marriage and parenthood. But increasingly writers are teasing out the meaning of these markers when the transitions are unclear and uncertain, evident in the changes from school to work, from living with one's parents to independent living, from financial uncertainty to financial security, and indeed from 'carefree' youth to 'responsible' adulthood.

Development and change

In adolescent psychology, development is a central concept. Development results from continuous change over time in the way that the person perceives and interacts with the environment, and the direction of development is towards greater complexity, greater differentiation and greater organization of cognitive, affective, social and conative processes. Early frameworks explained development in terms of the satisfaction of needs, which were often related to the notion of biological drives, and needs continue to feature in modern texts on adolescent psychological development, such as the need to develop autonomy and gain a refined sense of identity. In the youth work field, Button (1974) applied the concept of needs to group work with adolescents. He listed four needs for youth workers to recognize and foster in adolescents: the need for companionship and affection, the need for security in order to manage uncertainty, the need for significance, and the need for adventure and new experience. In the work of Ryan and Deci (Ryan and Deci, 2000; Ryan and Powelson, 1991), three needs are emphasized as central to well-being: autonomy, competence and related-ness. The nature of these needs is explained as follows:

> The need for competence is fulfilled by the experience that one can effectively bring about desired effects and outcomes, the need for autonomy involves perceiving that one's activities are endorsed by or congruent with the self, and the need for relatedness pertains to feeling that one is close and connected to significant others.
>
> (Reis *et al.*, 2000, p. 420)

In education, a concept that has been influential is that of developmental tasks (e.g. Havighurst, 1972); these are socially defined needs or goals whose mastery is required by society. The developmental tasks concept is associated with a lifespan view of development, and portrays the young person as an active agent in their own development. Recent formulation of lifespan theory by Hendry and Kloep (2002) has particular merit for the topics and age range discussed in this book, because it interprets the nature of a person's development in terms of resources for meeting the challenges that are posed by changing social contexts. The authors acknowledge a debt to the work of earlier lifespan theorists (e.g. Elder, 1998; Havighurst, 1972; Smith and Baltes, 1999), both in the way they portray the relation between the individual's lifecourse and the requirements of society, and in 'the interconnections between earlier and later developmental events' (Hendry and Kloep, 2002, p. 15). In normal circumstances, the individual is guided in dealing with developmental tasks by the normative nature of the timetable, as well as by advice and support from others. However, the increasing destandardization of the lifecourse can disturb the orderly nature of such task management, so that concerns that were resolved at an earlier point now reappear.

Arnett (2000) provides a positive perspective on young adult development. He suggests that 'emerging adulthood' is a time of life when future directions remain fluid and when the social roles associated with adulthood have yet to be adopted. Instead, there is an 'experimental and exploratory quality' (p. 471) to young people's lives, expressed in particular in three 'domains of self-sufficiency' – love, work, and world-views. What is interesting is the distinction that Arnett makes between the 'transient and tentative explorations' in adolescence and the 'focused explorations' linked to choice behaviour that are detected among young people in their early twenties. For example, in the love domain, he contrasts the brief romantic attachments that occur in adolescence, which are based on recreational activity, often within group contexts, with the serious and more enduring romantic relationships established in emerging adulthood, which are focused on feelings and communication. In the work domain, he contrasts the adolescent attitude towards jobs as being for pay rather than for skill development, with the attitude of older youth, where a job is valued for what it contributes to their future direction and the discovery of what kind of work they like and are good at doing.

Young people in transition

Current research views adolescence, youth and early adulthood as connected periods comprising a series of transitions, with each constellation of transition events requiring some reorganization of behaviour, role, or psychological functions. Transitions common to young people include the transition to secondary school, from school to the workforce, and leaving home to live independently. These changes in setting expose people to new roles and relations that require social and psychological adaptation. For example, a young adolescent wrote about the personal changes that accompanied her entry into secondary school in these words: 'I have grown up in the last few weeks more than I did all last year.'

This book explores the psychosocial transitions associated with different periods of the lifecourse from adolescence to young adulthood, and acknowledges that the social development concerns of young people vary in salience across these different periods. For young adolescents, attention is directed to their social world in and out of school, in order to appreciate the significant changes in friendship that occur, and their wider consequences. By examining the patterns of adolescent interaction within friendship cliques, we are able to understand the value and importance of peer acceptance and friend intimacy, and the devastating consequences of peer rejection on individual young people. Similarly, attention to the classroom experiences of adolescents in the early years of secondary school can supply insights into the process of disengagement that leads some young people to drop out before they have completed their schooling.

Older adolescents and youth experience a different set of transitions as they spread their wings beyond the home and school and encounter more diverse groups of people. Environmental changes include the social and academic adjustments to college and the first job, and exposure to leisure settings where heavy drinking of alcohol is featured. Youth also come into contact with adults outside their family, some of whom become mentors or models for them. The implications of leisure settings as influences on health risk are discussed, as well as the potential of new settings for positive youth development through opportunities for involvement in youth citizenship.

In an essay on transitions from a developmental psychology perspective, Graber and Brooks-Gunn (1996) draw attention to the potential for transitions to affect individual young people in different ways, depending on such factors as timing of the events, the cumulation of effects, and whether certain characteristics of an individual are highlighted or subjected to particular pressure. They discuss transitions from a lifecourse perspective, including the concept of *trajectory*. Developmental trajectory includes the direction of change, using knowledge of factors and influences observed over a considerable period of time to assess how much the individual lifecourse follows a predicted path. There is an implication that transitions follow an orderly and predictable succession. When circumstances are at odds with this sense of order, young people encounter disrupted or fragmented transitions, which may seriously affect their individual development.

The notion that the trajectories are predictable through adolescence, varying only in terms of social class, gender and ethnicity, is challenged by research in the youth field. Recent evidence suggests that the trajectory of development is far more varied and unpredictable and that the transition from adolescence to adulthood extends well beyond the teenage years into young adulthood. For example, the difficulties associated with the extended transition to work have 'created exceptional problems for beginning workers' (Roberts, 1997, p. 348). Roberts recalls that in the mid-1980s the ESRC longitudinal research program chose to focus on the 16- to 19-year-old age group with the assumption that by the age of 19 years, the majority of the cohort would have completed the transition to employment. By the end of the twentieth century, it was obvious across the developed countries that such optimism was ill-founded, and that young people were taking much longer to attain employment stability.

Evidence that youth are more vulnerable to unemployment than is generally true for adults comes from the 1997 OECD figures for twenty countries. These show that the rate of unemployment for young people aged 15 to 24 years was on average 2.4 times the unemployment rate for those aged 25 to 54 years, and ranged from 1.1 (Germany) to 4.0 (Greece). In Australia, 37 per cent of the unemployed in the first three-quarters of 1998 were young people. Clearly, the prospects of stable and full-time employment in many western countries are not altogether rosy for the youth generation. However, unlike youth during the 1980s, today's youth are drawn from a smaller birth cohort, making their problems less visible than would be the case if they were more numerous. Indeed, in the summer of 1983, the proportion of adolescents in the US population was exceeded by the proportion of persons over 60 years of age for the first time in the country's history.

Social commentators have noted that the standard paths to a defined adulthood have dissolved in recent times, and that the certainties of previous generations about the connection between future, present and past for the assembly of one's biography are no longer evident. They refer to the erosion of a linear view of time, replaced by an emphasis on 'randomness' (Sennett, 1998) where planning for the future has no meaning. Chisholm and Du Bois-Reymond (1993) questioned whether 'youth' as a classically understood label for a whole age-cohort still exists, given what they saw as the fragmentation of the *rites de passage* from childhood to adulthood. Wyn and Dwyer (1999) comment that, 'Life experiences and future prospects of this generation are more complex and less predictable than those of their predecessors' (p. 5). Experts on youth speak of a 'choice biography', drawing attention to the 'destandardization' of biography (Brannen and Nilsen, 2002) and the removal of agreed markers of adulthood. Some celebrate this for the freedom and flexibility it offers youth; others warn of the psychological costs on youth of continual exertion and watchfulness. Delay in commitment is characteristic of a choice biography, so that people strive to remain flexible rather than be boxed in by a job, a place, or a relationship. What intrigues Du Bois-Reymond (1998) is that European youth do not like the concept of adulthood; they equate it with 'dullness and routine' and are fearful that as adults they will 'lose their playful attitude and become serious, boring and responsible' (p. 74). Brannen and Nilsen (2002) remarked that, for some youth, adulthood is seen as a phase 'reserved for the distant future' (p. 522).

Moreover, uncertainty regarding the future extends well into their twenties, even for young people who have tertiary qualifications or impressive employment histories.[1] Writing about youth in Britain, Ahier and Moore (1999) argue that social changes in work and family and changes in government policies relating to young people 'combine to make the situation of youth less secure, less predictable and structured, enforcing a much more protracted period of ambiguous dependency' (p. 516). Furlong cites uncertainty in young people's lives, their separation from adults, and the lengthening of the pre-adult phase of life as contributing to 'the increased length and complexity of youth as a phase of the life cycle' (Furlong, 2000, p. 130). Brannen and Nilsen (2002) conclude that 'the way that young people navigate the transition to adulthood is influenced by their perception and experience of time' (p. 531).[2] From interview material, they suggest three approaches to adulthood taken by youth: deferment, adaptability, and predictability. Only the last of these shows planning and progression to adulthood; the other routes reveal reluctance to engage with the future or restless pursuit of change and impermanency. These restless patterns of non-engagement with the future, in the generation labelled twixters, kippers, freeters, and boomerang kids (see Grossman, 2005), have deep implications for society. Already the reverberations are widely detected among adolescent students in motivational problems in school and in the decline of job commitment among young adults.

This portrait is not restricted to the experience of young adults; it affects younger adolescents and youth in educational settings as well. They hear about the twixters; they see older siblings not yet settled; they listen to stories from youth who have left school. They realize that education is no guarantee of economic security, and that the separation of school and work is an artificial one. The perpetuation of a division between school as a place to learn, and work as a place to apply what has been learned, makes it difficult for modern youth to balance the competing claims made on their lives. Post-school, their lives are fragmented into casual work, part-time study, and a series of living arrangements where they juggle their time between the demands of work, study, family and friends.

The consensus view is that the modern economy is full of contradictions. On the one hand, the economy is pictured as deregulated, de-structured and managerialist, where market forces rather than governments determine labour-market opportunities and employment practices; where union power is eroded; where career paths are de-standardized and permanent jobs are replaced by casual ones; and where workers are hired on individual workplace agreements that stipulate few rights and many obligations. On the other hand, there is an anomaly: young people themselves are optimistic about their future, confident in their own ability to navigate the complexities of a 'marketized' and 'contingent' labour market. They express optimism and confidence about their own future prospects, even when confronted with the uncertainty and unpromising nature of labour markets. Indeed, Johnson (2002) has described the high job expectations of modern youth as indicators of 'over-ambition'.

One consequence of this individualistic thinking is that young people can be less aware of social structural changes that affect them, less willing to believe that their personal experiences are common to other young people, and more inclined to attribute the blame for any failure to achieve their goals to a fault in themselves. According to Brannen and Nilsen (2002), the research focus on youth agency and individualization 'assumes that adulthood is unproblematic' (p. 515). These authors reason that young people need structured pathways, or at least signposts, in order to construct their own biography. Where are these signposts for youth, and who provides them? Paul Simon sang of this concern with the loss of role models in 'You can call me Al'. Ahier and Moore (1999) propose that, in the negotiated lifepath, it is important for young people to have access to social resources. Accordingly, 'youth transitions must be understood in terms of networks of relationships' (p. 517), mainly intergenerational, which can provide these resources. We return to this issue in the last section of the book.

What then is the significance for researchers and practitioners of delays in the attainment of adult status into the mid- to late twenties, reported by scholars from many different countries? Let me make three suggestions. First, it means that the period known as youth 'has become a more prominent stage of the life course' (Furstenberg, 2000, p. 899). Second, extension of the period of adolescence and youth into the mid-twenties has implications for those who conduct youth research, or who determine public policy. Third, those who work with youth must be prepared to deal with the diversity and unevenness evident in youth pathways towards adult responsibilities.

The social and the personal

Whereas social network thinking allows us to examine social relations at broad levels of the ecological environment, other theoretical concepts are needed in order to explain aspects of importance in understanding the nature of young people's social and personal relationships, such as the value of group connection and the impulse for expressing themselves through group behaviour. Two theories are enlisted for the work of explaining social bonding and connection, and social and interpersonal influences on behaviour: attachment theory and social identity theory. Both of these theories deal with motivational systems and social relationships, and their concerns overlap in some respects, for example in their mutual interest in how individuals are bonded to others. Their theoretical insights are also highly relevant to the developmental tasks that are important to young people, such as forging meaningful relationships with others, achieving a distinct personal identity, and establishing purpose and direction for one's life.

Attachment theory

Attachment theory provides a useful framework for discussing the motivations underlying young people's personal relationships. It focuses on the individual's relationships with significant others, and provides theoretical insights into the nature of intimacy, trust, and emotional security. Bowlby (1969) defined attachment as an emotional bond between two people that extends across time and space. Initially the concept of attachment was applied to explain the bond between an infant and its caregiver, although Bowlby regarded attachment as continuing into adulthood. Over time, the concept has become increasingly used to explain relationships outside its original domain of caregiver–infant interaction, and beyond the dyadic level, to the extent that it has been employed by some writers to depict the individual's relation to the group (e.g. Smith *et al.*, 1999). Research on attachment now spans a period of more than fifty years, and reflection on its importance allows us to state with confidence that attachment is a fundamental force in human nature, which is active across the entire lifespan. People of all ages readily form relational bonds with others with remarkable ease, and are very reluctant to break them. Attachment is a powerful motivational system that impels us to seek contact and connection with others and to establish close relationships, from which we derive a sense of psychological security (see Baumeister and Leary, 1995).

Bowlby described four features of the expression of attachment in infancy. These attachment behaviours are: seeking proximity to a caring other; finding security in the safe haven that the caregiver provides; showing distress when separated from the caregiver; and venturing out from the secure base beside the caregiver to explore the world. While these four defining features of attachment (proximity seeking, safe haven, separation distress and secure base) are manifestations of attachment bonds in infancy, they remain relevant for older age groups too, where attachment finds expression in close relationships (Thompson, 2005). An observation study conducted by Fraley and Shaver (1998) on couples separating at airports is illustrative, and confirms the continuity of attachment behaviour from childhood into adulthood. Separation elicited high levels of attachment behaviour, and was particularly noticeable among couples who had been involved in their relationship for shorter periods of time. In contrast, where couples were not separating, their attachment behaviour was 'subdued'. The majority of responses to separation could be described as proximity-maintenance, such as embracing, clinging onto the partner, prolonged holding of hands, and maintaining eye contact over a distance. Other attachment behaviours included separation protests such as crying, following, and resisting the farewell contact, as well as avoidance behaviours, where the partner sought to hurry the separation by breaking off the contact or turning away. Fraley and Shaver (1998) interpreted the attachment behaviours from an evolutionary perspective, noting that the situation seemed to trigger attachment responses even when the separation of the couples was both foreseen and inevitable.

Attachment theorists argue that our relations with others are shaped by the organization of attachment behaviour. People have mental models of relationships, assembled from interpersonal experiences early in life and consolidated through further experiences in childhood and adolescence. The importance of these 'attachment representations' is that they regulate people's behaviour (e.g. Carlson *et al.*, 2004; Sroufe and Waters, 1977). Carlson and her colleagues argue that these representations 'carry forward previous social experience and provide structure for subsequent encounters with the world' (2004, p. 67); they shape attitudes and expectations concerning the emotional quality of later relationships. Attachment styles derived from these models have been found to consist of two major dimensions: anxiety and avoidance. *Anxious attachment* describes a person who is either anxious to be accepted and fearful of abandonment, or over-concerned about approval; and *avoidant attachment* describes a person who is either aloof and avoids closeness, or highly dependent on others for closeness. Kafetsios and Nezlek (2002) note that studies have found securely attached people to be more comfortable with self-disclosure than insecurely attached people, whereas individuals with anxious or preoccupied styles 'desire more intimacy than they find in their social interactions and tend to be indiscriminate in their self-disclosure, [while] people with avoidant styles tend to limit their self-disclosure' (p. 720).

While few would deny the central importance of attachment for understanding personality development, attachment researchers warn of the dangers from overstating the claims of attachment theory and applying it to all kinds of relational experiences. For example, van Ijzendoorn (2005) restricts the application of attachment to 'the affective relation with one or a few significant others in a child's social network' (p. 85); and Sperling and Berman (1994) argue against defining peer relations as attachments, preferring to describe them as 'affiliations' on the basis that attachment bonds are specific relations and not interchangeable. However, it is clear that in adolescence and adulthood, some people have relations with a group which bear the hallmarks of attachment relations. This was noticed by Weiss (1982), who suggested that adolescents and adults 'seem sometimes to display attachment to a small, cohesive, reliable and accepting group of peers rather than to an individual' (p. 177), and in this sense the attachment bond would appear to be group-based, rather than directed at individuals.

A shift in attachment is evident during early adolescence, away from parents and towards friends as preferred companions and as sources of emotional comfort (Nickerson and Nagle, 2005), and a similar pattern of preferences for friends over parents was found among college youth (Fraley and Davis, 1997). For example, proximity seeking with friends is expressed during early adolescence through long conversations after school on the family telephone, although increasingly today on personal mobiles (cell phones). Moreover, when attachments to peers are lacking or denied, individuals experience loneliness, grief and despair. A word of caution is that the preference for proximity to peers rather than parents does not eliminate parents as providers of deeper forms of comfort, reassurance and support. An insight of Weiss (1982) deserves mention in this respect. He suggested that when adolescents and youth leave home, they may 'relinquish' their parents as attachment figures (which may be painful for the parents at first), but they hold the parents 'in reserve'. This kind of attachment at a distance is something that many can testify to: the long-distance phone calls for advice, or simply for a sympathetic ear, continue well into the adult years. Moreover, the young person's growth of understanding of networked relationships assigns new value to their continuing attachment to parents – as the social capital to be mined from access to their parents' social network (see Chapter 11). In these ways, attachment theory contributes to understanding adolescent and youth friendship; it offers valuable insights into the contributions to personal development of trust, intimacy and close communication (e.g. Nickerson and Nagle, 2005).

Attachment theory may also help explain adolescent group relations with peers, fraternities and sports teams. Smith *et al.* (1999) argued that the psychological systems that regulate affect and behaviour in personal relationships are similar to those that regulate people's feelings and actions within groups. In both kinds of relationship – that with an individual friend and that with a group – the person is faced with the task of regulating closeness and separation. Individuals differ in how they relate to others. Some are worried that others will not accept them and are constantly on the alert for signs that they are unwanted. Others are relaxed about group acceptance, and do not even entertain the possibility of being rejected. These youth, who have low levels of attachment anxiety and avoidance, are secure in their groups. Their behaviour will signal to group members their sense of security with the group as well as their enjoyment of the group, in contrast with the attachment behaviour of people who are anxious or avoidant. Securely attached group members will be relaxed in other people's company, and will initiate or reciprocate attachment behaviour without recourse to attention-seeking or jealous remarks, whereas avoidant youth and adolescents will behave as if they don't need a group. They will shrug off attempts by peers to befriend them and ignore invitations for them to join in group activities.

Differences in attachment style may help explain the variations found in individual susceptibility to group influence. While avoidant attachment may explain the imperviousness of the loner or social isolate to group influence, anxious attachment provides a very different profile on the susceptibility of young people to adverse forms of peer influence. For example, Smith *et al.* (1999) suggest that a person who is anxiously attached to a group may identify strongly with the group for fear of being left out or rejected. This could include engaging in greater risk-taking in order to be noticed and accepted, even by a group that they do not actually belong to.

Social identity theory

Social identity theory deals with relations at the group level, and is concerned with the social construction of group membership. It enables group influences on behaviour – both those that occur within groups and those between groups – to be examined in terms of social categorization and group identification processes. Initially the theory arose from research into prejudice and the study of social stereotypes. Social identity was defined as 'that part of an individual's self-concept which derives from his knowledge of his membership of a group (or groups) together with the value and emotional significance attached to the membership' (Tajfel, 1978, p. 63). Using illustrations of racial, ethnic and economic disadvantage, Tajfel showed that value differentiations between groups are not far below the surface at any time. When people act as a group, their behaviour is best understood not as different members of the group acting in terms of their personal identities, but as 'individuals acting in terms of a shared identity' (Turner, 1991, p. 155). In these respects, social identity theory is more closely linked to sociological than psychological perspectives on behaviour, leading Hogg and Abrams (1988) to describe it as an approach that examines 'the group in the individual' (p. 17).

Tajfel suggested that the psychological value of belonging to a group is derived from its status relative to that of other groups. The effects of social categorization, in segmenting the individual's social environment into her/his own group and other groups, provide a basis for broader social comparison than merely comparing oneself with other individuals; and this form of comparison contributes to social identity by noting the positive characteristics of one's ingroup and its distinctiveness from the outgroup. The categorization is not neutral, but follows an ingroup–outgroup distinction, where people engage in finding fault with other groups while praising their own group.

It was further suggested by Tajfel that social behaviour could be arrayed on a continuum from interpersonal to intergroup. At the interpersonal end, people interact according to their particular personal qualities, whereas at the intergroup end, their behaviour is affected by their social group membership. Some environmental conditions assist the process of social categorization by what is termed *meta-contrast*, the tendency in certain situations for group differences to become accentuated. For example, where people share a common neighbourhood but have markedly different customs or religious practices, the adjacency of groups contributes contrast which makes the social categories more salient, and people are perceived as members of distinct social groups more than as individual persons. That is, their social category membership becomes more important for defining others than their individual attributes, in what amounts to social stereotyping. At the same time, they define themselves according to the group attributes, in a process of self-categorization that resembles self-stereotyping. For example, in south Jakarta, the close proximity of private, public and technical schools accentuates the differences between the schools to the extent that inter-school hostility develops, sustained by groups within the schools and expressed in a form of violent intergroup fighting known as *tawuran*, which has seen dozens of student deaths over a period of several years. The salience of category membership can also be increased by political activity, like that witnessed in Kosovo, where people who had lived together as neighbours for many years, despite their ethnic differences, were redefined into friends or enemies by a policy of ethnic cleansing.

Social identity theory has particular relevance to our understanding of group influences on individual behaviour and of intergroup relations, and provides insights into health risk behaviour, mass crowd behaviour, and discrimination against minority groups. A central tenet of social identity theory is that, where groups are differentiated, a person will favour the group that s/he belongs to. Whether such ingroup favouritism leads to intergroup discrimination or conflict will depend on other factors in the situation. Preferring one's own group and enjoying the social experiences offered by that group does not necessarily create any disharmony with other groups, unless the basis of group membership heightens negativism towards an outgroup. Thus a group of college students noisily strolling along a street late at night may generate intergroup hostility from a gang who resent their happiness and markers of social privilege.

What is also important is the applicability of social identity theory to reducing intergroup conflict and fostering social integration. For example, Dovidio *et al.* (1998) conducted a series of experiments to reduce intergroup bias by manipulating the status of the groups in a scenario where the groups had survived a plane crash and had to decide whether to stay by the plane or hike to safety. They were successful in eliminating intergroup bias when each group's expertise was differentiated and also valued as having equal importance for the survival plan. They concluded that, 'When members of each group perceive that the other group's contributions are necessary for their own success, members may develop the respect for the other group … and the inclusive group representations that can produce positive intergroup attitudes' (p. 118).

Socially situated personal biography

In summary, attachment theory and social identity theory provide complementary frames for understanding the young person's relationships. They are employed in the following chapters in tandem with social network thinking so as to contribute essential psychological insights into the nature of young people's relationships and influences on these. These three theory pillars underpin the arguments put forward in this book.

How can young people's networked social relations be mapped and described? How do the patterns of linkage evolve, and what do the patterns mean? How can young people's social relations be understood? What are the sources of social influence on young people's behaviour and personal development and how do these influences operate? What is their significance for the individual's development towards mature adult responsibility? Questions like these may be asked by the individual young person or by the practitioner. The challenge for this book is whether, and how well, the questions can be answered.

2   The science of social networks

The purpose of this chapter is to describe the major characteristics of social networks and some of the methods that are employed to map them. In writing this chapter, I am mindful of the interests of teachers and youth workers in identifying the networks of young people familiar to them, but I have included examples from research that employ sophisticated methods and techniques for those readers seeking an introduction to more extensive analysis. However, this is not a technical book on network theory and analysis; there are some fine texts on this topic, written by experts in the field, and it would be presumptuous of me to pretend to possess their expertise. Appreciation of the quality of the 'dish' that is served in this chapter may be related to the distinction between a cook and a chef. What follows, as I identify the ingredients and add them to dishes for the reader to taste, is the work of a passable cook. I am confident the menu will prove to be enjoyable, but for those with more discriminating palates, the chefs should be consulted from the list found in the chapter notes.

The study of groups by social scientists has a long history. For the most part, these were organized groups and institutions (corporations, political parties, churches, government bodies), and were studied in terms of roles, positions, and institutional norms. In the 1950s researchers in social anthropology at Manchester saw that the institutional structures were mediated through personal relations, and they adopted the term 'social network' to describe these interlinked relations. They compared the formalized relations among people in the workplace, church, and community organizations with the personal relations of the same people as friends and neighbours, and noticed that people interact with the local policeman, the teacher, and the grocer, rather than with the institutional systems that they represent – such as those of the law, education, and the economy.

At first, the Manchester anthropologists tended to think of social networks as group-like entities that had a particular shape and that were located on a continuum somewhere between the institutional structures in society and the individual person. But they soon came to realize that networks differ from groups; for example, networks may contain a number of groups, but networks are found within groups as well. Network thinking helped the researchers to notice that people were often linked to one another in ways that were independent of social position or role, and which depended instead on the nature of the interaction content; they might be linked, for example, through exchange of information, expressions of neighbourliness, material assistance, or social advocacy. Moreover, these exchange contents could overlap, creating multi-stranded links, so that for a given set of actors who at first were not friends, the links could evolve into friendship over time. Barnes found that the people he studied in a Norwegian island community in the early 1950s were linked to one another by ties of friendship, acquaintance, and community responsibilities, to form a social network where 'each person has a number of friends, and these friends have their own friends' (Barnes, 1954, p. 43). Another definition of the social network is 'the actual set of links of all kinds among a set of individuals' (Mitchell, 1973, p. 22). Networks are not merely metaphors describing the way social relations possess distinctive patterns; they operate, as do physical networks, to channel resources and transmit information. In the preface to their book on network analysis (Boissevain and Mitchell, 1973) Boissevain wrote that a network functions as 'a set of relations which persons use to achieve their ends' (p. viii). He neatly captured this idea in the title of his book, *Friends of Friends* (Boissevain, 1974).

Networks may be approached in two different ways: as total networks or as the network radiating from an individual person. The term 'social network' applies in a strict sense to the total network approach; whereas the individual approach captures the 'personal social network'. The latter is a slice of the total network in which the ties are linked to one person, and just as it is possible to dissect a total network into the links that attach to a particular individual, it is also possible to arrive at a total network from assembling the personal networks of members of a population. The total network approach is favoured by researchers in fields such as public health and anthropology, who study whole communities, and where paths of influence or information flow can be traced. The personal network approach is more popular among researchers in fields such as child development and counselling, where individuals are the focus of enquiry, and where the goals are to detect the adequacy of a person's social support.

The practitioner who is interested in understanding and applying social network approaches is faced with an inside–outside problem – ties or networks, depending upon the way the practitioner encounters young people in the discharge of their professional duties. As a youth worker,

I encountered young people individually, and it was only after I had assembled sufficient information on the pattern of their social ties that I could place the individuals into a network. In my career as a teacher, my dealings with students were in classes and large groups, and the challenge was to understand the behaviour of individual students against the background of larger groups. I had to observe these groups to detect the patterns of relations and where individuals fitted into these structures. There are strengths in each approach, and these are acknowledged in my treatment of networks and social ties in this chapter. The topic is not, however, exhausted in the discussions that follow, and is taken up in different ways in later chapters.

Towards an appreciation of a network

Social networks are graphs, consisting of points and lines. The actors are represented as the nodes in the network graph and the lines represent the relations (ties) among them. There are many kinds of relations: they could represent characteristics such as kinship, friendship, association, physical proximity, or academic citations, or they could represent actual social interactions. Thus the relations portrayed could represent brief interactions through to long-term links between persons, such as membership and kinship. Clearly, differing content in the relations will generate different social network structures.

Scientific analysis of networks is based on graph theory. Difficulty arises for readers who are interested in the utility of social network analysis to their professional field, but who lack the mathematical knowledge to understand the technicalities that one encounters in many research papers. Concern was raised as early as the 1970s that specialization of social network research could lead to the field becoming overly technical, prompting Barnes and Harary (1983) to write a defence of technical tools as scientifically valuable for network research. They traced the use of graphs 'to express … the configurations of social bonds' (p. 237) to the study of genealogies, which were discussed as far back as Cicero's time. Graphs do feature in the present book, but it is not written for a technical readership. My purpose is descriptive rather than analytical.[1]

Let us begin this appreciation of the nature of social networks at the deep end, where we so often find ourselves in life – for example, as a young person at a party where we 'hardly know a soul', or as a fledgling worker or manager on our first day in a new job, or as a new student in middle school or secondary school. Confronted with a mass of anonymous others in any of these settings, we urgently want to fit in, to belong. Our tactics are to look for a way to link ourselves into the social group, by contact with at least one of its members. When the network structure of the party, workplace or school is revealed through our tentative efforts, we feel less anxious, more confident.

A useful point of entry into the study of social network structure is Salzinger's field study of the social ties established among students at Harvard University (Salzinger, 1982). She mapped the ties to trace the evolution of 'clusters'[2] within the larger student population, and how these ties bound them into social networks. The appeal of this study is twofold: it is field-based, and it employs simple methods of analysis to identify the networks and the structures within them. A cluster was defined in terms of network configuration, as 'a group of three or more people who each have at least one friend in common, and who *in toto* have more ties within than outside the group' (p. 126). Features of cluster relations may be appreciated through examination of the theatre network in Salzinger's study, shown in Figure 2.1.

Inspection of the overall network graph reveals that the majority of subjects denoted as theatre people are males who are linked to one another by friendship and acquaintanceship ties, but these ties spread out from Subjects 2, 3 and 4 to link them to others who are in turn linked to other networks. (The friendship ties of people in these outlying regions are not recorded.) Subjects 1, 2, 3, 4, 5, 6, 7, 11 and 278 were identified as belonging to a cluster, but variations in their links to others are evident, with Subject 4 having the majority of choices with persons inside the cluster, whereas Subject 3 has more ties to people outside the cluster than inside it, and is indeed linked to another sector of the college network, which Salzinger shows in another graph. The network diagram shown here reveals features of the social field of these students, showing where they are located within it, including their location with respect to clusters within the network. It invites speculation on the significance of the location of individuals and of specific relationships with other network members.

Network elements

Actors and ties

At its most elemental level, a social relation occurs when a person A is linked to another person B in some way, perhaps by a tie of affection, association, or proximity. That is, persons A and B like each other, or are members of the same club, or live or work near each other. The relations of association and proximity are reciprocal: if A lives near B, clearly B also lives near A. However, the relation of affection is directional: A may like B but B may not like A, or one may have strong feelings of friendship towards

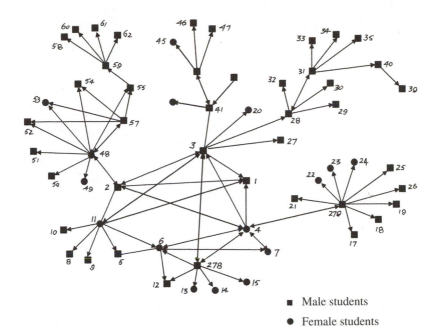

■ Male students

● Female students

Figure 2.1 College students' theatre network

Source: Redrawn from a figure by L. L. Salzinger in *Social Networks*, *4*, p. 130, copyright (1982), with permission from Elsevier Ltd.

the other which are not fully reciprocated. The strength of ties and whether the relation is reciprocal are considered later.

Social networks contain different orders of social relations. In a personal network, first-order relations are those direct links that actor A has with a number of others, while extending from these ties with actor A are other ties that are indirect. For example, Figure 2.2(a) shows that actor A has direct ties with actors B, C, D and E. These ties together comprise what Barnes (1969) called 'the primary or first-order zone' of A's social relations, in that all members of the group have direct or first-order relations with A. But other relations exist among the actors B, C, D and E, different from those existing with A. This layer of contacts with A (shown in Figure 2.2(b)) is an example of second-order relations. For example, A is tied to C, but in addition C is tied to F and G. These ties of C occur at a second-order level. A is also tied to D who is tied to H and J. Thus the actors F and J are not in direct contact with A but have indirect links to A through A's ties to C and

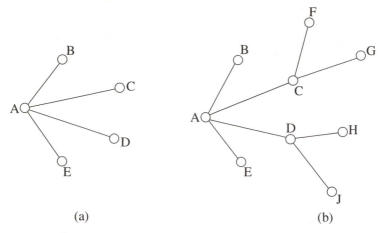

Figure 2.2 Network growth from first-order to second-order relations

to D. Further relations could exist at third, fourth and subsequent orders of relation to actor A.

What do these graphs suggest about the influence of A on D? If we assume that the relation between A and D is strong, then we could perhaps conclude that A can influence D say 90 per cent of the time. But at a second order of relation, for example, between D and J, the influence of A will be weaker, even if D's relation with J is as strong as D's relation with A. The strength of influence of A on J can be calculated as the product of the two relations A on D and D on J (90% × 90% = 81%). At further distances or path lengths from A, the influence of A will be further diminished. Youth workers know this well, in their attempts to influence young people. For example, a youth worker who befriends A will probably have more success in influencing D than in influencing C, because A's influence on C could be weakened by C's separate relations with B and E (who are also linked to A) and possibly also by C's relations with F and G. However, with knowledge that some redundant paths exist in the ties that link A, B, C, and E to one another, the astute youth worker may be able to build positive relationships with each of them so that they mutually influence one another. After all, if the ties are based on friendship and liking, they will also undoubtedly serve as conduits for the flow of information.

Bridging ties

In a typical network graph there are areas where points are joined together by lines and other areas where lines are absent. The resulting pattern

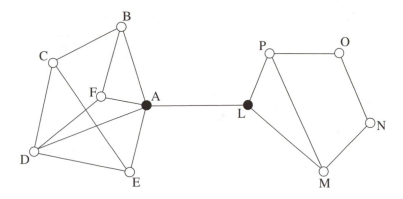

Figure 2.3 Bridging tie between two subgraphs

creates subgraphs. A line that connects separate subgraphs or components of a network is known as a *bridge*, or bridging tie. Burt (2002, p. 337) refers to bridges as ties that straddle 'a structural hole' in a network, such that a structural separation exists between people who 'circulate in different flows of information'. The location and function of a bridge across such a structural hole is shown in Figure 2.3. The diagram shows two subgraphs ABCDEF and LMNOP, where actors A and L are connected to one another by a bridge. Transfer of information from one subgraph to the other can only occur through this bridging tie. One of the most famous of these bridges was between 'Deep Throat', the Watergate informant, and Bob Woodward and Carl Bernstein from the *Washington Post*. The identity of this bridge was only revealed in 2005 as Mark Felt, who was second in command of the FBI at the time. This bridge provided key information from inside the Nixon Administration about the details of the Watergate break-in that implicated the president and finally led to the resignation of President Nixon himself. History may have been different if that bridge had been identified and eliminated.

Regions and bridges

Analysis of networks is concerned with the study of their structures, a point that Crossley (2005) emphasized when he wrote that 'the concept of "network" equates to the concept of "structure"' (p. 355). The Salzinger study discussed earlier was concerned with identifying dense clusters of friends within the larger college network. The ability to identify such clusters, whether they are friendship cliques, gangs, or larger cohesive components

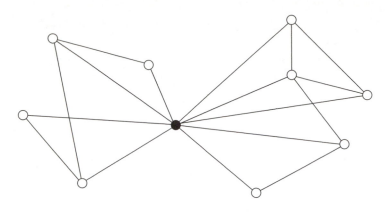

Figure 2.4 Cutpoint linking nodes in a graph

of a network, is a fundamental concern to researchers and practitioners in many social science and health fields.

How does one identify the component structures within larger networks? The simplest approach is by visual inspection of a network diagram, in which a broader network structure may contain subgraphs or components, so that its overall structural integrity depends on links being maintained between the components by a single actor or bridging tie. Figure 2.4 shows a situation where a single actor links two components of a network, such that the removal of that actor would eliminate a number of the links that maintain the overall structure of the graph. In network terms, this is called a *cutpoint*, which emphasizes that the graph can be cut at this point into two subgraphs by the removal of one point or node.

The cutpoint can be identified in the team structures of some sporting games. For example, in Rugby the halfback is the single player linking the scrum of forwards and the backs. In American football the quarterback has a similar role, and the opposing team that can stifle this key player is able to starve the running backs of quality access to the ball. In history, the king often served this role of tying the separate factions of lords and barons together, so that the death of a king often resulted in the disintegration not only of the royal household but of the kingdom; indeed in those days the king was indeed the 'kingpin'. Research examples of the importance of key actors are given in Chapter 3, including the example of a girl who was equally popular with girls from three separate cliques so that she was the key to maintaining the integrity of that social network.

Strength of ties

Social ties can be distinguished according to their strength. In an oft-quoted paper, Granovetter (1973, p. 1361) made the distinction between weak and strong ties in these words: 'the strength of a tie is a (probably linear) combination of the amount of time, the emotional intensity and intimacy (mutual confiding) and the reciprocal services that characterize the tie'. Thus strong ties are generally equivalent to close relationships, intimacy and emotional support that have built up over time, and are usually limited to family and close friend relationships. However, strong ties can at times exist outside these relations if they arise from experiences where people regularly interact with one another in different settings. For example, if the relation between two work colleagues Diane and Cheryl extends beyond their workplace to include membership of the same church choir and of the same swim club, they are most likely to form a strong tie, based more on the regular interactions than on emotional closeness.

Granovetter does not spell out exactly the nature of a weak tie as distinct from a strong tie, beyond treating acquaintances as weak ties, but weak ties are generally understood to refer to 'relationships characterized by infrequent interaction or low intimacy' (Bian, 1997, p. 366). Indirect ties are inevitably weak ties, thus leading to the conclusion that modern life generates a large acquaintanceship volume of weak ties.

Estimating a person's social network depends upon the ability of investigators to assess the weak ties in their 'contact net' (de Sola Pool and Kochen, 1978). However, research has consistently shown that weak tie relationships are less likely to be reported. Infrequent contact and differences in people's understandings about the meaning of the word 'friend' can explain the under-reporting of weak ties. For example, Mary may omit to list Julie because Mary has little social contact with Julie, or because in her view Julie is Kate's friend, not hers. Others may have few really close friends but a wide circle of casual friends who are linked by weaker ties. By omitting to name many of these other friends, they fail to reveal the true size of their personal network. Thus by under-reporting the extent of their friendship ties, perhaps because of the high standard they set themselves for defining a friendship, some people may be judged to have few friends when in reality they have many casual friendships.

The importance of weak ties is that they greatly extend the pool of contacts that comprises a person's social network. It is this ability of weak ties to penetrate domains that are different from ego's familiar domain that has attracted the interest of researchers. Through weak ties, the reach of an individual is extended to relatively remote contacts of possible importance to her/him, either for the influence that they can exert or for the information that they can provide.

Granovetter's reasoning on the strength of weak ties (SWT) theory deserves direct quotation:

> The overall social structural picture suggested by this argument can be seen by considering the situation of some arbitrarily selected individual – call him Ego. Ego will have a collection of close friends, most of whom are in touch with one another – a densely knit clump of social structure. Moreover, Ego will have a collection of acquaintances, few of whom know one another. Each of these acquaintances, however, is likely to have close friends in his own right and therefore to be enmeshed in a closely knit clump of social structure, but one different from Ego's. The weak tie between Ego and his acquaintance, therefore, becomes not merely a trivial acquaintance tie but rather a crucial bridge between the two densely knit clumps of close friends. To the extent that the assertion of the previous paragraph is correct, these clumps would not, in fact, be connected to one another at all were it not for the existence of weak ties.
>
> It follows, then, that individuals with few weak ties will be deprived of information from distant parts of the social system and will be confined to the provincial news and views of their close friends. This deprivation will not only insulate them from the latest ideas and fashions but may put them in a disadvantaged position in the labour market, where advancement can depend, as I have documented elsewhere (1974), on knowing about appropriate job openings at just the right time.
>
> (Granovetter, 1983, p. 202)

An interesting test of SWT theory was conducted by Weimann (1983) on the entire social network of a Kibbutz population. Tests were made of the speed and accuracy of information transmitted through both strong ties and weak ties. Strong ties were superior *within* groups in the Kibbutz, but *between* groups, weak tie links were faster in disseminating news, gossip, innovations, and consumer information. Interpreting these results, Weimann referred to the 'structural advantage' of weak ties as bridges between separate groups. He reasoned that the low multiplexity of weak ties makes their contact nets more diverse, whereas the higher multiplexity of strong ties creates more redundant paths within the network and so 'creates segmentation' which limits their capacity for 'expansiveness' beyond the group.

Small worlds

The small-world concept allows us to think of the world, or a large population, as a sparse network of people who are linked by relatively few ties that act as conduits of information or control. The actual location of these ties may remain unknown to the observer. At the heart of the small-world phenomenon is the principle that people belong to social networks that are linked to other networks by weak ties. Actors in the movie industry constitute a small world, comprised of a clustered population (n = 226,000) with a sparse set of links among them. Indeed a study has been conducted on the number of steps needed to reach any actor from Kevin Bacon, who appears to be linked indirectly to everyone!

The small world refers to the reachability of one person to another through acquaintanceship chains when the persons involved are socially and physically remote. It has generated the phrase 'six degrees of separation' and a play and film with that title, to capture the popular notion that everyone on the globe is reachable in five or six contacts. A small world is defined by Robins *et al.* (2005) as 'a graph that has low density, is highly clustered, but has short characteristic path lengths' (p. 900). The two key features mentioned here relate to local network structure (the clustering level) and the global network (path length). Bonacich (2004) argues that 'small world models are useful when there is a natural tendency to cluster' and that 'networks with a high degree of clustering may or may not be small worlds, depending on the patterns of weak ties in the network' (p. 287).

Whereas weak ties are sometimes viewed as active modes of contact, as I have illustrated and as others have shown in establishing the small-world concept, an aspect of particular interest is the passive expression of weak ties, through the spread of seditious activity or the spread of infectious disease. Modern society contains relatively dense clusters of people within an overall network of low density. All that is needed for disease transmission across clusters is a single bridge. In the Great Plague of the seventeenth century, the disease carrier to the relatively isolated village of Eyam in Derbyshire was a cloth merchant, bringing infected wool into the village. The result was decimation of the inhabitants. The village priest, Rev. Mompessom, realized that the only way of controlling the spread of the disease was to confine it within its bounds, by imposing quarantine on all inhabitants of the village. The contagion was controlled, but at the cost of great local loss of life, including the priest's entire family. That historical event saw its modern expression in the SARS outbreak of 2003, where short path lengths linked the carrier to large populations scattered around the globe.

Watts (1999) has modelled the small-world effect on vectors of disease. He writes, 'It is the size of the largest connected component that drives the spread of disease across a population' (p. 519). His models of network parameters reveal the flaws in our assumption that infectious diseases like Asian bird flu are confined to isolated groups in a population and thus are remote from our concern. His message is disturbing; the clustered and interlinked nature of the small world means that the risks of disease outbreak are very close.

Methods of identifying networks

Social network data may be collected in a number of ways. These include field observations, interviews, diary records, newspaper reports, class lists, minutes of meetings, and archives of the membership rolls of organizations. The focus of enquiry may be individuals (Who is friends with whom? Which persons are board members of which corporations?), groups (Which companies provide services to which corporations?), or nations (Which nations trade with one another?). Social network research is time-consuming. It puts heavy demands on the energy of researchers, because to do it well, painstaking collection of minutiae is required, and where interviews are undertaken, care is needed in deciding what questions to ask. Moreover, network analysis generates lots of data. For example, the number of ties among members of a network is calculated as $(N \times N-1)/2$; this means the undirected ties linking 10 persons are 45, and rapidly increase along with an increase in network size, so that the complete number of undirected ties linking 100 persons is 4450.

Most network elicitation methods begin by focusing on the personal social network. Respondents are asked to list the names of people they know, or like, or communicate with. Having listed the names, respondents are then asked to describe the persons listed and the nature of their relationship with the person named. This procedure enables the investigator to describe the content of the relationship as well as its direction. The format for eliciting the network information may consist of a ruled sheet, which allows the respondent to list each person on a row and then describe her/his relationship with that person by checking information set out in a series of columns. This information may refer to the kind of relation (relative, friend, work colleague), the length of time known, the frequency of contact, and the importance of the person on some criterion.

A variant of the mode of elicitation is to use a set of cards in a simple interview. As the respondent names the persons in their network, the interviewer writes each name on a separate card, numbered on the back. When the listing is exhausted, the interviewer can give the name cards to the respondent and ask her/him to select the cards of people according to a social relation, for example 'friendly with', 'hang out with', or 'seek advice from'. The numbers of the cards are recorded each time. Another variant is more visual, and is related to the support functions of network members. It uses a chart showing a set of three circles radiating from a single point (ego), so that the circles represent differing degrees of closeness or importance to ego. The respondent is asked to write on the chart the initials of each person previously named so that the position of the names represents their relation to ego and perhaps their relation to one another as well.

Elicitation of the total network by a cumulative approach is generally known as snowball sampling. Once a person's social ties have been listed, names are randomly chosen from the list, and these new people are interviewed to determine their personal networks. The procedure is then repeated. A variant of this procedure is the random walk, described by McGrady *et al.* (1995) and used to obtain a broad sample of adolescents in a survey of HIV transmission in several cities.

Where the names of the target population are known, as is true in schools and defined communities, a list of names can be drawn up and given to each respondent so that the total network is assembled from the personal network data provided by each of the respondents. A comprehensive approach is to provide each respondent with all the names, set out in matrix format, and obtain from each informant a description of the network ties of all the others named, as these are perceived by that informant. This task is a daunting one when the list is long, and some researchers have taken shortcuts on this approach by asking a select group of informants to peruse the list and each indicate which persons listed are linked to others in the list in terms of the relation of interest.

Reliability

Among the issues to be resolved when ensuring that the network information obtained is reliable are accuracy of recall, and reducing fatigue. A persistent problem in recall-based eliciting of personal network ties is forgetting. The consequences of omitting some names can distort the estimation of network size and restrict the identification of network ties that may be important for tracing a particular link (as in infectious disease research), or for estimating the effect of social influence processes, for example on smoking. Brewer (2000) argues that people forget a significant proportion of even their close contacts, and they are more likely to forget weak ties than strong ones. He suggests that where a list of potential members cannot be provided, investigators should apply techniques that will enhance recall, such as the use of multiple name generator questions, non-specific prompting, and re-interviewing.

In eliciting a young person's personal network, attention needs to be given to the wording of the instructions so as to ensure that the respondent is clear about the pool of contacts that is of interest to the investigation, so that the list of names obtained is as complete as possible. Interviews are superior to questionnaires. Liebow *et al.* (1995), for example, began with the following preamble, which was followed with a specific set of questions to elicit the names of network members according to different kinds of 'relational domains':

> I'd like you to think about the main people in your life. These are the people who matter to you (in a good way, a bad way, or both). They also include the people who care about you, and who you make a difference to. They are people you know, and who know you. They can be relatives, friends, enemies, neighbours, people at school, people you do things with, and so on.
>
> (Liebow *et al.*, 1995, p. 269)

In her study of Dublin youth, Kirke (1996) used two name generator questions in order to remove any possible ambiguity about the people to be included in the list of an adolescent's friends. Her first question asked the respondent to name her/his friends, defining different kinds of friends, from best friend to boy/girlfriend, other good friends, and anyone else who is a friend; in a separate question she asked respondents to name others 'you pal around with'.

Another factor that may limit the reliability and accuracy of network elicitation is respondent fatigue. Researchers who gather social network data from young people generally restrict the interview time to less than an hour in order to minimize fatigue. Other strategies have been employed as well. For example, Bo (1989) employed a method intended to reduce fatigue as well as to increase the pool of names that was recalled, by conducting the data-gathering over several days. At the conclusion of the initial interview, Bo left the name list open to addition: the boys were able to take a copy of the list with them so that they could add any names to it that they may have initially forgotten. The final list and relational detail were consolidated at a second interview some days later. Another approach to minimizing fatigue was that taken by Kirke (1996). She asked a small number of questions about all the names listed by each adolescent, and then followed up with detailed questions about a few names on their list.

It is interesting to note that researchers who conduct interview-based surveys of young people's personal networks in a careful and sensitive way report high levels of compliance. Kirke (1996), for example, was able to interview almost every adolescent in the target population. McGrady *et al.* (1995) reported that not a single interview was abandoned by request of the respondent, and that young people willingly answered sensitive questions, giving them confidence about the validity of the risk-related data they obtained (see also Liebow *et al.*, 1995). What can be concluded is that when substantial 'up front' efforts are made, such as ethnographic fieldwork, or door-knocking to establish the population, and when additional care is taken in the interview and follow-up, efforts to elicit accurate youth social networks are rewarded.

Matrix

Raw data obtained from data collection are transferred to a matrix for analysis. The matrix is known in sociology as a sociomatrix and in network analysis as an adjacency matrix (in recognition that nodes are said to be adjacent when joined by a line). Typically it is square, containing the names of actors arranged in k rows and k columns. Where several relations between persons (actors) are of interest, each relation (for example, liking, advice, help) is entered as a separate matrix. Another kind of matrix has different entries for its rows and its columns, and is known as a two-mode network. An example is an incidence matrix, which contains nodes plotted against lines that link the nodes, so as to show which lines are 'incident' with which nodes. For example, the matrix could show the connection between student association with one another and college residence, with rows r1 ... r25 nodes representing students and columns c1 ... c6 representing 'resides in the (name) college'.

Affiliation networks

An interesting kind of two-mode network is an affiliation network; it allows actors to be studied together with the events that they attend or the environments that they inhabit (see Figure 2.5). Event data for assembling such a network can come from observations of young people's attendance at local events, or from interviews concerning their use of haunts and hangouts. Other data sources include membership lists of school clubs, sporting groups and community organizations. In an affiliation matrix the row entries consist of persons, while the columns contain the entries for events, locations or memberships. The matrix allows an analysis to be made of how the actors are linked to the events that they attended as well as how the events are related to the actors who attended them. That is to say, membership of the same organizations, or attendance at the same event, supplies the basis for establishing network ties. The resulting networks are established through associations between subsets of actors rather than through ties between pairs of actors, as is the case for one-mode networks.

What is shown in Figure 2.5 is that attendance at certain events, or membership of particular groups or clubs, provides a basis for association, and the information can be applied to establish a social network. Two kinds

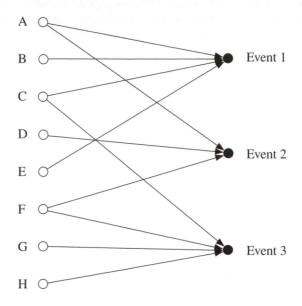

Figure 2.5 Connections between persons and events

of networks can be detected, one being the ties among persons derived from common attendance at certain events or in certain locations, and the other being the ties among locations and events based on similarities in membership or attendance. The film *Four Weddings and a Funeral* illustrates the intersection of persons and events. The same group of friends was found at each wedding, and presumably not at weddings attended by other guests, so their network connections could be discovered through their common attendance. Of course, lists of all attendees at the focal events are needed before a matrix can be constructed. This necessary if tedious impediment protects an observer from too quickly jumping to conclusions about possibly salacious associations.

Environments and networks

Network thinking emphasizes that each individual is connected to others through direct and indirect social ties. People are simultaneously linked to the groups that those persons belong to, through the environments that contain them. The point is that social environments foster network growth. How do they do this? Different environments (workplaces, neighbourhoods, churches) contain different groups of people. Connections between environments provide linkages that connect their separate memberships. Fischer *et al.* (1977) emphasized the links between environments and social networks in the title of their book, *Networks and Places*.

The issue of environments is important to discuss for practical reasons, such as the relationship concerns of emerging adults. For example, how do you find friends when you take a new job, or move to a new town? Drawing on the concepts of social milieu and social circles introduced by Georg Simmel in the 1920s, Feld argued that social ties are organized through a *focus*, which he defined as 'a social, psychological, legal or physical entity around which joint activities are organized' (Feld, 1981, p. 1016). His examples of 'extra-network foci' included workplaces, hangouts and voluntary organizations. How does a 23-year-old guy meet a nice girl? Answers to such a question include making contact through network links, such as the blind date and the internet chat-room, but another strategy is to take Feld's advice and exploit the social network possibilities of different social milieux, such as the workplace, a sports event, a friend's party, or the evening social hour at the local pub. The film *Wedding Crashers* dramatizes how two young men exploit the milieu of weddings to contact single young women.

Feld's argument is that a focus is organized around a particular set of interests and activities, and people whose own interests are compatible with those of the focus will encounter others who share the same interests. One young adult explained to me his focal strategy for finding his type of girl: 'If you are a sports type, and you want to meet a girl with similar interests, you get involved in sports clubs; if you are intellectual, you join intellectual groups or go to events where people talk about art or history. But you won't find too many librarians at basketball games!' The point being made here is that each social setting contains a population that has common interests. When a person enters a new setting, the possibility arises that the range of network others will be increased. Feld reasoned that people who belong to few foci will tend to have dense networks, whereas people who expand their personal network by connecting to new foci will have networks of lower density, because in the latter case fewer persons are tied to one another. The pull of obligations to network members in dense networks is a retarding force on individuals who may want to break into a new social circle. Because the social tie that provides the link to a new focus is likely to be weakly connected to others and to ego, people in dense networks discourage their members from cultivating weak tie contacts.

Environments create network opportunities through expanding the pool of acquaintances. Evidence that network opportunity contributes to the growth of friendships comes from a study of Dutch youth in Groningen, a university town, by van Duijn *et al.* (2003). They studied the emergence of friendship ties amongst students beginning college. Environmental features of the town included student accommodation and eating places that were scattered across the town, and the concentration in the one building of the academic program, the classrooms, the faculty offices, and the canteen. These physical locations juxtaposed focal settings that fostered social contact amongst the students. The authors monitored network growth by a series of seven questionnaires across the year. They plotted the acquaintanceship ties from these data sets at the beginning of the year, after three weeks, after six weeks and after thirteen weeks. Dramatic changes occurred in network size and connectivity as early as three weeks, by which time 'the group of strangers is transformed into a group of persons who know one another and start doing things together' (van Duijn *et al.*, 2003, p. 172). These changes were independent of psychological factors.

Network measures

I describe in this section some of the most common terms in social network analysis, to enable discussion to proceed in this and the chapters that follow. The chapter notes provide key references that should be consulted for fuller descriptions and technical explanation.

- *Size* is a measure of the number of actors (nodes) in a network.
- *Composition* refers to how the network is comprised, based on the kinds of relations in the network: kin, friend, business associate.
- *Density* is a measure of the number of actual ties in the network as a proportion of the total possible ties among its membership. Larger networks tend to be less dense than smaller networks, so that comparisons between networks in terms of density need to control for network size.
- *Reachability* refers to the number of intermediaries enlisted to reach one part of a network from another in the most direct fashion. To determine if it is possible for Actor F to get a message to Actor A, a path must exist between them, linking them in a network graph, based on some relation such as liking or acquaintanceship. If such a path exists, Actor A is said to be reachable from Actor F.
- *Betweenness* refers to the extent to which an actor occupies an important position in the network such that others are dependent on this actor for transmission or receipt of information to or from other sectors of the network. Actors who operate as brokers between sectors of a network, or as gatekeepers, have a high betweenness score.

- *Centrality* is a measure of the impact that an actor has on others in the network. Several kinds of centrality measures are described by McCarty (2002). *Degree Centrality* is 'a measure of network activity' and indicates the extent to which an actor in a network is directly linked to other actors. *Closeness Centrality* is 'a measure of independence from the control of others' and indicates how close an actor is to all the others in the network. *Betweenness Centrality* is 'a measure of information control' and refers to an actor's key location 'between' the others in a network graph, and carries the sense of 'go-between' and 'middle-man'.

How do these network measures apply to young people's social relations? Do students who have dense network ties find it harder to adapt to a new school or college? Does network cohesiveness explain something about bullying – namely that bullies are well connected, and victims are not? Is peer popularity a constraint on one's freedom to be oneself? Are acquaintances sometimes more helpful than close friends? Questions such as these are explored in later chapters.

Portraying networks

In recent years, a body of research tools and techniques has emerged that provides the analytical firepower to examine and display specific properties of social networks. These tools and techniques have benefited from developments in physics and mathematics, particularly graph theory, as well as from improved computer graphics, and have come to be known as *network science*, a cross-disciplinary field that is concerned with studying 'the relations among actors, and the nature of individual functioning within structured social relations' (Klerks, 2001, p. 58). Particularly exciting are the developments in graphic presentations that model network structures in visually powerful formats that are highly communicable to researchers and practitioners.

Remember those molecular structures in the chemistry lab at school, with their rods and billiard balls? The original researchers on the structure of DNA relied on such cumbersome model-building methods to portray molecular structures. Reasoning that networks resemble complex molecules, Klovdahl (1981) in the early 1980s adopted a similar approach to portray connected social structures, using computer graphics. Improvements since then in the visualization of social networks have increased the ability of researchers to understand patterns of relations and to communicate these, either by drawing two-dimensional diagrams showing the links among actors, or by generating three-dimensional models. Freeman (2000) has traced the development of this visualization facility from Moreno's hand-drawn points and lines of the 1930s up to the colour graphics of modern times, illustrating the progression of display methods in vivid images, and including examples of Klovdahl's images. I have drawn attention to Freeman's paper to underline the value of visual portrayal of social network structures for guiding both researchers and practitioners towards a richer understanding of the patterns in social relations. As we find in recent research on health risk, visualization of patterns can elucidate meaning, as well as alert the investigator to structures that are not easily detected by computer analyses.[3]

Conclusion: moving beyond the metaphor

The widespread acceptance of networks as a way of describing intercon-nected systems ranging from telecommunications to terrorism is evidence that the network metaphor is easily understood. There is a risk, however, that the use of network as metaphor may undermine genuine network analysis. The early popularity of social network research certainly caused Mitchell (1973) to be concerned about the dangers of confusing a metaphor for a method. Social science is replete with metaphor, and practitioners must constantly be on guard against reifying the concepts they employ, including network, ecology and identity, lest the extra baggage attached to favoured concepts causes them to sink under their own ponderous weight. Care will be taken in the following chapters to limit the meaning of key concepts, so as to avoid overloading the saddlebag with unnecessary terms. Where re-searchers have employed network analysis, the measures will be explained and discussed, so as to provide a common basis for understanding and to reduce confusion arising from the rampant use of metaphor.

Vigorous development of network analysis techniques, associated with improvements in computing capacity and programs, has enabled rapid expansion and sophistication of the field. However, a good deal of network research remains focused on refining the tools of analysis, almost as an end in itself. Inspection of any issue of the journal *Social Networks*, for example, will yield articles that are devoted to improving the methods of data collection or testing measures of reliability for key concepts such as centrality. True, there are applications of network analysis to substantive issues such as AIDS, crime, and delinquency, but for network thinking and network analysis to achieve greater strength and power, what seems to be required is an injection of growth hormones from theoretical advances occurring in other fields, including education and social psychology. Some of these advances, or the possibilities for these as they relate to young people, are discussed in this book.

The purpose of this chapter and the previous one has been to canvass some of the social concerns that confront young people through the adolescent years and into the period of emerging adulthood, as backcloth to the application of network science and network thinking to particular youth concerns. An argument made in the chapters that follow is that social network growth enables the young person to develop the competencies required for participation in adult society. The strengths of network analysis methods for understanding youth concerns are outlined below.

First, social networks are useful for describing the structures and sets of relations found in an individual's social landscape and for identifying key figures and groups in a person's social field. Friendships are seen to be embedded in a broader system of relations through the social ties of each friend with others. The degree of overlap between the social network of one person and that person's friends is critical in determining their access to new people. Social network analysis deals with the geography, as it were, of social relations.

Second, group cohesiveness can be assessed by social network methods, and group structures identified. For example, peer networks that are comprised of many overlapping ties among the members and few ties to peers outside the group tend to be self-sufficient, insular, and impervious to outside influence, because members' energies are directed towards maintaining the network structure rather than investing in new relationships. Thus once a teenager has joined a sect or a gang, attempts by adults to dislodge her/him from the group by undermining the links and weakening its cohesiveness are likely to fail.

Third, network analysis provides structural insights into social influences, for understanding both peer pressure and adult influence on young people's behaviour and decisions. Peer influences are assumed to be strongest where social network ties are strong, and where members are linked through multiplex ties. From such a perspective, youth workers who have not established multiplex links with particular street youth will have difficulty making a positive impact on their lifestyles.

Fourth, social support can be understood by examining network structures. Different kinds of network supply different kinds of support. Strongly tied dense networks are able to respond faster in times of emotional crisis. In times of transition and uncertainty, loose networks of weak ties are more appropriate, because they contain more diverse resources, and contacts that are bridges to other groups.

To conclude, social networks are not just metaphors; they are active social arrangements that create community, confirm identity, and prevent loneliness. 'People belong to networks as well as to categories', wrote Wellman (1988, p. 32). Social networks reflect the regularities of how adolescents and youth actually interact in regular social exchanges. They operate as miniature social systems structuring the individual's social opportunities, and linking them to others who can provide various social resources. The versatility of social network analysis is that it offers a means of describing the structures in social relations from both an individual and a group perspective.

Part II
Social networks

3 Networks and groups

The goal of this chapter is to describe the range of social structures inhabited by young people, from cliques to social networks, and in so doing, to move beyond *the peer group* as a catch-all term for describing sociality structures among young people. Traditionally, *the peer group* has been a convenient identifier for all kinds of collectivities where youth are found, and has been invoked to explain all kinds of behaviour from risk-taking to school truancy and fashions in clothing. In my opinion, *the peer group* is a vague term that has been overworked, and it is overdue for retirement. After all, the term does not adequately represent the variety of group alliances that young people form with their peers; and the structures serve different social purposes that it is important to distinguish. Ennett and Bauman (1993) lamented this vagueness in terminology. They commented that, 'Despite pervasive interest in the peer group, the literature reflects a surprising lack of clarity in conceptualizations of the peer group and little consideration of peer group structure' (p. 227). This chapter enlists social network approaches in order to outline the different structural forms found in young people's social relations. The group structures include cliques, peer crowds, and loose groups as network components. Each is described and its relations to other structures discussed. Moreover, information about a young person's location in these structures is employed in order to understand aspects of individual development and a young person's susceptibility to social influence.

Adopting a networks perspective

Whether or not we belong to a group, we are inescapably linked to others through network ties. The networked nature of our social existence is easily overlooked because we are prone to think of our social world in terms of face-to-face relations, located in observable group formats, while the network in which the relations are anchored may not be obvious to us. A network perspective shows that groups are not bounded entities but are linked to one another through the social ties of actors with overlapping memberships. What may seem to be a distinct group of persons when briefly observed in a single setting soon loses its shape when tracked across time and space. Longer observations of these 'intact' groups reveal that someone leaves the group, or that others join it, or that the original group splits into two groups.

Social networks and groups co-exist, but as different social entities, although the terms appear at times to be interchangeable. Groups are based on particular social relations; networks open out a panorama. Groups are tamed and corralled; networks are wild things, not easily roped in. Groups are the same for each member; networks vary for each member, because each has a unique location and a distinct set of ties to others. Networks contain groups that overlap and whose boundaries change, so that individuals can be linked to several groups. While people may choose whether or not to join a certain group, network membership is inescapable. In summary, network membership is less precise, less categorical, and more fluid, which makes it sometimes hard to determine the nature of the links between people. For example, situations arise where people may not have activated some social ties for a considerable time, so that certain links in their network may lie dormant. Thus a person's social network tends to be much larger in size and more varied in scope than the sector of the network that is active at a particular time.

Moreover, networks are independent of the individual. The choice of another person as a friend links you with that friend's social network, and thus to a system of relationships beyond your control. Thus we have the axioms 'A friend of a friend is a friend' and 'A friend of an enemy is an enemy'. Salzinger (1982) emphasized this point when she wrote: 'First, [people] cannot control the degree of connectedness within their immediate networks, and second, they cannot control the configuration of relationships in their friend's networks. In fact their "free choices" have linked them to a larger system which they cannot control, and which will significantly affect their lives' (p. 119). Social networks connect us to others who have no direct connections with us, by links that can affect our fortunes. The point was humorously treated in the 1999 Hugh Grant film, *Married to the Mob*, where Grant's character (Michael Felgate) can't work out why his girlfriend Gina won't marry him, even though she loves him. What Michael is unaware of is that Gina is concerned to keep Michael from meeting her mobster father. Inevitably, the two men meet and become friendly, with the consequence that Michael finds himself doing favours for the gangsters through his job as an art auctioneer.

This chapter applies network approaches to identify structures in young people's social relations. Network thinking is not hostile to group concepts. What it offers is insight into the ways that persons are linked to groups through their personal ties, and that groups are nested within other groups. The embeddedness of groups within networks was evident to the young informants in a study of adolescent smokers. One teenage girl explained it this way: 'But we have ... we have groups within the group as well.' Her friend agreed: 'Yeah. So we've got this big group of like twenty people or something ... and we're just little groups' (Abel *et al.*, 2002, p. 330).

Groups observed

I begin with observations of young people in public places, which is the usual point of exposure for most practitioners who work with youth. Likely locations in any large town or city are the open plazas and pedestrian malls. On a Friday or Saturday evening these are crowded with young people intent on meeting up with others before going off to some activity or entertainment. Notable are the groups and collectivities, characterized by much coming and going. The group boundaries are unclear and constantly changing, as individuals follow shifting patterns of alliance. Smaller groups break away and then rejoin the main group, suggesting the existence of substructures such as friendship cliques. The process of assembling the larger group is often noisy and accompanied by displays of affection (hugging between girls, slapping and high fives among boys), as well as shouts and squeals of surprise when members see other friends or acquaintances, who are persuaded to join the group. The whole buzz of noise, movement and shifting alliances found in this collectivity of youth resembles the flocking pattern of lorikeets in the trees outside my window.

The questions for the researcher or youth worker are: what are the underlying social structures in this seething mass of young people, and how can they be identified? The simplest methods of describing social structures in the field are topological ones, and they have long been employed by researchers and practitioners to impose order and pattern on naturally occurring social phenomena. The patterns observed are easily communicated, and the method connects us to the earlier field studies of youth that were reported by Dunphy (1963) in Australia and by Sherif and Sherif (1964) in the United States.

An illustration of the topological approach follows, based on observations of youth in the central pedestrian mall of Brisbane. The observer's focus was on a group of ten adolescent boys about 15 to 16 years of age, who stood out from the buzzing confusion of young people in the mall because of their casual relaxed manner. Their main purpose seemed to be to 'hang around' and 'check out the talent'. For a time they stood chatting together and

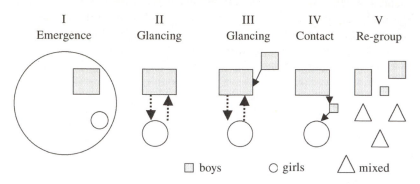

Figure 3.1 Changes in group structure following clique contact

glancing around, but then their attention took focus on a nearby group of five girls who were also casting glances at the boys. In this period of group attentiveness and appraisal, which lasted for some minutes, the boys' group swelled with the addition of several new arrivals. The glances between the groups continued, accompanied by smiles from the girls, in a manner that seemed 'flirtatious' to the observer. Following the continued glances between the two groups, the body language of group members 'became intense' and the glancing looks became bolder, with shuffling and jostling among group members. Eventually, after about half an hour, one boy broke away from his mates and walked over to talk to the girls. Other boys then followed the leader to join the girls' group. The observer quit monitoring the group at that point, but later that same evening saw various group members, now in smaller subgroups. These cliques had formed from the merging of high-status members from the male and female groups, while the remnant of the boys' group had broken into two smaller groups. The history of group contact and structural change is sketched out in Figure 3.1. It shows in simple form several structures: the single-sex clusters observed within the large collectivity of young people, and the emergence of mixed-sex cliques, with remnant single-sex cliques.

Similar topological approaches have been used to portray clique patterns within classrooms. An example is that of Griffiths (1995) who observed the way that cliques influenced girls' seating locations, and portrayed the group structures ('interaction sets') in the classrooms to show the separate classroom territories inhabited by girls and boys. Use of these simple sketch-maps of girls' seating locations allowed Griffiths to discuss the tenacity with which the girls maintained contact with their clique, even when they had been separated by the teacher for some misdemeanour.

Critical comment

To this point, the discussion has traversed territory that is common to many older texts on adolescent social relations. The group structures inferred from the field observations are interesting enough, but they are impressionistic; and the information is familiar to anyone who has firsthand experience with young people's social lives. Much more is required of this chapter to enable readers to identify with any degree of accuracy the structures of young people's social relations, and to gain analytical insights into what the structural patterns may mean. For that goal to be met, what is needed are more systematic methods of enquiry into the patterns of social relations among young people. Social network analysis provides a fresh stream of ideas about structures in social relations as well as an extensive and sophisticated set of tools for analysing them. Network analysis can trace the ties that link individual persons to one another, and can examine the patterns of association that emerge. Importantly, network analysis is capable of detecting the structural components of networks, as well as the links that connect the actors within them.

A pioneer of network thinking within the field of adolescence is Robert Cairns. In 1998, he and his colleagues (Cairns *et al.*, 1998) listed what they saw as the goals of social network analysis. They are stated as follows: 'To identify groups of people who affiliate with one another, how groups are related to one another and to the system as a whole, and whether some individuals are members of several groups' (p. 30). These goals admirably serve our purposes in this chapter. I begin with small groups and discuss the ties that link people together, and progress to the examination of intergroup relations, before discussing the analysis of whole networks and their components.

Cliques and clusters

Adolescent cliques

Cliques are natural groupings of peers. Members are of similar ages, have similar interests, communicate easily with one another, and spend a great deal of their time together simply enjoying one another's company. Although cliques remain valued sociality structures all our lives, associating in cliques is distinctively an activity that has importance in adolescence. The cliques are exclusively same-sex in early adolescence; it is only in later years that mixed-sex cliques form. For the most part, male and female adolescents don't hang around together, generally preferring their own gender for company. These gender preferences remain well beyond the adolescent years, so that even among college groups, cliques are predominantly single-sex, as Salzinger's network analysis shows (see Chapter 2).

In network terminology a clique is defined as a subset that contains three or more actors who are all linked to one another, which makes them the 'optimally cohesive subgroup' (Frank, 1995, p. 29). However, in real life, cliques are rarely so cohesive that they are exclusive social groups; one finds that some clique members are tied to others who are attached to other cliques. As a consequence, network analysis rarely delivers clean well-defined groups. The problem of overlap in the clique boundaries means that the investigator must decide on the most appropriate boundary to apply to define the cliques. Visual inspection of a network diagram may be sufficient for the practitioner to make such decisions, but researchers prefer to rely upon a statistical approach.

Rules for determining clique boundaries are similar for the various network analysis programs[1] in use by researchers. The NEGOPY network analysis program requires that at least 50 per cent of the reciprocated ties are to members within the same clique. Other programs such as UCINET and GRADAP employ similar rules but allow the investigator to modify them so that looser cliques are produced than the standard clique. Allocation of subjects in a survey population to specific groups will always leave some dangling between groups, and others left out of groups altogether, simply because the amount of information about particular people is too limited to allocate them to a clique with any degree of certainty. It is also possible that the degree of success in forming cliques from the data varies from one program to another. Choice of the most appropriate methods depends on the researchers' particular objectives, and the different network analysis programs will produce slightly different cliques, because of variations in the rules employed. Finding the most appropriate program for a particular data set thus involves a certain amount of trial and error.

The problem of clique identification is illustrated in a study by J. Moody (2001) which employed several different network analysis programs to determine the clique boundaries within the same set of data (see Figure 3.2). What can be seen in the figure is that, while there is a great deal of agreement between the results produced by the NEGOPY and RNM programs that Moody used, in terms of the assignment of actors to cliques, differences in the assignment of a single actor to a particular clique produce clear differences in clique boundaries. These differences need not be regarded as problematic; indeed, scrutiny of the differences in clique boundaries might be informative in explaining the ambiguous affiliations or divided loyalties of particular actors.

In the Ryan (2001) study of young adolescent friendships, which used UCINET, respondents could be members of only one type of group; those

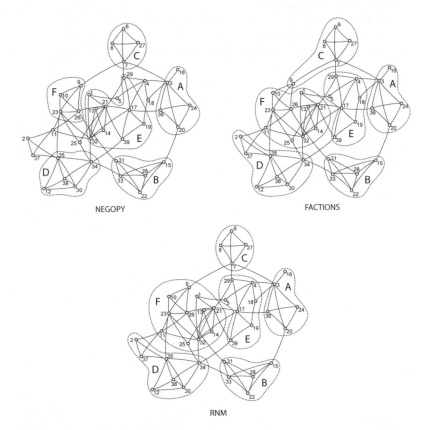

Figure 3.2 Clique boundaries in a prison network determined by different methods

Source: Original figure appears as Figure 8 in an article by James Moody in *Social Networks*, *23*, 2001, pp. 261–283. Used by permission of Elsevier Ltd.

who had social ties to more than one group were assigned to the one that contained the greatest number of their direct and indirect ties. On both testing occasions, 83 per cent of students' direct ties were with their group. Hallinan and Smith (1989) used the program COMPLT, which allowed them to merge two subgraphs if two-thirds of the members overlapped. In the six surveys on cliques that they conducted across the school year in twenty-six racially mixed classes, this procedure resulted in them detecting between sixty-two and sixty-seven cliques containing at least three members.

The average size of cliques reported by network studies of adolescents is remarkably similar, and ranges from about five to six members. For example, Ryan (2001) reported average clique sizes of slightly less than five, and Ennett and Bauman (1993) found similar sizes: 5.3 at Wave 1 and 5.0 at Wave 2. The clique size reported by Liu and Chen (2003) for Chinese adolescents was 6.0, and the size of cliques in the Shrum and Cheek (1987) research averaged 6.5 members for Grade 7–8 students and 6.3 members for Grades 9–12. Hallinan and Smith (1989) found that the cliques grew larger across the school year, averaging 4.9 early in the year and 6.4 at the end. There were three distinct cliques on average within each class of students. The consistency of these sizes across time and culture is convincing, and compares closely to the average size (6.2) and range in size (from three to nine) reported by Dunphy (1963) in his fieldwork observations of forty-four cliques in Sydney, almost fifty years earlier.

A requirement of network analysis programs like the NEGOPY program is that friendship choices be reciprocated; and that at least 50 per cent of an individual's ties should be to other members of the clique. This rule ensures that cliques are comprised of actors who are closely tied to one another. However, cliques in real life are not always so tightly knit, and they can only be identified where the rule for inclusion is relaxed. Social network researchers have devised a number of ways of relaxing the requirement for interconnectivity so that looser groupings that are of interest to the analyst might emerge within a network. Some of these methods are briefly cited here, but interested readers should pursue the original sources for detailed explanations. One approach is to increase the admissible path length of the clique so that indirectly linked actors (that is, those who are connected by a path length of 2, not 1) are able to be included in the clique, resulting in what is known as an *n-clique*. An alternative strategy was proposed by Seidman (1983), known as a *k-plex*. Instead of focusing on the path length, the rule imposes limits on the number of actors that each member must be connected to, so that a 2-plex is a graph that allows inclusion of a person if connected to at least two of the other clique members.

Researchers in adolescence prefer to speak of 'loose groups' rather than use the network terminology of *n-cliques* or *k-plexes* and similar terms to describe adolescents who associate with one another without reporting a mutual friendship, and thus are 'loosely connected' to one another. The descriptions given of loose groups by Urberg *et al.* (1995) and by Hallinan and Kubitschek (1999) refer to groups that fail to meet the clique criteria imposed by NEGOPY because there are insufficient mutual ties between members, although ties may exist between them which are not reciprocated. Earlier, Granovetter (1973) had drawn attention to the existence of groups where some affective ties are weaker than others. He noted that if A and B are friends, and if A and C are friends, then B and C must at least be acquaintances. Clique rules that require at least half the ties to be reciprocated eliminate the weakly tied persons from group membership, and also change the shape of the clique, whereas a looser group can be identified where persons are linked because each interacts with at least one fellow group member more than with any person outside the group. Freeman (1992) examined the consequences of adopting Granovetter's weak tie rule, and applied it successfully to the detection of group structure from known data sets.

Another method of studying clique structures and their inter-relationships is the Galois lattice (Freeman, 1996), which reveals the structures formed within a social network as individual actors are progressively linked together into increasingly more inclusive clusters. A Galois lattice is a mathematical procedure for tracing the relation between two sets of elements (for example, actors and groups, or actors and events). The lattice captures changes in the relations between the two sets of elements as the actors are progressively grouped by the program, from the initial point where all actors are distinct individuals, through a succession of groupings, to the concluding point where all actors belong to the one group.

For small networks, the lattice structure is easy to visualize. It resembles a birdcage, with a meeting point at its top and a joining point at its base, in between which is the broadening cage that displays the lattice structure. The top part of the cage represents the emergence of different subsets with their contained elements, and the bottom part of the cage shows their submergence in broader groups. The lattice has considerable potential for tracing change in social relations, for example gang membership or the integration of students into a school or college environment. An example applied to a small network is found in Freeman (1996). An application to a large social network is reported by Falzon (2000), where the network linkages between actors and groups were shown separately for each layer of the lattice. Accuracy of group allocation was high; Falzon was able to confirm the validity of the group composition obtained by the lattice technique with the members of the fifteen groups themselves.

Peer crowds and social clusters

The Galois lattice procedure is a reminder that adolescents and youth not only belong to cliques of friends but that, because of the overlapping nature of cliques, they also belong to broader groupings of peers. These groupings have been given various names, such as peer crowds, friendship networks and social clusters. The common feature of these groups is that they are broader than the typical clique. They may contain several cliques, or include a pair of friends in the cluster, and/or individuals who do not belong to any particular clique. Researchers have recognized that groups other than cliques are important in young people's social worlds. Sometimes these broader groupings are called networks. For example, Cairns and his co-workers encouraged researchers to extend their study of peer relations beyond friendship cliques so as to 'include the pool of relations from which friendships emerge, namely, the social networks in which children are embedded' (Cairns *et al.*, 1995, p. 1341).

The peer crowd[2] is a type of social network that contains several cliques, loosely linked together. Our knowledge of the structure of these groups owes much to the fieldwork of Dunphy (1963) in Sydney in the late 1950s. Dunphy spent lengthy periods of time hanging out with young people in milk bars and on beaches in order to gather data on these peer crowds. He reported that the twelve crowds he studied ranged in size from fifteen to thirty adolescents and youths, with an average size of twenty members and an age range of 13 to 21 years. It should be recalled that the youth recruited in his research were connected to 'sponsored youth organizations' (Dunphy, 1963, p. 232), and the pattern that he detected, where young people going to these clubs would call by one another's houses and gather their friends together on the way to the club, may have led to Dunphy's assertion that 'groups [i.e., the cliques] were clearly recognizable as definite entities' (p. 233).

Dunphy's major contribution to the literature was in identifying distinctive differences in the structure and function of cliques and peer crowds. He argued that peer crowds were entirely composed from cliques, so that clique membership was the required ticket of entry. However, it seems surprising to me that the peer crowd would not include pairs of friends as well as some isolated adolescents who were not even part of a clique, because how would a youth club grow if individuals were unwelcome? Was a condition of entry that you had to bring at least two friends with you? Unfortunately, his descriptions do not supply enough detail for his claims about the relation between cliques and crowds to be challenged, so that the difficulty remains of defining boundaries around clique and peer crowd membership, and of understanding exactly how these two kinds of groups are inter-related.

Evidence that adolescents associate within broader clusters more than in discrete cliques comes from a large survey conducted by Shrum and Cheek (1987). Social relations data were collected on almost 2500 students from Grade 3 to Grade 12 in order to describe the structures of adolescent groups, and to observe whether these structures changed across adolescence. Among the findings that Shrum and Cheek reported was that clique membership declined across the grade levels, particularly during the junior high school years. They argued that the small friendship clique was not the major group structure among adolescents. Instead, youth move away from membership in small tight-knit cliques to associate with a wider range of peers in a more open and diffuse structure. Shrum and Cheek labelled this process 'de-grouping', and noted that while group membership may vary from one particular event to another, there is an overall continuity of association with the larger group and a sense of group belonging among its members.

The study of social clusters by Salzinger (1982) bears further mention, because some of the network structures she identified among Harvard university students fit the loose group pattern. Salzinger gathered her data by a three-phase snowball sampling method, where questionnaires were mailed to a large core sample, and then subsequent mailings were sent to people who were not in the original sample but who were named by her respondents. This approach begins with the personal networks of each respondent and then traces the ties that connect them into the larger social network. Salzinger's paper reports details on eight 'clusters' (sub-networks) that she identified by means of friendship preferences. Some of these were relatively tight-knit structures based on the pattern of reciprocated choices, while other clusters were more loosely structured. Salzinger was interested in whether the structure of social ties in the groups affected how many people the students would know. She found that the social ties of students in the looser networks, compared with those in the more tight-knit networks, were spread across a wider expanse of the student community, so that people in these loose clusters got to know a larger and more diverse range of friends. The effect of being in tight-knit clusters, in contrast, was to 'reinforce their own structures by supporting the relationships they contain at the expense of their members' access to people outside the cluster' (Salzinger, 1982, p. 140).

Understanding of how social ties operate in loose group structures can also be gained from observations of social interaction. Zisman and Wilson (1992) explored whether differences in the permeability (structural looseness/tightness) of groups might affect the extent of inter-racial contact at school. Observations were conducted in the lunch period in the school cafeteria. The observer, Wilson, found that cliques with loose structures functioned differently from those with tight-knit structures. The tight-knit groups were smaller and racially homogeneous. Their members would always eat together in the cafeteria and rarely did they visit others or get visits from them. In contrast, the loose-knit groups contained a core membership which functioned like a clique, but 'unlike the cliques, the core does not shield its members from interacting with non-core members' (Zisman and Wilson, 1992, p. 205). Zisman and Wilson noted that the latter groups operated like 'social waterholes' with much coming and going of members, so that the composition of these groups was more racially mixed and less constant from one lunch period to another. The openness of these social clusters provided an opportunity for adolescents who were not core members of cliques to 'table-hop' into and out of a particular clique without the application of strict sanctions on them. Adolescents who were described as 'table-hoppers' moved between groups and could 'gain entrance to the conversations at more than one table during the lunch period'. From the descriptions given here, they closely resemble what other researchers have termed 'liaison' people.

Liaisons

In some networks there may be a single actor linking different sectors or regions. The connections across different sectors of the network are dependent on the activity of this liaison person as gate-keeper or go-between. The importance of liaisons is recognized in the world of business (e.g. Burt, 2001), as bridges spanning a 'structural hole' in a large network. In adult life, these persons include the 'fixer' in any community, who is the key person to approach in order to get things done, or the person to see if you want cooperation within a community or organization. Within the kinship system, certain actors – perhaps a grandmother or an uncle – connect separate components of the network and maintain its overall cohesion. In day-to-day matters they have the role as mediator or go-between, so that when some lines of communication are soured or broken through ongoing family jealousies and feuds, resulting in separate factions within the broad kin network, they ensure that communication is possible.

Adolescents who occupy these positions in a network have been called 'group peripherals' (Pearson and Michell, 2000), or 'liaisons' in the NEGOPY network analysis program (Richards and Rice, 1981). These youth are not friendless, but instead they have friends who belong to more than one clique or cluster within the larger network. Their significance as links across a network is not immediately apparent from the diagrams given in research papers, where liaisons tend to dangle from a clique, because the total network has been inadequately mapped. They may 'float' between groups, perhaps because they are unwilling or unable to commit solely to one group. The liaison role is important in young people's social relations, because a liaison person enables connections to be established between groups without being closely involved in the groups themselves. Research on adolescent relations has been slow to understand that actors who do not belong to a particular group but who interact with members of several groups can be important players in group life. Indeed, they may be influential network members by virtue of their betweenness and the diverse nature of their connections with group members. Damico (1976) had earlier noticed that adolescents who filled these liaison roles by maintaining their friendships across groups were more socially competent than their peers;

but the focus by researchers on clique-based notions of peer popularity seems to have led to that insight being subsequently ignored.

Research suggests that liaisons comprise a substantial proportion of an adolescent network, but estimates of the number of liaisons are inconsistent. For example, Shrum and Cheek (1987) found that the proportion of liaisons in junior high and senior high school increased, from a figure of 30.4 per cent of students in Grades 7–8 to 47.4 per cent in Grades 9–12. Urberg *et al.* (1997) identified 29 per cent of their sample who fitted the definition of liaison because they were members of more than one clique. Ennett and Bauman (1993) also found a sizeable proportion of liaisons among Grade 9 students, ranging from 18 to 42 per cent across the five schools they studied. In contrast, studies of Chinese students by Fang *et al.* (2003) and by Liu and Chen (2003) identified a relatively small proportion as liaisons (7 per cent and 11.5 per cent in the respective studies), with higher proportions amongst the boys. The figures from the American studies (those by Shrum and Cheek (1987), Urberg *et al.* (1997) and Ennett and Bauman (1993)) seem awfully high, given what we know from field observation about cliques and larger clusters. A plausible explanation is that many of those classified as liaisons in the American studies are clique members of lost cliques,[3] whose other members were not identified because of weaknesses in the research methods (read the study by Kirke (1996) on this point).

There is also the possibility that the reported increases in liaison persons found in the American studies from about Grade 9 are related to the American practice of dispersing students across different classrooms for different school subjects. This explanation was the one that was offered by Shrum and Cheek (1987). They suggested that dispersal across classes in a departmentalized school could be a factor in creating weak ties across non-overlapping groups, where many choices of friends are not reciprocated because the constant change in class membership undermines the class unit as a basis for friendship formation. In contrast, the practice in Chinese secondary schools (and in European ones as well) is to preserve classroom units. Views differ on the merits of the American practice; Ennett and Bauman (1996) take the view that the effect is to create a social network that is more open and less segregated. Others argue that it is important to foster a sense of belonging in students through building strong-tie relations among students within defined and stable groups.

Network components and connectors

Discovering network structures

The first step in locating persons within network structures is to gather data across the entire population of interest. If researchers neglect that step, some of the ties that exist between individuals are ignored, and unnecessary boundaries are placed around many of the persons studied, to the neglect of others who merit inclusion but fall outside the boundaries. Such an approach makes it difficult to get a proper grip on young people's full social relations. A network approach starts at the broadest level. The benefits of this approach were argued by Wellman (1988): 'By starting with networks rather than with groups, analysts are able to study both ties that do not form discrete groups and networks that are, in fact, sufficiently bounded to be termed "groups"' (p. 37). When a large network has been surveyed, the challenge facing an investigator is how to partition the network into dense regions and thus identify its component clusters. Researchers rely on statistical guidelines such as grouping distances, and network properties such as centrality, calculated by the network analysis package, in arriving at a decision. Large networks (of, say, a few hundred persons) have until recently posed serious data-gathering and data-management problems, as Scott (2001) has pointed out, so that apart from the research on risk networks, there is little published work that takes a total network approach to studying young people. What I find commendable about the studies described in the following paragraphs is their whole of network approach to their chosen topic.

Given that networks are social structures, they can be explored in terms of their level of cohesion – the extent to which the links among their members hold the network together. Concepts such as tight-knit structure and network density capture the notion that networks that are bound together will lack any breakaway substructures. More commonly, people are unevenly connected to one another in a social network, so that the overall pattern of ties tends to result in areas of density together with areas that are relatively empty and spanned by few ties. Networks may be cohesive, even with a low density, if the links within the network are evenly distributed so that actors are connected to one another by different paths. A study of network structures by Friedkin (1981) found that with network sizes of 20, cohesion was achieved when the density was <0.20; and with network sizes of 60, the minimum density measure for cohesion dropped to <0.08. The effect of indirect ties within networks means that 'comparable levels of structural cohesion are achieved at lower levels of network density in large networks than in small ones' (Friedkin, 1981, p. 44). More advanced methods of determining structural cohesion have emerged in recent years which take account of connectedness among sets of actors in a network. For example, Moody and White (2003) used a large data set from the Adolescent Health survey to generate a measure of structural cohesion based on student 'nestedness' within a school network. They employed a procedure to identify the components of the school network, progressively isolating more

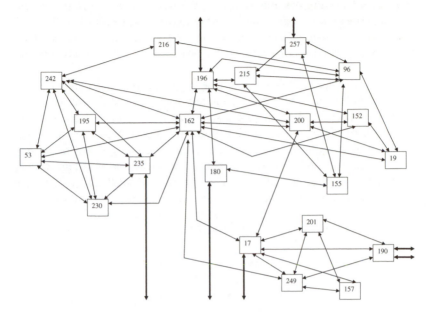

Figure 3.3 Section of a network depicting NEGOPY-defined liaisons

Source: Original figure appears as Figure 1 in an article by G. Abel *et al.* in *Drugs, Education, Prevention and Policy*, 9, 2002, pp. 325–338. Used by permission of Taylor & Francis Ltd, http://www.tandf.co.uk/journals.

and more connected structures within the overall network. They found that the nestedness of each student in the resulting groups was related to the student's sense of attachment to the school, thus demonstrating that their measure of network cohesion reflected the student's actual experiences of school attachment.

Other questions of interest include those relating to the connections between components of the network. For example, what component networks exist, and what are their characteristics? How robust is the network structure, and what enables it to resist dismemberment? A network that contains clusters or cliques joined to other clusters or cliques by ties to a few key members or to a sole liaison person (critical node) is more easily dismembered than one where the ties are widely distributed. In graph terms, the critical node is a cutpoint, crucial to linking the network together, so that its removal will result in the disintegration of certain ties and lead to the network separating into distinct components. An interesting case of a liaison (cutpoint) is found in the research of Abel *et al.* (2002), where the importance of the liaison person 162 (shown in Figure 3.3) was only appreciated when the researchers visually examined the network structure. Inspection of the network diagrams revealed that a highly popular girl tied the twenty-one-member network component together.

In this instance, actor 162 could be regarded as influential on girls' smoking, given her high centrality, but her discovery could have remained undetected because the structure shown in the diagram did not fit with NEGOPY rules. Her numerous ties to others prevented the program from resolving the clique structure. The crucial role of this girl in linking the three cliques was only discovered when a graph was drawn of this section of the network. With her removal from the network analysis, as required by NEGOPY, three separate cliques emerged that had previously been excluded in the analysis (Figure 3.4). For our purposes, her importance lies in her inclusion because of her influential ties to all three cliques.

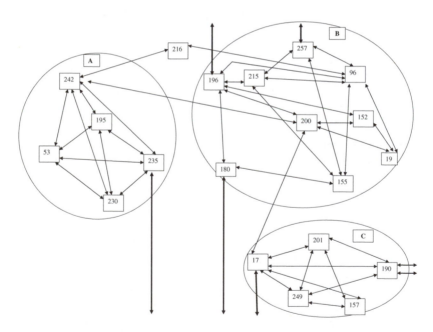

Figure 3.4 Cliques identified after removal of a critical liaison

Source: Original figure appears as Figure 2 in an article by G. Abel *et al.* in *Drugs, Education, Prevention and Policy*, 9, 2002, pp. 325–338. Used by permission of Taylor & Francis Ltd, http://www.tandf.co.uk/journals.

HIV and drug networks

Liebow *et al.* (1995) undertook a survey in two cities, San Juan and Atlanta, to map the social networks of young adolescents aged 12–15 who were seen to be at risk for HIV-related health risk behaviour. They adopted a link-tracing method (a variant of snowball sampling) to capture representative members of the network of at-risk youth in an economical manner. The procedure began with a door-knock of neighbourhoods. Youth who were initially contacted by this method were interviewed about health risk and asked to provide a list of their contacts. The next step was to randomly select a name from each list of contacts obtained from the first round of interviews, and this person became the subject of the next interview. The link-tracing method was continued in order to yield a third node and then a fourth. This method spreads the network widely in a minimum of steps.

The investigators then analysed the personal networks of respondents as well as the structure of the social network that connected the entire sample. Our interest here is in the latter aspect, where they found 'striking differences' between the structure of social relations in the two cities. For example, they found that adolescents living in San Juan were much more highly connected to one another than was the case for adolescents living in Atlanta. Nearly everybody in the San Juan network could reach everyone else in a mean distance of five steps, whereas in Atlanta only half of the interviewees could reach one another through any number of links (the reachability index for San Juan was 0.883 whereas that for Atlanta was 0.513). These differences in reachability relate to the network structures. Whereas the networks identified in both cities were of similar size (about 1000 persons), the San Juan network contained a dense core of social ties in a structure where almost every person was connected to others. By comparison, the social network of adolescents in Atlanta was less dense, and members of the network were also less well connected.

Studies of disease transmission in large networks are interested in finding the key connecting links between network components, and then identifying the actors in these positions. Bearman *et al.* (2004) used data from the Adolescent Health survey of 1994 to detect the structure of sexual networks among high school students. A feature of this study is that it included saturated fieldwork in fourteen high schools, where extensive home interviews were sought with all students enrolled in those schools. In these interviews, adolescents were shown a list of all the students enrolled in the school and asked to identify their romantic and sexual partners. The study analysed the romantic links among students in one large rural high school in order to determine the structure of the sexual network. Investigators found that 573 students had been involved in a romantic or sexual relationship over the past eighteen months. A graph of the sexual network was created, and the network components were examined. The investigators found that over one-third of the romantically involved students were located in network components of two or three members; another 13 per cent were in components ranging in size from four to fifteen members; and more than half the population of romantically active students were linked into a large component that contained 288 members. The investigators described this large network as very broad, and resembling 'a chainlike spanning tree', with 'numerous short branches' attached to the chain but growing away from it at a point (or node) on the chain, so that the span of the total network was very broad. Indeed, the investigators found that the greatest network breadth was thirty-seven steps, meaning that HIV infection could travel a very long way through the network.

What is the significance for HIV prevention of this discovery of a large sexual network among high school students in a small town? The investigators put it bluntly: 'The size of the large component of connected nodes (i.e., adolescents) identifies the worst-case scenario for potential disease diffusion within the population' (Bearman *et al.*, 2004, p. 59). In fact, the sexual network described in this study is a small world, where clusters of students are linked by single ties that bridge to other clusters in the chain. Crucial to the containment of HIV or STD infection through such a network is the sexual health of the students who tie the clusters together. If infection occurs, it will quickly spread through all those with whom they are in contact, and infiltrate adjacent network components. Accordingly, prevention of infection from spreading through the whole network depends on its containment within a component.

An excellent example of the importance of network analysis for detecting key connecting links in the spread of HIV infection comes from the Colorado Springs Project (Klovdahl *et al.*, 1994). It should be noted that this was a study of adults, not of youth networks. Researchers examined network patterns and processes at the personal (or microsocial) level of the network and also at the group (or macrosocial) level. Information on the personal network was collected from interviews, and included getting the name of 'the associate of an associate' in order to trace weaker network ties, as well as listing at least one social environment where network members got together. The large network that was assembled from the personal network data comprised more than 600 persons. When the research team analysed the core of the connected region, they found that one of the three positive HIV persons in the network was in this region. Examination of this person's ties to others showed that he was able to reach half of the 106 members in the network core within three steps of HIV infection, and all of them in six steps (three personal associates directly in one step, twenty-seven persons in two steps $(3+24)$, seventy in three steps, ninety-eight in four, and 102 in five). Moreover, everyone in the larger connected region, including the 563 other linked persons, was less than seven steps away from HIV infection. The practical importance of the analysis was in identifying the person in the network core who was a personal associate of the HIV carrier, but not in sexual contact with him. Because of this person's key location in the larger network, the investigators reasoned that for this associate to become infected would trigger 'a veritable explosion of disease' (Klovdahl *et al.*, 1994, p. 87), and they recommended that resources should be allocated to protecting this person, despite the fact that no sexual contact existed between this person and the carrier.

Knowledge of the connecting ties between network components has been employed by a project in Connecticut in the United States to enlist adult drug users as prevention agents (Weeks *et al.*, 2002). The first task of the investigators was to produce a comprehensive map of the macrosocial network of the Hartford drug users. From the network information obtained, they traced the transmission paths through the network to identify persons who could act as 'prevention linkages', that is, key people within the network structure who could be employed as peer educators in drug intervention. The study utilized a combination of methods for documenting the social networks, including observation, drug-use site tracking, and social network interviewing. The researchers even included people's photographs, with the participants' permission, in order to improve the reliability of the fieldwork in tracking people across sites. The social network of drug users assembled by these methods included a major network component that contained 193 connected individuals, as well as several minor components. The major component, shown in Figure 3.5, comprised about two-thirds of the total sample of participants.

Inspection of the network diagram of this major component shows that it is comprised of three distinct social clusters, with very few linking ties between them. They represent three ethnic groups. Weeks and her colleagues were interested in identifying network members who were located at key points of linkage within the ethnic clusters of drug users, because of their potential role as agents in drug prevention and health promotion. They applied measures of degree (both indegree and outdegree) in order to identify these persons. The rule they employed was that if a person was to act as a drug prevention linkage, that person should be able to reach a novel set of ties not reached by other persons selected. They found that a minimum of fourteen people were required in order to reach half the people in the connected component.

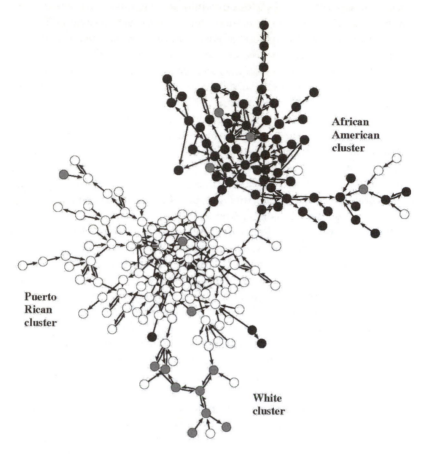

Figure 3.5 Ethnic clusters and bridging ties in a drug-user network

Source: Original figure appears as Figure 1 in an article by M. Weeks *et al.* in *AIDS and Behaviour*, 6, 2002, 6, pp. 193–206. Used by kind permission of Springer Science and Business Media.

Tracing change in a network

Social relations are never static. Friendships flourish, new acquaintances are made, workmates become companions; and then circumstances alter, and people move on to new jobs and neighbourhoods, or their interests and social activities change. The photo album is a silent witness to the changing membership of our social world. Social networks are not static structures: they are vibrant and changing, with some ties being constantly activated and others dormant but in a state of readiness. When displayed as graphs, the dynamism of networks is lost and they seem solid and fixed, like family trees or maps of the rail network that comprises the London Tube or the Paris Metro. When studied across several weeks, months, or years, the change and growth in networks are as noticeable as those seen in time-lapse photographs of water flooding in a myriad of rivulets over a parched landscape. It is the flow of relationships through time that network methods are able to capture.

Friendships are particularly vulnerable to change during the educational and social transitions of moving into secondary school, entering college or university, and leaving home to begin a job in a new town. For young adolescents, friendship changes make the transition into middle school or junior high a major period of adjustment. Prior to the change, they have mixed emotions: they are fearful for the loss of old friends and anxious that they will not make new ones, yet excited and curious about the possibility of interesting new friends. Research in the adolescence field has explored the extent of stability and change in friendships, using lists of friend nominations at each time period to generate scores of new and old friends for each respondent. There are numerous studies of friendship changes, and that of Cantin and Boivin (2004) is a particularly good recent example. They traced the changes in network size, membership, and adolescents' support from peers across two years from the end of elementary school to the second year of junior high school. They found 'significant declines' in the number of social ties to peers following adolescents' transition into junior high, but by the second year the networks had recovered to their size in elementary school.

Several social network studies have been conducted at the university level, tracing changes in student relationships over time. These have tended to be examined as individual cases. An example is Subject 11 in the Salzinger (1982) study (shown in Figure 2.1 in the previous chapter). This student had the same nine friends in January as in October, although the rankings of his friends changed. What Salzinger noted was that the rankings matched closely with the network structure at each occasion, so that in January the informant's four best friends as defined at that time were in the central part of the cluster, his next best friends on the periphery, and his least close friends not connected to either sector of the cluster. From her analyses of cases like Subject 11, Salzinger concluded that the relations within clusters were 'enhanced' while those outside the clusters were weakened.

Research by Degenne and Lebeaux (2005) traces changes across a six-year period in the personal networks of sixty-six young adults by means of three surveys. The merit of their longitudinal approach is the ability to register ties that are important in one period, but not in a later period, as well as ties whose importance can only be judged at later periods.[4] They treat each person as a case study, so that specific network ties can be examined. In the examples shown in their paper, the graphs display the social field containing all network members, and use bold shading and lines linking certain members to indicate which relationships were active at the time of the survey. Regrettably, their method of portraying the networks does not allow a reader to gain a full appreciation of the evolving structure of the network, a point they admit; instead, the graphs resemble three phases in a sequence of Christmas lights, where different sets of lights are illuminated in each phase. Nevertheless, the network graphs of the five cases selected are quite dramatic, and prompt questions to guide investigation of multiplexity and the effects of centrality on the stability of network ties.

Van Duijn *et al.* (2003) employed a similar 'join the dots' outline of network nodes in graphing the evolution of a friendship network within a college in Groningen, but their focus is the social network, not the egocentric network of selected students. They produced a series of graphs showing the progressive development of student acquaintanceship contacts (MEETING) and student friendships (MATING). Each graph displays all the respondents, with different symbols for males and females as well as for the two college programs they were enrolled in. Over time, more of the dots (the network nodes) are linked, and more lines appear, linking the dots. The effect of this sequential display of network growth is similar to watching the emergence of text written in invisible ink, or a photograph appearing in a developer tray. They noted that among the initial set of thirty-eight students, only five friendships existed; most students were unknown to one another. Within a bare three weeks, all students have met others and formed acquaintances with them. Over time, their analysis shows that social ties established in the initial meeting stage decay, and the network becomes segmented into subgroups, as relationships are refined.

Just as a college may be regarded as a small world, so can a Shakespearean play. Network analysis has been applied to reveal the social structures in Shakespeare's plays, and sequential analysis of the contacts among the characters from scene to scene yields insights into the changing relationships – whether the play is a comedy or a tragedy. Stiller and Hudson (2005) view Shakespeare's plays as small worlds, and show that they are structured in a way that assists memory and reduces the information-processing demands on the audience. The structural aspects include limiting the number of actors in scenes and the size of conversational groups to sizes that are familiar in everyday life, and ensuring that characters are 'socially linked' from scene to scene by only a few intermediate characters. Moreover, the social relationships between characters can be inferred from interactions among scene cliques, in similar ways to those that occur in real life. Examples of characters in *Troilus and Cressida* with strong links to a select few (that is, those with 'high cluster coefficients') are Menelaus in the Greek camp, and Priam in the Trojan camp. In contrast, Iago in *Othello* has a large number of weak links to cliques that are themselves not connected, which highlights his gossiping nature and lack of loyalty to any one clique.

The Shakespearean tragedies are mentioned because their small world structure condenses a great deal of change in social relations. Particularly interesting is how the great tragedies show that the main protagonist (Othello, Lear, Hamlet, Macbeth) becomes increasingly isolated from his family and his friends as the drama unfolds. Paul Mutton analysed changes in the social networks of the protagonists in Shakespeare, based on the strength of relations between the characters in the play, and recorded these changes in video clips of network graphs. These video clips of network ties provide a social network window into the unfolding tragedy. Othello is isolated by his jealousy, Lear by his folly, Hamlet by his depression, and Macbeth by his sword and dagger. The tragedy of Lear sees his decline from a king with an army of knights to become a lonely mad figure on the heath in a great storm, with only his faithful Kent and the blind Gloucester for company; even his jester is dead. On stage, the tragedy of the heroes is palpable, accentuated by scenery and the acting itself; but network analysis provides a graphic perspective of what Mutton calls the 'temporal decay of social networks' in Shakespeare's tragedies.[5]

Concluding comment

What I have sought to do in this chapter is demonstrate that knowledge of how networks are structured and familiarity with the tools of network analysis, are necessary if researchers and practitioners are to gain further understanding of the social relations among young people. Relationships do not arise from nowhere. They are located within social systems; and the network structures that link people together are contexts for the active pursuit of various types of social and personal relationships. Moreover, if people are linked to one another in specific ways, we can expect that they will share certain behavioural characteristics with the group with which they are associated. However, there is more to understanding social relationships than a map of their structures: other matters to be considered concern the dynamics of interactions among the individual actors. It is to these aspects of social relationships that we now turn.

4   Friends and mates

Said Romeo of Juliet:
She hasn't left school yet;
We're friends, just friends.
> (Music hall song by Michael Flanders and Donald Swann, 1963,
> used by permission)

This chapter explores the nature of friendship. It describes how relationships with close friends as well as with groups of friends are felt and expressed, and it draws on research to show how the intertwining of shared experiences with friends shapes young people's lives. The lifecourse for today's young people is no longer straightforward and predictable; it is said to have become a 'much less collectivised experience' (see Brannen and Nilsen, 2002). Youth are charged with creating their own biographies, where the experience of older generations can offer little direction. In these circumstances, friends become increasingly significant as guides and fellow travellers and as supports in establishing identity, because they are moving along in the same part of the stream of history. The friendship network has thus become a key context for young people's development, not only through the qualities of personal relationships with particular friends but also through connections to the social resources contained in different sectors of the wider social network. The focus on friends as sources of companionship and social validation and as intimate attachments offers insights into the influence of friends as agents of socialization and as convoys for social support.

Most of our knowledge of friendship is based on research on pairs of close friends, apart from what is known from our own biographies. Little is known beyond that horizon about interactions with other kinds of friends. Yet a range of friendships does exist: not only are there the close friends but also the friends who are not so close, as well as the pals and mates, and together they constitute the friendship network. This chapter is concerned with exploring the qualitative features of friendship and examining how different kinds of friendship meet different social needs. It has two broad goals: first, to describe the forms that friendship takes, within the wider friendship network; and second, to explore the nature of friendship, in what friends do together and in how they express their friendship. Together, the discussions emphasize the central importance of friends for companionship, support and guidance in navigating a lifepath and creating a satisfying personal biography.

The swirl of friends

Some people have a large circle of friends; others can quickly name their friends on the fingers of one hand. What exactly do young people mean when they call someone a 'friend'? A range of meanings is contained in the word, including best friend, close friend and casual friend. Collective terms such as pals, mates, buddies, us girls, our mob, our crowd, are also designates for friends. Young people seem profligate with their friendships; they quickly make new friends and they share their friends with others, rather than hoard them to themselves. Their philosophy is that friendships, like jewels, lose their lustre when hoarded away. Indeed a feature of adolescence is sociability: they want to be friendly and meet new people as well as enjoy their existing friends. And in the company of their friends they are happy, relaxed and uninhibited. Indeed, when the group is large, young people seem to glow. It is this openness and lack of restraint when with their friends that is an endearing characteristic of youth and young adults.

While being friendly should not be mistaken for being friends, the meaning of friend is clearly not restricted to close relationships. Fischer (1982) noted that adults commonly used the term 'friend' to define any unrelated member of their social network, and found that friends comprised 83 per cent of the non-relatives in his respondents' social networks. Montemayor and van Komen (1985) studied adolescents in natural groups, and found that the term 'friend' accounted for almost 92 per cent of the persons identified. These studies suggest that several types of friendship can be found within the average person's social network, and each type holds some importance for understanding friendship relations.

Peer crowds and social clusters

While many young adults trace their close friends back to their school days, a new network of friends is often generated from the first few post-school years, as one begins a job or attends university. In many cases the friends are cultivated from a larger group of mates who supply companionship. For example, I met some of my friends at university through acting in a play,

where we also built the scenery and made the costumes. From the continuing contact that was fostered by the production of this play, a social cluster[1]
of about twenty people was formed, which absorbed previous friendship
cliques and pairs of friends into the new network. Our cluster's larger size
and greater social mix was ideal for social outings such as swimming or
going to a movie or holding a party. Some network members were celebrat-
ing their twenty-first birthdays that year, so there were larger gatherings
for this purpose, with the celebrations held in public halls and attended by
numerous relatives, with musical entertainments, food, dancing and party
games. I recall playing a charade at one of these parties, where I was stuck
between floors in a lift with several 'screen personalities' including Tarzan,
Henry Kissinger and Marilyn Monroe, and we were required to make intelligent conversation. I asked about Jane. Cold war politics (Kissinger style)
left me cold.

Our cluster offered each member a very different social world from that
in their clique. The loose structure tolerated clique components within the
cluster, but the boundaries were permeable, so that people could associate
with one clique for a while and then move into another clique. The broader
cluster membership offered its own social benefits, including romantic
attachment; it was not in competition with clique relationships, and did
not deny individual loyalties to a clique or to particular friends. Moreover,
an advantage of the cluster was that the presence of all members was not
essential for it to function. Thus if some friends were unavailable for a
particular event, the group was still sufficiently large and diverse to pursue
its agenda. Different groupings among our cluster would occur, depending
on who was available for a particular social event, and on these occasions
we could be mixing with people who were not in our own close circle of
friends. The bonus from these arrangements was to discover that the event
was enjoyable without our best friends, and that we had got to know one
another better. Thus new attachments were made to others in the group.
From a network viewpoint, the advantage of these social gatherings was that
while members retained close ties to their own clique, they could confidently
make new friends with members of other cliques in the larger cluster.

Friendships were cultivated both on and off campus. While on campus,
we shared some classes and met together on the lawn daily for lunch. Off
campus, we gathered at house parties where food, conversation, jokes and
music were the usual fare. Our strongest drink was coffee. We treasured
these regular contacts and shared social experiences, where there were
opportunities for self-disclosure and thus to discover that others had similar
concerns and hopes. Moreover, simply airing a complaint or concern
seemed to reduce its power. The friendships we forged in those two years
transformed our university lives. They were our 'salad days', and although

within a short time we had parted to follow our separate careers, in some cases by travelling to the far corners of the earth, some of those friendships have endured until the present time.

Clusters are popular among older adolescents and young adults because there is more fun in larger numbers. They may eat out together or go to clubs and dance parties in large groups, often progressing from one venue to another. The large group atmosphere heightens the arousal potential of activities, where enjoyment bubbles up and sometimes seems to generate an internal echo effect through the audience available. This further increases each member's enjoyment at being part of the group and its activities. The benefits of the social cluster were well known to earlier generations. From about the early 1920s, summer would see large numbers of Australian youth and young adults of my parents' generation book in for their entire vacation at guest houses at Australian beaches at Bondi, Manly, Portsea, Victor Harbour, Coolangatta, or Noosa (to mention a few), to join in beach parties or house parties. The parties went on for weeks! At these beach venues young people would eat together in large dining rooms, sleep dormitory-style six to ten per room and participate in indoor and outdoor activities such as group games, swimming competitions, dances, and fancy dress parties. This form of group enjoyment retains its appeal for modern Australians, who may join up with a bunch of friends at the beach (although the grand old guest houses have disappeared), or at a ski resort, or go outdoor camping. Backpacker tourism is a commercial form of leisure activity that exploits the large group excitement that young people in particular derive from being part of a social cluster.

Large crowds

Some social experiences are particularly associated with youth affiliation with a really large crowd or mass crowd, for example at rock concerts, folk festivals, or street parties. Selzer (1989) is one of the few writers who have drawn attention to the distinctive need of young people to associate with large numbers of others of their own age. She argued that such a crowd is a sociality structure worthy of discussion in its own right, and applied the term 'peership' to the social experience of belonging to a large crowd as 'a corollary to' the experience of friendship in the small group. From surveys of over 1100 high school students on the social contacts of young people and their preferences for large crowd affiliation, Selzer found that the average number of people her respondents said 'hello' to at school was 107; the average number of peers at the last party they attended was 63; and the ideal number of friends they would like to invite if they held a party in the school gym was 160. Clearly, these preferred numbers suggest a very broad network of peer associates, and that her respondents valued being immersed in a large crowd of peers at a party because of the additional buzz that accompanied them.

The size of the gym party is dwarfed by the populations in events such as rock concerts, carnivals and New Year's Eve street parties. What are the particular social provisions of being immersed for a few hours in a large crowd? People's thronging at these events resembles the herding instinct of mammalian species to gather closely together in large numbers, and throngs have a distinctive appeal to people of all ages, where shared emotion creates a common bond. Mass events have a magnetic attraction for young people, perhaps because the energy associated with the combination of music, colour, and hubbub of sound wraps around everybody to include them in its welcoming embrace. And as people come inside the magnetic field of the event, its energy seems to agitate and magnetize them, so that they adopt more extroverted kinds of behaviour – smiling, rocking their bodies to and fro, and waving their arms, as they echo the rhythm of the scene and imbibe the celebratory spirit of their surroundings. There is a feeling of freedom and abandonment, and a loss of inhibition. Individuality is for a brief period submerged in the throng. Each person is part of the collective and yet at the same time remains to an extent a spectator of the scene; and because the event has a momentum of its own, individuals are relieved from any obligation to be responsible for the proceedings. In my study of adolescents at the World EXPO held in Brisbane (Cotterell, 1991), informants clearly preferred the crowded leisure venues of the Riverstage concert arena (which catered for crowds up to 12,000) and the Funpark arena of rides and floorshows (where populations numbered over 1000). These venues functioned as magnet settings for youth, where 'most young people go' because 'it's a good meeting place' which provided excitement as well as social stimulation.

Romantic relationships

While relationships with friends of the same sex retain their primary importance for the vast majority of adolescents and youth, interest in members of the opposite sex triggers casual friendships, as well as romance, that can be traced through the early years of adolescence to young adulthood and beyond. Extension of youth lifestyles into the mid-twenties and the associated delay in marriage, described by Côté (2000) as 'arrested adulthood', mean that opposite-sex friendship and romantic attachments now take on greater developmental significance as forms of friendship. It is therefore not surprising to find that research into various aspects of romantic relationships has blossomed in recent years.

As opposite-sex friendships and romantic relationships become more common in middle and late adolescence, these friendships contribute benefits in companionship and intimacy of the kinds that are found in adult relationships. Kuttler *et al.* (1999) found that for adolescent boys, the distinctive benefits of friendships with girls were that the boys 'felt good about themselves'. Whereas adolescents of both sexes stated that companionship was derived predominantly from association with close friends of the same sex, adolescent girls reported that they derived friendship intimacy just as much from opposite-sex close friends as from close same-sex friends.

Do close friendships become supplanted by romantic relationships as sources of friendship intimacy? Some scholars, such as Seiffge-Krenke (2000), argue that intimacy relationships between a close friend and a romantic partner can co-exist in adolescence, and that close friends are not necessarily replaced by the girlfriend or boyfriend, either as sources for intimate sharing or for companionship. However, displacement of the close friend does seem to be more common by late adolescence. Kuttler and La Greca (2004) flag the possible erosion of girls' same-sex friendships by the dating relationship. They examined the links between romantic relationships and friendships in girls age 15–19, by comparing the quality of friendships among girls who dated casually with those among girls who rarely dated and girls who were serious daters. What they found was that the networks of casual daters contained more opposite-sex friends and also more friends who had boyfriends, compared with the networks of both those who rarely dated, and those who were serious daters. Thus casual dating actually expanded the friendship network, whereas serious dating reduced the size and diversity of the network. The investigators concluded that, 'As romantic partners become more central in the lives of adolescent girls, more time is spent with boyfriends, leaving less time for friendships' (p. 410).

Another adolescent study (Connolly *et al.*, 2000) explored the effects of network composition on fostering girls' romantic relationships. They found that adolescents who belonged to larger social networks of mixed-sex friends had more close friends of the opposite sex. Moreover, as in the Kuttler and La Greca study, the gender mix of the social network seemed to contribute to adolescent girls' later involvement in romantic relationships, in that the size of the opposite-sex peer network in Grade 10 was linked to romantic companionship in Grade 11.

The qualities of friends

In this section we turn to what young people expect from friendship and the qualities they value in friends, particularly close friends, so that we can appreciate the powerful influence that friendship exerts on a young person's behaviour and sense of well-being.

A useful way of viewing the qualities of friends is in terms of 'social provisions' (Weiss, 1974) for meeting people's needs. Weiss suggested that these provisions occur continually in social and personal relationships, rather than being restricted to social support provided in situations of distress. They satisfy major psychological needs and protect us from loneliness. Weiss listed six social provisions – attachment, social integration, reassurance of worth, reliable alliance, nurturance, and guidance – and suggested that different members of our personal network supply the provisions for satisfying our needs. This does not, however, mean that certain network members exclusively supply certain provisions; indeed, friends can be considered as contributors to all of the provisions that Weiss listed. The difference between the roles of friends, parents, siblings and spouse is more a question of degree. In their work on measuring friendship quality, Mendelson and Aboud (1999) defined six functions of friendship: namely, stimulating companionship, reliable alliance, help, intimacy, self-validation, and emotional security. These functions have clear similarities with the Weiss concept of social provisions: they describe distinctive qualitative aspects that are important for sustaining a friendship, such as sharing in enjoyable activities, being loyal and available, being ready to assist, being sensitive to the friend's feelings, expressing confidence in the friend, and providing comfort and optimism in times of difficulty.

Two particular social provisions that are supplied by friends as a group are social integration into a friendship network and reassurance of worth through the social validation of friends. These provisions can be submerged by general notions of belongingness; they describe social processes that are not fully captured by 'fitting in' and 'feeling accepted' because they include an element of social identification together with a psychological sense of mattering and belonging. We will return to the social dimensions of feeling at home and identifying with the larger group in later chapters. This discussion is focused on the most common provisions of youth friendship: companionship and intimacy. While different members of the social network supply these provisions to children and young adolescents, Furman and Buhrmester (1992) reported that by late adolescence friends had become the major providers of both companionship and intimacy. The importance of these friendship provisions increases in young adulthood. A study of young adults by Carberry and Buhrmester (1998) found that close friends were the most frequent providers of the whole range of social provisions when the young adults were single, but that following marriage, friends became 'secondary sources of provisions' (p. 401) as they relinquished their major provider role to the spouse.

Companionship

The most fundamental form of friendship is companionship, where friends are partners in leisure activities and adventures, such as ice-skating, cross-country skiing, horse-riding, swimming, surfing, or watching movies. I know of a group of 20-year-old young men who decided to ride their bikes to Sydney (1000 kilometres away) to watch a cricket match. Their adventure caught the imagination of people in the towns they travelled through, so that they were made welcome and given hospitality along their journey. Just as important is friends' joint participation in inactivity – sitting on the front step talking about nothing in particular, or lying on the floor listening to music, or camped down by the creek whittling a stick or skimming stones off the water – simply content in one another's company. The common feature of activities with friends is that enjoyment arises from the shared nature of the experience.

Companions serve different purposes from close friends; you can enjoy the company and sociable qualities of your mates without regarding them as close, and without needing to entrust your worries and concerns to them. Rook (1987) argued that companionship provides positive emotional benefits such as affection, humour, and relaxation from tension. Companionship is the glue of social relations. Researchers have found that young adults express reluctance to become adults, out of fear that entry into adulthood will rob them of the sense of fun and closeness that they enjoy with their friends, and replace it with the routine dullness they detect in the lives of older generations around them (Du Bois-Reymond, 1998).

Intimacy and disclosure

Intimacy or closeness is a valued quality of friendship. Not all kinds of friends are regarded as intimate friends, even if they are good friends, because, as Shulman *et al.* (1997, p. 613) have explained, 'Adolescent friends must negotiate the extent to which an individual is allowed within the emotional closeness of the relationship'. They propose that intimacy is comprised of three aspects: first, the elements of closeness, affection, disclosure and commitment; second, the practice of partners adapting their behaviour to that of the other to preserve closeness; and third, realization of the importance of balancing one's own needs out of respect for others. Parks and Floyd (1996) asked their adult informants to define closeness, and state whether they experienced different kinds of closeness with their same-sex and opposite-sex friends. The meanings given ranged from feelings to relationship states to communication. The predominant definition of closeness was self-disclosure, and was cited by over two-thirds of the respondents. Other features were the provision of help and support, shared interests and activities, relational expression, and comfort and ease of interaction. Women mentioned each of these provisions in relationships much more than did men, except for the issue of comfort and ease of interaction, which was rated equally by male and female respondents. What was interesting was that closeness characterized friendship relationships whether the other person was a romantic partner, a best friend, or just a friend. Half the respondents said they would use the word intimate to describe their friendship, and there was no gender difference.

In general, however, male friendships do not appear to achieve the same level of expressiveness as female friendships. Findings from a range of studies indicate that females engage in greater disclosure of their innermost thoughts and feelings than males. By the time girls reach adolescence, they regard their relationships with girlfriends as providing considerably more intimate forms of sharing and companionship than their relationships with parents. Jones (1991) found that females reported greater levels of disclosure and more trust in their friendships than did males, although both sexes valued similar core provisions of friendship. Girls' greater use of telephones for the pursuit and maintenance of friendships through extended conversation is well known, but it is not the preferred method of contact for boys, who are more likely to cultivate their friends through shared activities. In a study of intimacy in close friendships among young adolescents and young college students, Radmacher and Azmitia (2006) found that males reported a sense of closeness and intimacy with close friends in the context of shared activities or practical help, whereas females more readily disclosed their intimate feelings and expressed support towards their friend 'as a regular aspect of the friendship' (p. 443). An interesting finding was that the college men were more ready to disclose their inner feelings in conversations with female friends than they were with male friends, with whom they used shared activities as a means to disclose their thoughts and feelings. The key to intimate self-disclosure appears to be the friend's ability to communicate trust and supportiveness.

Loyalty

Few studies have investigated conflicted loyalties among friends in a way that takes into account the social context of the friendship network. Thus the importance of wider contexts for sharing stories and gaining validation and acceptance is ignored. As couples enter into relationships, they erect psychological boundaries around themselves which can separate them emotionally from the larger group of friends. For example, a group of friends are out together when one member's mobile phone rings. The member withdraws from the others to converse on the phone, and the clique structure is briefly altered as the others wait for the friend to rejoin them. If the caller makes demands on the friend that compete with her loyalty to the clique, the clique structure may alter and the evening's plans may change, with negative consequences for the remaining clique members. If the clique is male, and the call results in the addition of the friend's girlfriend into the clique, issues of loyalty and closeness may be compromised, to the extent that there is a shift in the balance of liking. Introduction of a girl into his group of mates requires some loosening of the male group rules of exclusive membership. Perhaps the unspoken concession is 'We'll let you include her as long as nothing changes in our friendship or social life.'

Some of these tensions between loyalty to friends and loyalty to a romantic partner are raised by Baxter *et al.* (1997). They collected accounts from adult informants of situations where they faced competing loyalties in friendship and romantic relationships. The loyalty dilemma was proposed as one where the informant encountered contradictory demands from the relationship itself and from an external source of some kind (a new job, the group of old friends). Baxter *et al.* found that in friendships and in romantic relationships the most frequent loyalty dilemmas were concerned with demands on the informants' time. An example given of a general time dilemma concerned competing claims on a young man's free time from his mates and from his girlfriend:

> There is constantly the issue of my partner wanting to spend time alone together versus my desire sometimes to hang out with my friends. This is a problem when some of my mates ask me ahead of time to do something on the weekend, and although I don't have anything planned I'm afraid to commit for fear of pissing off my partner.

A particular example of conflicting loyalties to the girlfriend and to the group of mates was described by another male informant in these words: 'I was supposed to go out to the bars with my friends but at the last minute a girl, who I care for, altered these plans. I instead went out with her and broke my plans with my friends' (Baxter *et al.*, 1997, p. 664). Analysis of these dilemmas was concerned with how the informants would manage them. What is interesting for our purpose here is the interaction between the protagonists – girlfriend, mates, and ego – and how the strength of ties among the various players would affect the decision. In the second dilemma, the scenario suggests that ego has almost blown it with his mates. Does he crawl back to them or give up his group of friends? Is the girl's friendship worth the loss of his mates' friendship? What do you think? Faced with this dilemma, what would you do or advise your friend to do?

Communication among friends

Attachment displays

Noticeable among cliques of friends in public places are actions to bond the group and distinguish it from other people. These actions may be interpreted as forms of intragroup attachment, but to the extent that they include other markers (for example, clothing styles) that distinguish the group from other groups, they qualify as expressions of group identification. Young males often express their identification with their clique by adopting unconventional behaviour. By doing things that are different (for example, draping their arms and beach towel around a statue or street sign; joining in a conga line and copying the steps of the leader; chanting a group slogan or war-cry, and doing so as a group) they display their creativity and announce that a sense of fun is a quality that binds their clique together. For example, at sports events such as cricket matches, cliques can be seen wearing clothes that make them distinctive. One clique of seven or eight males in their twenties had adopted a summer clothing style for watching cricket that consisted of blue 'Jackie Howe' singlets, football shorts, thongs (flip-flops) and Aussie bush hats complete with dangling corks. Another clique of young men were clad in gold T-shirts and green shorts and wore huge Mexican straw hats. A group of fifteen male and female teenagers of about 17 years of age arrived at the cricket match wearing singlets declaring they were the Boonies (after a former Australian cricket star, David Boon, now a national selector). The boys had names written on their singlets, like Ian Boonbarrel, Boonerang Bob, and Tom Happy Boonday. Each group member also had David Boon's trademark moustache painted on their faces – including the girls, whose shirts carried the message 'Check out my Boonies'. In the company of their friends, these young people are very happy and relaxed, and as they declare their group identity they radiate good humour which spills over to the onlookers.

Another striking feature of friends' interactions is laughter. The presence of laughter, joking, teasing, carrying on, and displays of general euphoria among teenagers was very widespread among the Australian 12–18 year-olds that we observed in public settings, and these displays can be interpreted as expressions of friendship intimacy. Our field notes of observations of young people in public settings contain descriptions like these: 'much noise and laughter', 'loud talking and laughing', 'talking and joking', 'fits of laughter', 'raucous laughter erupts from the entire group'. Other observers of peer interactions have also marvelled at the extent to which joking and various kinds of humorous behaviour feature in adolescents' daily conversations with peers (e.g. Sanford and Eder, 1985).

A third feature of interaction among friends is touching. Whether the clique of friends is male, female, or mixed, and whether it is mobile or stationary, there is an amazing amount of touching and jostling of bodies. Among girls it ranges from stroking, hugging and back-patting, plaiting another's hair or painting her nails, to lying sprawled out on the lawn shoulder to shoulder. Males also engage in similar kinds of contact comfort, but are more likely to express their attachment through vigorous forms of body contact including pushing, wrestling, punching and karate chops or kicks. In our observations, these forms of interaction were directed to others within the group, rather than to youth outside the group, and they commonly occurred among peers of the same sex, rather than as displays for the opposite sex. A good deal of these expressions of attachment emerged when a new member joined the clique. Girls when meeting up with their friends engaged in emotion-laden hugs and embraces, accompanied by loud greetings. Boys greeted a newcomer by giving him a punch in the chest, several bangs on the upper arm or back, or a clip over the ear. Teenagers 15 years of age or younger tended to be more vigorous, whereas older adolescent males were more subdued in their mode of physical contact with friends. Other observers have described these actions as signalling behaviour, and have also noted that they are more exaggerated among younger adolescents. For example, Moore (1995) observed girls' flirtatious behaviour in public settings such as shopping malls, ice-skating rinks, and school sports events. She commented that girls employed the same signals towards males as adult women did, such as primping and pouting, but that adult women were more practised and proficient in 'courtship signalling'. For example, a woman would toss her head and glance in the direction of the male in a definite but subtle manner, whereas an adolescent girl took longer and used broader movements to achieve the same goal. The adult women were also more successful in obtaining a male response. Adolescent girls were both less skilled and 'much less attentive' to boys, and directed much of their signalling to their own group members.

It is clear that physical contact is very important to adolescents as a way of expressing attachment, and also as a means of identification. Whether expressed as a gentle and light brushing of the arm or body, or as a vigorous thump in the back, touching is a highly important means of communication. Moreover, touching provides feedback; it seems that being able to touch someone else in the group or receive such contact gives adolescents a great feeling of acceptance among their friends. The frequent physical contact among young people, together with group actions such as joint laughter and the group adoption of similar clothing and distinctive patterns of public behaviour, suggests that adolescents and youth see that group attachment and belonging are important to their emotional well-being.

Talk

A region that is hard for outsiders to enter is friends' talk, where individuals can share feelings, hopes, fears, and joys. When friends are engaged in conversation as a group, they may joke, tease, interrupt one another, burst into laughter, argue, disagree, and then change their opinion, to arrive suddenly at a point of full agreement punctuated by strong murmurs of assent. Friends also gossip about other young people, often in language that is devoid of self-policing and seldom politically correct, but frank, open, vigorous, and sometimes scandalous. They engage in story-telling, recounting incidents that may have been embarrassing to them or that were physically risky at the time. The tale may be one that has been told before, but the re-telling allows for embellishment and dramatization, with others joining in, encouraged by an audience ready to be impressed and entertained. Participation in stories is a form of myth-making that boosts the egos of the tale-tellers as each takes up the story and adds a contribution, in an exercise that Mitchell (1998) has wryly called 'synchronised self-deception' (p. 125).

Talking or gossiping with a group of one's friends promotes group solidarity. It allows each friend to 'rave on' and contribute to the gossip, and celebrate their common interests; and the mutual exploration of a topic strengthens the friendship bond. Eder (1988) provides examples of these 'collaborative narratives'; she describes how a group of female friends were observed using 'a collaborative style of talk in gossip or teasing' (p. 226). One of her illustrations is a story of how some of the group pulled in a dead catfish when out rowing a boat. Two girls share the story-telling, and the effect is to verify the details as well as confirm that the story deserves to be told. The second story concerns an incident in the choir where the group made fun of a girl because she was overweight. For this incident, five girls joined in the group story-telling, adding brief statements and even repeating certain offensive remarks in a highly collaborative manner.

The topic of the talk is irrelevant to group purposes, as Bucholtz (1999) shows from her recording of snatches of talk among a friendship clique of six nerdy friends at high school. The importance of the talk lies in strengthening attachment within the group, in much the same way that mutual grooming is utilized for bonding by primates. Bucholtz reports that the trigger for the group's lunch-time talk was when one of them noticed the sesame seeds on a bagel. They debate what the seeds are, and argue and joke about the origin – from a tree? One friend parodies the scientist discourse, with appropriate voice, and pseudo-biological and anthropological details inserted into the banter in the style of a classroom television documentary. The others participate by playing up the theme, to sustain the frame of an intellectual debate. By this means, an idle remark about the seeds on a bagel generates a group performance, with talk binding the group together, and where laughter 'keys the tale as play' (Bucholtz, 1999, p. 216). These microsocial studies of friendship interactions are instructive in the insights they provide as to the importance of talk as a means of expressing attachment. They help to explain why teenage girls in particular will phone each other as soon as they get home from school, despite having spent much of the day in each other's company, and also why adolescents talk so much in class, regardless of the admonitions by teachers to refrain from doing so. Talk is attachment behaviour: it reaffirms a social bond.

Interestingly, talk between friends has a number of interaction cues that distinguish it from talk between acquaintances. The distinctiveness of these cues is something that we have all noticed if we have inadvertently overheard a friend's telephone conversation with an acquaintance or perhaps with a 'cold-caller' and have detected a different tone of voice from their normally friendly one. Planalp and Benson (1992) tape-recorded conversations between friends and conversations between acquaintances, and then asked a group of students in their communication classes to judge excerpts of these conversations to see what distinguishing cues they contained. The researchers generated thirty-one propositions underlying the cues that were identified. All except three cues were very clearly associated with conversations of either friends or acquaintances. The distinguishing cues are interesting. Among the markers of friends' conversation were that 'friends interrupt each other', 'friends use more slang', 'friends converse at a faster pace', 'conversations between friends are more relaxed', 'friends express more negative judgements, such as criticisms, insults, etc.'. Compared with acquaintances, friends are more informal, and more intimate; they share the conversation, talk about a single topic more, and interrupt each other more. In addition, friends laugh more, talk faster, and show more involvement and interest in each other.

Gender differences in talk

Observation of conversations between best friends seems to confirm that girls' friendship relationships are more personal than those of boys, and that their talk with friends deals with the more intimate and emotional aspects of relationships. For example, Tannen (1990) noted that discussions by males were less personal and more abstract than those by their female counterparts. The latter were more interested in emotionally-charged topics such as relationship difficulties with other people, including parents, where-as boys discussed their topics, even where relationships were at issue, in an emotionally neutral fashion. Girls' talk was more tightly focused on the topic, and engaged their listener in the feelings they experienced on the issue; boys' talk in contrast was more diffuse, and did not seem intent on involving the partner in the dialogue. Boys seemed to be giving a report of someone else's experience. Girls' conversation had a distinctive style. A notable feature was the exaggerated intonation, which has the effect of injecting emotion and dramatic emphasis into what would otherwise be a bland account. For example, the girls would say, 'I couldn't believe it', 'It was like, God, it was bad', and 'It hurts when you lose your best friend.' Accentuated speech patterns of this kind were absent from boys' talk.

These features illustrate what Tannen calls the 'cultural' differences between girls and boys. Having chosen an issue to talk about, girls elaborate on a common focus of concern, building joint understanding through mutual clarification of the issue, whereas boys take a different approach which leaves each partner more independent. Instead of each discussing the other's concerns, the boys seemed determined to maintain a focus on their individual preoccupation. Each would respond to the other's account by describing his own concern, as if engaged in a tacking duel between sailboats, with each changing tack to match that of the other. When one boy was recounting the events associated with his personal dilemma, the other appeared to give little input by way of feedback or reflection on the account; and when any comments were made, they seemed intended to downplay the seriousness of the situation described by the friend. Tannen noted, however, that neither boy appeared unhappy or dissatisfied with his friend's responses.

The way that the partners arranged their chairs was an analogue of their mode of discussion. Girls sat opposite each other, in keeping with a joint focus on the concerns raised by one party, and tracked each other's story with emotional punctuation as described above. Boys faced outward and made little eye contact, and each maintained a separate focus on his own concerns. The obvious differences in empathic communication invite value judgements about the lack of empathy in male relationships, in contrast to the greater level of engagement which appears characteristic of female interaction. Tannen cautions against hastening to such a conclusion. What appears at first to be a failure on the part of boys to listen actively to one another may be *a difference in style*. Boys seek to downplay the seriousness of the friend's problem; they provide reassurance by affirming to the listener that 'you're OK; you'll be alright; it's not all that dreadful, so you needn't feel so bad about it'. If one accepts that the style of supportive communication between males and females is different, it may help to explain the frustrations experienced in communications between friends of the opposite sex.

A study by Galliher *et al.* (2004) of couples' conversations suggests that males and females see relationships differently, with consequences for their communication. Sixty-one couples aged 18–19 who had been dating for less than two years were videotaped discussing two hypothetical situations, and then were asked to view themselves on the film and code their social behaviour. Their interaction patterns were then related to their overall ratings of the relationship. What is interesting is that the global quality of the couple's relationship was related to different interaction loci according to the gender of the participants. For girlfriends, minimizing conflict is important for the harmony of a relationship, whereas boyfriends seem more accustomed to conflict and take less notice of disagreement as a factor in a harmonious relationship. Girls judged the overall quality of the boy–girl relationship in terms of perceptions of *their boyfriend's* conflictual behaviour. Boys, on the other hand, assessed the relationship in terms of *their own* behaviour and their capacity to influence and if necessary mollify their girlfriend. Thus a boy thinks that if *his* behaviour is reasonable and supportive, the relationship is going along fine. Girls, in contrast, tune into *their partner's* behaviour for clues about the overall quality of the relationship; if they sense that their partner is showing more conflict and negativity, they interpret the relationship in a poor light.

Sex differences are seen both in the topics which friends choose to discuss, and in the style of the conversation itself. The difference is highlighted in a study by Johnson and Aries (1983) of 18–19-year-olds. Conversation topics between female friends were more 'personally oriented' than those between male friends; for example, females were much more likely to talk about family problems, personal problems, and their private doubts and fears. Discussions on these topics were also treated at greater depth by females, although there was some discussion of these personal areas by males. Male conversations, in comparison with those of females, are more concrete and event-based, which is consistent with the reliance of males on grounding their exploration of relationships and identity in the recounting of events and the analysis of activity. The main topics discussed between male friends were sports and reminiscences about things they had done together in the past. The apparent lack of depth in male sharing with their friends led Johnson and Aries to speculate whether males' friendly banter and story-telling 'may replace a deeper sharing between friends' (1983, p. 235), with the consequence that males are less well equipped to resolve complex relationship problems. A challenge to these stereotyped views of gender differences is mounted by Thurlow (2002). He writes:

> Whereas girls tend toward a more *affective* notion of 'real communication,' boys tend toward the more *effective* 'good communication.' Girls in my study consistently prioritized friendships and the interactional bases of communication (e.g. in terms such as personal qualities,

trustworthiness, problem solving, understanding); boys, on the other hand, prioritized more transactional concerns, thinking in terms of computers and technologies of communication and more technical or formal qualities (e.g. skilful orator, being knowledgeable, speaking good English).

(Thurlow, 2002, p. 55)

I agree with him. Males and females talk about different things, and males are more activity-focused than relationship-focused. I for one would prefer to celebrate *la différence* than to delve for male communication deficiencies.

If males express their feelings differently from females, it is possible that the methods used by researchers do not do justice to male forms of expression. Indeed, Giordano (2003) has drawn attention to that possibility. She has suggested that the research measures typically employed in the study of friendship can be considered 'more resonant with girls' styles of intimacy'. Thus, males tend to be compared against a female-centred standard. To correct for possible bias, Giordano advocates the use of assessment tools 'more appropriate to male adolescents, even though the sharing of intimacies may not be as frequent or pervasive' (2003, p. 262). For example, Guerrero (1997) points to the subtle sex differences she observed in nonverbal communication. Women are more expressive than men: they touch more than males, stand closer when conversing, make more eye contact, and display greater amounts of affect such as smiling, nodding, and vocalizing emotions. In addition, people from different cultures and from different walks of life differ in their extent of communication display, and even in their signals of involvement. The typical Aussie male's style of conversation is to adopt a parallel stance with his friend, and stare at the distant horizon or stub at the soil with his foot, while conducting a monologue devoid of emotional expression. The listener's only involvement is to punctuate the pauses in the monologue with a droll 'yeah'. Boulders have more personality. However, this should not be construed to mean that males are insensitive or not in touch with their emotions. Rather than argue in terms of stereotypes of male impassivity and male deficiencies in communication, it may be more fruitful to acknowledge that males and females express intimacy in different ways.

Opposite-sex contact

How do young adolescents feel about talking to someone of the opposite sex for the first time? The prospect of speaking to a member of the opposite sex whom they find attractive is daunting. The uncertainty of asking a person of the opposite sex for a date is tinged with fear of failure. The adolescent male rehearses his speech over and over in his head, and then when the prospect arises of talking to the chosen one, away from her friends and before his mates find out what he is up to, he becomes tongue-tied. The bus or train arrives; the critical moment is lost; and the chance of asking for a date is gone. He resumes the role of admiring her from afar, and begins afresh to work up the courage for another meeting. The day drags along. As the crucial time draws near, and there is only ten minutes left in the last lesson in the afternoon, he reviews his strategy, which requires careful positioning in the target zone, social nonchalance, smooth delivery, and exquisite timing. As he pictures the situation in his mind, he approaches her, sees her turn and look at him with those devastating blue eyes and the wisp of fair hair across her brow, and just as he is ready to speak to her, a voice booms out from two metres away, 'Are you listening, Jones?' and the classroom surroundings return with a jolt: Thursday afternoon Chemistry with Mr Todd.

Asking girls for a date, after one has eventually managed to meet them, is a further challenge because adolescents start from a position of what Jackson *et al.* (2001) call 'restricted relevant experience' which is pretty well beyond the scope of parental help, and cannot be learned from books. The strategies of setting up the first date are explored in Jackson *et al.*'s absorbing study of the social cognitive abilities of 14-year-olds. The work is a model of good discovery research. It begins with an interesting real-world problem – first dating – asks young people about their experiences, and then explores these step by step, refining the situations identified so they elicit genuine responses. The final list of situations relevant to dating was compiled from those chosen by at least 45 per cent of respondents. Examples included: 'a girl/boy you do not know if they like you', 'a girl/boy who is a few years older than you', 'a girl/boy you fancy but who is going out with another'. Among the actions chosen by respondents as appropriate responses were these: 'Talk it over with your friends', 'Be as often as possible in the same group or place', 'Join a big group where you can meet her/him easily'. These actions can be compared with those recommended by experienced daters, which included: 'Decide to take some risks', 'Try to communicate your feelings non-verbally', 'Do things to make you stand out from the crowd', 'Change the way you normally behave'. Friends were listed as sources of advice and information on aspects such as the following: what they think about the boy/girl, how to approach them, what to talk about, and the chances of success.

Reprise: adolescent emotional expression

It is generally assumed that male friendships operate at a lower level of intimacy and disclosure than female friendships. A body of research exists to confirm that assumption: girls talk more about personal relationships than boys do, and girls are more able to articulate their feelings. However, this should not be construed to mean that males are insensitive or not in touch with their emotions. Rather than preserve stereotyped views of female emotionality and male impassivity and communication deficiencies, it may be more fruitful to acknowledge that males and females express intimacy in different ways.

The issue of inappropriate interpretation of male emotional life has practical consequences, particularly for teachers. If the female-centred frame is applied to male verbal outbursts in school, given the predominance of female teachers and counsellors in high schools, it may explain why males are far more likely than females to be in trouble for bad behaviour. Males are more likely to cope with frustration and tension by explosive outbursts of anger – swearing, throwing down their book (or their tennis racket in a tournament). Males are more likely to react belligerently to teacher intervention and defend themselves by confronting the teacher, although on further admonition they may adopt passive aggressive strategies. They may get sin-binned, but rarely is the target of their outburst the teacher or official; their anger is misdirected, and a sign of frustration with their own inadequacies. The target of their anger is often themselves. Their avoidant style is interpreted as hostility, not as an attachment signal and a plea for help. Similarly, when a male feels betrayed by a friend, or is 'dumped' by a girlfriend, the internal tension, anger and frustration often finds vent in object-related ways – intense sport, fast driving, or watching violent movies. Parents or teachers who witness such antisocial displays and take exception to the responses as rudeness or challenges to their own authority are missing the point entirely. The solution lies in improved communication to recognize the attachment need.

Conclusion

This chapter has explored adolescent friendship as a social experience of companionship and closeness, and described some of the features of different types of friendship. Romeo and Juliet were more than just friends: their relationship was an audacious romance that bridged the networks of warring families. But behind the audacity of their love lay the inevitable tragedy of conflicted network obligations and allegiances. The lovers constituted the only bridging tie between separate family networks, while their ties to their families bound them into segregated societies that denied their right to find love outside the boundaries. There was no way of moderating the attitudes so that Juliet's family could accept a traditional enemy as a friend, on the basis of her love for him.

The individual lifecourse is often portrayed in eulogies and biographies as a line threading its way through time, dotted with points of individual achievement, where the group context of family and friends is simply the background. But the social and the individual are intertwined in life. Each person is a player in an unfolding and somewhat improvised drama, the meaning of which derives from interactions with the other players. On the stage of life, each of us is linked through the actions of our friends, so that the quality of our shared history extends beyond the scenes in which they took a leading part. The relationships with friends constitute one of the richest and most varied domains of human experience.

5   Loners and outsiders

Socially, these boys were generally isolated and rejected by peers. Most had poor social and coping skills and felt picked on or persecuted. In most cases, they had an antisocial group of friends. They were neither outstanding students nor committed to school ... As a group, they lacked social support and prosocial relationships that might have served as protective factors .... In all cases, violent intentions were clearly communicated to others, often including the time and place of the attacks. These were not taken seriously by peers .... The assaults were all committed in school settings where there would be a large number of observers .... These were very public acts of violence.

(Verlinden *et al.*, 2000, pp. 44–45)

In any group setting, there are young people who don't seem to fit in easily and who remain on the fringe. In network graphs they are the isolates, positioned on the perimeter of the social network or disconnected from it. They stand apart from their peers because they are different. Some are unusual looking, some very shy, some aggressive. Some are newcomers, foreigners, perhaps refugees. Some are gifted. While some draw attention to themselves, others are almost invisible to the casual observer. Many of them are lonely. Their experiences are the subject of this chapter.

The first part of the chapter describes young people who are isolates. A distinction is made between a loner, as a person who prefers to be alone and avoids the company of others, and an outsider, as a person who is not recognized as belonging to a particular community or who is denied membership in a group. The term 'loner' is commonly used, but it is imprecise, in that it has been employed to refer to different kinds of social isolates, both those who are invisible and those who have conflict with peers (Kreager, 2004). Outsider carries the meaning of foreign, stranger, and estranged, and these meanings derive from the French word *étranger*. Both types of persons are isolated from the majority, whether they are isolates by choice, or isolates through the actions of others.

The second part of the chapter examines why young people who are loners or outsiders are excluded or rejected. In particular, it explores the extent to which peers are involved as a group in ostracism, rejection and harassment of individuals. The discussion extends beyond school settings into youth and young adulthood, to the experiences of neglect and betrayal among close friends and romantic partners, and relates these to feelings of loneliness. Some of the questions of interest to the chapter are: What are the characteristics of loners and outsiders that distinguish them from their peers? What factors in the behaviour of others contribute to the social isolation of some young people? What are the psychological costs of being rejected and excluded from group life?

Loners

Adolescent loners were virtually an ignored species in academic research until the shootings in April 1999 at Columbine High School in Colorado, although a longer cast of history would reveal that assassins have often been described as loners – for example, in the assassinations of President Kennedy, Mahatma Gandhi, and Archduke Ferdinand. The Columbine killers were described as loners, and one was said to have been rejected by a girl at school. Being a loner was also a defining characteristic of three Scottish-born serial killers, according to McKay in the *Scottish Daily Record* (14 January 2005), and it aptly described Martin Bryant, the Australian who destroyed so many lives at Port Arthur in April 1996. The message of films such as *Elephant* and *Bowling for Columbine* is that rejection and social isolation are linked to violence – in extreme cases – and that schools and communities should view social rejection seriously.

The film *The Station Agent* provides a window into the world of the loner. Its central character is Fin, a dwarf who inherits a railway station in a small New Jersey town. And the trains still run by! Fin is a loner of sombre demeanour, who protects his privacy and is content with his own company. His self-contained lifestyle arouses the curiosity of other isolates in the tiny town, including Joe, a loquacious hot-dog seller, Rachel, an unhappy teenager, and Virginia, an erratic artist. They intrude into his life and he is drawn reluctantly into theirs. The experience of their companionship leads Fin to relinquish his solitary existence and open himself to friendship.

Adolescents may be loners because they are socially inhibited or socially inept. Because they do not mix easily with others, they hang around on the fringes of the group, avoid social contact whenever they can, and cope by giving little cause for offence. They choose not to be involved in social activities, and become anxious if forced to interact with others. Some loners, like Fin, are sensitive and protective of their space, and react to intrusions in a prickly manner. They gain a reputation for being difficult, and challenge the tolerance of others in the school or workplace. For example, Schuster (1999) suggests, on the basis of her study of German adolescents in different schools, that some youth react in a defensive manner to the pranks and teasing of others so that they invoke a hostile response and subsequent group rejection.

A personality characteristic of some loners is shyness, described as 'feelings of uneasiness and behavioural inhibition in unfamiliar situations' (Asendorpf and Wilpers, 1998, p. 1542). Young adults who are extremely shy have been found to report more depression, loneliness, fearfulness, social anxiety, and lower self-esteem as well as more psychosomatic illnesses. Shyness has also been linked to peer rejection in a large study of Dutch adolescents (Scholte *et al.*, 1997). Although the cluster of traits most strongly predictive of peer rejection was defined as aggression-inattentiveness, Scholte *et al.* report that adolescents who appear to be anxious, insecure, shy and withdrawn 'are likely to be rejected by their peers' (1997, p. 551). A boy I once taught named Bob was extremely shy. At school he preferred to be left to himself, and when given any attention by the teacher in class he would become visibly uneasy and display avoidant behaviour. Because he was a good student, a fine athlete, and good-looking, his shyness did not seem to be an impediment to his relations with peers, to the extent that they would exclude him from their company.

The social networks of loners tend to be small with low density, because they do not seek out others to interact with at the same rate that positively regarded individuals do, and consequently there are fewer connections among members of their network. In a network study of the growth of relationships among university students by Asendorpf and Wilpers (1998), students kept diaries of their interactions with others which allowed the number and extent of contacts to be examined over time. When the networks of shy students were compared with those of students who were outgoing and sociable, it was found that it took fifteen months for shy students to make as many new friends as others had managed to do within three months. They recorded lower levels of daily interaction than the sociable students, interacted less with peers of the opposite sex, had fewer romantic interactions, and reported more contact with their families. Interestingly, the personality effects on social relationships were still detectable after eighteen months. The investigators commented that 'most of the effects were enduring', although the levels of shyness did decrease across the period of the study, as student unease with the unfamiliar university environment gradually diminished.

Deeper insight into the personality of loners comes from the work of psychiatrist Sula Wolff, who reported a detailed study of a select group of people whose social life marked them out as different (Wolff, 1995). Her insights are valuable because she studied their lifepaths through childhood until well into their adult years. In childhood, the children she called 'unusual' were distinguished socially from other children by their solitariness, their social wariness, and their emotional detachment. They preferred their own company, were preoccupied with their own solitary interests, and had real difficulty interacting with their peers, to the point of being antisocial. Some had unusual language and an unusual fantasy life. To children of their own age, their lack of sociability made them appear strange: they lacked empathy and did not appear to enjoy any kind of close relationship. Moreover, they were poor at sizing up a social situation and reading the social cues. Not all were shy or uncommunicative, because Wolff detected the disorder in mild as well as severe forms, but the overall pattern of their behaviour closely resembled the descriptions given by Asperger.

Wolff struggled to equate the behaviour patterns she had observed over the years in these children and adults with those found in the clinical definitions of disordered personality. She concluded that these loners possessed 'schizoid' personality traits, on the basis of the clinical description given by the ICD-10 (World Health Organization, 1992) and the DSM-IV (American Psychiatric Association, 2000). The incidence of this personality disorder is about 2 per cent of the population, and the personality pattern is present in boys almost four times as often as in girls. Wolff noted that schizoid personality traits are 'most troublesome during the school years ... but once school is over, the majority manage to find a more congenial way of life ... [and] occasionally contribute to unique and original achievements' (Wolff, 1995, p. 170).

A word of caution is needed here. 'Normal' covers a broad range of personality types; but despite this breadth there are people who do not quite fit into the normal range. Even among the personality types described by Wolff, there are degrees of oddness, so that some people could be regarded as 'a bit odd or unusual' while the habits of others would attract comments of weird and bizarre. We should not assume that Wolff's study captures all the kinds of people who may be described as loners, but it goes a fair way in highlighting the importance of personality disorders in explaining the socially isolating behaviour that is our concern in this chapter. It is also a reminder that personality disorders lie on a continuum, grading from mild to severe, and that social difficulties underlie many disorders, such as oppositional disorder, obsessive-compulsive disorder, and various anxiety disorders.

Among the surveys that have focused directly on adolescent loners and their attitudes and behaviour is that conducted by Demuth (2004) on adolescents from the NYS database. A loner was defined as 'an adolescent who is socially isolated and has limited friendship ties'. Demuth found that 6.5 per cent of the sample fitted this description of loners, and 70 per cent of them were male. Loners were less involved in antisocial activities, perhaps because they had limited contact with the larger peer culture, and were less dependent on the approval of friends. The loners had similar beliefs to other students on the importance of schooling, but were performing poorly, which suggests that their poor school achievement may have resulted from feelings of isolation at school rather than from lack of study.

Outsiders

Being different and not blending into the group marks the outsider. The outsider has been romanticized in Clint Eastwood Westerns such as *A Fistful of Dollars*, *High Plains Drifter* and *Pale Rider* as the lone rider who materializes from the desert, rights the wrongs, and then disappears into the heat haze. The outsider character has no history, remains aloof, and in control; he confides in no one, and then vanishes into the desert; so the question lingers that perhaps he is a spirit and not a real person. Eastwood's characters are made even more enigmatic by being called 'the stranger' and 'the man with no name'. The outsider character is similarly captured in the *Mad Max* movies, again with the backdrop of an arid landscape. Mad Max is a brooding lone figure, utterly determined and physically dominant. The lives of these movie characters are given a certain heroic dimension, hardened by their solitariness; they do not seek our understanding or our sympathy, but remain unknown and apart from the community.

In real life, people are outsiders because they are culturally excluded and the targets of prejudice,[1] and there is nothing particularly heroic about their existence. They don't belong. They don't fit in. Their life is unknown. Their history is not open to the host community. There is no bridge of feeling or common experience. The bridge is closed and defended by the community, whose members are suspicious of the outsider and unwilling to make her/him welcome. A person with no clear social tie to any member of the community is a stranger, a blow-in, an unknown quantity, a foreigner. S/he has no claim on the territory and on other social and material assets enjoyed by community members.

For young people, whose central concern is fitting in and being cool, being an outsider is a social liability. No one wants to be socially out of place, and no one likes to be reminded of their shortcomings. Of course, outsiderness is a fact of social existence. Each time that people move into new settings and new communities, they are confronted with the challenge of fitting in and gaining acceptance. Each change in school, or change in town, or change of job, brings to the surface the insider–outsider uncertainty. For example, young adolescents entering secondary school voiced their uneasiness to us (Power and Cotterell, 1979) about their new surroundings: 'I felt like I was entering a new land.' They felt diminished by the strangeness of the setting and their outsider status: 'I felt like I was just a drop of water in a stream. There was nothing significant about you.'

These feelings of disjuncture and dislocation following change of situation are temporary, but adolescents who are perceived as different by their peers remain outsiders. They do not fit in and they know it. The adolescent period is characterized by a rich language of rejection, employed to differentiate those who are members of the group from those not 'in' the group, and this language serves as a means of social control. Terms like thick, dweeb, dork, dropkick, drongo, mental, loser, moron, spaz, deadhead, faggot, foetus and numerous others (an extensive list is found in a study of outsiders by Thurlow (2001)) are part of an ever-changing litany of insult that rains down upon individual adolescents from their peers every day.

Migrants

The most typical experience of being an outsider is a cultural one, and arises from the status of immigrant. A common thread that runs through history is that immigrants are troublemakers. For example, the Chinese miners who flocked to the Australian goldfields in the 'rushes' of 1851 and later years encountered fierce prejudice and racial hostility. Their industrious habits, their thrift, their collaboration and their separateness were resented rather than admired, and these resentments were linked to racially based slurs concerning their appearance and their lifestyle to further exclude them from the mainstream. The resentment was so strongly felt by the mix of European miners that outbreaks of violence occurred on the goldfields, and resulted in a number of Chinese being killed.

The White Australia Policy, introduced in 1901, enshrined in the laws of the new Commonwealth of Australia the exclusionary practices that were found on the goldfields, and enabled successive governments to exclude people on racial grounds from migrating to Australia. The policy was officially abolished in 1966, but exclusionary attitudes remain. For example, following a surge of refugees attempting to enter northern Australia in small boats in the early years of the twenty-first century, new laws were introduced to restrict the arrival of such people, and these laws were generally approved by the electorate.

Similar toughening of immigration laws has occurred in Europe as well. Pettigrew (1998) provides an extensive review of the recent responses of European governments to the 'new minorities', comprising people from former colonies, guest workers, refugees, and 'accepted' illegal migrants. He documents the extent of prejudice towards these minorities, in blatant as well as in subtle forms, which highlights their continuing status as outsiders.

The eruption of extended rioting in the northern outskirts of Paris in October and November 2005 (*les émeutes*) drew the world's attention to the particular economic hardships of those youth and their families who had migrated from North Africa, which arose from their lack of real acceptance by French society. One young Muslim man who was born and raised in France captured the link between the rioting and the denial of the opportunity to feel included as a crisis of identity. He asked 'How much more French can I be?' (Graff, 2005).

Sport can divide and also unite disparate groups. The 2006 FIFA World Cup attracted interest around the world, and an unprecedented level of public attention in Australia because our team had made the finals, a feat last achieved in 1974. In a country where footballs are oval, the round-ball game is called soccer, and its growth through post-war migration meant that soccer was not seen as a truly Australian sport, but as something foreign. Indeed, its association with migrant groups once attracted the insult 'wogball'. However, there is a growing tolerance for the game, no doubt assisted by Australia's recent successes at the World Cup. This attitudinal shift prompted one television commentator, himself a migrant, to express his newfound sense of inclusion. He wrote in his blog from Berlin: 'I realised that I've never felt more Aussie than I did tonight. As a "new" Aussie I've struggled at times to find a true identity among the true-blue Aussies, but tonight, cosseted with Berliner beer and awash in a sea of Strine emotion, I felt like I belonged.'

Bullying and rejection

Harassment and victimization

Peer harassment and victimization are used interchangeably with bullying in the literature on peer aggression, to refer to a range of persistent and ongoing acts intended to annoy, hurt, humiliate, or intimidate the target, usually someone of about the same age. In their extensive review of research on peer victimization, Hawker and Boulton (2000) distinguish several categories: physical, verbal, indirect, and relational. Indirect forms of bullying are disguised, enabling the aggressor to remain invisible and avoid sanctions. Examples are: writing anonymous letters attacking the person one is angry with; spreading rumours and slanders about a person; and revealing confidences to a third party. Relational aggression is a peer-related type favoured by girls. Examples are: making a friend jealous by associating with someone else; organizing peers to exclude the target person; and sending the target to Coventry, and ensuring that no one will talk to her. Mobile phones (cell phones) and e-mails are powerful tools for these indirect and relational forms of victimization, because they accelerate the spread of malice (and thus increase its impact in a brief period of time) while leaving the victim powerless to retaliate. Moreover, the instigator can be anonymous.

What is the extent of victimization? One of the most comprehensive surveys was undertaken in Britain by Whitney and Smith (1993) and sampled twenty-four middle schools (2623 pupils) and seven secondary schools (4135 students). The secondary school students reported being bullied 'once or more per week' at the rate of 4 per cent for girls and 5 per cent for boys. It is likely that these figures underestimate the extent of the problem, if we accept the authors' assertion that 'Half of those who are bullied do not report it to anyone' (p. 21). Their claim finds support in another large survey of British secondary schools, which reported that repeated bullying was experienced by 7 per cent of adolescent students (Glover *et al.*, 2000). The most common types of bullying described by Whitney and Smith (1993) were name-calling (57 per cent of cases for boys and 71 per cent for girls), being threatened (boys: 26 per cent; girls: 24 per cent) and being the victim of rumours (boys: 20 per cent; girls: 30 per cent). Actual physical assault was 34 per cent for boys but 16 per cent for girls. The prominence in the survey results of verbal and indirect forms of bullying, particularly among girls, exposes the fallacy of the old saying that 'names will never hurt me'. Name-calling is the worst form of bullying, according to some experts, because it undermines the person's sense of identity.

The importance of the group context in victimization and rejection owes much to the pioneering research of Olweus (1978) and his fellow Scandinavian researchers. They have shown that when the peer 'constellations' are examined, we gain a greater appreciation of the destructive power of victimization on the target, and also of the dynamics of the peer networks themselves, given that bullying and victimization comprise one of the key features that bind young people into their peer networks. Victimization in adolescence generally occurs in a context where an individual is the target of bullying within a group of others, usually with a single bully and a group of urgers. For example, Whitney and Smith (1993) found that groups were involved in the victimization of individual adolescents in 53 per cent of cases reported. The aggressor was a single boy in 47 per cent of cases reported by boys and in 21 per cent of those reported by girls.

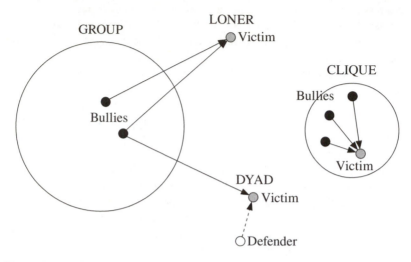

Figure 5.1 Bullying roles in peer networks (after Salmivalli *et al.*, 1997)

Researchers have noted that the group context of bullying accommodates a number of different participant roles. They include being an active participant in bullying, acting as an assistant or as a reinforcer, being a neutral bystander, sympathizing with the victim, and acting as a defender. Salmivalli *et al.* (1997) draw attention to the different peer configurations that support bullying: the large group with its target the isolate (loner) or a dyad; and the small clique with its target a clique member. These are shown, together with participant roles, in Figure 5.1. Almost half the loners identified in the study were victims, whereas all the defenders were in a friendship network.

The figure draws attention to the important influence of onlookers on how the bullying is conducted. In some cases, the onlookers include other victims. It is the memory of this latter group of onlookers that still haunted Manning Clark, the Australian historian, some sixty years later as he recounted his experiences of being initiated as a new boy at Melbourne Grammar in the 1920s. He recalled the circle of senior boys and their brutality, his own powerlessness in the face of the public humiliation they inflicted, and especially the fact that his fellow initiates offered no sympathy, but instead averted their gaze. Being bullied by a group, where no one among the watchers will intervene to halt the process, increases the victim's sense of isolation.

In the situations outlined here, bullying is a means of establishing group identity, through differentiation between adolescents who are inside the group and those who are made to feel outsiders and different from others. One teenager who was not included by the group expressed the feeling that 'I wish I could change myself'.

Recall that the boundaries of adolescent networks are imprecise and constantly changing, as we have seen in Chapter 3. These young adolescents are learning about the power of the group as a source of belonging and acceptance on the one hand, and as an instrument for ostracism on the other. Indeed, the research of Schuster (1999) in German secondary schools provides justification for the claim that group bullying helps establish and maintain group coherence. An interesting finding of her studies is the identification of one or perhaps two victims per class, regardless of the grade level or the type of school. Given that the same students were victims in different classes, it seemed to her that 'one scapegoat may suffice' for the purpose of maintaining group coherence, and that certain students were singled out for this purpose.

Research undertaken by Sunwolf and Leets (2003) has been directed at the social dynamics within the group that silence individual peers from voicing any criticism about the practice of peer exclusion. They call this 'communication paralysis' and it applies to any group situation where individuals choose to remain silent in the face of unfair or cruel behaviour because of their own uncertainties about secure membership of the group. The Sunwolf and Leets study analysed responses from adolescents aged 14–18 to situations of peer exclusion in which they had participated. The researchers found that adolescents' decision to support the exclusion was rarely based on specific qualities of the rejected person. Instead, despite regretting their actions, they justified their silence from fear of losing their place in the group, or of being seen as 'uncool' or 'different' or 'stupid'. Their reluctance to voice disagreement mirrors 'groupthink', where the individual keeps quiet and agrees with the majority out of a misperception that a view that differs from everyone else's undermines group harmony, and that it is more important to fit into the group than to emphasize points of difference.

So strong is the need to belong that few young people want to be seen as different from the majority. Safety lies in fitting in, by wearing the same style of clothes, having the same kind of hairstyle, holding to the same kinds of attitudes and values. Individuality is fine in adolescence – up to a point – but to be seen as a bit different risks being rejected by one's peers, and perhaps becoming a target for harassment. Just as there are benefits from belonging and fitting into the group, there are costs of not belonging. The darker side of relationships between the individual and others is evident in the denial of attachment – through ostracism, social rejection, and peer victimization. Individuals who do not belong to a group may become prey, from the tendency of groups to strengthen group bonds by hostility towards outsiders. An adolescent boy explained to Martino (1999) that 'to be in the group you have to be hassling someone else' (p. 246).

Victim blaming

How is peer victimization justified? A series of studies of young adolescents by Juvonen (1991, 1992) poses the interesting possibility that the majority of peers believe that kids who are targets of bullying are themselves responsible for what happens to them; in short, 'He was asking for it.' The victims stand out so clearly from the rest of the students that they may as well be wearing a shirt with 'hit me' painted on it. They are the bait, and we are the predators! Juvonen's research is concerned with identifying those who are regarded as 'different' by the majority, and finding out why they are victimized. Investigations carried out in Finland and in California analysed the role of student perceptions of deviance (that is, difference from the norm) as justification for negative feelings such as anger and irritation towards the students who were different. The prompts given to students in order to identify the different kids were: 'some may look different or act different from most others'; and 'those who you think are most different from your other classmates'. The most common defining characteristics of the 'different kids' were composites: shy and small, or aggressive and hyperactive. Responsibility was broadly defined as having personal control over one's actions, as *volition* ('Does X want to be that way?') and *fault* ('Is it X's fault that he's like that?'). The hypothetical classmates who were judged to be personally responsible for their deviant characteristics were more disliked, attracted more anger from respondents, and were more likely to be rejected.

The basis for victimization may lie in the kind of relationship that exists between the victim and the group. For example, an individual who is an outsider may be victimized because s/he acts in a way that shows disrespect for the group, perhaps by seeming aloof or 'stuck up' or in some other way ignoring its members or failing to accord them the respect they think they deserve. Of course, ignoring can operate at different levels. It may be a simple case of not noticing their existence and thus denying them recognition, or it may be overtly contemptuous of the group. Group reactions are likely to vary according to the extent to which the group feels a threat to its dominance. Within a clique, victimization may be employed as a means of controlling an errant member and restoring group cohesion. If a group member is perceived to behave in ways that are contrary to the group so as to restrict its functioning, sanctions may be enforced. Examples of individuals who defy or thwart the group include failing to conform, denying loyalty to the group, ignoring or directly opposing key members of the group, or upholding a view or value position that is intolerable to group members.

Graham and Juvonen (2002) examined victimization in terms of the peer group context. They investigated what is known as the 'social misfit' effect, which views the likelihood of a person being harassed or rejected by others in terms of the fit between the person's behaviour and the norms of the majority. Thus an adolescent who is a loner or an oddball may be seen as a misfit in one peer network and attract victimization from its members, whereas in another network s/he may be tolerated and left alone. Graham and Juvonen's study was undertaken in a high school which had large populations of African-American and Latino students and smaller populations of White, Persian and Asian groups and students from a mixed ethnic background. The researchers were interested in the effect of ethnic status (majority or minority) as a context for harassment. The different ethnic groups held different values about being aggressive, further allowing analysis of the effects of ethnic group norms on individuals who deviated from the group norm – both in terms of their risk of harassment and rejection, and also in their degree of adjustment or maladjustment. They found that in the major groups, which upheld aggressive norms, there were fewer victims of harassment than in the minor groups. Approximately four times as many White and Persian students were described as victims rather than aggressors, whereas aggressors outnumbered victims in the African-American and Latino majorities. Moreover, being a victim of harassment was strongly associated within each ethnic group with peer rejection, lack of acceptance and being uncool.

What are the effects of group victimization? Few investigators have examined the immediate effects, but they are traced in an Australian study by Owens *et al.* (2000). The sequence suggested is as follows: first, there is confusion; this is followed by victim denial and attempts at covering up; and next there is an admission of the hurt and pain. Following this admission to herself, the girl engages in 'catastrophizing self-talk', where she blames herself and expects the worst from anything she attempts. This undermines her capacity to cope and leads into further fear and loss of confidence and a desire to escape from the whole sorry situation. It is at this point that the girl is likely to attend her medical practitioner, accompanied by her mother. Sadly, in my experience, schools are reluctant to take any notice of what the doctor may write to them, so that the family's recourse is to put up with it or withdraw their daughter from the school.

What are the longer-term consequences of victimization? Hawker and Boulton (2000) reviewed twenty years of research, and concluded that the findings were so convincing that 'there is little need now for further cross-sectional studies' and that 'it is now time for victimization research to move on' (p. 453). Their summary noted that, regardless of gender, age, or the type of aggression, 'victims of peer aggression feel more anxious, depressed, lonely and worse about themselves than do non-victims' (p. 453). Moreover, evidence has emerged in recent times on the long-term effect of bullying, which suggests that people who had difficulty in coping with bullying at school are more at risk of being victimized in later years. A survey undertaken by Smith *et al.* (2003) of over 5000 adults from various workplaces in Britain reported that those who were victims or bully-victims at school experienced higher workplace harassment in adult life. Analysis of the coping strategies of these people revealed an increase in strategies such as 'tried to make fun of it'. Schafer *et al.* (2004) traced the long-lasting effects on loners of being victimized at school in adults from Spain, Germany and Britain and found that the isolation they experienced in bullying contexts continued to shape their view of life into adulthood, so that they were 'lonely in a crowd'. Of those who had been victims of bullying at school, one in twenty adults reported 'recurrent or intrusive memories' of being bullied, and only one in seven reported the absence of such memories. Respondents who were 'stable victims', that is, they were victimized at primary and also at secondary school, had 'especially low' general self-esteem in adulthood, which suggested to the researchers that the critical effect is the duration of the victim experience rather than its point of onset. As adults, they remained wary of others and found it difficult to trust them, 'fearful that they could be hurt if they allowed themselves to become too close' (p. 389).

Social rejection

Many of the insights into peer rejection come from research on children, conducted during the 1980s and 1990s. Peer rejection was defined in terms of sociometric status. A rejected status was assessed where peer nominations for disliking a child outnumbered those for liking. While the research in this tradition has resulted in productive insights into *children's* behaviour, its applicability to adolescents and young adults is doubtful. One reason for this doubt is that there may be excess meaning in the term rejected when it is based on a sociometric procedure that merely indicates which children are not preferred, rather than which ones have been actively excluded. In the adolescent years, rejection takes more overt forms, in some cases closely resembling relational aggression (see Box 5.1). These active peer practices are a stark reminder of 'the unexpressed pain inflicted on children and adolescents by peer group rejection' (Sunwolf and Leets, 2004, p. 196).

Sunwolf and Leets (2004) examined the real-world group rejection experienced by adolescents. They gathered hurtful accounts of being excluded

---

Box 5.1 How to make you feel you're an outsider

Ignoring:	Failing to hear your greeting and averting their gaze
Diminishing:	Talking through you, as if you don't exist
	Differentiating you from others by affective forms
	(e.g. enthusiastic greeting to friends vs. 'Oh, it's you')
Confidences:	Forming groups that separate you from others
	Moving on when you arrive
	Sharing secrets but excluding you from them

---

from peer groups from 90 per cent of the 682 participants in the study. Active rejection strategies by peers fell into five categories: (a) ignoring; (b) disqualifying; (c) insulting; (d) blaming; and (e) creating new rules. I like that last one: if all else fails, change the rules. The illustration they give is of an unpopular boy who is waiting to get picked for the team. The teams are six a side, and only twelve players are available. Determined not to include him, the team leaders change the rules, so that one side has six and the other five players, and the boy is omitted! The illustration of rewriting the rules shows the desperate lengths to which a group will go in order to protect its boundaries. After analysing the communication patterns in peer rejection, the authors' conclusion is sobering; they note that 'penetrating peer group boundaries ... may be more painful to all children and adolescents than previously acknowledged' (Sunwolf and Leets, 2004, p. 213).

Other researchers have defined rejection by employing the notion of psychological distance. For example, Lease *et al.* (2003) generated a social distance map of students using multi-dimensional scaling. First, they obtained measures of perceived similarity for every member of each peer group identified, on characteristics such as odd, cool, fun to hang around, excluded, communicates, cooperative, bully, shy, inattentive. Distance scores were calculated from the similarity/dissimilarity between pairs of persons on these characteristics. They found that when the scores were plotted, there was a difference between the rejected peers who were located on the periphery of the group structure and the rejected peers who were located in more central locations within the group. The rejected peers who were located on the margin of the group lacked positive social characteristics, and they also possessed 'substantial negative characteristics in addition to being perceived as odd and not very fun to hang around'. The authors add the comment that, 'in early adolescence when learning to fit in is important, being perceived as dissimilar to peers certainly carries a negative connotation' (p. 211).

Rejection and aggression

A major reason for being rejected by one's peers is aggressive behaviour. Children who are disliked or unpopular are more aggressive than other children (e.g. Asher and Dodge, 1986; Parkhurst and Asher, 1992). However, aggression and popularity are not mutually exclusive characteristics, at least in adolescence. Some young people use aggression as a means of achieving group acceptance and exercising leadership. For example, Cairns *et al.* (1988) found that highly aggressive 10–11-year-olds and 13–14-year-olds had similar numbers of friends compared to their non-aggressive peers, and rated themselves as being as popular as others, even though they were less liked than the latter. Moreover, an analysis of the social networks of the aggressive adolescents showed that they occupied very similar positions in the networks to those of non-aggressive controls. However, there was a tendency among the 13–14-year-olds for similarly aggressive adolescents to hang around in the same cliques, an example of 'birds of a feather' flocking together. Other investigators (e.g. Giordano *et al.*, 1986) have also reported this pattern, noting that aggressive teenage girls congregated with others who matched them in terms of socially deviant behaviour. Aggressive youth may have friendships within the group of aggressive peers, but they remain less popular with those who are not aggressive, as Xu *et al.* (2004) found, so that the relation between aggression and unpopularity remains. These studies suggest that an aggressive temperament does not prevent adolescents from having similar numbers of friends to their non-aggressive peers, but that when the wider peer network is considered, being aggressive is still an impediment to acceptance.

For some young people, peer rejection is accompanied by violence. The escalation in school shootings in recent years is a timely warning that peer rejection can prompt violent retaliation from its victims. From their study of ten school shooting cases in the USA from 1995 to 1999, Verlinden *et al.* (2000) concluded that, 'socially, these boys were generally isolated and rejected by peers; most had poor coping skills and felt picked on or persecuted' (p. 44). All of them blamed others for their problems, and all threatened violence to others as retaliation for their sense of isolation and rejection. Thus the image of the shooter as a loner has a basis in unsatisfactory peer relations. A later study (Leary *et al.*, 2003) explored the issues of rejection and ostracism more fully, and covered fifteen school shootings that occurred between 1995 and 2001. They report that in twelve cases there was evidence of a pattern of malicious teasing, ostracism or other forms of ongoing rejection directed at the victim, and in eight of the cases the violent offender had experienced acute rejection by a girlfriend or unrequited love. Many of the girls who had spurned the shooters were victims in the killings. The investigators created a profile of the typical school shooter. They noted that he is male, has been ostracized by the majority of his school peers for some time, and has been chronically taunted or harassed.

Williams and Govan (2005) are critical of the Leary conclusions, and point out that it is difficult to determine whether ostracism played a major role in the shootings, given the likelihood that 'there are probably thousands of students who are bullied and ostracized' (p. 54). Clearly, being bullied and ostracized is not sufficient cause for acts of violence, and Leary's team are well aware of this. They identified other factors that were also present in the lives and personalities of the school killers. Three key risk factors were noted in the profiles: an unusual interest in guns or explosives, a fascination with death, and psychological problems such as depression and/ or a personality disorder. The authors concluded, that 'Rejection is rarely sufficient to provoke premeditated violence …. Rejection alone … does not necessarily cause the violence' (Leary *et al.*, 2003, p. 211).

Relationship break-up

Among life's most emotional experiences are those associated with the break-up of a relationship with a close friend or romantic partner. Collins (2003) points out that romantic relationships are central to peer status, and they facilitate connection with other peers. From this viewpoint, a romantic break-up has a ripple effect that extends beyond personal rejection; it can undermine one's standing amongst one's peers, perhaps to the extent of losing one's place in a particular peer network, in addition to having broken up with one's boyfriend or girlfriend. Where investment in the relationship is high, people experience the greatest anguish following its dissolution. The level of emotional distress is also reported to be greater where the injured party sees no alternative (see Sprecher *et al.*, 1998).

Neglect and betrayal

For young people who have been neglected by a close friend because they have been replaced by a new relationship, or 'dropped' by a romantic partner, there is a sense of betrayal. The experience of rejection generates a wave of emotion and confusion. The loss triggers strong feelings of hurt, anger, guilt and self-blame. You feel gutted, and desolate. You go over and over the last scenes in your mind. Despite the inclination to challenge the person who has rejected you, when the significance of the rejection sinks in, you are flooded with intrusive thoughts directed at the self. These ruminations, like those detected in bullying situations, are critical and self-blaming: 'I'm a loser. There's nothing about me that is likeable.' There are also accusing questions, like these: 'What's wrong with me? Why doesn't anyone like me? How long have I been unaware that s/he/they didn't want me?' These questions are best *not* answered by a friend or sibling, although the Lucy character in the *Peanuts* cartoon was quick to point out Charlie Brown's obvious and irredeemable faults. Answers do nothing except generate a further cycle of self-blame, which finally ends in a sigh of resignation – 'Why bother?' – and the dismissal of friendly advice as 'whatever'.

A relational break-up creates a great sense of being alone, accompanied by feelings of emptiness that leave the person restless and dissatisfied. Recall the songs you have heard about this theme. Here are a few of mine as a young person: *Only the Lonely, Georgy Girl, Heartbreak Hotel, How Can You Mend a Broken Heart* (which contains the line 'How can a loser ever win?'), and *Cry*, the 1950s classic by Johnnie Ray that says it all in one tearful word. Moreover, dissatisfaction with the broken relationship is likely to impede social functioning at school or in the workplace. People are lethargic, unfocused, preoccupied. A young man in his mid-twenties explained to me that after he broke up with his girlfriend he just had to take a week off work because there was no way that he could give the proper attention to people in his job, given the emotional state that he was in.

Roth and Parker (2001) were interested in examining the emotions that younger adolescents experience when neglected by a friend who had begun dating, and whether their views were coloured by their role in the situation. The experiment required 14-year-old adolescents to empathize with a hypothetical adolescent who has been neglected by a friend. The adolescents were interviewed concerning their emotional reactions, taking into account their own similar experiences as either the neglected friend or the offending partner. The adolescents who were asked to view the situation from the neglected friend's viewpoint felt hurt, jealous, and angry. However, when asked to take the offender's perspective, they felt guilty. Thus their emotions changed, depending on the role they were given in the jealousy triangle. However, their own experience as victim or offender further coloured their feelings about being left out by a friend, either accentuating or neutralizing these emotions. Past experience of exclusion heightened their sensitivity to neglect, so these adolescents expressed greater anger, jealousy and hurt than others did. In contrast, the adolescents who in the past had themselves neglected a friend for a boyfriend/girlfriend downplayed the impact of their actions by neutralizing the emotions felt in the hypothetical case. What this study shows is the important role of feelings both in the interpretation of situations and in deciding a response to them. It is likely that for young people who have been neglected by a friend, feelings of hurt and jealousy and dwelling on the 'betrayal' may interfere with their ability to cope with school. Moreover, the conclusion that 'the tensions generated by the dating of one partner are not likely to be self-correcting' (Roth and Parker, 2001,

p. 292) suggests that adolescents may have difficulty accepting counsellor advice to be rational about their situation.

Fortunately, few young people are totally isolated from their peers and beyond the reach of friendship, as the character Fin discovered in the film *The Station Agent*. Friends are sources for building resilience, even to the extent of providing ground-rules for the conduct of relationships. It is through interactions with friends that the rules are established at an implicit level, and the task that remains is to communicate these rules to individuals. Much of friends' talk about romantic relationships could be considered to be an informal curriculum in learning the rules of engagement and acquiring the 'social reading' skills for how to relate to others. Some of these are captured in the studies of socialization by Baxter *et al.* (2001). The researchers encouraged university students to keep diary entries on incidents concerning their personal relationships, and from their stories the informants were asked to extract rules concerning how to relate to others. Two-thirds of the rules were found to apply in some way to romantic relationships, and a further one-sixth to friendships. Some of the rules generated from the contribution of informants are listed in Box 5.2, and further examples are found in Baxter *et al.*'s report.

Box 5.2 Rules for relating

Romantic – eligibility
Don't get romantically involved with someone if he or she is already in a romantic relationship.
Don't get romantically involved with a person who is on the rebound from a prior relationship.
Don't get romantically involved with a person if you are on the rebound from a prior relationship.
If a person is friends with your ex-romantic partner, don't get romantically involved with him/her.

Romantic – entry
Don't falsely lead someone on if you have no genuine romantic interest in them.

Romantic – established
Show respect for a romantic partner.
Don't take more than you give in a romantic relationship.

Source: Adapted from Baxter *et al.* (2001).

The rules that informants extracted from the diary events are guides to behaviour, sensitising them to the complexities of particular interpersonal situations. Clearly, those who are isolated from the network will have restricted access to such a social reading curriculum. Moreover, the loner and outsider have few opportunities to practise and fine-tune the signals that are given in social interaction, and as a consequence they can appear to others to be abrupt and tetchy.

Loneliness

Loneliness is a consequence of the various kinds of social exclusion, neglect, rejection, and peer harassment that are experienced through adolescence and into the adult years. Young people realize that by choosing to enter into any relationship based on openness and trust they are vulnerable to hurt and rejection. Thus the very intensity with which social relationships are pursued during adolescence and youth increases the prospect of exposure to loneliness when the desired level of satisfaction from friendships or from group affiliation is not achieved. For most young people, loneliness is intensely felt because it is intensely personal. Consequently it is an unpleasant experience to be avoided wherever possible.[2]

When loneliness is first experienced, it exerts a force that impels people to seek companionship and make social contact with others who are compatible. But if loneliness is prolonged, anxieties increase to a point where they inhibit action and reduce the motivation to make contact with others. In these circumstances, loneliness can reduce a young person's motivation to participate effectively in communal life, whether in the classroom or the workplace. Prolonged loneliness thus takes on aspects of depression, such as the feelings of emotional emptiness, and the sense of being shut off and separated from others. Rook defined loneliness as:

> an enduring condition of emotional distress that arises when a person feels estranged from, misunderstood, or rejected by others and/or lacks appropriate social partners for desired activities, particularly activities that provide a sense of social integration and opportunities for emotional intimacy.
>
> (Rook, 1984, p. 1391)

The merit of her definition is that it limits the term loneliness to distress arising from some persistent sense of separateness from others, rather than from a fleeting period of social withdrawal. It also reminds us that persons who prefer a solitary lifestyle – like some loners – are not necessarily lonely.

Social loneliness

From his clinical work with adults, Weiss (1974) distinguished between the loneliness of emotional isolation, which appears in the absence of a close emotional attachment, and the loneliness of social isolation, which appears when a person lacks access to a social network and to socially integrative relationships. Of interest here is the concept of *social loneliness*, which may be particularly acute in adolescence and youth, when identity is closely bound up with group belonging, and when ostracism is employed as a weapon of social control by peers.

Social loneliness refers to the sense of boredom, aimlessness and marginality associated with social isolation and a lack of affirmation by others. It often follows some kind of disruption to the social network caused by changed circumstances – for example, moving to a new town, a new school or a new job. It is also associated with the feeling of being rejected or ostracized, where the person feels misunderstood or alienated from the group. Social loneliness captures the notion of anomie, of not fitting in, of not belonging, of being an outsider, disconnected from those around you. Its destructive power was exerted in the ancient Aboriginal practice of pointing the bone. The victim was isolated and rejected by the tribe, and denied his very identity. Feelings of social loneliness and estrangement may also be experienced in everyday circumstances: for example, when you are not 'in on the joke', or when others are talking amongst themselves but you are excluded, or when you are left out of social activities. The prominence of social loneliness was detected in a survey by Chipuer and Pretty (2000) of almost 1000 adolescents living in urban and rural Queensland. They found that males were lonelier than females, and the loneliest group were males in rural areas. This finding underlines the nature of rural areas in Australia, where adolescent suicide is higher, and boys have limited opportunities to belong to larger peer networks.

Coping with loneliness

Research evidence shows that lonely people have poor self-esteem and lack confidence in their own abilities, and that they hold negative and disparaging views of others (e.g. Jones *et al.*, 1981; Levin and Stokes, 1986; Wittenberg and Reis, 1986). In these respects, individuals may contribute to their own loneliness. For example, over-concern with gaining acceptance makes them extremely sensitive to any hint of peer rejection and negatively distorts even the positive social messages that others are sending. Second, pessimism over the outcomes of social interaction colours their expectations of others' behaviour towards them, and contributes to their own social awkwardness and also the hesitancy of others to include them in social activities. Expectations and attitudes, both in respect of self (outgoing personality/social confidence) and in relation to others (non-judgemental attitudes to others, positive attitude to friendship), appear to contribute to peer acceptance and likeability.

Maladaptive coping with relationships seems more common among people who are lonely. Nurmi *et al.* (1997) suggest that people who feel lonely have generally negative attitudes to social reality, to their view of themselves, and to the coping strategies they employ. They choose to be pessimistic. For them, the glass is half-empty, rather than half-full. They seem to be more self-focused and less able to refer to the other person. The Finnish young adults (average age 21 years) in the study were shown cartoons of two social situations with positive and negative outcomes, and asked to write down their thoughts and planned actions. Nurmi *et al.* (1997) found that the more likely these young people were to employ a pessimistic avoidance strategy, the more loneliness they reported a year later. They conclude that 'a social strategy characterized by failure expectations, negative feelings, avoidance, and self-handicapping leads to dissatisfaction with social relationships' (p. 771). Earlier, Peplau *et al.* (1982) had reported that lonely people have a self-blaming style that is intolerant of their own faults: they apologize frequently. This makes them vulnerable to doubts and to falling levels of confidence whenever they do make attempts to become socially active.

When Cutrona (1982) traced the experiences of loneliness in beginning college students she found subtle differences between those who remained lonely all year, and those who overcame their initial loneliness. The latter students held higher expectations about finding friends than the students who continued to be lonely. As the year wore on, the lonely students lowered their goals, deciding that they didn't need a lot of friends, and that they would focus on their work rather than on their social life. Some took a radical path, and reasoned that, since there was little hope of group acceptance, the only way of avoiding loneliness was to go for broke and seek an intense romantic alliance.

Observations of social interactions report that lonely people are less talkative, ask fewer questions, and recall less of the other person's conversation than non-lonely people. They may have real conversational difficulties in initiating conversations, in engaging in intimate communications, and in making appropriate kinds of self-disclosure. Moreover, during periods of loneliness they tend to adopt a non-social pattern of coping. Roscoe and Skomski (1989) report a greater use by lonely adolescents of coping strategies such as 'listen to music, read, write letters or a diary, forget it, sleep, or take a drive'. In contrast, non-lonely adolescents were more likely to talk with someone, go out, or find something to do. For males, 'going for a burn' in a car may relieve the sense of angst and boredom. Females may prefer to go shopping to relieve their loneliness and get a boost at the same time from social stimulation.

The internet is an avenue for lonely individuals to make social contact. Indeed, some researchers assert that the lonely are drawn to the internet because of the possibilities it offers for companionship in (cyber) communities. Chat-rooms and blogging offer many possibilities for a person not only to communicate anonymously, but also to assume any kind of personality they wish. Research suggests that internet use, unlike television, appears to benefit some lonely individuals and is potentially liberating for those who feel stigmatized and rejected. Morahan-Martin and Schumacher (2003) found that internet use enhanced the social behaviour of lonely adults, so that 'their behaviour was less inhibited, they were friendlier and more intimate', and their online friends were emotionally supportive and fun to know (p. 668). However, 'the Internet is so new that we really don't know what will happen to people as they begin to use it over an extended period' (E. J. Moody, 2001, p. 396).

Implications for practice

Social skills

A theme that has been mentioned in this chapter is the importance of 'social reading' – that is, the particular set of social skills a person employs in order to understand a social situation and tune in to its social nuances, so as to choose the appropriate responses to make in interacting with other people. Courtesy, politeness, respect and consideration of others are values upheld in most societies. Social or cultural insensitivity is often interpreted by others as rudeness and bad manners rather than excused as social clumsiness or forgetfulness. The exceedingly rich, the immensely gifted, and the fabulously famous may ignore the social norms, but even they are not immune from public condemnation. However, tolerance and understanding are required in our dealings with young people who are loners by reason of their personality, or who are socially isolated through the kinds of experiences that have been described in these pages. Just because a person is unusual or socially inept, and shrugs off the gestures of friendliness of others, is no excuse to treat them as social lepers. When we accept that some people have 'slow to warm up' temperaments, and that some find the proximity and noisy behaviour of others both stifling and unpleasant, we are more able to tolerate their retreat and social distancing as forms of social coping. When they are free to determine their own social space, rather than be pressured into groups and settings that they find to be distressing, their awkwardness diminishes.

While loners and outsiders would profit from greater tolerance and better understanding of their behaviour by the majority, the need remains for socially isolated youth to become more aware of the subtle social signs that a person needs to read in any social situation, as well as the social signals they give that put other people offside. There are numerous formal programs that focus on social skills training, and one that was mentioned in the first edition of this book was that of Lindsay (1987). The program emphasized three skills areas: (1) recognizing and interpreting communications, both verbal and nonverbal; (2) conversation skills, including the strategies of initiating conversation, continuing a conversation, and breaking into a conversation group; and (3) situation management, which teaches adolescents how to be assertive, how to keep out of trouble with peers, and how to handle authority figures. Each of these skills areas is relevant to the topics that have been discussed here. In addition, there are social reading skills important for the classroom (see Alschuler, 1980).

Concluding comments

The particular focus of this chapter has been the adolescent or young adult who is isolated, through the deliberate actions of others, because of an emotionally distressing event, or by dint of their own personal make-up. They are lonely in the crowd. Often they are invisible, their plight unnoticed and their pain unrelieved. In our concern with managing groups in school or in youth work it is easy to overlook the person on the fringe, the one who stays in the background and is never a willing participant.

From the group perspective, the topics discussed are a reminder that there is a darker side to social and personal relationships, and that many adolescents and youth at times experience hostility, betrayal and ostracism from their peers. The significance of social rejection and peer victimization has both immediate and long-term effects. Coping and adjustment are impaired, self-worth is reduced, and the capacity to function in everyday situations is stalled. While isolation and rejection are not uncommon experiences in life, and loneliness is not the preserve of the few, this chapter has shown that the denial of attachment and of opportunities to belong is psychologically damaging to the individual. Moreover, the experience of rejection and betrayal in close relationships can affect one's ability to make commitments to others in the future.

The youth worker knows that it is natural for groups to close in on themselves and show intolerance towards outsiders as an act of protection, just as a clam closes up when it is disturbed or feels threatened. Fortunately, few groups are as tightly closed in on themselves as a clam. Once they feel safe, they become less defensively self-protective, and like the clam they open out to savour what is offered by the wider environment. The question for the youth worker is how to prise a group apart so that it is open to accepting new members.

The challenge for the teacher practitioner is to recognize the power of social relations to hurt as well as heal. It is said that some students can be described as phantom students; that is, they are so silent and unnoticed that when they are absent from class, no one seems able to detect who is missing. That is a sorry state of affairs. Similarly, students who are isolates may be unnoticed by their teachers. Certainly this was the conclusion drawn by Ward (1982) in the Junior High School Transition Study. She wrote that, 'the characteristics of the isolate suggest that the difficult and unpleasant situations of these students may be completely overlooked', and if this is the case, 'teachers may need to have such students pointed out to them' (p. 387). This chapter has drawn attention to their plight.

If isolated youth are to be catered for, serious attention must be given to the process of inclusiveness. Indeed, inclusion should be the watchword in designing classroom tasks or youth work activities, so that all young people feel welcome, wanted, and valued for themselves. Communicating respect and valuing the group and its members are ways of building trust, and with greater trust comes greater openness and tolerance towards others. Teachers and youth workers can model inclusiveness, and encourage other adolescents to be accepting and tolerant of socially isolated youth; and they can ensure that the group structures they put in place contain levels of safety that ensure that the social risks of involvement by loners are manageable for them.

When teachers and youth workers[3] adopt inclusive practices, so that young people are acknowledged and valued, the benefits can be immense. At the recent graduation day at a junior high school to which I had been invited, one of the guest speakers was a former student who had taken remedial classes, and was now managing his own company. He spoke about what the school meant to him, and announced that he wished to endow a school prize for students like himself who achieve against the odds. The task for the practitioner is to communicate the values of inclusion to young people in their care, so that the positive influence of that young man's school becomes commonplace. Sunwolf and Leets (2004) observed that, 'All of us can become more intentionally thoughtful about changing how we socialize students in our classrooms' (p. 220).

Part III
Social influences

6   Antisocial behaviour

> Almost all research on antisocial youth concludes that being with simi-
> lar youth exacerbates their tendencies toward such behavior, yet most
> social programs for such youth put them all together in groups.
>
> (Petersen, 2004, p. 18)

Graffiti scrawled on post-boxes and bridges, broken glass on sidewalks,
slashed seats on trains, overturned litter bins in public parks – cities bear
these urban scars from Sydney to San Francisco, from Manchester to
Montevideo. Together with fighting among football fans, assaults on individuals, hostile confrontations with police, and car races in suburban streets,
they constitute some of the forms of antisocial behaviour that are perpetrated
by young people. How antisocial behaviour is expressed and instigated in
groups, mass crowds, and delinquent networks is the subject of this chapter.

What is meant by antisocial behaviour? Simply put, it is behaviour that
repeatedly violates established social norms. Cheating, swearing, and men-
acing others are some examples; others are vandalism, stealing, assault,
rape and murder. Use of the term antisocial behaviour allows inclusion of
acts engaged in by young people that fall outside criminal jurisdiction. It is
inappropriate, however, to describe an act as antisocial because it offends
particular sensibilities or social customs. For example, a boy who barges
past a teacher may be thoughtless, but the act is not an antisocial one; and
a student who hangs his head rather than look at the teacher, even when
ordered to do so, may be acting in accordance with his culture (as is true for
Aboriginal children). It would be wrong in such a case to describe the act
as either disrespectful or antisocial.

Onset and persistence

Estimates of the prevalence of severe behaviour problems in school surveys of children and youth range from 2 to 6 per cent, but general surveys

of adolescent antisocial behaviour report far higher incidence levels. For example, Baerveldt *et al.* (2004) report that almost 90 per cent of the 15–17-year-old Dutch students they surveyed admitted to at least one minor delinquent offence in the past year; and Emler and Reicher (1995) cite rates for English boys of 61 per cent for breaking windows in empty houses, 60 per cent for truanting, 51 per cent for smashing bottles, and 55 per cent for shouting insults at strangers in the street. Also of interest was their finding that one-third had damaged school property on purpose and one-quarter had participated in a group fight. The levels of antisocial behaviour reported by the Australian Institute of Criminology (Smart *et al.*, 2004) included fighting (30 per cent in early and mid-adolescence, reducing to 23 per cent in late adolescence), vandalism and graffiti (35 per cent in mid- and late adolescence), and truancy (43 per cent in late adolescence). Approximately half the total number surveyed had engaged in some form of antisocial behaviour within the last year.

Before we jump to the conclusion that our schools and communities are infested with vandals, bullies, truants and hooligans, a distinction should be made between an antisocial act and an antisocial person. The latter is a relatively rare species at school despite the rates reported above. Let me give a personal illustration. The author engaged in shoplifting (as a boy of 12), rode on a train without paying his fare (as an adolescent of 15), and climbed the fence into the school swimming baths for a night swim with his mates (as a youth of 17). These antisocial acts, all done in the company of others, do not make me a delinquent, but they would certainly have looked bad on my school report card.

Indeed, reports that violence among youth is increasing may be exaggerated, and may reflect changing norms and methods of classification rather than actual increases in prevalence. Drawing on two Swedish studies, one of social data and the other of school data, Estrada (2001) finds no evidence of an increase. Rather than an actual increase being found in the prevalence of violence, there has been an increase in media attention, as well as in the level of school reporting of violence. Estrada argues that the concern in society with youth violence is evidence of 'a marked shift' in the way that society interprets the actions of young people (p. 647). He is particularly critical of the role played by 'the media as actor' in amplifying the incidence of antisocial and violent behaviour among youth. His survey of ten European countries shows that, except for Britain and Germany, the rates over the past fifty years have been decreasing.

Because the scope of this chapter includes expressions of antisocial behaviour from adolescence to young adulthood, it is important to identify the themes that link the chapter together. These may be stated briefly as: the role of aggression in interpersonal conflict; the effects of social identification in accentuating intergroup hostility; and the extent to which association with deviant and antisocial peers influences antisocial behaviour. The focus on social influences is not to ignore individual tendencies for risk-taking and individual differences in self-control, but it is consistent with the emphasis found in this section of the book. Clearly, some social environments are more risky than others and some groups have more antisocial habits and tendencies than others. Knowledge of the nature of risk in these different groups and social environments should be of benefit both to young people and to those who work with them.

The spectrum of antisocial behaviour

Some authorities restrict youth antisocial behaviour to illegal acts, while others, like Rutter *et al.* (1998), take a wider view of antisocial behaviour to include delinquent behaviour together with non-criminal activity. Antisocial behaviour is the term preferred in this discussion, first, because words like crime and delinquency imply conviction, whereas the majority of antisocial acts by youth are not reported in crime statistics; and second, because it allows us to include types of behaviour at school and in the street that may be precursors to criminal acts but do not result in prosecution because of other circumstances, including the age of the perpetrator. Most texts on problem behaviour in school are disappointing in their treatment of antisocial behaviour, in that they either reduce it to classroom discipline or restrict their focus to psychiatrically disturbed students. Even the best of them (for example, Walker *et al.*, 2004) limit their discussion to the serious conduct disorders. However, Walker *et al.* make the telling point that, 'In a very real sense antisocial behaviour is about aggression' (p. 15). This statement can serve as our compass as we examine how aggression is expressed in the many types of antisocial behaviour, including community forms such as assault, reckless driving, delinquency and crowd disorder, as well as in school victimization and student conflict.

Anger deserves special mention, because it is an emotional accelerant to aggressive behaviour, and fuels many of the incidents of violent confrontation that are described in the following pages. Anger undermines self-control and allows free rein to hurtful retaliatory behaviour. Moreover, research shows that aggressive youth are hypersensitive to negative social cues and often misperceive neutral events as intentional attacks on them. In the context of violence and antisocial behaviour, the spotlight has long been directed at males, but there is evidence that girls engage in violence as well. Smith and Thomas (2000) interviewed a broad sample of violent and non-violent adolescent girls, and found that not only did the violent girls report more intense levels of anger arousal and more frequent occasions when they felt angry enough to hurt someone, but when asked what they were angry about, their answers were often vague and general. In contrast to the responses of non-violent girls, who were more likely to describe specific incidents, the violent girls seemed to display 'a free floating hostility' (p. 568).

Pub violence

The pub is a high-risk setting for violent assault. Surveys around the world show that pubs and clubs are the main locations for violence against young people. Using data from the 1998 Australian National Drug Strategy survey, Williams (2001) shows that verbal and physical abuse against males 14–24 years of age was experienced in pub settings by over half of the city respondents and over two-thirds of the rural respondents. Evidence from studies such as those by Leonard *et al.* (2002) in the USA and by Graham and Wells (2001) in Canada confirms the pattern of aggression among bar patrons, and supports Williams's comment that 'there is overwhelming evidence that drinking and antisocial behaviour are proximate' (2001, p. 12). Of particular merit are studies that delve into what actually happens in pubs that generates violent behaviour. For example, Graham and Wells (2001) identified 169 incidents of aggressive interactions in bars in which the majority of patrons were under the age of 25 years. Their findings reflect 'the essentially social nature of bar-room aggression' (p. 201). Incidents often escalated in size from two or three combatants to include a larger number. Fights that involved a group of five or more males, which comprised 'a substantial proportion' of the total fights, sometimes resembled a 'tag-team' format where an initial pair of fighters was replaced or joined by others, even to the extent that the originators of the fight became bystanders or left the area altogether.

In situations of crowded bars, populated by intoxicated young males, seemingly minor actions or remarks can provoke angry responses. In the research by Graham and Wells, aggressive incidents arose from disputes over a game, from a jostle or bump, or from taking another's chair. Congested areas in the bar environment had higher frequencies of incidents. The role of anger in pub violence was explored in greater detail in a later study by these authors (Graham and Wells, 2003). Respondents were interviewed and asked to describe a specific fight incident, and provide their views about what caused it, what may have prevented it from happening, and how they felt when it was over. An interesting finding was that some exaggerated an angry emotion as a pretext for aggressive action. The researchers also found instances where the emotional reaction *followed* the decision to fight, giving it stimulus and increasing the level of intensity. Respondents referred to 'instant anger' and commented that 'a man's temper's very hot'. It was also evident that some young men found fights rewarding, and made little effort to avoid them. Both the presence of alcohol and the atmosphere of the bar setting itself contributed to aggressive behaviour. Among the rewards that were identified were a sense of righteousness, feeling like a hero, gaining respect from others, a sense of power, and group bonding. While grievances were often the pretext for aggression, the key motives were maintaining male honour and group loyalty, and fighting was viewed as part of the fun of drinking in bars. Graham and Wells concluded that for young males, 'public drinking occurs in a highly volatile and aggressive social context not unlike the general context for males who spend a lot of time on the streets' (2003, p. 561).

Buddie and Parks (2003) also focused on the social behaviours exhibited in bars. Of particular interest was the likelihood of a woman experiencing aggression in a bar setting where groups of young men are present. They asked, 'What is it about bars that increases an individual's risk for experiencing aggression?' They found that women experienced more severe aggression when they frequented bars that contained younger patrons and when they behaved in certain ways that increased their risk. The specific behaviours of women that were associated with the risk of aggression included heavy drinking, mixing with less well-known individuals, and talking to larger groups of individuals in the bar context rather than staying in a small group of known friends.

Gatecrashers

Gatecrashing the parties of young people has become commonplace in many countries. Armed with mobile phones, these antisocial youths cruise the streets looking for houses lit up with festive lighting; and the word is spread in minutes, giving the location of their target. The strangers barge into the house and rampage through the rooms – taking what they want of food and drink, and responding with violence and abusive language when ordered to leave. Confronted by antisocial groups, parents feel powerless to expel the intruders and bewildered at how to control their own child's party. Numerous reports of gatecrash incidents can be found in the Australian and New Zealand press, with incidents reported from Cairns to Canberra, Adelaide to Auckland, Perth to Wellington. The level of disorderly behaviour of the gatecrashers ranges from throwing rocks and bottles to attacking others with knives, needles and bats. A Brisbane youth was stabbed in the chest after he had been chased down the street by a gatecrasher. In Gerringong, south of Sydney, drunken youths who had gatecrashed a party in December 2005 then brawled in the street and smashed shop windows.

A resident told reporters that he saw a teenage boy dragged into the middle of the street outside his house, where four others 'laid the boot in for a good ten minutes'. Chief Inspector Wayne O'Keefe sent ten police cars and the dog squad to Gerringong, where they herded the troublemakers onto buses, accompanied by police officers, 'to make sure they left', he said.

A party that was gatecrashed on the Queensland Sunshine Coast became so violent that the windows of police cars were smashed, and police took three hours to restore public order. Another party in Perth was gatecrashed by about 120 youths and young adults, and it required thirty police in riot gear to restore control. A police inspector said of the Perth party that it was a typical teenage party that got out of control because of alcohol, and that 'idiots, when they become affected by alcohol, become a problem for everybody' (*Sunday Times*, Perth, 29 February 2004). The rise of these incidents has prompted the Victorian Police Department to devise a Party Safe program which gives tips to parents on the steps to follow in planning a safe party, including how to register the party with police.

Networked telecommunication influences can be detected in gatecrashing. Mobile phones enable gatecrasher gangs to communicate a text message across a loose network and to assemble quickly at a chosen venue. Once at the party address, the separate groups of gatecrashers merge into a larger force.

Reckless driving

'Grass is made for mowin' and rubber is made for smokin'', and car hoons express themselves in donuts, burnouts and street drifting races. Driving at speed at night around a town in a car full of friends is tremendously exhilarating. Putting 'the pedal to the metal' in street racing and taking wheelies at high speed with the tyres screaming in protest brings a rush. A hotted-up car is an excitement machine, and danger is part of the excitement.

However, the danger may not be commensurate with the risks. Twenty per cent of all driver fatalities in the USA and 63 per cent of passenger fatalities occur when the driver is a teenager. Road accidents per mile among 16–19-year-olds in the USA are four times the national average, and the crashes per mile for 16-year-olds are three times those of 19-year-olds. If the road accident statistics fail to bring young drivers back to reality, the actions of police may do so: 'When we tell them if they race here we're going to crush their cars, it gets their attention' (California Police spokesperson).

Both research and observation confirm that, for young people, risky driving occurs in a peer context. Similarly, joy-riding in a stolen car is most fun when undertaken by a group (Scott and Paxton, 1997). Wherever street car racing is found, there is the watching crowd of peers – those who compete with their car, and those who can't afford a car and serve as passengers and onlookers. 'Burnouts always attract an audience', said one car enthusiast. Another stated that, 'It's much more fun when you've got your mates there, flying round corners, going fast – it's really good' (Stephen and Squires, 2003, p. 152).

Some authors link cars, speed and danger to masculinity, and describe driving performance as the use of 'public space as theatre' for showing off (Kenway *et al.*, 2006). A study by Sarkar and Andreas (2004) suggests how peer influences may work as risk contexts. The respondents were adolescents attending traffic school because of a traffic citation. The researchers obtained self-reports of their driving, to explore whether their risky driving was affected by their exposure as passengers to others' reckless driving. Twenty-seven per cent said they had driven recklessly, 20 per cent reported drag racing, and 17 per cent had driven a car when drunk. Moreover, they found that adolescents' exposure as passengers to reckless driving was associated with their own reported levels of risky driving. For example, those who had been a passenger in a vehicle with a reckless driver were more likely to have also been exposed to drag racing and drunk driving, and were more likely themselves to have engaged in drag racing.

Reckless driving is not confined to the teenage years. Bradley and Wildman (2002) found that the pattern was continued among their sample of emerging adults (aged 18–25 years) in Australia. Similarly, Arnett (1998) noted a 'strikingly high' prevalence of high-risk driving patterns among young adults. In his study of 21–29-year-olds, 77 per cent had driven 20 km/hr over the speed limit (41 per cent more than five times); 55 per cent had driven when intoxicated (half of these more than five times); and 29 per cent had engaged in racing their car (17 per cent more than five times). Moreover, peer influence on reckless driving was also evident. Bradley and Wildman (2002) concluded that, 'the reputedly *adolescent* [*sic*] characteristic of peer pressure influencing antisocial behaviour continues to have an important influence into emerging adulthood' (p. 263).

Although no direct examination of peer influence was made in these studies, the poor risk perception shown by these young people of their own driving would seem to be derived from their association with other risky drivers, assisted by the different roles taken by participants. For example, some members were designated as the car-jackers, others as the drivers, and others still as the navigators and passengers.

A further aspect concerns the psychological benefits of car theft and risky driving for some young people. In their detailed interviews with car thieves, Stephen and Squires (2003) uncovered a common theme, 'the issue of control of the car as a metaphor for their lives' (p. 157). They interpreted comments of informants such as 'you're in control of the car and can do anything' as revealing a sense of agency that was not usually present in the daily experience of these youth 'on the margins'. The risks and excitement of car activities provided relief from the insecurities of their everyday lives, the heaviness of which was summed up by a youth who was facing four years of prison: 'Adults don't realize how sheltered they are' (p. 160).

Delinquent gangs

Whereas the instances of hooligan behaviour so far mentioned involve loose groups and collectivities, other antisocial behaviour is generally associated with delinquent gangs. There are different understandings about what constitutes a gang. Attempts to differentiate between the American notion of criminal gangs and the European concept of street groups of youth produced an international conference on the topic of the 'Eurogang paradox' (Klein *et al.*, 2001), where American gang scholars met with their European counterparts. What was helpful from the discussions at that conference was recognition that the American notion of youth gangs is relatively rare in Europe. In contrast to the true criminal gangs, which tend to be older and more organized, youth gangs are loosely structured groups that engage in minor delinquent behaviour, such as vandalism, graffiti, theft, and fighting. Klein put the difference clearly in the preface: 'Street gangs are, by and large, qualitatively different from other youth groups' (Klein *et al.*, 2001, p. 10). The participants concluded that the neglect of non-gang groups by American researchers has contributed to over-identifying of gangs as the predominant form of street group for youth. The delegates agreed that 'gangs exist at one end of a continuum of youth groups' (p. 333), whose common basis is antisocial behaviour.

Networks and delinquency

Thornberry *et al.* (2003) see youth gangs as the 'prototypical deviant social network' (p. 166). Loose groups are formed around existing pairs and cliques, but weak ties may link them to others through past affiliations, so that the gang grapevine may be much more extensive than the apparent size of the group at a particular time. Gang involvement in early and middle adolescence may be erratic, and engagement in antisocial activities may be spasmodic – rising during the school vacations and dropping away during times when adolescents have heavy demands on them from, say, school examinations or part-time jobs or sporting activities. In addition, we need to appreciate the nature of delinquent friendships as possibly 'friendships of convenience'. For example, Snijders and Baerveldt (2003) found that adolescents with similar levels of delinquency formed friendships more quickly and dissolved them more quickly than did non-delinquents. Curry *et al.* (2002) explored the extent of these brief associations among St Louis middle school students. They reasoned that, 'When gangs are loosely structured manifestations of collective behaviour, one should find, in addition to members and non-members, a population of youths who are neither completely members nor non-members, but something in between' (p. 280). Their predictions were confirmed: they found a large number of adolescents who associated briefly or occasionally with gang members. In addition to the 15 per cent who said they were in a gang, over half of the remaining adolescents (59 per cent of the boys and 55 per cent of the girls) – those who said they were not in a gang – reported at least one gang involvement; that is, they were associated with a gang at some time.

Research on youth gangs is clear in showing that gang membership fosters delinquent activity, and the evidence shows that 'this relationship is remarkably robust' (Thornberry *et al.*, 1993, p. 55). Thornberry and his colleagues (Thornberry *et al.*, 2003) examined the delinquent careers of youth in relation to their gang membership. Their longitudinal design allowed them to trace membership histories of individual boys, before, during, and after their involvement in gangs, and to compare their level of delinquent activity with that of non-gang youth. When they compared boys who at any time had been gang members with those who were never in a gang, the rates of delinquency in each of the three years were substantially greater for gang members – four to five times as high. The researchers found that during periods when adolescents were active in a gang they had higher rates of violence against others than did non-gang members; whereas in periods when they were not active in the gang their rates of assault were much lower, and comparable with those of youth who were not in gangs. This study highlights the role of gangs as convoys for delinquency and confirms that the group context itself facilitates antisocial behaviour, over and above the antisocial coping styles typical of these adolescents.

Other studies have produced similar findings, noting that, while in the gang, boys' delinquency increased. An example is Curry *et al.* (2002), who compared the rates of delinquency of 'gang associates' with those for gang members and those for adolescents who had never been in a gang, and found that the delinquency of associates was intermediate between the other groups. Another longitudinal study of youth gangs, that by Gordon *et al.* (2004), identified the periods of a boy's history before, during, and after gang membership. Access to ten years of follow-up data meant that the researchers were better able than Thornberry *et al.* had been to untangle potential confounds arising from misclassification of boys as non-members at the beginning of the study. The quality of these data enabled them to clarify the effect of selection as well as the influence of peer socialization;

in summary, boys are more delinquent during the period when they are gang members (socialization effect), but the boys who join gangs are already more delinquent than the boys who never join (selection effect).

Delinquency research was slow to adopt social network approaches to peer influence. Peers were recognized as sources for the transmission of delinquent attitudes and behaviour, but their identities were obscured as 'delinquent peers'. Although Krohn (Krohn, 1986; Krohn et al., 1988) had earlier applied network concepts to delinquency, the structural characteristics of friendship networks were ignored by the field of criminology. It took another decade before network measures were applied; yet the use of network analysis is still not widespread. Sarnecki (1990) had earlier shown that delinquency was related to network centrality: the stronger the connection that delinquents had to delinquent networks, the more substantial, serious and long-lasting was their delinquent behaviour. Baron and Tindall (1993) used measures of network structure to predict that youth who occupied central positions in a gang network would hold more delinquent attitudes than peripheral figures. Interviews were conducted over a period of several months with thirty-five members of a punk gang, and from the information so obtained, Baron devised measures of closeness (degree centrality) and betweenness centrality. Consistent with his predictions, members who were more central to the gang held more deviant attitudes. This analysis of group structure indicates that while each person in the gang is vulnerable to the views and expectations of other gang members, conformity pressures vary with location in the network, being stronger in the core area than on the periphery.

Recent studies using large data sets from the Adolescent Health database to construct social network measures have confirmed the Baron and Sarnecki findings. Haynie (2001) used three measures of network structure – density, centrality and popularity – to assess the association between individual delinquency and that of the friendship network. She found that properties relating to the individual's position in the network explain this association. For example, the peers' level of delinquency has a stronger association with an individual adolescent's delinquency when their network is very dense (or cohesive), when the individual is located in a central position in the friendship network, or when they are popular in the sense of receiving a high number of nominations from others. Conversely, the association between peers' delinquency and the adolescent's delinquency is weak when they occupy a peripheral position in their peer network. The research of Schreck et al. (2004) also showed that these structural features of friendship networks were associated with victimization risk among delinquents. They found that adolescents who were centrally located within delinquent peer networks had a high risk of victimization compared with those on the periphery, and the risk level increased as the level of delinquency of peers increased. In contrast, adolescents with high centrality in conventional (non-delinquent) networks had reduced exposure to violence, through high levels of support. These contrasting experiences are discussed in terms of the mistrust and suspicion that permeate delinquent networks. Centrally located delinquent individuals are sensitive to any threats to the network from competitors. They are more at risk of victimization because of their centrality, and also because they are aggressively active in the business of maintaining their position and control.

Attachment and belonging

Researchers note that youth gangs generally form as the response of young males to the need to protect themselves from hostile group attacks, often racially motivated. Apart from the motive of protection through group membership, there is the benefit of belonging to a social network that already contains admired friends and relations, together with the excitement of joining in gang activity. The main reasons for joining a gang are reported by Esbensen *et al.* (1999), derived from accounts provided by approximately 10 per cent of adolescents aged 13–14 years who were gang members in their large survey. The sample consisted of almost 6000 students in forty-two schools across eleven US cities. The reasons given were protection (51 per cent), fun and excitement (47 per cent), and to get respect (46 per cent). Esbensen *et al.* (1999) found that girls in general had lower self-esteem and a greater sense of social isolation than the boys, and this was more pronounced among gang girls. A further finding was that gang girls' attachment to the gang, while modest, was stronger than that of the boys; girls endorsed statements of 'being like a family' and 'feeling like I belong somewhere' (p. 45). Perhaps membership of a gang provided them with some compensation.

I have mentioned that several delinquency researchers, notably Hagan, Krohn, Baron and Sarnecki, have applied notions of network ties to explain the integration of youth into street gangs and criminal gangs. This work shows that as links are established with others who are involved in delinquent behaviour, the individual adolescent becomes isolated from conventional groups of young people and from legitimate employment sources, and increasingly linked to antisocial forms of 'employment'. Just as part-time jobs link youth to people in the workforce and to work-related social structures, a delinquent career is furthered by part-time delinquent jobs and by links with other antisocial youth.

So what are the mechanisms of peer influence in antisocial behaviour? Clearly there is not one simple process as the term peer pressure may suggest. Association, affiliation and identification, as well as emotionally charged forms of social bonding like those described as attachment and belonging, are present. The research evidence suggests that delinquent adolescents are no different from others in respect of caring and trust (Giordano *et al.*, 1986; Pleydon and Schner, 2001). But we have not resolved the question of influence by finding that delinquents have friends. Social learning approaches (Poulin *et al.*, 1999) suggest that the quality of the friendship is immaterial to delinquent behaviour among antisocial boys, in the sense that it is not a driver of their delinquency. Rather it seems that their friendship arises *as a consequence* of social interactions: their problem behaviour provides an entry ticket to link them to a peer network. Once in such a group, it is the group dynamics of joint participation in delinquent activity rather than friendship quality that fuels their delinquency. This reasoning is consistent with what was found: the 13–14-year-old boys with low-quality friendships had escalated their delinquency the most when assessed at 15–16 years of age. The group context is emphasized in another longitudinal study of boys aged 13–19 years by Lahey *et al.* (1999). They see gangs as providing a convoy for increasing levels of delinquency among already antisocial boys, which they suggest is 'the next developmental step' in their escalation of antisocial behaviour.

Developmental changes in susceptibility

The second aspect concerning peer influence is the extent to which antisocial behaviour follows a developmental pattern that is linked to the nature of adolescent development. A long-term finding in research on delinquent behaviour is that it peaks at the age of 17 but falls away rapidly after that, so that by the age of 28 an estimated 85 per cent of former delinquents are no longer committing offences. Drawing on longitudinal data from a birth cohort of children in Dunedin, New Zealand, Moffitt (1993) traced the growth in antisocial behaviour from childhood across the high school years. The prevalence rate in antisocial behaviour grew from 5 per cent at age 11 to 32 per cent at age 15, and continued to increase, so that by age 18, as many as 93 per cent of adolescent males in the sample had engaged in some form of delinquent activity. In an endeavour to explain the growth and decline of delinquent and antisocial behaviour, Moffitt (1993) devised a twofold typology of antisocial behaviour in adolescence, each with a distinctive developmental pathway. The first group (comprising 7 per cent of the sample) displayed delinquent behaviour traceable to their early childhood, and their behaviour persisted into adult life. This is the *lifecourse persistent* group. As adolescents they had marked levels of social alienation: they lacked closeness; they were callous; they felt that they were being victimized, and were vigilant and suspicious of others. By the age of 18, compared with normal adolescents they reported more incidents of dangerous driving and unsafe sex, and higher levels of unemployment. A second and larger group (24 per cent of the sample) only became involved in delinquent behaviour in adolescence, but the behaviour was temporary and arose from their association with delinquent peers rather than from social malfunctioning or individual psychopathology. Moffitt named this the *adolescence-limited* group. During the adolescent years, the two groups were indistinguishable in terms of the variety and frequency of their delinquencies, and without knowledge of their childhood there would be no way of telling them apart.

Moffitt's essay is thought-provoking in what it suggests about the influence of the small number of truly antisocial adolescents (the lifecourse persistent delinquents). Moffitt explains the 'tidal wave of adolescent onset' of antisocial behaviour by referring to social network changes (1993, p. 678). Whereas the lifecourse persistent were marginal to the friendship networks of normal kids in childhood, during adolescence they became more linked into peer networks, more tolerated despite their antisocial tendencies, and more interesting to the adolescent majority because of their unconventional attitudes and deviant ways. It seems that in adolescents' general shift away from conformity to adult expectations these antisocial youth become influential models of deviant behaviour for others to mimic, more from curiosity than from liking. As their 'in-your-face' defiance and tough behaviour become more and more interesting to their adolescent peers, the antisocial adolescents become tolerated, if not liked. The shift towards their greater centrality in the peer networks increases their influence as models of antisocial behaviour.

In contrast to Moffitt's focus on delinquent behaviour, Fergusson *et al.* (1996) drew on another longitudinal data set in New Zealand to examine the developmental pathways in conduct disorder and oppositional defiant disorder. Like Moffitt and her colleagues, they found that affiliation with deviant peers was a key factor in distinguishing those with early onset of these antisocial behaviours from those who displayed no problems. However, some who displayed conduct problems in early childhood no longer showed these problems by mid-adolescence. They compared this 'remission' group with a group who only began to display conduct disorders in adolescence (the 'late onset' group), and found that affiliation with deviant peers 'played an influential role in determining the behavioural discontinuities' (p. 549). What this finding suggested to the researchers was that peer relations may 'act as a turning point event' (p. 550), insofar as attachment to deviant peers leads to onset of hostile, defiant, and oppositional behaviour, while avoidance of deviant affiliations leads to the absence of hostility or a remission in such defiant behaviour.

Antisocial behaviour in school

How is antisocial behaviour manifested in schools, and how do schools deal with it? Schools are important social places for young people, and their influence on students' antisocial as well as prosocial behaviour cannot be ignored. Through the school curriculum, organization, educational resources, classroom activities, and teacher–student interactions, schools are daily engaged in both absorbing and minimizing antisocial behaviour, and, for the most part, the level of antisocial behaviour is extremely low. A visitor to a high school would be impressed by how schools perform 'a minor miracle' each day, effectively managing large numbers of adolescents with the minimum of fuss and conflict; and throughout this book there are references to the positive effects of schools on young people's social attachments and social development.

This section looks at the antisocial behaviour of students in school. Its purpose is to examine the prevalence of school-based antisocial behaviour and to trace the possible links between school problem behaviours such as defiance of teachers and aggression towards other students. Recent increases in student violent outbursts at school, as well as assaults on teachers, underline the seriousness of antisocial behaviour. Calls for greater protection for teachers and greater powers for schools were linked to the proposal by Britain's Minister for Education to establish a task force in 2005 to examine the problems of antisocial behaviour of students in school (see Box 6.1).

The issues relating to antisocial behaviour are not widely canvassed in texts on school effectiveness and curriculum. Instead they seem to be relegated to 'how to' books on classroom discipline and the management of student behaviour. The lack of scholarly examination of antisocial behaviour by educational researchers is lamented by Rutter and his colleagues, who note that 'The question of school influences (for better or for worse) on young persons' antisocial behaviour has received very little systematic attention in school effectiveness studies over the last 15 years' (Rutter *et al.*, 1998, p. 235). Of course, there is a considerable literature in abnormal psychology which explains these problem behaviours in terms of individual psychopathology. Our interest is with non-pathological populations and the contexts of the behaviours, including the social influence processes that instigate and sustain them, because these are the domains that are most accessible to school intervention. There is also a tradition in sociology that draws on subcultural and social class explanations to explain antisocial behaviour. The sociological view is that adolescent 'deviant' behaviour in school is evidence of class-based resistance to teacher authority. Although such a sweeping view finds support among the teacher unions, its claims remain unconvincing to me, as they do to others. For example, Grahame and Jardine (1990) have pointed out

---

Box 6.1 Headlines demanding action against antisocial students

'Prosecute violent pupils', says Minister (*Evening Standard*, 30 March 2005)
'Throw yobs out of our schools' (*Leicester Mercury*, 30 March 2005)
'More powers to tackle violent pupils' (*Western Mail*, 31 March 2005)
'Teachers call for protection' (*Western Morning News*, 5 April 2005)
'Task force to tackle discipline in schools' (*Guardian*, 21 May 2005)
'Kelly's Task Force to tackle unruly pupils' (*Daily Mail*, 21 May 2005)

---

that most disruption is brief rather than long-lasting, and is more an expression of adolescent play and mischief than malevolence.

Davies (1999) presents a detailed critique of the Marxist theories of resistance and rebellion that are best represented by the work of Willis (1977), crucially noting that writers in this tradition produce no real evidence of just how the cultural influences on young people are supposed to be transmitted. Moreover, the schools are blamed for projecting a middle-class culture of individualism and failing to connect with these youth. In his studies of Canadian students, Davies found little evidence to corroborate the resistance theorists' claims, and he concluded that 'resistance theory's emphasis on the class nature of student opposition is misplaced' (Davies, 1999, p. 197). He found that lack of academic success 'widely predicted deviance'. The students who became dropouts were those who had put less effort into study, had difficulties coping with the work, were more disruptive, and had friends who were dropouts. Others concur with this viewpoint: McEvoy and Weller (2000) conclude that 'academic failure and antisocial behaviour exist in a reciprocal relationship' (p. 131). They are critical of the contribution of ineffective classroom practices to the cycle of failure; for instance, class exclusions that remove students from unpleasant schoolwork reward inappropriate behaviour and at the same time deny students the opportunity to learn. These school practices actually operate as deviancy training systems: they confirm antisocial attitudes by rewarding bad behaviour. Moreover, they create outgroups of disaffected students: by rejecting them as bad apples and isolating them in a barrel with other bad apples such school management practices amplify antisocial behaviour.

Anger outbursts

The common expressions of antisocial behaviour in the classroom are defiance and reactive aggression towards the teacher, and there is little doubt that these kinds of behaviour have increased in recent times. Defiance may result from a student's sense of deep disaffection with the subject matter, the teacher or the school itself, so that a point is reached where the student gives up and refuses all entreaties to participate. It may also arise from an emotionally charged situation. For example, a student finds himself hedged in by classroom rules and frustrated because things are not working out for him, and vents his frustration by an angry outburst, initially directed at his desk or his books, but when admonished for his display of temper and lack of control, the teacher may become the target of angry defiance. The adolescent's reactive aggression is a rudimentary defence against being controlled or ordered around, and is an attempt at self-protection rather than a retaliatory response.

Some young people do have a short fuse. When something does not work out for them (they are not selected for a team, or they can't solve a technical or logical problem, or they are criticized over some matter), they blow up and put on a tantrum. Angry outbursts may also have their origin in depression, and depression is common among adolescents. Klingman and Zeidner (1993) analysed anger-related situations in five junior high schools in Israel. They found that there were two kinds of coping responses adopted by adolescents to teacher-evoked anger: an avoidant response and a hostile-aggressive one. The more common form of coping was internalization of their angry feelings. Those who coped with anger aggressively displayed acting-out behaviours: they created a disturbance in the class, slammed the door, or tried to hurt the teacher. The percentage of these responses was extremely small. However, whereas only 8 per cent were prepared to confront the teacher, and only 1 per cent displayed physical aggression, half of the respondents frequently felt hatred towards the teacher when they were provoked to anger. The extent to which adolescent students feel a deep resentment towards their teacher because of some classroom incident where they have been humiliated, insulted, or unfairly treated, reminds us that many young people may feel angry over something in class, even if they rarely express this feeling in violent ways.

Truancy

Given the terms by which truancy is known by young people, such as skipping, skiving, wagging it, suggesting a mixture of mischief, fun and adventure, it seems sour grapes to describe truancy as antisocial. There is a delicious sense of freedom as you 'nick off' from school and leave everybody else stuck in class, slaving over a hot equation. Yet the fact is that poor or erratic school attendance is a reliable indicator of the presence of various problems in young people's lives, whether they are medical, social, legal or educational. Truancy is also 'a substantial risk factor for delinquency' (Rutter *et al.*, 1998, p. 232), including stealing, car theft, substance abuse and sexual activity. Indeed, truancy is consistently included in descriptions of delinquent lifestyles. When Hansen (2003) studied the crime-age profiles of 16–25-year-old males in England and Wales, she found that school truancy was one of the most important factors distinguishing the persisting crime-age profiles of less educated youth from the declining crime-age profiles of more educated youth. Two key school factors (whether they had truanted, and whether they had been excluded from school) were strongly associated with all three crime clusters: property offences, handling offences, and violent crimes. Hansen comments that, 'for someone who is interested in bringing the crime rate down' among 16–25-year-olds, 'the first more easily targeted and probably most obvious [policy] is to encourage youths to stay on at school' (2003, p. 156).

The most common form of truancy is skipping lessons, or class cutting. Fallis and Opotow (2003) report that in some schools in major American cities like Chicago, Boston and New York, two-thirds of students cut at least one class every day. To their surprise, the investigators found that the schools did not regard this kind of truancy as a matter of priority. Teachers viewed class cutting as a nuisance and an individual student matter; they did not conclude that if the students are absconding, this indicates a serious mismatch between the program and its clients. From interview data gathered in focus groups over a period of four years, Fallis and Opotow identified the characteristics of the schools where class cutting was rampant as indicative of 'structural violence'. They chose this term to emphasize the harm being done to students by educational structures that were 'sterile, bureaucratic, disrespectful of students' pedagogical preferences or goals, and that did not value student contributions' (2003, p. 108).

There is a certain logic when students react to the unpleasant aspects of school life by becoming truants. Truancy is, after all, an avoidance behaviour. Commenting on the experiences of a group of habitual truants who had been institutionalized for their offences, Cullingford (1999) writes: 'Schools are disliked. They contain, for a minority of people at least, all the ingredients of threat' (p. 62). Others, like O'Keeffe (1994), urge a rethinking of our image of the truant, in order to accept that the majority of truants are not as disaffected with school as is supposed. Indeed, O'Keeffe's major report on truancy in Britain showed that most students who truanted at secondary school actually liked school and on the whole accepted the school curriculum. They absconded for specific reasons, usually to avoid a particular lesson or teacher, and 'the greater the frequency of truancy, the more intimate its links to pupil dissatisfaction over aspects of specific lessons' (p. ix).

Given that truancy commonly occurs in company, detailed examination of student absences, including the days when they occur and which students are absent on the same day, can provide information pertaining to delinquent activity. Regrettably, detailed attendance data are not kept in many school systems, and cross-checking on truanting in peer networks remains a pipe-dream. A national report on truancy in Australia (Australia, 1996) drew attention to the lack of detailed and accurate records of student attendance in the nation's schools. As a consequence, it is estimated that up to 80 per cent of truants are likely to go undetected.

Bullying and standover groups

The most common kind of antisocial behaviour in school is bullying. While much has been written in recent years on individual bullying, little attention has been given to group bullying in schools. Bukowski and Sippola (2001) have commented that groups use victimization to establish group cohesion, and individuals who thwart the group in some way or fail to show respect become targets of victimization. Group bullying finds expression at high school in the victimization of younger students by older and bigger students. An old established practice is robbery on demand. In Queensland we found that standover tactics were used by older boys to extract money from students new to school. The practice was known as 'jewing' or 'scunging', where the victor acquires status as tough, and the loser is seen as soft (Power and Cotterell, 1979). Groups of older boys would single out a Year 8 boy, often when alone, and threaten to bash him if he didn't comply. Few victims were prepared to challenge the group; the menace in the threat was enough to create apprehension. One realist told us: 'When Year 9s jew off a Year 8, they say "your money or your life" and mean it.'

Group bullying traditions are particularly robust in boys' boarding schools, where one could imagine at times that nothing has changed since *Tom Brown's Schooldays*. At one school, senior boys make a new boy stand against a wall for ten or fifteen minutes, with his nose and toes touching the wall, and punch him whenever his body moves away from the wall. Another practice is the 'wedgie', where a new boy is lifted by older boys who grab his trousers and hoist him into the air. An informant bragged to me that his wedgie was so successful that he hooked the victim onto the wall by his collar. 'What did the boy think of it?' My chuckling informant replied, 'He didn't like it much. But he was a tool [a person of no significance].' A common initiation rite is the close encounter with the toilet bowl – widely known as 'the royal flush'. Initiation practices continue at university. As a member of a college board, I was appalled to discover that freshmen were initiated into our college by being forced to drink large quantities of beer that were literally poured down their throats; and if they resisted, their heads were held under water in a swimming pool till they were close to drowning. To dismiss these actions as simply initiation practices and group bonding is to gild the lily; they are brutish and stupid.

The best sources of research on group bullying are from Norway and Japan. The Japanese word for bullying is *ijime* and refers to group bullying (Yoneyama and Naito, 2003), and Japanese research finds that only 8 per cent of bullying incidents are carried out by lone offenders, in contrast to the much higher estimates reported by Olweus in Norway and by Rigby in Australia. Moreover, the Japanese researchers point out that 'bullying often involves the whole class' (p. 319), and that classrooms are the contexts for bullying in 75 per cent of the cases reported. Other notable challenges to the prevailing western view of the single bully include the fact that peer victimization often occurs *within* the group of close friends, rather than as attacks by an outsider or by an outsider group of bullies. Moreover, the perpetrators are 'good' students or 'ordinary' students rather than problem students. This perspective is a salutary reminder to us that appearances can be deceptive – the good kids may indeed be the bullies.

Further evidence of group bullying comes from the Norwegian study by Salmivalli *et al.* (1997), mentioned in Chapter 5. Social network analysis was employed to examine the structure of the bullying system, and maps were drawn of each classroom, identifying loners and clique members. Results confirmed the existence of bullying within cliques as well as by the clique on victims outside it, whether the victims were loners or pairs of friends. Salmivalli *et al.* note that 'the sizes of the network may vary, some children belonging to large "gangs" and some preferring to be with one or two friends' (1997, p. 306). Moreover, different bully roles were identified (see Figure 5.1, p. 102). The largest groups contained bullies, reinforcers, and assistants, and the smallest groups were comprised of victims and defenders. Salmivalli and her co-workers draw attention to 'a new picture of what bullying is', as not so much 'an affair between an aggressive tormentor and his/her victim', but more like 'aggression of a group which includes the bully and his/her supporters on one side, and on the other the victim(s) with perhaps some supporters and outsiders' (p. 311).

Another worrying aspect of group bullying is revealed in the Japanese studies: it concerns the role of teachers as supports for group bullying. Yoneyama and Naito (2003) cite Japanese research which found that teacher bullying of students had occurred in 11–15 per cent of reported cases, according to the students, and in 11–14 per cent of cases reported by the teachers themselves. Teacher bullying of students was greater in classrooms where teachers emphasized the collective responsibility of the whole class for the actions of a few, and this suggests that the 'commune-like' classroom environment is to blame. Yoneyama and Naito paint a picture of classrooms where teachers and students collude in regulating and manipulating the members of the class in the name of group cohesiveness. Is this pattern of classroom coercion limited to Japanese culture, or is it found in classrooms around the world? Recall the Pink Floyd song about the teacher in their Wall series, where they cry, 'Teacher, leave them kids alone!' It seems they were pretty close to the mark.

Antisocial behaviour in crowds

When young people are part of a large group or mass crowd some are willing to behave in socially unacceptable and even violent ways that would be out of character for them in normal situations. We should not underestimate the importance of the mass crowd as an extra-individual context capable of altering the normal behaviour of its members. Milgram and Toch (1969) remarked that, 'Many actions which seem beyond the range of human capability, both from the standpoint of heroism and of destruction, come to light in collective episodes' (p. 507). The crowd context of antisocial behaviour prompts a series of questions. Are crowds of fans or protesters comprised of antisocial individuals, or does the crowd context in itself induce deviant behaviour? If antisocial crowds instigate law-abiding people to engage in vandalism and violence, how are the group norms transmitted, and why do these norms rather than peaceful norms gain acceptance by the wider crowd membership? How does the crowd context provide opportunities for things to get out of hand? Does it provide mutual reinforcing conditions? Or does it supply a cloak of anonymity where troublesome youth can behave in outrageous ways? A full consideration of these questions of crowd influence on antisocial behaviour merits a book-length treatment, but some aspects are explored here in relation to mass crowd influences on young people.

For our purposes, let us distinguish three types of large crowds: the festival type, the protest crowd, and the sports crowd. These crowds differ in specific ways, and some of these differences are attributable to features in the setting itself. The festival setting is characterized by fun, goodwill and celebration, producing what Reicher (1987) called 'spontaneous sociality' (p. 171). People gather to enjoy themselves and watch the spectacle of colour and sound in the carnival procession, including the costumes and music of the performers, the humour of particular groups, and the reactions of other spectators as well. A partnership is established between the

performers and the crowd so that crowd members applaud the performances and even interact with some performers, and also show by their own
festive clothing, flags, and face-paint that they want to share in the celebratory atmosphere. In rock and folk concerts, music and dancing allow more
extroverted expression of enjoyment, and as people join in, they abandon
their social reserve. The setting norms seem to get ramped up over time,
so that participants may be motivated to outperform others by accentuated
displays, such as frenzied dancing, doing handstands, crowd-surfing, or
throwing lighted flares.

The sense of inclusion and common cause that is characteristic of such
festivals and carnivals can be found in particular spectator crowds, for example those watching the Olympics or those attending most college football
in North America. In these sports settings, there is a shared interest in the
athletic contest, but the spectators do not see themselves as participants
in the contest they are watching. On the other hand, European football
crowds are emotionally involved in the game almost as participants, and
are divided into separate camps by their loyalties to the different teams; the
intergroup context makes the social identity of the supporter groups salient: 'At the game it is your shirt, not your face, that counts' (Reicher *et al.*,
2004, p. 561). Similarly, protesters are radicalized by the actions of police
into adopting a crowd identity that unites them against the police. Stott and
Reicher (1998) write that, 'We have repeatedly noted a pattern of collective
interaction where an initially heterogeneous crowd has come to be treated
as a homogeneous whole by the police' (p. 512). In their study of a protest
against construction of a motorway in London, Drury and Reicher (2000)
found that the psychological shift towards confrontation by the protesters
with the police occurred 'only when the police were seen to act illegiti-
mately' (p. 598), with the effect that their attempts at crowd control produced greater polarization of values around a shared social identity.

A second aspect of crowd behaviour is how a mood spreads rapidly and
spontaneously across the whole crowd, whether the mood is one of euphoria
or one of hostility. This phenomenon of rapid transmission of mood and behaviour is traditionally referred to as behavioural contagion, and its spread is
compared with the spread of an infectious disease. An eye-witness account
of the beginning of a riot by football hooligans (Buford, 1991) traces the
deliberate and rapid escalation of involvement in vandalism and violence
as the rates of those joining the hooligan throng doubled, trebled and quad-
rupled. Patten and Arboleda-Flórez (2004) apply a mathematical model to
simulate behavioural contagion, and suggest several factors that increase
the contagious transmissibility of behaviours. These are: social identification (enhanced by wearing team colours, carrying flags, and chanting or
singing); incidents that increase emotional arousal (such as a bad refereeing

decision or a police baton charge); and the consumption of alcohol (which inhibits self-control). Rheingold (2002) offers an interesting view of how contagion operates to communicate shared understandings in modern street protests. He shows how mobile phone technology is being used by protesters to rally 'smart mobs' through the interconnectedness of the small world.

A commonly held viewpoint among those who study unruly crowds has been that immersion in a mass crowd provides individuals with a cloak of anonymity and an associated reduction in their sense of personal responsibility for their actions. The classical view of crowd influence, based on the writing of Le Bon (1896/1947), argues that individuality is lost and submerged in the mob: the individual's sense of self is subsumed by the more powerful social identity derived from the crowd. This process has become known as de-individuation.

These interpretations of crowd psychology may be contrasted with those based on social identity theory, which argues that people do not lose their self-awareness when their individual identity is replaced by the social identity of the crowd. Instead, the person allows the crowd social identity to override her/his individual identity. As Spears *et al.* (2001) point out, 're-sponsiveness to a group norm is not a mindless or irrational process ... but may be a conscious and rational [one] relating to a meaningful sense of identity' (p. 336). The argument is elaborated by Drury and Reicher (2000) who explain crowd influence as a shift 'from behaving in terms of their individual identities to behaving according to a "contextually specified common identity"' (p. 581). Their emphasis on the specified nature of this crowd identity reminds us that each crowd context is different, and that the context is fluid, so that actions by protesters and by police produce modifications to a crowd protest. Actions play an important part in mass crowds. Unlike groups, where communication can occur through discussion and deliberation, the acquisition of norms in crowd situations can only occur by induction. Membership of the crowd is established through individuals behaving in conformity with what they perceive to be the norms of the group, and their own actions provide information to others as to their understanding of the crowd. Actions such as clapping, singing and chanting become criterial attributes for identifying the actors as members of the crowd. In an antisocial crowd, chanting racial abuse, taunts that 'cops are pigs', rhythmic handclapping, throwing bottles and hurling stones are all forms of action that serve as markers of crowd identification.

Violence by crowd members is often initiated and sustained by small groups within the crowd, rather than spread across its extent. These groups of antisocial youth may shelter under the umbrella of the apparent crowd unanimity of goals in order to pursue their antisocial objectives. In this respect, the bystander component of the crowd is important as an audience that either overtly or tacitly approves the violent and destructive behaviour of these hard-core elements. Although the majority of onlookers may react with puzzlement and dismay to scenes of violence and destruction, the absence of direct condemnation of the rioters in a mass crowd may have the same effect as approval for them. In his extended essay analysing the riot at the 1999 Woodstock Festival, Vider (2004) provides valuable insights into the psychology of crowd violence and the relevance of social identity interpretations. His conclusion is suggestive. By describing the rioters as both spectacle and spectators, he encapsulates the public dimension of disorderly behaviour. Participants in a riot are fully aware that their rioting will attract the notice of others and be reported by news media, even when the acts in question are destructive.

Interethnic violence

The past decade has seen an increase across the globe in interethnic tensions and hostile acts, often associated with religious fundamentalism. Examples include the bombing of the London Tube in July 2005, and the murder in 2004 of Dutch film-maker Theo van Gogh by a Moroccan-born man after the release of a film critical of Islamist attitudes to women. These violent events have been accompanied by a political shift to the right in many western democracies. For example, the Australian government has strengthened its border protection so as to exclude refugees arriving in small boats from Asia; and European countries moved in 2006 towards creating 'an immigration moat'. Government ministers from Britain, France, Germany, Spain and Italy were reported to be requiring new migrants to sign a commitment to integration and respect for the values of the host nation as a condition of their acceptance.

Ahmed, a Sydney psychiatrist, argues that in the multicultural state, 'identity will increasingly be the issue' (Ahmed, 2004), and where young men feel excluded from Australian culture and disconnected from society because of their ethnic background, they are turning to Islam out of the desire to belong. A similar view was expressed by President Chirac in his address to the nation in November 2005, concerning the riots by youth from North African families that had erupted across France. He highlighted the problem of 'la fracture sociale' which left minority youth estranged from mainstream French society, and emphasized the value of social cohesion.

Rival social identities were central to the explanations given by politicians and police for the gang violence that occurred over several days in mid-December 2005 on Sydney's southern beaches. The rioting was apparently triggered by a dispute between two or three lifesavers and a large group of Lebanese youth, which led to a fight where the lifesavers were bashed. A week later, a text message was sent to hundreds of mobile phones calling for surfers to 'get down to North Cronulla for a Leb and wog bashing day and show them this is our beach and they're never welcome back'. Carloads of angry young men began arriving at the beaches around Cronulla, and over the following week engaged in 'smash and bash' rioting that was racially-based territorial protection. Such was the extent of crowd violence that 2000 police officers were deployed in roadblocks and patrols at beaches in Sydney and nearby cities, and fifty-nine arrests were made, together with the confiscation of knives, swords, axes and baseball bats. Prime Minister John Howard saw the violence as 'a manifestation of tribalism', and right-wing groups interpreted the riots as 'a people's rebellion – a rejection of the anti-Australian policies of Multiculturalism and Third World immigration foisted on us by lousy politicians, academics and journalists'. Moves to defuse the intergroup tensions were implemented swiftly. A public statement was issued by the Assistant Commissioner of Police in New South Wales which said, 'I can absolutely assure you it is not an offence to be a Lebanese person on a beach in New South Wales.'

Among youth themselves, actions were quickly taken to address the intergroup hostilities; within a few days of the rioting, members of the Lebanese community met with members of the surfie gang at Maroubra ('the Bra Boys') to proclaim messages of tolerance. Muslim youth worker Saeed Kunawati said, 'These people that do these things are really nothing but, you know, thugs, you know? And hooligans. So we can reach out to 'em now. So the message that we want to bring across to them is that both sides of the spectrum are not going to tolerate it' (ABC Radio: AM – Thursday, 15 December 2005).

The principles for resolving intergroup and interethnic conflict have been outlined by several social identity researchers. They include changes in social categorization. For example, decategorize and personalize relationships with people from other ethnic groups. This means that you cease to regard them by means of a category and instead see them as real persons with names and families and with the same daily concerns as you. Second, recategorize the separate groups or ethnic minorities at a more inclusive level, so that the differences between you and them are dissolved in a more general 'we'. Third, employ a process of mutual group differentiation, where differences are not erased or swept under the carpet but are accepted and used to define the characteristic strengths and limitations of each group and culture.

Simon (2004) suggests that social integration of minority groups is best achieved when two complementary processes are present, which he terms *adopt* and *adapt*. That is, the migrant/minority group adopts the basic values of the host community, and the host demonstrates a willingness to adapt its institutions and procedures so that they fit more easily with the beliefs and practices of the migrant/minority group. Improved intercultural contact is needed if these strategies are to operate at the interactional level.

Concluding comment

The subject matter of this chapter is far-ranging, and has taken us from bar brawls to interethnic violence. It has described various kinds of anti-social behaviour that young people engage in, and has examined the group processes at work in different situations. A motivation for much antisocial behaviour is that associated with an identity derived from the individual's place and sense of belonging in the network or group. It is explained by Emler and Reicher (1995) as reputation management, which they describe as self-presentation where the person is mindful of the audience, and knows that the audience brings to each new encounter a history of the person's reputation, established from previous encounters. Within the group, a person may have a specific reputation for toughness or for daring, which the person has to maintain. Emler and Reicher emphasize that for the delinquent adolescent, reputation management 'must be seen in the context of group process' (1995, p. 194). By taking part in delinquent activities, the individual not only acts in an appropriate manner but shows to others that s/he possesses the appropriate qualities to belong to the delinquent group. Three requirements for reputation management are listed: choosing behaviour that is consistent with the reputation one seeks; publicizing one's actions and achievements to friends and other relevant people so that the association with one's reputation is clear; and protecting one's reputation from harmful influences, including 'repair work' to correct any comments or actions that could undermine it.

A long-time concern of schools and communities is what to do with the seriously antisocial. Some suggestions can be derived from the topics discussed in this chapter. They are as follows:

1   Apply social network analysis combined with knowledge of territories and settings to identify antisocial groups, using affiliation matrices.
2   Use knowledge of social networks to avoid linking difficult students with other antisocial students in school. Dishion *et al.* (1999) alert us to the possibility that such quarantining practices exacerbate the problem, even when intervention is involved.
3   Establish and maintain detailed records on student behaviour, from the adolescent's entry into the school system, so that the persistence of learning and behaviour problems is known, and spikes in these can be identified. Data are the basis of science.

4   For the small number of seriously difficult students, employ multi-agency resources and close consultation among them. The South Australian Education Department has a system of weekly case-conferencing within each school region which links the school system to mental health and social work agencies, and this works effectively.

5   Devise innovative ego-affirming school and community programs which allow seriously difficult students to gain visibility for prosocial reasons. This would include connecting adolescents to adults as guides and mentors. Schreck *et al.* (2003) talk of 'social guardianship' as a protective strategy against victimization at school. What they mean is that a student who builds social bonds with other students and also with their teachers is socially protected by this pool of guardians.

7   Academic motivation

Stand at the school gates and watch the school day begin. Observe as adolescent students empty from the buses, carrying their bags and books, and amble along the paths into the school-grounds and halls, where they gather in loose groups with friends to talk and socialize before moving to assembly or dispersing to their classrooms. Be aware that each day the pattern is repeated, as the adolescent tide drains from the neighbourhoods to flood into the school precincts. Within the jurisdiction of the school these individual young people are transformed into a community governed by rules and conventions intended to organize and control their behaviour, where teachers attempt to engage their minds in academic tasks. Operating alongside the formal system of schooling there is an informal system of social network relations; and both exert influences on adolescent motivation to shape their school experiences.

Peer influence on academic motivation is the subject of this chapter. Of particular interest is the extent to which social relations affect adolescent attachment to school and academic motivation within the classroom. We are guided by the following questions: How is peer influence manifest? Is it pro-school or anti-school? What roles do peers and teachers play in shaping student motivation in the classroom? What are the features of the school structure and of adolescent society that affect adolescent social relations and their experiences in school?

Schools and adolescents

Schools are motivational environments whose educational rationale depends on the successful creation of settings that promote student development. The academic life-blood of schools is the curriculum: it defines the knowledge domains of student learning and how these are expressed as concepts, learning activities, and forms of assessment. But the sad reality is that for many young people the curriculum fails to ignite their imagination, whet their interest, or harness their idealism. The classrooms are often unstimulating, and the learning tasks pedestrian. Raven (1994) put it bluntly: 'American high school students spend most of their time in boring, noncumulative, routine activities.' Discovery that the school curriculum falls short of one's expectations comes early for some; a 12-year-old Australian boy expressed his disillusionment to us after just six weeks at high school: 'It was good the first couple of weeks, to change classrooms every half-hour. It was easy to get lost. But now it's just the same. We do everything the same, every day' (Power and Cotterell, 1979, p. 115).

Schools are also networked communities, and through the school network flow different kinds of motivational influences. In a school of a thousand students, there may be ninety teaching and non-teaching staff. The school network links staff to one another as well as to individual students, in a model of the small-world phenomenon, so that it is possible for a school principal to contact and quickly communicate with any individual student or member of staff/faculty and also to know personally a great number of teachers and students. In addition, each student's personal social network extends beyond the wider group of friends and classmates to include students in other classes and year levels, as well as some teachers, counsellors and non-academic staff. Thus each adolescent student inhabits a multi-layered community where some relational ties are uniplex (perhaps with a student in the same basketball team) and others are multiplex (such as those with friends and perhaps with a teacher or two).

Publication of the Coleman Report (Coleman, 1961) with its emphasis on the power of 'the adolescent peer society' as a negative influence on student motivation exploded like a grenade on the field of secondary schooling, and the shrapnel still lies embedded deep within educational bodies. Coleman's claim that a monolithic adolescent subculture operated in high school to exert a powerful anti-education influence on adolescents ensured his report a prominent place in a generation of texts on education. Terms like the 'leading crowd' drew attention to the adolescent peer group as a force wielding enormous power over adolescent students to undermine their commitment to academic values. From a networks perspective, Coleman assigned significance to the adolescent peer society as a powerful social influence on academic motivation. Where earlier research had seen value congruence between family, school and the peer group, Coleman suggested that adolescent interests, values, and even their goals for schooling were not identical with those of adults. The Coleman Report is my starting point for examining the concern that is central to the teacher's life: how to motivate adolescent students in the classroom.

Motivation and classroom life

Although motivation is a central factor in classroom teaching, it is not an easy thing to grasp. Motivation includes broad values and beliefs about the relative importance of different life goals and lifestyles, as well as attitudes about people, events and activities. It comprises feelings, attitudes, value judgements and understandings. There is no shortage of research on student motivation, but much of it is highly psychological and tangential to the concerns of classroom teachers. Somehow the motivation research manages to bypass the complexity of classroom life, where adolescent students are free agents and not always willing to submit to the repetitive nature of classroom activities, or remain focused on the long-term goal of graduation. It skirts around the everyday actions of teachers in working with students and dealing with topics listed in the curriculum, constantly under pressure from timetables, resourcing, and of course the next round of assessment. Concepts of mastery versus performance goals, of locus of control or self-efficacy, are attractive to researchers; but they are individualistic ways of interpreting the multi-layered world of teaching and the complex social psychology of adolescents in schools. Researchers seem to talk in a different language from that used by teachers to describe the daily challenges that they encounter (see, for example, Denscombe, 1985; Frances, 1975). It is not that the psychological theories are irrelevant; rather, they are just hard to apply to the mix of students, activities and social relations that teachers encounter in lesson after lesson every day. Sit the researchers down in the classrooms for a few weeks; invite them to the teachers' staffrooms for a few days; send them out to mingle with the students during recess. In a short space of time they will discover, as the ethnographers have already found, that there are rich layers of meaning in students' classroom experiences, and that adolescent students are knowledgeable players and astutely aware of what happens in their classrooms.

Classroom teachers would understand student motivation to include aspects such as these: interest, curiosity, enjoyment, enthusiasm, concentration, selective attention, decision and reflection, together with self-system qualities of self-regulation, self-referencing and self-criticism – attributes that are brought into play in the process of selecting, judging and evaluating the difficulty of a task, the effort expended, and the quality of one's achievement. Teachers also understand that motivation is not simply an individual attribute of students, but a product of social interaction. Involvement, participation, and persistence are motivational words that imply a connection between the person and an activity or group. To focus on academic tasks or locus of control on their own in a discussion of motivation leaves unanswered the question of how the tasks are related to broader meaning contexts. These contexts include the social network of adolescent students. Clearly, motivation is not a straightforward concept. If it were, says Dornyei (2000, p. 519), 'It wouldn't be interesting.'

Motivational theories have largely been concerned with choice, and have limited value in school contexts where student choice is often a chimera. The aspects of motivation important to students and teachers occur *after* a choice has been made. Recent writers have distinguished between choice, which occurs in the pre-decisional phase of motivation, and will or commitment, which is activated during the post-decisional phase. It is in this phase that being willing to put in the effort and persist is of central concern to teaching. Maehr (1976) had previously referred to these behaviours as part of 'continuing motivation' (p. 443). Writing about motivation in educational settings, Dornyei (2000) draws attention to time, a forgotten dimension of motivation that is particularly relevant in school. Classroom tasks are budgeted a certain amount of time, and require continued application of student effort and attention over those periods of time – sometimes to the point of endurance. The aspects of motivation that we are talking about belong to what Dornyei calls 'the actional phase'. Some of the action control mechanisms that he lists relate to strategies that individuals use in order to 'enhance, scaffold or protect learning-specific action' – for example when the going gets tough and when learners find that they are getting stuck and their progress is slowing, or they have lost track of what they were told to do. When the array of these mechanisms is considered, they are extensive and complex. Moreover, they engage affective as well as cognitive features, and require that these features be activated in the public arenas of classrooms. Together, these elements comprise the motivational zone that teachers occupy in their daily work.

Classroom behaviour

Behaviour in class is a barometer of adolescent motivation. Students are said to be 'off-task' when they whisper, pass notes, signal friends across the room, read magazines under the desk, project missiles onto the ceiling, or switch off by staring out the window or by listening to music through an earpiece. However, from time to time they engage in active forms of dissent that are directed squarely at the classroom protocol. Banding together by students for 'stirring', 'mucking up', or 'goofing off' is a collective yet often spontaneous response of restless bodies and minds to tasks that are boring or irrelevant or monotonously predictable. The actions cover a wide range – making noises such as loud sighs and yawns and orchestrated fits of coughing, throwing or shooting things, or acting in unusual ways – the overall effect being that it generally annoys or 'bugs' the teacher. For example, before the teacher arrives, the students may re-arrange the desks and chairs so they face the opposite end of the room, or stack the chairs into a pyramid in the middle of the classroom. They may put drawing pins in the whiteboard duster, or attach the duster to the table with superglue. In one school that I taught in, there was an outbreak of shrieks and squeals from the girls in the adjacent classroom. They had discovered bulky brown paper bags on the shelf under their desks, and the bags were moving! My class of boys immediately volunteered to help; and lo and behold, the bags were found to contain large repulsive-looking cane toads! How could they have possibly got there? And what did my gallant boys know?

Other collective behaviours may be directed at having fun at the expense of a particular teacher, in a playful rather than malevolent way, as relief from classroom tedium. In my high school days, we had a French teacher who was terribly short-sighted but refused to wear spectacles, so one day our class of boys decided to test her eyesight. The plan was simple. Each time she turned to the chalkboard or looked at her book, we shifted to an adjacent chair, so that we progressively moved away from our usual place in class. Whenever she asked a question and called us by name to answer, each respondent would do so from a location that became increasingly remote from his customary seat. We linguists had a great time of it. We were proud of our success. It proved our belief that she was as blind as a bat. Unfortunately for us, our teacher never gave a sign that she had even noticed the prank. Her equanimity remained undented, and her lack of surprise denied us much of the satisfaction that our clever plan deserved. Was this possibly by design?

Actions such as those I have described are playful reactions to boredom rather than markers of resistance or eruptions of antisocial behaviour. Although not tolerated by school authorities, few would be listed as offences in the published school rules. They are ripples on the surface of classroom life, rudimentary expressions of misrule not intended to overthrow the regime or undermine the teacher's authority. As a form of release and harmless fun, such acts resemble the expression of adolescent high spirits seen in public places. Although they are spontaneous, they do not occur randomly in school: they need certain favourable conditions to flourish. Everhart (1982) noticed that goofing off required an appropriate group climate, based on the presence of sympathetic classmates. Moreover, it didn't occur in maths, where the work was highly individualized and a group climate was absent. In short, goofing off is a group expression, arising from a collective awareness among one's peers of a common state of mind; and peers provide an audience as well as the necessary group solidarity to trigger the action. Such actions are not marks of deviance or resistance.

Grahame and Jardine (1990) bring a refreshing tone to the elaborate sociological arguments about youth deviance and resistance that have been popular in recent times. They interpret classroom behaviour of the kinds described here as play and diversion, rather than as an expression of youth counter-culture or organized resistance. They are reminders that the classroom serves as a theatre where different class members perform in character. The cast may include not only the class clown, but others as well: the kid who is guaranteed to ask the dumb question, the kid who regularly forgets his book, and the kid who acts as class memory and can be relied on to tell others (including the teacher) an important detail for the next lesson. Their performances derive meaning from students' daily life in a school class and are 'contributions to the production of a playful structure' (p. 301). What's more, they are signs of life.

Wise teachers ignore student mucking up (like my French teacher) or respond with humour and tolerance. They know the cast of characters. They are comfortable with student asides and red herrings, because they see the value of these in bonding the class together. They read the instances of mucking up as signs of students' need for relief from unchallenging classwork, and redress the balance so that classroom harmony is soon restored. In contrast, anxious and controlling teachers go ballistic; they extract grudging compliance but lose respect. The capacity to maintain 'proportion' in judging students' behaviour is one that the students value. Tolerance, understanding, respect, and acceptance of an adolescent's point of view were important qualities sought in teachers by the adolescent essayists who wrote to the *Observer* (Blishen, 1969) about school. However, these teacher qualities remain elusive, according to a recent study of Swedish youth and young adults. Only one-third of Swedish 18-year-olds were of the opinion that their teachers had a sense of humour, and only one-quarter of the 25-year-olds could remember this trait in their former teachers (Andersson and Strader, 2004). Teachers who are unbending, intolerant, or lacking a sense of humour may exaggerate the antisocial features of a harmless prank and escalate their response to it, so that they provoke dissent and passive resistance from generally cooperative students and reap hostility and overt rebelliousness from the less cooperative ones. To despise and belittle adolescent students is a foolish power trip; to credit them for playful inventiveness is not weakness, but wisdom.

Micropolitics of classrooms

From the student's perspective, classrooms are social spaces, peopled by personalities like Mozza, Jurg, Grack and Lakey, and teachers like Hoppy, Shiner and Brutus. However, from a school perspective, classrooms exist to achieve curriculum objectives through the concept of work and through the teacher's exercise of power. Work and authority permeate the language of schooling, and classroom relations reflect these workplace concerns. Not only do teachers speak of schoolwork, group work, and homework, but school reports commend student work habits; an inattentive student is told to 'get on with your work'; and students get into trouble for disrupting others' work. Clearly, schools are meant to be places of serious work, where effort is expended on academic tasks. The contrasting perspectives on classrooms adopted by schools and by their students – workplaces versus social spaces – supply a framework for appreciating student behaviour in the classroom. At the social level, student relations are paramount, and adolescents strive for attention, acceptance and approval from their peers. But another process is being activated at the micropolitical level, where concerns about power and authority, justice and respect are played out in teacher–student interactions.

Micropolitics is 'the use of formal and informal power by individuals and groups to achieve their goals in organizations' (Blase, 1991, p. 11). Any action, consciously motivated, may have 'political significance' in a given situation. Both cooperative and conflictive actions and processes are part of the realm of micropolitics. The concept has usually been employed at an organizational level, but it is relevant to classrooms as well, particularly where there is an orchestrated student challenge to a teacher's authority, as the following examples show.

McFarland (2001) suggested that when students engage in everyday forms of misconduct, it 'can potentially transform the classroom setting' (p. 614), and the clique structure determines which students 'have the greatest political opportunity' (p. 618). Students who are central in the clique are more able to defy the teacher, confident of their friends' support. In the survey of classrooms that was included in the study, popular students (that is, with high centrality) in close-knit networks displayed higher levels of classroom resistance. While one factor in the micropolitical process is the social resources derived from centrality in the social network, another factor that McFarland identifies is social opportunity, which arises from inappropriate instructional formats created by the teacher. These formats generate student dissatisfaction. He describes a class where the mathematics teacher conducted group work that allowed students to work in friendship cliques on their maths problems, but the teacher failed to supply instructional advice and leadership when students were unclear about the concepts they were expected to use. This failure to explain the concepts eroded students' level of interest in the work, and reduced their compliance to teacher demands. At the same time the clique structure supplied a source of support to counter the teacher's power. By the second semester, the cliques had grown increasingly confident. Individual students now mocked and defied the teacher. When the teacher corrected one student, 'the entire clique replied' (p. 625) and the teacher's authority was left in tatters.

When a whole class rebels against a teacher, it may be appreciated as an act of last resort within the micropolitics of the classroom. In my own experience as a student, I can recall only a single incident. It arose from a sense of mass outrage by our Grade 10 class to the intimidatory actions of a young physics teacher. He had attempted to control us with a rubber truncheon, so that if a boy spoke out of turn or failed to pay attention, he was whacked with the truncheon. We were the brightest boys in the school, and we were not amused. No other teacher had ever threatened us, let alone hit us. Our relations with teachers were harmonious. The most ominous warning we had ever been given was from Shiner, our geography teacher: 'Continue doing that, and you and I will fall out.' We never did explore what he meant. Before long, a plan was hatched. Someone suggested a tactic by which we could make our views about classroom conduct known to the physics teacher. On the next occasion that a boy was menaced by the truncheon, we all produced our own pieces of rubber hose, and waved them in the air! I can still see us waving our truncheons, and the mortified look on that teacher's face. The lesson ended in pandemonium. The following week, we had a different physics teacher.

From his observations of adolescents in the classroom, Alschuler (1980) decided that the 'central conflict' in teaching is a motivational one, captured in his phrase 'the battle for students' attention' (p. 26). Moreover, these battles 'often consume more than half the school day' (p. 38). A one-dimensional view of the micropolitics of classroom behaviour places major store on the intentional nature of student misbehaviour and interprets non-compliance as deliberate. Accordingly, acts that are defiant, disruptive and oppositional are perceived as deliberately challenging the teacher's authority in order to transform the classroom structure. Student expressions of boredom or passive resistance are interpreted as deliberate but covert challenges to the teacher's values and rule-structures. The limitation of such a control view is that it allows no room for considering student misbehaviour as unintentional (inappropriate, but simply clumsy or thoughtless) or immature (angry reactions to teacher controls), or that it may actually be adaptive to the situation. For example, day-dreaming and time-wasting may challenge the teacher's definition of the situation, but from the student's viewpoint they may be reasonable forms of coping with classroom boredom or with an instructional format that is confusing.

Student 'misbehaviour' is rarely confrontational, challenging or violent. For example, Denscombe (1985) detailed 101 incidents of disruptive behaviour reported by teachers, and found that only nine of them could be classified as very serious. Most of the incidents were concerned with 'boisterousness and minor infringements of rules' (p. 32). He concluded that 'what troubles teachers more than anything are acts which challenge their authority – indiscipline, such as lack of co-operation or inattention during lessons, dumb insolence, noisiness, cheeky comments' (p. 32). The greater seriousness assigned to overt forms of misconduct is probably related to the public nature of teachers' work: confrontation is perceived as more rejecting of authority than are evasive tactics; but both are interpreted as *intended resistance* to legitimate teacher authority. Moreover, teachers who personalize their teacher role are likely to perceive any inappropriate behaviour in the classroom as student misbehaviour, and to construe such behaviour as being intentionally directed at them, to challenge their authority.

When teachers misinterpret student behaviour as rebellious and challenging to their authority as teachers, their reactions can become personal retaliations that undermine the motivation of their students by attacking their group or individual identity. This is the darker side of classroom life. The significance of being humiliated by a teacher is that it occurs in the context of one's peers. Several authors have remarked on the indignation of female adolescents at being 'shown up' by a teacher 'in front of everybody'. Girls resented teachers who accused them of being a 'tart' or a 'slut' because the stigmatized identity denies them their right to a normal one. Adolescents are very sensitive about such disparaging treatment, and the memory of being humiliated by a teacher lasts well beyond one's schooldays. Recalling years later why she didn't feel like working in her senior maths class, a young woman wrote to me: 'The teacher humiliated me in front of the entire class, questioned why I was in his class, and asked me to answer questions in a sarcastic way that implied I wouldn't know the answer. Is that enough?'

Disconnection

When adolescents become disconnected from school, they cope by escaping from its confines: they truant or drop out of school. Indeed attendance is one of the key indicators of school connection, and its association with dropping out of school has been confirmed in a large body of research. Some authors refer to identification (e.g. Finn, 1989) in discussing adolescent connection with school, and others speak of attachment to school. Mouton *et al.* (1996) interviewed adolescents in Grades 9 and 10 who were defined as 'low-attached' to school. They reported that these adolescents valued education but felt out of place at school, as if they were outcasts who did not fit in. This sense of disconnection came from their social experiences with peers and with their teachers. They spoke of not having friends and said that 'no one wants to talk to me'. Their teachers made them feel dumb, talked down to them, and acted as if they did not want them in the class. When they missed school, 'the teachers don't notice'.

With little experience of mastery and success, the curriculum becomes increasingly irrelevant and they become disengaged. At first they achieve some relief by withdrawing into a world of their own creation, but if the disconnection between them and the school continues, they eventually escape by removing themselves from the classroom altogether. Cullingford (1999) interviewed twenty-five young people aged 16 to 21 who had been institutionalized for habitual truancy. His goal was to try to understand why they had become alienated from their schools. In his opinion, the truant's sense of exclusion 'begins far earlier than actual truancy' (p. 65), and could be traced to their experiences of failure and not being able to handle the work in class. The public nature of this failure (on view for the members of their class), together with the teacher comments and peer jibes that they were stupid or thick, made them angry and humiliated (Box 7.1). The growing sense of not belonging, and of not being accepted because they didn't measure up, led them to feel they were outsiders. This sense of exclusion from their classmates soon extends out from the classroom to lead to their disconnection from the school itself.

Academic difficulty is compounded by the striving of adolescent students for a more equal partnership with their teacher, one where they can relate on more or less the same level. Students resent being treated as kids and reminded of the power difference between teacher and student. An adolescent essayist wrote to the *Observer* of her wish for 'a school where the teacher is regarded as a friend and yet respected; where the barrier of the desk is overcome' (Blishen, 1969, p. 63).

Teachers who create conflict situations are those who allow no room for negotiation and no space for a young person to make mistakes without being criticized or balled out. They accentuate the distance between themselves and their students. In contrast, teachers who are effective in relating to the same students are often described as having a sense of humour, 'being able to joke with you'; that is, they are able to see things in proportion. These teachers have the ability to fill out their role, monogrammed with their own personality and an easy style of relating to students. As a consequence they are described as being 'alright', real people who are 'tuned in' to where the students are coming from, who can tell the difference between mischief and malice, ratbags and rebels, and who see everybody in the class as 'basically good kids'.

Box 7.1 School experiences of habitual truants

- Having to take orders, being told what to do, being treated like a kid.
- Feeling stupid when the work was too hard or not understood.
- Being identified or paraded in public as a failure.
- Lack of self-control, so that the slightest provocation triggers retaliation.

(adapted from Cullingford, 1999)

Social networks and motivation

Classroom cliques

My theme is that the group dimension of classrooms affects student motivation, and that the fluctuations in individual motivation find expression in the everyday events of classroom life. While there has been a long-held view that adolescent peers have negative influences on academic achievement, their positive influences on motivation and achievement need to be acknowledged as well. There is research evidence that the security provided by clique membership has benefits for academic achievement. After all, given that similarity of interests and values is the basis of friendship, it seems natural for classroom cliques to form around common levels of school motivation and achievement.

Nichols and White (2001) investigated whether academic achievement was related to clique attachment in thirteen classrooms, in which they identified *clique members* and *pairs* of friends in forty-one friendship cliques and dyads. They also distinguished students who were the *floaters* (those named by several different cliques), as well as the *loners* (those named by a few classmates but who made no choices themselves), the *ignored* (those who named others but were not named by them), and the *invisible* (those who were named by no one). They found that the achievement of students who were attached to others (clique members, pairs of friends, and floaters) was greater than that of the unattached students (the loners, ignored, and invisible), and that the students who were attached to several cliques (the floaters) had higher achievement levels than those who were members of a single clique. These findings, based on student nominations, suggest that not only may peer affiliation affect achievement, but 'successful achievement may be a factor that initially draws students together to form a clique'

(p. 271). In the teacher nominations of students to the categories, a further category 'overlooked' was added for students whom teachers had difficulty placing in a designated clique. The researchers found that the highest achievers were those not bound to particular cliques but attached to them in looser ways (the floaters), and that the achievement of overlooked students fell between the attached students and the unattached ones. Clique attachment was thus seen as beneficial to academic achievement, because youth who were unattached and on the network periphery had lower academic performance.

Ryan (2001) was also interested in the role of the peer group as a socialization agent for academic motivation. She employed social network methods to map changes in peer groups among adolescents in transition into middle school, and tested whether changes over time in peer group membership were related to changes in their motivation. She found that peer group affiliation accounted for declines in motivation and declines in achievement as well. Because students were separated from their previous cliques, they had to make new friends. Even where they selected friends with similar achievement levels, the achievement and motivation characteristics of the cliques they belonged to accounted for changes over time, the difference being one of degree. Those in cliques of high achievers recorded less of a decline in motivation than those in cliques of low achievers; while those who belonged to cliques who disliked school showed a greater decline in enjoyment of school than those who associated with peers who liked school.

Clique affiliation also fosters classroom involvement. A student's status within the classroom network and security within a friendship clique can affect their attention and participation. How aware are teachers of the cliques within their classroom? Teacher awareness is often limited to those aspects of classroom life salient to the *teacher's* definition of the world, so that a teacher may be blind to the peer relationships and shifting clique alliances that are occurring under their nose. For example, 'Lyn' was a 16-year-old girl in my literature class who was constantly turning around to talk to the other girls who sat behind her in class. She was not defiant, just distracting and inattentive, and I found myself constantly asking her to pay attention during class discussions. Finally I arranged to meet her at recess, and we talked about her behaviour in class and her persistent chatting to other girls. Lyn was apologetic. She explained that it had nothing to do with the class material or my teaching, but that she was trying to get the attention of the girls in the back seats because she desperately wanted to be accepted by their group. I had underestimated how important friendship was.

Exposing the clique structures within the classroom requires systematic observation. My own early ventures in sociometry with a class of 15-year-old boys were informative. Using three questions – one asking them to nominate the peers that they liked, the second to nominate the peers who could get them to do what they wanted, and the third to nominate the boys whose help they would seek on schoolwork matters – I identified three quite different group structures in the classroom, based on affiliation, power, and academics. Knowledge of these structures and the location of particular boys within them improved my teaching and my relations with these tough boys immensely.

Ethnographic studies of classroom cliques have noted how seating arrangements reflect the pattern of clique relations. Where students could choose their own seats in class, the cliques occupied different sectors of the classroom and utilized the seating to define their territories and preserve clique boundaries. Moreover, the different cliques engaged in very little contact with one another. In her book, Griffiths (1995) refers to 'hierarchies of preference' (p. 103) in choice of seating that girls applied across the different school subjects (that is, where the class membership changed). Preferences began with their best friend, then moved to others in their clique, then to girls not in their clique, and last of all to boys, in a pattern of choices that suggests that these girls made use of relational ties within their network that extended beyond the clique of close friends. Griffiths noticed that clique members preferred to interact with others in their own clique even when separated from them. They would ignore those seated nearby in order to talk to or pass notes to more distant friends, and share pens or swap books with them. In some cases classroom interaction with the teacher was carried by members of a single clique, with some assistance from clique isolates. The position of cliques within the classroom often corresponded with their level of class participation, following the T-shape of interaction reported by observational research in the 1970s. Thus the active cliques were near the front and centre of the class, while the inactive ones were found in the back row and side margins. Teachers who understand the importance of these clique 'interaction sets' can utilize this knowledge to build a cohesive and happy classroom.

Social crowds and social identity

What insights into motivation can be gleaned from knowledge of social network influences in school? Schools are comprised of different adolescent crowds, which are reputation-based collectives of young people with distinctive value systems and lifestyles. The social crowd resembles in many ways Coleman's 'adolescent society' insofar as these crowds are not regarded as actual groups but as cognitive abstractions (see, for example, Brown and Klute, 2003). Research in this tradition has been concerned with the impact on peer relationships of status differences between the crowds, rather than with the implications for academic motivation of a student's affiliation with a particular friendship network. It is the motivational significance of crowds as social stereotypes that is explored here.

The significance of crowd types for adolescent motivation is derived from the social identities that adolescent crowds supply, and may be appreciated as follows. Adolescent students are seen to affiliate with particular social groups within the school. These social groups are arrayed in a hierarchy according to popularity or status, based on a system of social categorization of the adolescent crowds within the school. Each social crowd has a distinctive character or style; it brings with it certain attitudes, values and status which not only provide a group identity for its affiliates but also distinguish that identity from other social identities in the school. The crowds operate like a social blueprint or identity template for adolescents to apply to others as well as to appropriate for themselves, generated by the adolescent's need for significance in the mass of fellow students at school. They supply positive differentiations of certain groups from others and provide a system of interpreting the behaviour of other target adolescents according to the category or group to which the target belongs (or the group to which the observer belongs). Brown *et al.* (1994) argued that, 'crowd defines what a person is like, more than who she or he "hangs around with"' (p. 124).

Crowd stereotypes are cognitive constructions made by adolescents about others; from a social identity perspective they are not distortions but judgements of people 'in terms of their group memberships' (Turner, 1999, p. 26). That is, categorizations are made on the basis of characteristics of the group as a whole. Hogg (1996) discusses the social categorization processes at work in defining group membership, and explains the use of prototypes to represent social groups. These concepts, shared among group members, are 'fuzzy sets' rather than lists of attributes. They are often based, they suggest, on 'exemplary members' or are abstract 'ideal types'. They supply templates of group membership which can then be applied to assess the fit of real members to the prototype, and these co-exist with social identities. Hogg writes: 'People form relatively enduring group memberships/identities which prescribe situationally appropriate behaviours' (1996, p. 74). Social identity theory suggests that by garnering to themselves the attitudes and values that are assumed to attach to a particular social crowd, adolescents may be influenced by a perceived mutuality of identity.

Categorization proceeds by social comparison; this means that for a group to establish its own distinctive identity, comparisons with other groups must provide features that are favourable to the group (known as ingroup favouritism) – for example, 'we play fair, but they cheat', 'we respect teachers, but they are rude to them'. In short, the positive aspects of a social identity only acquire force in comparison with other groups. Not surprisingly, the studies of adolescent crowds generally report that a large proportion of respondents fall in the middle, with labels such as 'regular' or 'average' students. Turner *et al.* (1987) refer to the process as 'referential informational influence'. The individual, through observing the behaviour of students who typify a Jock crowd or a Party-Animal crowd, derives information about crowd attitudes and values which serves as reference group norms. Crowd stereo-types may also inhibit adolescents from being themselves, particularly in early adolescence, when young people are more categorical in their think-ing, more active at group boundary maintenance, and more sensitive to the viewpoints of others in determining their self-concepts. For example, being one of the brainy kids may be viewed as a liability in the peer system of a middle school or junior high.

Social identity theory provides a social-psychological explanation for the way that adolescent crowds may influence individual motivation in schools and classrooms. My argument is that the crowds supply stereotype identi-ties for real groups of young people to use when creating their image or style. The categorization processes that are associated with crowd types are imported into the working relations of cliques, where they are applied like blueprints to guide and shape categorizations of people in real situa-tions, as adolescents navigate various social identities in the shoals of peer relationships at school. These crowd identities are relevant only to the ado-lescent society and to what is salient for differentiating between young people according to youth culture values. They are played out on the stage of school, but they are unrelated to the academic culture of the school or to achievement in school-related activities.

Peer status is based on popularity and coolness. This means that if you belong to a popular crowd, the popularity is likely to be linked to looks, personality and partying rather than to academic performance. If you are labelled as a brain because you fit the brainy crowd type, you aren't espe-cially valued for being clever or for abilities useful for a future career, but are classified as lacking the valued attributes of sociability and coolness. While crowds as collectivities may not exert direct social pressures on ado-lescents concerning academic goals, crowd stereotypes may nevertheless offer adolescent students a motivational template that diverts them from fo-cusing on school achievement, quality schoolwork and classroom participa-tion. The discrepancy between reputations created by the adolescent society and those accepted by adult society is illustrated in the character of the Fonz in the 1970s sit-com *Happy Days*, still running on Cable TV. Initially, a 'laddish' role was claimed and this became elaborated into a social repu-tation through clothes, hairstyle, and speech mannerisms that together con-veyed the Fonz 'attitude'. Notice that the Fonz does no schoolwork, but always keeps ahead of the game. He is the centre of attention, directs the agenda, and always looks cool.

A study of the stigmatizing effect of peer labelling on motivation was reported by Hufton *et al.* (2002). They compared adolescents in the USA, Britain and Russia and found that the peer norms relating to school study and achievement differed markedly across countries. In the British and American schools, students' attitudes were anti-academic and directed at undermining teachers' efforts; adolescents in these schools had pejorative names for students who were hardworking and successful in class, calling them 'swots' in Britain and 'nerds' in the USA. These students were seen as outside the peer culture and were resented by the majority for showing up their own academic efforts and achievements in a poor light. By contrast the Russian students respected and admired fellow students who were high achievers, and they shared many of the teacher's views about appropriate classroom behaviour. There was no 'us and them' division between students and their teachers. A further area of difference was in the level of effort made by students in class. Trying too hard was seen by the British and American adolescents as undesirable, as the peer norms were about not working hard; instead, the students placed greater emphasis on adolescent pursuits of a non-academic nature. The authors comment that their British and American informants saw no problem with their attitudes to school-work, because 'the majority actually appeared to believe that they *were* working hard' (p. 283).

Ethnic minorities

The influences of social categorization processes are particularly evident in school motivation and performance. For example, studies of adolescents in Dutch schools (e.g. Verkuyten and Brug, 2003) confirm that ethnic minority youth perceived greater levels of discrimination from their teachers and were more disengaged from academic efforts in class. The level of psychological disengagement was related to teacher feedback; when the feedback more accurately reflected the student's ability, adolescents tended to be more engaged with schoolwork. Verkuyten and Brug found that perceived discrimination added a further dampening effect on student motivation, which they interpreted as prompting in minority students 'a defensive detachment of the self from the school domain' (2003, p. 197).

Adolescents from ethnic minority groups may also actively resist the labels that others assign to them. When they actively challenge these labels and adopt an identity of their own making, they may encounter sanctions from school authorities, as Lei (2003) reports. Her account provides a sense of the struggles that students encounter in establishing a valued social identity. For example, a group of black girls adopted Loud identities as expressions of independence and as a defence against the perceived unfairness of the school authority system. Their assertive style was confronting for some teachers. Occasionally a teacher would respect their choice of a Loud identity, accepting that these girls 'tend to be more self-confident and don't back down'. Similar defiance is found in Lei's account of the Hard identities adopted by Asian males as protection against threats from other peer groups at school. She quotes one student explaining the sense of security that comes from belonging to a group that 'acts tough' in a male peer system where tough is good. 'Walking in a group, it's not that they're not going to mess with you; it's just that you are more comfortable' (Lei, 2003, p. 176).

What are the effects of ethnic differences on motivation at the college level? Apart from studies of college dropout, the college research does not deal directly with academic motivation, but focuses on prejudice and its effects on self-esteem and adjustment; thus inferences concerning motivation must be drawn from these. Given the large numbers of international students now enrolled in colleges and universities in western countries (there were approximately half a million international students in 1998 in the USA alone), adjustment is important not only for successful academic performance, but also for students to benefit more widely from their college education. Therefore, as Spencer-Rodgers (2001) explains, 'Understanding the nature and structure of attitudes towards foreign student visitors and attempts to alter these attitudes are worthwhile endeavours' (p. 628). She found that the stereotype characteristic of foreign students most salient to American students was how non-American they were. Their foreignness was regarded negatively and linked to notions that the students were somehow deficient, handicapped, out of place, and socially maladjusted. At the same time, they were regarded academically as clever, adventurous, hardworking, and eager to learn. The mix of these two conflicting stereotypes may actually increase the stress on foreign students and explain why they prefer to socialize within their own cultural group. The strategy of building strong ties within their ethnic communities is a logical one, and according to Al-Sharideh and Goe (1998), an effective way of coping with the demands of the new college environment. They suggest that students from overseas countries 'undergo a disruptive cultural experience' in dealing with 'cultural frames of reference' that are different from their own (p. 704). This disruption extends beyond the lectures and tutorials and examinations, into the food, social customs, religious practices, and forms of entertainment that comprise one's culture. Not surprisingly, then, members of minority groups build social ties with those in similar circumstances. Schmitt *et al.* (2003) comment that identification with a minority group 'provides individuals with a social and psychological "place" within which they can establish a sense of identity' (p. 3). Through identification with other minority students, they experience a sense of inclusion that is not available to them from the host community.

The style of adjustment adopted by overseas students through ethnic group contact has been described as the 'detached observer' (Al-Sharideh and Goe, 1998). That is, they establish social network ties with other foreign students as a buffer against the pervasiveness of the host culture and experiences of prejudice, while making some links with members of the host community. In terms of optimal adjustment, the degree of immersion in the ethnic community has to be balanced with integrating into the host community. In Al-Sharideh and Goe's study, strong ties within the ethnic community were primary, but these 'co-cultural' ties contributed to self-esteem only up to a threshold point, beyond which strong ties with American students were required to further boost their self-esteem. Too much involvement in the ethnic community 'began to inhibit his or her ability' to engage with the American social environment and to benefit from learning to meet its demands (Al-Sharideh and Goe, 1998, p. 721).

However, multiculturalism in universities has its costs, as Sidanius *et al.* (2004) have shown. They provide evidence that the creation of ethnically diverse campuses in the USA increases the tendency for students to form ethnic enclaves as a means of ingroup affirmation and protection, through accentuating ethnicity as the basis for social identification. When white students were conscious of the presence of minority groups, they joined 'Greek' letter sororities and fraternities where their majority characteristics were emphasized and their identity enhanced. The researchers found that membership in these white ethnic enclaves had the effect of strengthening their negative attitudes to outgroups. Moreover, it hardened their opposition to ethnically diverse campuses. Thus multiculturalism may have the opposite effects to those intended by the arguments for fostering interethnic contact. Readers should however be mindful that the study was conducted at UCLA where there is a high level of racial heterogeneity (there were 154 ethnic organizations), so the effects may be less dramatic in campuses with fewer minority groups.

Stereotypes and harassment

Crowd status and prestige are derived from adolescent concerns with appearance, personality, and social confidence; by contrast, stigmatized identities are assigned to individuals who show little interest in these concerns, or who challenge their validity by espousing the values of education and career, study and hard work. In this sense crowd stigmatizing is a form of group harassment that arises because more subtle forms of distracting motivational influence have failed. Kinney (1993) and Merten (1996a, 1996b) provide detailed analyses of how crowd labels can operate as tools of peer victimization in middle schools. In these cases a person automatically gains the reputation associated with the crowd label, whether or not the characteristics of such a label accurately represent that person's attitudes, values and behaviour. Tajfel (1981) wrote that for us to adopt a social psychological view of stereotyping requires an appreciation of 'the competitive and power relations between groups' (p. 157). These kinds of social relations are not far beneath the surface in some middle schools and junior highs.

The account given by Kinney (1993) of the peer society of a middle school underlines the importance of crowd affiliation for social identity in early adolescence. It appeared to Kinney that the peer culture of the middle school he investigated was primarily shaped by the concerns of the sportspeople, the cheerleaders, and their friends. The visibility and prestige of the 'Trendies' and 'Jock-populars' within the school allowed them to define who were part of the ingroup and who were consigned to the outgroup, and to orchestrate the peer harassment that followed, which included making fun of the outgroup, calling them Nerds, and shunning them. Kinney interviewed older adolescents who had been regarded as Nerds in Grades 7 and 8, and he draws attention to the oppressive peer culture that operated when his respondents were in the middle school. So rigidly defined were the social categories that the peer society gave little room for alternative routes to popularity. One interviewee stated, 'You had one route [to becoming popular] and then there was the other. And we were the other' (p. 27). The effect on these so-called unpopular students was to make them feel outsiders and social outcasts. They judged themselves by the values of coolness displayed by the Trendies, which led them to conclude that there was something wrong with them, and they were continually afraid of offending someone. One reported, 'I was just a loser. I didn't have many friends' (p. 28). Things improved for the Nerds when they moved from middle school into the more open environment of high school, where they were free of the rigid group categories that existed in the middle school. Instead of one powerful and exclusive trendy group dominating the value system of the peer society, there was a greater variety of groups in the high school, and accordingly more routes to visibility. The Nerds reported that they felt 'relieved they were in high school'. They became more confident, were able to shrug off the negative social identity they had acquired, and became Normals.

Perhaps unwittingly, Kinney traces a sequence of development from Nerd to Normal that denies individuality and rewards conformity – its message being that if you're a bit different, you'll suffer at school. Nerds are pilloried for being different. We know from Chapter 5 that there are serious consequences for students who don't fit in at school; what we don't know is how rigid or how tolerant the school climate is for those who are different. Bucholtz (1999) is clearly disappointed with Kinney's argument that Nerds need to undergo a process of 'recovery of identity' in order to fit in at school, such as being more sociable, dating the opposite sex, and participating in school extra-curricular activities. She sees this formula as a remake of their identities into Jocks. Why do high schools pander to the Jocks? Bucholtz challenges the assumptions that Nerd is a pejorative label for someone who is 'a failed Burnout or an inadequate Jock' (1999, p. 211). She argues that Nerds are not failures or misfits, and that the social identity of Nerd is as valid as that of Jock or Burnout. She suggests that Nerds consciously reject the values of coolness and the identities based on it, and deliberately choose an identity that is distinctive, 'through language and other social practices'.

Merten (1996a) described the peer rejection of four boys who were labelled as 'Mels' – a term that was derived from a boy at school named Melvin, who was considered to have childhood interests and attitudes. The experience of moving into junior high was an unhappy one for these boys, because the Mel label that they had acquired in their Grade 6 class became a crowd label across the school when they moved to junior high. The boys were quiet and obedient in class and did not adopt the agenda of the majority of their peers, who were attempting to distance themselves from their childhood selves and 'get on with their adolescent future'. Rather than choose the immature adolescent style adopted by the peer majority, the Mels saw junior high as an invitation to adopt a more mature approach to their future. Their nonconformity marked them as different from their peers, and as belonging to the despised Mel group. For the peer majority, the Mel label had scapegoating value; it served as a category for others to avoid. The four boys found that others were responding to them not as people, but as a social type. The problem lay not in the individual boys but in the social categorization practised by their adolescent peers. One boy found that his Mel reputation was sufficient justification for others in the school to pick on him whenever they felt like it. He adopted the strategy of psychological withdrawal, despite the fact that his attempts at being invisible tended to emphasize his outsider characteristics and confirm the Mel label. William, Scott and Les (the other boys studied by Merten) determined to change their Mel image, but found it very difficult to do so.

In reflecting on the difficulties of altering such stereotypes as the Mel, Merten makes a compelling point, that 'being categorized as a Mel gives salience, even existence, to characteristics and behaviours that can be interpreted as Mel-like' (1996b, p. 41), even if others with the same characteristics escape the label. The mischief of assigning a crowd category to an individual is that the person is confirmed by the stereotype and denied the freedom to step outside it and be themselves. There is no doubting the destructive power of stereotyping if it is allowed to run unchecked by school authorities. If some crowd identities are valued over others, so that the Jocks and the cheerleaders are celebrated, while the Brains and the Nerds are widely regarded as negative identities to be avoided, schools become coercive institutions that value preferred identities and reward conformity. What should be of concern to educators is the use in schools of stigmatized identities, implicitly or explicitly, to maintain social cohesion.

Social identity and coping

How do crowds as abstract concepts influence academic motivation? Crowd labels find expression at school within actual cliques and social networks. They operate by providing adolescents with exemplars of attitudes towards school. While social crowds remain stereotypes, formed through the process of social categorization, generalization occurs from the crowd type to adolescents whose group shares some of the crowd characteristics. It is therefore possible to find adolescent cliques that resemble crowd types, and to discover that in this way crowd types exert influences on specific classroom behaviour, through the workings of actual groups. Evidence that they remain reference points appears in adolescent discussions of crowds; informants readily assign crowd labels to others, but prefer to describe themselves as members of the 'ordinary' or 'normal' or 'average' crowd, whose defining features are less distinctive. Hendry *et al.* (2002) found 'no cases of self-identification with crowds' (p. 370), apart from the normal association mentioned. Among these Scottish youth, group labelling seemed to be used not so much to find an identity as to exclude negative identities.

Jackson (2003) and Francis (1999) both adopt a feminist frame to explore 'laddishness' as a protective identity adopted by adolescent boys in British schools against negative labelling by their peers. They explain laddish behaviour as a defence, although the nonconforming and mucking-up classroom behaviours that Francis describes have been a route for expressing an alternative identity among boys for almost as long as schools have existed. Being one of the lads is very important; it means that you aren't different from the rest, and you don't stand out as a diligent student or as too serious at school. Lads hang around together and enjoy having a laugh; according to Jackson's informants, lads 'go around taking the mick out of people' (p. 586). They concealed the efforts put into school assignments for fear of being regarded by their mates 'as a Geek or a Swot or something' (pp. 588–589). They also expressed a fear of looking stupid or thick to their mates, and so they adopted a strategy of concealment. They would hide away a low mark that they gained on a test, and if discovered by their peers, would make up an excuse to protect their self-concept; for example, they might claim that they didn't study for the test.

A similar protective strategy was described by Martino (1999) among 15–17-year-old Australian boys, who sought a 'cool' identity as protection against being labelled a 'Squid' or a 'Poofter'. The cool boys, like the laddish group, concealed their academic efforts; they publicly rejected schoolwork and devalued striving for high academic achievement, possibly because they feared being too different from the dominant footballer-surfie crowd at school. 'To be in the group you have to be hassling someone else …. There are quite a few groups like that at this school' (p. 246). A Kentucky student told Hufton *et al.* (2002) that, 'Most people, like, they think it's cool to be bad.' The presence of the group affirms the individual's work-avoidant reputation. Evidence that the available social identities are operationalized in the clique comes from a comment by 'Adan', who explained that when he negotiates between an academic identity of Squid and a socialite identity of Party Animal, his crowd affiliation changes: 'Whichever one you choose also determines what friendship group you're in' (Martino. 1999, p. 255).

Clique enactment of social identities

The image or identity is a general type to begin with; it requires a whole set of behaviours before the identity can be filled out, like that of a performance on stage. The cliques within the classroom and in the school-grounds enable adolescents to experiment with these crowd identities. Mucking up is part of this performance. Classroom behaviours are tried out, polished, and retained, and reflect gender-based differences. Whereas girls may engage in quiet talking, or surreptitiously do their nails or read a book, boys are more extroverted in their behaviour. They are more restless and more vocal. Warrington *et al.* (2000) singled out their noisy joking and clever remarks, and their greater restlessness. Through these action routines, endorsed by the clique, adolescents establish a behaviour style that is attached to a particular identity and reputation. Cliques are alert to any behaviour that deviates even slightly from the established style, so that their fellow clique members are punished for any aberrations. Any discussion with adolescent students will quickly confirm how sensitive they are to every nuance of behaviour, and how well they know what little details depict various identity types.

A theme of these British and Australian studies is the importance for boys of their image, and how their concern to maintain their image and preserve a reputation that is acceptable to their mates can affect their academic motivation. The preservation of group affiliation is an important matter: by maintaining certain patterns of behaviour that are consistent with a cool image, such as nonchalance, an adolescent avoids being labelled as a Swot

or a Nerd when he gets praised by a teacher for the high quality of his assignment. The groups cited are classroom-based, but carry crowd labels: for
example, the Cool boys or girls and the Sad boys or girls, or the In crowd
and the Squares (see Warrington *et al.*, 2000). The negative labels vary,
with adolescent students in some schools speaking of Swots and others of
Boffs when referring to students who are studious types, but the common
theme is that for boys, 'being part of the crowd and living up to its expectations was really important' (p. 403). Understanding how cliques refine
the crowd-based reputations and how they support avoidance patterns are
important tasks for teachers.

Whether crowds exist as prototype identities in high schools outside
North America remains a moot point, but it is clear that social categorization occurs among adolescent students. It seems, however, that most school
communities are not polarized along a single dimension of judgement, and
instead contain a diversity of viewpoints and sentiments about other people.
When schools allow room for a variety of crowd identities to flower, the
destructive force of negative crowd identities is undermined. Where there
is a lack of consensus about the specific features that constitute the crowds
in their school, adolescents have no definite prototypical crowd identity to
imitate. Robinson's (1995) discussion of consensual and non-consensual
prototypes is helpful in explaining why some crowd types fail to create
specific social identities. He argues that people who belong to groups strive
to conform to their representation of the group norm (that is, the subjective
prototype). Where there is consensus with respect to the prototype, members will agree on their opinions and attitudes, and behave in similar ways.
However, where there is a diversity of representations of the prototype,
members will differ. The latter situation arises where people are exposed to
different comparative contexts and receive different information. Schools
that encourage and respect different identities rather than favour a few will
have created the conditions that counter group polarization and intergroup
conflict. This seems to be the case among most adolescents surveyed by
researchers outside North America, who report loose boundaries for the
crowds named in their school.

Self-handicapping and social identity

An avoidance pattern that is related to social identity at the classroom level
is self-handicapping, a form of reputation management that occurs when a
person seeks to deflect the cause of poor performance away from scrutiny
of their own lack of competence. Self-handicapping is pursued through a
combination of 'image management' and 'achievement-undermining behaviours' (Urdan *et al.*, 1998, p. 116). For example, a young person may

avoid asking the teacher for help when the work is unclear. They may explain away their poor performance on a test as a case of forgetting that there was a test, rather than be seen to lack the ability to pass it. The motive that underlies self-handicapping is to protect one's reputation as academically able, reasoning that, 'If I ask for help, others will think I'm dumb.' There is debate among researchers as to the audience, and whether students are concerned with not looking stupid to their classmates in general, to their close friends, to their teacher, or to all of these audiences. But what is agreed is that students who are uncertain about their capacity to be successful in the classroom will, under some circumstances, engage in ruses and deceptions to protect an image of themselves as capable – even at the risk of undermining their academic achievement. Students who are most vulnerable are those who are self-focused (ego-oriented) rather than task-focused. That is, they view success for what it conveys to others rather than for any value in the success itself. Thus their vulnerability is exposed in motivational climates that emphasize achievement and competition and the possibility of failure, particularly where their performance is visible to others. Their self-concerns lead them to ignore what the test reveals about their task performance, and to focus only on what others think about their ability and how they can deflect any negative appraisals. The priority of these students is to 'protect their sense of ability and to try to influence others' evaluations of their ability' (Martin *et al.*, 2003, p. 617). The point to be made about self-handicapping is the salience of a person's extrinsic motivation, and in particular their concern with how others view them. Elliot and Church (2003) put it this way: 'self-handicapping occurs when guarding against the negative implications of failure is more important than actually attaining success' (p. 370).

Self-handicapping not only occurs during a test; it is also a motivational problem for time-management and assignment work of the kinds associated with university study and office work among young adults. While all of us are aware of ways of avoiding work that is hard, the self-handicapping student or worker takes every opportunity to engage in distractions. For example, the student procrastinates: s/he puts off study for a test, or preparation for an assignment, by rearranging a set of folders or by watching television. In the office, the legal clerk or junior town planner delays making a concentrated effort on the files on his desk that concern a difficult problem, and instead makes a sixth cup of morning coffee and then strolls across the room to gossip with others. Their reasoning may be as follows: 'If I leave it to the last minute, then I've got an excuse if I didn't do well.' It's easier to say 'I failed because I didn't put enough work into it', than 'I failed because I'm not good at it' (see Martin *et al.*, 2003, p. 621). The public nature of achievement in school and in the workplace affects motivation and task performance among those who have an overriding concern with preserving their image and reputation rather than with the achievement itself.

Concluding comments

What has been explored in this chapter is the social and contextual basis of motivation. Motivation has even greater importance to modern-day youth as they spend longer periods of time at school and college. For example, Andersson and Strader (2004) note that Swedish youth now spend one-third of their lives in educational settings, but they question whether such a lengthy period of schooling is in the students' best interests. Despite major attempts at educational reform over forty years, the Swedish school curriculum and school organization remain relatively unchanged. If Sweden, which sets the benchmark for educational reforms, has found it difficult to drive the school system forward for the benefit of youth, how much more difficult is it for change to occur in other countries? A friend once put it to me that 'It is easier to move a cemetery than change a curriculum.' Perhaps he was right.

Rather than discover that there is an anti-school adolescent culture, where peers seek to undermine motivation, what can be concluded from the research reviewed in this chapter is the influential role of the teacher in establishing a healthy partnership with students. True, negative peer influences do occur, but they generally arise from frustration with poor teaching and from motives of self-protection. The process view of motivation suggested by Dornyei (2000) directs our attention to classroom relations, and is consistent with seeing teacher and learners in a partnership, rather than taking a corporate or managerial view. It casts classroom life into a series of intellectual journeys undertaken together by the teacher and the students, based on mutual respect and joint responsibility. For school to be relevant, young people need to connect not only to the curriculum material but to the teacher and fellow classmates as well.

Seifert (2004) reviewed the major theories of motivation and summarized their key principles to create five broad motivation patterns, comprising a mastery pattern and four patterns of avoidance: failure avoidant, learned helplessness, bored and work avoidant, and hostile and work avoidant. The failure avoidant adolescents strive to preserve an image; the learned helpless believe that no effort they make can change the outcome; the bored do the minimum of work to get by in school; and the hostile do little work in order to get revenge on others. These avoidant patterns underline the importance of personal meaning for adolescent motivation, and point to the key role of teachers in helping students to find meaning in their work. According to Seifert, 'The critical factor may be how the teacher and students interact', and 'this depends on the teacher's ability to be nurturant, supportive and helpful' (2004, p. 148). From interviews with gifted but bored high school students, Kanevsky and Keighley (2003) concluded that boredom evolved out of a lack of challenge, complexity and control. The teachers who were described as caring respected adolescent needs for challenge; they prepared their lessons so that students had freedom to discuss, question, explore, and apply ideas, and also demonstrated an interest in them as developing persons.

8 Smoking, drinking and drug use

It is during the adolescent years that nearly all alcohol and drug use begins. This bald fact leads many parents and teachers to want to know how they can protect their young people from the dangers of illicit drugs and from the health risks of alcohol and cigarettes. Peers are often blamed as influencing adolescents' health risk behaviour, as a visit to any website on substance use will confirm. However, few investigators subscribe to the popular notion of peer pressure, where naive and helpless youth conform to irresistible peer forces exerted on them. Social influences are far more subtle, and young people far more aware and autonomous, than the popular notion of peer pressure would imply. It is the subtlety and complexity of peer influence that receive close examination in the following pages. The chapter examines the nature of peer influence on drinking, smoking and drug use, by reviewing research on the influence of best friends, the friendship clique and the social crowd, as well as the critical factors that make young people vulnerable to health risk. The existence of a substantial body of scholarly research on these topics is a reminder of the complexity of the issues, and that any attempt to find clear water where the currents of drug use meet those of health and education requires exceptional gifts in navigation. But the sails are set, the day looks fine, and the breeze is in the right quarter; so let's head into the open seas.

Health risks

Smoking, drinking and drug use are of central importance in the adolescent period as markers of the social transition to adult lifestyles, but each has serious potential for harm. While there is a persisting belief that marijuana is less harmful than tobacco, this is not true: marijuana use carries serious risks for deteriorations in memory and judgement as well as for health dangers to the brain and the pulmonary system. Alcohol is the major drug of abuse in society, and excessive alcohol use has deleterious effects on the brain, liver and kidneys, apart from its association with violent assault, drownings and traffic injuries. Alcohol and drug use are implicated in about 40 per cent of all road fatalities (data from the US Department of Health, 2002), and while overall fatality rates have been declining in most western countries over recent years, they have been increasing among young drivers. The Australian rates for road trauma for males aged 17–24 are almost three times those for female drivers of comparable age. It is not known what proportion of car accidents among youth or how many work-place fatalities are related to intoxication and drug use, but it is surely not an insignificant figure. As for smoking, the harm done to health has resulted in tobacco advertising being banned in many countries. Smoking is prohibited in all Australian government buildings, airports, public transport and domestic aircraft, and is banned from pubs and clubs. Yet despite controls on cigarette sales to minors, the problem of underage smoking persists in many countries. For example, American teenagers illegally buy 150 million packs of cigarettes a year, and every day approximately 3000 of them join the ranks of smokers.

According to the World Health Organization, tobacco is the only legally sold product that brings about the deaths of half of its regular users. Currently about one in ten people using tobacco die from smoking-related diseases each year, amounting to 5 million people worldwide, and the figure is on the rise. In Australia, deaths from smoking-related diseases occur at a rate of fifty persons per day – approximately two classrooms of school students (Table 8.1). Treatment of smoking-related disease currently consumes over 900,000 hospital bed days in Australian hospitals at an estimated cost of A$700 million. While it has long been known that smoking shortens one's lifespan by more than five years, recent medical research has drawn attention to the impact of smoking on the ageing process: smokers age more quickly – by between eight and twelve years. This means that smokers die younger but look older!

Adolescent usage

Health authorities estimate that 80 per cent of smokers begin smoking before they are 18 years of age. The peak years for smoking experimentation are from 13 to 16, and 'the lines of friendship are often characterized by smoking behaviour' (Kobus, 2003, p. 37). In the United Kingdom, every year 114,000 people die as a result of smoking, and every day about 450 children and adolescents start smoking for the first time. In most western countries the smoking rate for adolescent females now exceeds that for males. The percentage of 15-year-old smokers in Britain is estimated as 26 per cent of females and 18 per cent of males. Australian estimates in 2002 of adoles-

Table 8.1 Australia: health statistics 1996–1997

	Tobacco	*Alcohol*	*Illicit drugs*
Hospital-related episodes	149,834	95,917	11,240
Deaths	18,224	3,668	832

cent smokers aged 14–19 years were 16.2 per cent for females and 14.1 per cent for males. Canadian smoking figures in 2002 for 15–19-year-olds were 18.9 per cent for females and 17.7 per cent for males. In both these countries, the rates for smoking among those aged 20–29 are higher than these figures, being 23.7 per cent (Australia) and 22.7 per cent (Canada) for females and 23.7 per cent (Australia) and 28.5 per cent (Canada) for males.

Adolescent alcohol consumption and binge drinking are further issues of major concern. Alcohol consumption and heavy drinking are higher in the early twenties than at any other period of life, reaching a peak around the age of 21 years. The New South Wales Alcohol and Drug Service estimates that about 40 per cent of boys aged between 12 and 18 years, and about 30 per cent of girls, regularly engage in binge drinking, which is defined as five standard drinks in a session. Drinking is almost a curriculum component at universities: Davey *et al.* (2002) estimate that 90 per cent of Australian university students drink alcohol, and about half of them get drunk on a weekly basis. Similar figures could be obtained in other countries, and they represent tremendous costs to society. For example, the costs associated with underage drinking in the United States were estimated in 1999 to be US$58 billion (US Department of Justice figures).

Nature and origins of peer influence

There is no doubt about the importance of peer influence on adolescent use of tobacco, alcohol and illicit drugs; support can be found in hundreds of research studies. Large-scale surveys and interview research all conclude that peers are implicated in young people's initiation into substance use and in the maintenance of substance use patterns, as well as in resistance to them. Oetting and Beauvais (1987b) put the argument forcefully: 'the single dominant variable in adolescent drug use is the influence provided by the peers with whom an adolescent chooses to associate' (p. 206). Elsewhere they expand the argument in these words:

> When drugs are actually used, it is almost always in a peer context. Peers initiate the youth into drugs. Peers help provide drugs. Peers

talk with each other about drugs and model drug using behaviours for each other, and in doing so shape attitudes about drugs and drug-using behaviours.

(Oetting and Beauvais, 1987a, p. 137)

Despite the confident language of these authors, assessing the nature of peer influences and how they affect the individual adolescent's own behaviour is a complex matter. Smoking and drinking alcohol are social activities, and they occur in social leisure settings. Influence is both direct and indirect. Direct forms of persuasion often occur in concert with others, where standards are set and compliance reinforced by group actions. Peers may support a particular activity by urging and teasing, or discourage it by criticism or shaming. Indirect influence is exerted through relationships, where individuals are linked by attachments based on common interests, so that each person is motivated to behave according to a desire to fit in and is guided by perceptions of how others behave. An additional factor is the constructive role that tobacco and alcohol use play in the psychosocial transitions into adolescence and from adolescence into young adulthood in many societies. Alcohol and tobacco are part of leisured social activity, but like the Trojan horse they bring pain and suffering to many who welcome them inside their lives. The goal of this section of the chapter is to review the leading arguments concerning the nature, origin and extent of peer influence, referring to research on the use of tobacco, alcohol and illicit drugs.

Defining peer influence

One problem in defining peer influence is the lack of a rationale for how peers should be defined. Are young people more likely to be influenced by the peer network or by their best friend? Notions of 'peers' vary considerably in the literature, and range from 'other pupils in your school' to 'current acquaintances', 'your five closest friends', or 'your best friend'. Oetting and Beauvais (1987b) emphasized the importance of *subgroups* of closely linked peers: 'peer clusters' with a shared lifestyle that supports a group identity, in this case one that incorporates health risk behaviour. Morgan and Grube (1991) proposed that social influence varies according to the *closeness* of relationships. They distinguished different sectors of the peer social network so as to separate peer acquaintances and casual friends from best friends, and then compared adolescents' susceptibility to influence from these different peer relationships. Their longitudinal study of 13–18-year-old Dubliners found that the strength of peer influence on smoking, alcohol use and illicit drugs was consistent with the level of closeness, so that the best friend was more influential than other friends, and the wider peer network had little influence. Kandel and Davies (1991) highlight the aspect of friend closeness in relation to illicit drug use in adults in their late twenties who had been followed up since they were 15–16 years of age. These studies emphasize that substance use occurs for many young people in their close circle of friends, and provides a sense of relaxation, group bonding, and shared emotional experience. The significance of group attachment for drug use is captured in the Beatles song 'With a Little Help from my Friends'.

Another problem is how to measure peer influence. Studies often rely on respondent reports of their friends' levels of smoking or substance use. These perceptions of peer use have been found to predict the individual adolescent's use or intentions to use tobacco, alcohol and marijuana (e.g. Iannotti and Bush, 1992; Sieving *et al.*, 2000; Moss *et al.*, 2003). However, the correlation between perceived peer use and the individual's use is deemed a 'false consensus' because the respondent overestimates the extent to which others are like him, or projects his own behaviour onto that of peers. Indeed Rice *et al.* (2003) found that respondents' estimates of peer drug use were highly inaccurate, when compared with actual peer behaviour. Some researchers have approached the influence question by including a measure of the respondent's susceptibility to peer pressure. For example, Schulenberg *et al.* (1999) designed a series of questions that tapped such a trait, arguing that individuals who are highly susceptible to peer pressure to misbehave are likely to be influenced by others who misbehave when the conditions are favourable. They found that peer susceptibility in sixth graders predicted excesses in alcohol use at Grade 7 and again at Grade 8. Their data suggest that susceptibility to misbehave is a stable individual characteristic which increases in early adolescence, and is likely to affect 'selection of certain types of peer group' and consequently how individuals respond to peer influence (p. 131).

Selection versus influence

The extent to which adolescents are influenced by their peers or share similarities with their peers because of selective association is not easy to tease apart. The distinction between peer influence (pressures to conform) and selection (birds of a feather) is an important one for health education, because prevention programs that are focused on protecting young people from harmful peer influences may be interpreted by their hearers as attempts to undermine their existing connections to peers. Influence implies change in lifestyles and behaviour. If selection processes are predominant, young people will show similarities with those with whom they associate simply because they are attracted to others who have similar interests to themselves. On the other hand, if influence processes are predominant, young people will change their behaviour to mirror that of the peers they regularly hang around with, or of the particular social crowd they are identified with. If influence is transmitted by peers, it is important to understand the processes by which group norms are established and how individuals are rewarded for adhering to the behavioural standards of their peers.

Tolson and Urberg (1993) found that the most important characteristics shared by friends were observable attributes and behaviours rather than attitudes or values, and that older adolescents were more similar to their friends in their smoking behaviour than were younger adolescents, suggesting that both selection and mutual influence may be operating, with the effect that these strengthen friend similarity over time. A longitudinal study by the same investigators (Urberg *et al.*, 1998) compared stable friends with about-to-be friends. The design allowed the effects of friend similarity to be examined separately from peer influences in relation to cigarette use, alcohol use and delinquency, because similarities could be identified before the adolescents became friends. The researchers concluded that pre-existing similarities in adolescent levels of substance use and delinquency explained why they later became friends. However, I have reservations about their conclusions. These arise from their measure of friendship (best friend and other friends you hang around with, gathered at one time-point each year), limitations on the sample (only 33 per cent of the sample were matched up), and their suggestion that 'friendships may be organized to a large extent around shared activities' (p. 709). What is ignored is that, within these shared activities, peer influence may flow via existing network ties between stable friends and about-to-be friends. Unless social ties are comprehensively mapped in adolescent studies so that second- and third-order relations are mapped, many links of significance (such as those with about-to-be friends) may be omitted.

In order to control for the effects of selection and thus ensure that the effects of peer influence are not overestimated, Urberg *et al.* (1997) propose three rules. First, examine adolescents in pre-existing friendships; second, focus on a new behaviour; and third, within a longitudinal design control statistically for common variance between the subject and the friend. Maxwell (2002) followed these rules in her study of health risk behaviours, which included smoking, drinking and marijuana use. She reported her findings in terms of the likelihood of change in an adolescent's level of risk activity at a later time-point, based on the earlier risk behaviour of a random same-sex friend. She found that, in general, adolescents were twice as likely to engage in risk activity if the friend had previously done so, but that the extent of influence depended on characteristics of the particular health risk activity. For smoking and using drugs, which are addictive activities, influences of a user friend were stronger on non-users than on those already engaged in these activities; whereas for alcohol use, influences of a user friend occurred in both directions – encouraging the adolescent to begin or maintain drinking, or urging her/him to avoid or cease drinking.

Kirke (2004) is critical of approaches that assume peer influence occurs if adolescents' substance use behaviour becomes more similar to that of their peers, because selection and influence have not been separated. She adopts a stringent definition of peer influence, based on two indices: 'whether the adolescents had been in the company of their peers, and whether the adolescents had been provided with the substance by their peers' (p. 8). What is clear is that much more needs to be known about the process of peer influence and its relation to friend selection, which is difficult given the instability of adolescent peer relationships and the limitations of survey research. Kobus (2003) suggests that if research into substance use is to advance, it should become less 'one-dimensional' and 'take a much closer look at peer relationship dynamics and the influences therein' (p. 52). Information of the kind discussed in Part II of this book could assist in understanding the twin processes of inclusion and exclusion in cliques and networks, and examining the structures of networks themselves, as Kirke herself has done. The dynamics whereby young people are selected into a clique or excluded from it on the basis of their smoking or substance use are elaborated later in this chapter.

Peer influences on drinking

Initiation into drinking

The purpose of this section is to consider the social and environmental influences on young people that induct them into drinking. Initiation sometimes exposes the raw elements of peer pressure, but there is more to initiation than this: it seems in some ways to resemble the conjunction of the planets, where the contributing factors include access, opportunity, social atmosphere, and peer encouragement. In an open society, young people are inevitably exposed to a mix of these factors, amongst which the distinctiveness of peers as sources of influence may seem fairly obscure and insignificant.

It has been found that adolescents who regularly attend parties and other peer outings at clubs, discos and dances adopt drinking patterns at an earlier age than the majority of their peers (Margulies *et al.*, 1977). A major condition affecting susceptibility to alcohol-related risk behaviour is the absence of adult controls in these unstructured settings, which have been associated with heavy alcohol use, illegal drug use, and criminal behaviour (Osgood *et al.*, 1996). This may occur because the venue chosen for leisure activities is one where adults are seldom seen, and where adult prohibitions on drinking are less likely to be enforced. An example is 'O-Week' – the Orientation week activities that inaugurate the academic year at Australian universities, where large numbers of 18-year-old students new to university life are initiated into a drinking culture. The supply of 'free kegs' of beer prominently situated on campus is intended to encourage heavy drinking among new students, whatever their normal level of alcohol use, and to put pressure on non-drinkers to 'have a couple'. Harford and Grant (1987) have remarked on the relatively greater 'wetness' and prevalence of student binge drinking at time-out events located at the beginning and end of the academic year. For many young people, special events like the Toga Party at the University of Queensland each mid-February in O-Week, and the Faculty Balls in the middle of the year, are thinly disguised modern orgies, and are understood as such by many students.

The importance of peers, particularly friends, in introducing adolescents to alcohol and in reinforcing drinking behaviour has been widely noted, and is confirmed by research. Adolescents whose friends are drinkers begin drinking at a younger age (Hawkins *et al.*, 1997). Moreover, early adoption of drinking in adolescence increases the likelihood of heavy drinking in young adulthood (Barnes *et al.*, 1992). The risk of early drinking is underlined in the Hawkins study, which found that 'the younger individuals are when they begin drinking alcohol, the greater their level of problems associated with alcohol misuse' (Hawkins *et al.*, 1997, p. 288).

Older youth play a crucial role in inducting younger ones into drinking, as Stattin *et al.* (1989) showed in a study of Swedish youth. Taking the view that drinking is an instance of a social transition, they proposed that students who associated with peers who were older, or who were working, were exposed to experiences outside the normal age-range of schoolmates, and would be more likely to engage in adult behaviours like drinking at an earlier time. They reasoned that adolescents whose networks contained these 'nonconventional' peers would be experiencing different social environments that were likely to 'accelerate psychosocial transitions' (p. 229). The peer socialization processes would be different, and would influence the timing of when regular drinking habits were acquired. The longitudinal data in the Swedish study give special point to its findings, which show that associating with older peers or working peers was related to earlier drinking and to more reports of drunkenness among respondents. The pattern was consistent for both sexes. In contrast, those whose peers were all schoolmates reported stronger sanctions against drunkenness and less permissiveness from their peers concerning alcohol use.

Binge drinking

Much of the harm associated with alcohol is linked to binge drinking or 'getting wasted', where large quantities of liquor are consumed on a single occasion. The consequences can be tragic: a student in a residential college adjacent to my own was drowned when attempting to swim the river after a drinking session with his mates. Binge drinking is assisted by the tradition of the shout, where one group member buys a round of drinks for the others. If the group is large, a young drinker may well find that by the time it is his turn to buy the round, the room is also going around. Peers in these settings thus promote motives for drinking that increase their exposure to risk. Most tellingly, the normalizing effect of these social leisure settings is that youth 'did not see the issue of alcohol use or abuse as an important one' (Broadbent, 1994, p. 33).

Links between youth networks and heavy boozing are found among working young people as well as college youth, and confirm the association between youth transitions and heavy drinking. Lindsay (2001) surveyed non-college Australian young people aged 15–25 who had jobs in sales, clerical offices, and building trades. She reported that 60 per cent were regular drinkers and that 15 per cent of the males and 31 per cent of the females drank quantities that were 'hazardous to their health', with one in five reporting that they drank thirteen or more drinks in a session. An American study by Weitzman *et al.* (2003) reports that two-fifths of college students binge on alcohol, and that one-quarter had binged three or more times in the past fortnight. Students' heavy drinking appears to be supported by their own 'inflated definitions of binge drinking'. Respondents defined binge drinking as 'consuming eight or more drinks' for men and 'six or more drinks for women' (p. 29), which is well above the accepted definition of five standard drinks in a single occasion (four for women). College drinkers were also more likely to belong to Greek letter organizations and live in a 'wet environment', one where the majority of their peers drank alcohol, endorsed alcohol use, and engaged in binge drinking.

Alcohol-fuelled settings

In considering the conditions that may influence drinking alcohol, a primary factor is a young person's access to alcohol, and a secondary factor is the encouragement for drinking that comes from the drinking environments themselves. Sieving *et al.* (2000) emphasized that the strength of influence on drinking and other drug use is related to features of the context. In contexts where the prevalence of drinking and drug use is high, peer influence may be 'potent', whereas in contexts where the overall rate is low and most peers are non-users, the influence of drinking friends may be less powerful because it is non-normative.

The social contexts of drinking deserve mention because alcohol consumption is a leisure activity: it occurs at parties and on special occasions, and in narrowly defined time-zones within the weekly round of activities. In some instances, young people gain access to quantities of free alcohol – at weddings, sporting celebrations, and college special events – in an environment where adult sanctions are relaxed, so that 'having a drink' is the norm, and to refuse a glass would seem churlish. The role of the social setting for drinking activity is highlighted by Harford and Grant (1987), who showed that, across a variety of social contexts, the frequency of drinking was best explained by normative support from peers ('my friends drink') and from parents ('my parents like a drop'). Thus, for many young people, the social settings of private parties and special occasions induce them to behave in an unconstrained manner, including drinking more than is wise. These settings can expose them to social and health risks well before they have attained the legal drinking age.

Liquor outlets also affect individual opportunities for drinking. Casswell *et al.* (2002) report that the quantity of alcohol consumed at age 18 by New Zealand youth, and the patterns of visiting bars and nightclubs, could be predicted from the person's ability at age 15 to purchase alcohol. For adolescents at school, patterns of alcohol use may be affected by its availability in the outlets near the school. Swiss research shows that access to alcohol sales outlets increases the probability of adolescent drinking (Kuntsche and Kuendig, 2005). The marketing of cheap alcohol is also linked to increased binge drinking among American college students (Kuo *et al.*, 2003), in relation to both off-campus and on-campus liquor access. From these studies across different countries, it is clear that easy access to cheap alcohol, made possible by the presence of local liquor outlets, promotes an atmosphere where regular drinking is normative, and where students are tolerant of heavy drinking.

What these studies highlight is that social networks link not only people but places. The research on drinking brings into sharp relief the importance of social network ties not just to other drinkers but to environments that contain drinking activities. Thus, the person who is a sports follower (football, cricket, basketball, baseball) is able through social network links to gain access to drinking facilities. In this case, similarity of sporting interests connects the individual to a network of others within a leisure atmosphere of friendliness and good cheer where social drinking is the norm. Studies link alcohol use with peer contexts where informal groups gather in leisure settings, rather than in organized cultural activities (Engel *et al.*, 1987; Pulkkinen and Narusk, 1987). In these situations the behaviour of some peers is likely to affect the individual's estimates of the amount of drinking of her/his own friends so that participants' estimates of the drinking norms become inflated. The Lintonen and Konu (2004) refer to adolescents' overestimation of peers' drinking as a 'misperceived norm' that is related to heavier drinking patterns. In three separate large surveys of 14-year-olds in Finland from 1989 to 2001, they found that those who were most influenced by a misperceived norm were the moderate drinkers – those who normally did not get drunk, but who were influenced by these perceptions to engage in greater intakes of alcohol.

Peer influences on smoking

Initiation into smoking

Models of the role of peers as influences on smoking have not stressed strongly enough the critical ages of susceptibility for initiation into smoking. Smoking is so addictive that once smokers have had a few cigarettes, they are hooked: the social influences on smoking then become less important for maintaining the practice than is the case for other substances such as alcohol and marijuana. The importance of the early adolescent period is underlined by evidence in the USA that over half the seniors in high school had begun cigarette smoking prior to the tenth grade. Smoking is a social act; Delorme *et al.* (2003) report from their study of the first time adolescents tried smoking a cigarette that it 'occurred in the presence of others in locations that were relatively inaccessible to intrusions by authority figures' (p. 487). Sensitivity to peer pressure has been found to be greatest among experimental smokers. In the research of Covington and Omelich (1988), non-smokers and experimental smokers felt more tempted to smoke as peer influences increased, whereas regular smokers were unaffected by peer influence. Moreover, adolescents progress rapidly from the experimental stage to becoming regular smokers – in a matter of one to two years. This means that intervention that is concerned with peer influences on smoking must necessarily focus on the initial experimentation phase, which occurs from age 10 to 14 years.

A longitudinal study of almost 18,000 adolescents by Van den Bree *et al.* (2003) examined adolescent initiation into experimental smoking and the progression to regular smoking in terms of a broad group of risk factors. Peer influence was not studied, but family and school experiences were included, including the role of school attachment. They found that initiation and progression to regular smoking for both genders, and initiation of experimental smoking in boys, could be predicted by a problem behaviour profile called 'trouble in school' (p. 178). This factor indexed such aspects as dissatisfaction with school, difficulty in dealing with school authorities, learning problems, and low academic ambitions. The significance of this finding is what it suggests about attachment to school. It would seem that school attachment functions as a protective factor for health risk for many young people, and education about the risks of substance use would be justified for them. For those who are in trouble, however, school-based health prevention programs are likely to have little impact, even if they are introduced at the stage of adolescent initiation into smoking and drinking.

Best friend influence

The central influence of best friends on smoking has been reported in several large studies, including the British study by Eiser *et al.* (1991), the Dublin study by Morgan and Grube (1991), the Waterloo Smoking Prevention Project (Van Roosmalen and McDaniel, 1989) and the Nebraska Prevention Centre survey (Gerber and Newman, 1989). In the Morgan and Grube study, initiation into smoking was predicted by the smoking behaviour of the best friend, as well as by that friend's approval or disapproval of smoking. Maintenance of smoking was explained by the best friend's smoking as well as by the smoking behaviour of other friends. This research highlighted the significant influence of the best friend rather than peers in general in initiating and maintaining health risk behaviour.

The study of Bristol adolescents (Eiser *et al.*, 1991) focused on close friends' influence by matching each respondent's rating of their friends' smoking and drinking with the reports of the friends themselves. They concluded that adolescent smokers were more likely to have smokers in their circle of friends. However, the friendship groups resembled one another in other ways as well, such as in their drinking behaviour and in their attitudes to school, suggesting that a selection process is at work. The breadth of the lifestyle pattern led them to conclude that, 'If peer group influence is at work here, it appears to have little specifically to do with smoking' (p. 346). Van Roosmalen and McDaniel (1989) also reported that when the best friend was a smoker, there was a strong likelihood that the respondent, whether male or female, was also a smoker. Moreover, adolescents were more likely to quit smoking if their best friend was not a regular smoker than if the friend smoked regularly. Another finding was that those who were smokers were likely to have many more friends who had tried smoking than was the case among non-smokers. Van Roosmalen and McDaniel interpreted these patterns as suggesting that the social environment of peers contains 'a degree of indirect pressure … upon the non-smoking adolescent to smoke' (1989, p. 807).

Urberg *et al.* (1990) compared pressures from friends not to smoke as well as pressures to engage in smoking. The adolescents studied included regular smokers, experimental smokers and non-smokers. Only one measure of peer pressure was found to be consistently related to adolescent smoking: normative pressure to smoke. It is the normative peer climate, including adolescent perceptions of their friends' smoking, that seems to provide the motivation to experiment with cigarette smoking, but Urberg and her colleagues found very few who were willing to admit that their friends directly encouraged them to smoke, even among those who were already smoking. They comment that 'it may be the absence of perceived disapproval from friends rather than the presence of perceived encouragement' that results in normative pressure to smoke (p. 254). Lack of friends' disapproval may thus be interpreted as tacit approval.

Crowd influence

Peer influence on smoking behaviour has also been attributed to identification with the wider peer group or social crowd. Social crowds function as social maps by which adolescents develop a status hierarchy of the peer society in their school, and then use this map to locate themselves within it. For these reasons they are better thought of as *crowd types*, to distinguish them from actual cliques or social networks. The distinctiveness of crowd types extends beyond general style characteristics relating to tastes in clothes, hairstyle, music and leisure interests, into what La Greca *et al.* (2001) call 'selective areas of health risk', so that styles of alcohol and substance use become associated with particular crowds – for example, drinking among sporty types, smoking among social types, and drug use among antisocial types. La Greca *et al.* found support for these style distinctions: Jocks were more sexually active; Populars had higher alcohol use; and Burnouts had high overall rates of health risk and illegal behaviours. Earlier studies using the social crowd concept (e.g. Mosbach and Leventhal, 1988) found that smoking use was much higher among adolescents who were identified with the Dirts crowd.

What the crowd research on health risk suggests is that social identity processes are at work, steering individuals towards the norms of the social crowd they affiliate with, assisted possibly by the social categorization activities of others. Thus, where smoking or alcohol use was regarded as enhancing an image consistent with a particular crowd, adolescents who identified with that crowd were likely to display higher levels of those behaviours.

Could both social crowds and close friends be important sources of influence on smoking? After all, adolescents are reported in some studies as having friends who affiliate with several different crowds, a factor likely to confound the analysis. The approach taken by La Greca *et al.* (2001) resolves some of this confusion. They found a close match between adolescents and their close friends in terms of crowd affiliation, with 69 per cent of best friends affiliated with the same crowd as the adolescent, while those having at least one of their close friends in the same crowd ranged from 80 to 94 per cent. Their conclusion does not deny the importance of close friends as influences on health risk, but by showing how these friends are generally nested within the same crowd as the respondent, they suggest that peer influences on behaviour are likely to be driven to some extent by crowd identification. La Greca *et al.* make a telling comment in this regard. Noting how females who identified with the popular crowd had relatively high rates of alcohol use, particularly binge drinking, which were often not linked to the drinking patterns of their close friends, they comment that 'Populars' support for binge drinking may come from influences other than close friends … [via] other peer crowds' (2001, p. 140).

Social network influence

Studies adopting social network concepts and methods of analysis offer a different perspective into the role of peer influences and friend selection. This research allows us to distinguish which young people are particularly vulnerable, as well as demonstrate how influences may be transmitted through actual social ties. Ennett and Bauman (1993) were among the first to use social network methods in studies of adolescent smoking, and their work is widely quoted in adolescent research. They found that smokers were over-represented among those defined as isolates (lacking ties to others), and explained their results in terms of selection processes. Because the majority of cliques were comprised of non-smokers, they reasoned that 'perhaps cliques excluded smokers' (p. 661). The problem with their findings is that the network analysis was faulty. Similar flaws are detectable in the assignment of adolescents to network roles by Urberg *et al.* (1997). For example, Ennett and Bauman (1993) used the rules in NEGOPY that require reciprocated ties for inclusion in cliques, and classified between 17.5 and 38.2 per cent of adolescents as isolates. There are problems not only with declaring such a large proportion of adolescents as 'isolates' but also with the category of 'liaisons'. Others, like Urberg *et al.* (1997), applied the rule that adolescents could be members of only one friendship group, and excluded isolated dyads and adolescents with no mutual friend. This rule excluded 29 per cent of students in one school. By imposing these arbitrary partitioning rules on network structures, so that large proportions of adolescents are defined as non-group members, researchers can arrive at erroneous conclusions. Their reliance on NEGOPY exposed weaknesses in

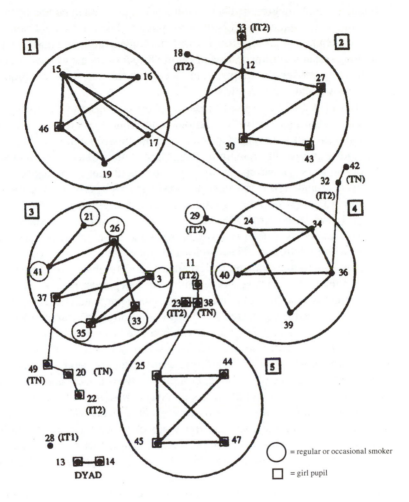

Figure 8.1 Relation between gender and smoking in adolescent cliques

Source: Original figure appears as Figure 3 in an article by L. Michell and A. Amos in *Social Science and Medicine*, *44*, 1997, pp. 1861–1869. Used by permission of Elsevier Ltd.

their approach, as the study by Michell and Amos (1997) and that by Abel *et al*. (2002) cited below make clear.

When network structures are drawn, the diagrams help the investigator to visualize how members are related, and overcome some of the problems mentioned above. Network diagrams were employed by Michell and Amos (1997) as case studies of peer group structures, to illustrate the links among members of smoking groups. They found that cliques tend to be homogeneous – comprising either smokers or non-smokers. The high school sample comprised ten non-smoking groups, three smoking groups, and four groups containing one smoker. Inspection of Figure 8.1 shows some of the cliques, and clique 3 (smokers) is sharply contrasted with the non-smoking cliques 1 and 2 (boys) and clique 5 (girls).

Abel *et al.* (2002) also used visual displays of the networks to try to understand patterns of network relations, and found that eighteen groups were homogeneous with regard to smoking, with thirteen non-smoking and five smoking groups. The remaining ten groups contained a mix of smokers and non-smokers. However, the diagrams revealed that some dense networks were excluded from the identification of groups by NEGOPY because they failed to conform to the NEGOPY definition of groups (mentioned in Chapter 3), while the NEGOPY rules excluded a total of 116 adolescents who were defined as isolates or liaisons. Abel and her colleagues were dissatisfied with these results. They decided to employ cluster analysis to seek groupings among the remnant adolescents, and were able to reclassify all bar six of them. The adolescents fell into four categories: *tryhards* – who had few reciprocated ties but made numerous unreciprocated ties; *populars* – who had several reciprocated ties but in addition many unreciprocated ties to them; *ordinary* adolescents – who had one or two reciprocated ties and some unreciprocated ones; and *loners* – who had no links at all, or one or two unreciprocated ties. They found that the loners, who are the true isolates, were *less* likely to smoke, contrary to what Ennett and Bauman (1993) had previously reported. Thus by considering individuals who are not directly connected to one another but have 'structural equivalence' (Scott, 2001), in that they have similar kinds of network ties with others, the New Zealand researchers have been able to show that roles like *being popular* or *being a tryhard* may explain adolescents' adoption of health risk behaviour.

The Abel *et al.* (2002) study demonstrates the particular merit of social network analysis for studying peer influence on substance use. Another study worthy of comment is the research by Kirke (2004). Where many studies of adolescents have restricted the scoping of peer networks to particular school year levels and classes and ignored any friends outside these bounds, Kirke mapped all the peer ties in the network, focusing the ties on the relation of interest – namely, initiation into substance use. Her study is an exemplar of what good social network research looks like: it is focused on the key relations; it allows respondents to name all the peers they are linked to, without limit; it maps all the peer ties in the sample, including siblings; and it uses interviews to gather the responses. Kirke's thoroughness may be appreciated when one finds that the sample of 14–18-year-olds was obtained by a house-to-house census of an entire Dublin electoral division, and that she successfully interviewed 267 of the 298 young people who lived there. The benefits of this careful data-gathering include the ability to detect an array of weak tie links together with strong ties, and through analysis of the weak and indirect ties, to isolate sub-networks as well as trace the 'chains' of peer influence through social networks. Even the geography was included, through sequential coding of streets and families. This meant that she could track the effects of proximity. Her report[1] includes a set of case studies of selected social networks, which enable her to conclude that: (a) in 42 of the 45 peer ties listed in chains 1–7 peer influence had occurred; (b) in 31 of these ties peer influence was between peers who were similar in the chains, and in all of these the peer tie had preceded the substance use; and (c) in 8 peer ties the links between them had formed *after* the first substance use of both of them. The detailed level of this analysis allows Kirke the authority to state that even for those adolescents whose similar substance use could be attributed to selection, 'they had, nevertheless, been influenced by their peers, but *not by the peers to whom they were now similar in these chains*' (p. 11; original emphasis). This is ground-breaking. Her conclusion is also worth quoting:

> As demonstrated in the case studies, the peer network contributes to the similarity of the adolescents in their substance use by linking adolescents, who are already similar in their substance use, to adolescents who become similar through their continued association with their peer in the peer network. Thus the chain reaction results from linking those who are similar with those who are not.
>
> (Kirke, 2004, p. 26)

The benefits from social network methods relate to increased understanding of how particular kinds of health risk behaviour are transmitted through a society, as was found in the SARS outbreak in 2003. That episode began simply, with the arrival of an elderly medical professor with a headache and sore throat at the Metropole Hotel in Kowloon on 12 February 2003. His chance meeting with two others in a lift was to have fatal consequences for hundreds of people in twenty-six countries across half the world.

Meanings and beliefs

Behaviour is influenced by the meanings and beliefs that are attached to it. Interviews with young people bring into sharp relief the perceived social benefits of drinking alcohol in teenage drinking contexts, such as parties

---

Box 8.1   Young people's views of drinking

- It's easier to talk to people if you have a few drinks.
- Drinking makes you popular and you get to go to more parties.
- If you don't drink you're not in the group.
- Everyone drinks at parties.
- If you drive carefully you can get home even if you're drunk.

---

and social outings, but not in adult settings – particularly where one's parents are present. The positive social functions attributed to drinking include helping to overcome shyness and signifying that one is grown-up. The benefits that binge drinkers reported to Sheehan and Ridge (2001) were: helping them relax more, helping them to be less shy, enabling them to be less socially inhibited, making it easier for them to talk to boys, and allowing them to feel more connected to the group (p. 361). These meanings are listed in Box 8.1.

A major reason for drinking among females is what Abel and Plumridge (2004) call becoming 'disinhibited'. This state goes further than feeling relaxed: it encompasses release from normal social decorum, displayed in weird and rowdy ways. One informant explained that, 'when you're pissed … you're more like to just want to run around and do all sorts of crazy stuff'. Another said, 'Yeah, it's fun, cause you do these really weird things and in the morning you feel funny … and everyone laughs at you' (p. 495). Johnston and White (2004) found similar motives in a group of Australian young women, who not only sought release of their inhibitions through binge drinking, but expected and accepted the negative side effects, such as behaving in an embarrassing manner, having a hangover and feeling sick.

The meaning of smoking for adolescents of all ages is tied up with images of coolness and the presentation of self. From interviews with the clique of 'top girls', who were self-confident, dressed smartly, and hung out with boys after school, Michell and Amos (1997) suggest that smoking was deliberately adopted by these girls as 'part of the top girl package or social identity' rather than from any explicit peer pressure to smoke. The 'pressure' was there, but it was more pervasive, and tied to social categorization and acquiring a popular social identity. They comment that 'girls of 11 and 13 associated going up the pecking order with smoking' (p. 1868) and with projection of an image of confidence and social maturity. Adolescents who are no longer at school use smoking as well as drinking 'as a facilitator of peer bonding' and as 'a marker of acceptable identity' (Wiltshire *et al.*, 2005, p. 614). Getting a job and moving into the different social spheres beyond school led to the initiation of some young people into 'social' smoking, while for the majority it increased and reinforced their smoking.

Abel *et al.* (2002) explored the motivations of *tryhard* girls, who were despised but thought that they could use smoking as 'a lever to group membership'. Their informants described their tactics for trying to get into the cool group: 'they bring smokes to the school and don't even know how to smoke them'; 'they try to smoke behind the bushes'. When asked why these girls and boys began smoking, the informants suggested that they 'wanted to be cool', adding that, 'I don't think it was peer pressure cos like they don't really press people into smoking … it's your own choice' (p. 331). Lest it be assumed that young people automatically equate high status with smoking and illicit drug use, these behaviours are not key markers of identity across the entire peer spectrum. Pearson and Michell (2000) explain that different groups of girls smoked for different reasons, and that health risk activities 'had no salience in the lives' (p. 32) of other peer groups.

Gender contributes to the complexity of the relationship between social identity and smoking. Plumridge *et al.* (2002) reported the experience of boys who refuse to smoke and still are regarded as cool, through the route to peer respect and acceptance that is available to them by sport. This route is not available to girls. The conclusion reached by these investigators is that the greater uptake of smoking by adolescent girls may be explained by their situation in terms of peer relations, where 'girls are struggling with fewer social resources than boys to accredit themselves as worthy' (p. 178).

Among young adults in college who are already smokers, a more complex set of influences seems to be operating. Kenford *et al.* (2005) studied the progression of smoking among experimental or occasional smokers at college. They found that the likelihood that they would become regular smokers was sustained by beliefs about the functional value of smoking together with features of the social realm and lifestyle of young adults.[2] The key influences on whether these college students were still smoking four years later was not the number of friends but the number of smoking *venues*, including parties, group activities, and studying alone in one's room. What is interesting in this study is that once young people have been initiated into smoking, they are not compelled to become daily users even when the habit is addictive; rather, their smoking behaviour is related more to 'the degree to which smoking became intertwined with daily experience' (p. 291).

Rethinking peer pressure

Given the research reported in this chapter, phrases such as 'peer group influence' and 'peer pressure' cannot continue to be bandied around as catch-all explanations for health risk behaviour. The notion of peer pressure has proven to be more subtle than the words imply. Given the evidence for peer influence, I suggest that we turn the question around, and instead of asking how do peers influence young people, enquire into the conditions that lead a person to behave in a way that is similar to that of her/his peers. By adopting this perspective, we acknowledge that influences on behaviour are complex and multiple, that they are cultural and setting-specific, that they can have positive as well as negative benefits, and that they are not constant.

Without a more precise appreciation of how peer influence operates on behaviour, those involved in health education programs are left with a concept that explains everything but clarifies nothing. Moreover, when intervention programs are considered from a motivational standpoint, we find that youth needs for acceptance and recognition, the role of social contexts as sources of stimulation, and the timing of interventions all come into consideration. For example, Delorme *et al.* (2003) found that their respondents described several forms of peer pressure when recalling their first experiences of smoking. Some experienced direct pressure in the form of goading or daring them to light up; others were motivated by a desire to be accepted by the smoker group or to gain the approval of a particular peer, such as a boy they wanted to impress. These accounts do not suggest that adolescents were pressured (that is, coerced) into having a smoke.

Where drinking is the issue, the peer pressure school of thinking assumes that young people are so unaware of the social context and so concerned about fitting in that they are 'easily led' into excessive drinking. Sheehan and Ridge (2001) demolish this argument. From their conversations with young women, they declare that we should give young women credit for their drinking choices, including their decision to get drunk. 'They plan their drinking, sometimes control their intake, or deliberately use alcohol to alter their mood' (p. 358). Sheehan and Ridge cite instances of how their interviewees adopted group protection strategies, 'looking out for each other' at parties and pubs. That meant the girls took it in turns to drink heavily, so that the sober one looked out for the binge drinker. They also made prior arrangements so that their friends were primed to intervene in order to prevent a girl from making a fool of herself in a situation where she had imbibed too much liquor.

Implications for intervention

What implications for intervention and prevention can be drawn from the research on peer influences? First, earlier claims of pervasive peer influence from an exclusive sector of peer society such as the best friend or small coterie of close friends are not supported by the research; and second, educational programs that emphasize the dangers of one group of peers while ignoring other sectors of the social network fail to understand young people's social worlds. Recent research points out that even where the evidence is clear that social forces are operating to influence individual behaviour, it does not necessarily follow that educational programs based on the social inoculation model, which alerts participants to this fact, will be effective. Some authorities doubt that it is possible to inoculate young people against peer influences arising from the perceived social benefits of smoking (e.g. Unger *et al.*, 2001). Educational programs that alert youth to negative peer influences on their behaviour are likely to meet resistance. Few of us find it easy to accept that our behaviour is influenced by group conformity: we prefer to explain our actions in terms of intrinsic motives and our personal choices. Indeed, the adolescents who were interviewed by Carter *et al.* (2003) emphatically denied that they were easily swayed by others. They argued, 'We're not sheep. We're individuals all of us ... we are our own people' (p. 233).

Rather than adopt a hostile view of the role of peers in socialization in smoking, it is preferable to note the value of peer relationships for healthy development, and recognize the folly of attempting to alienate adolescents from their friends in the misguided belief that youth are 'easily led' and socially naive. For young people, just as one finds for adults, friends are chosen on the basis of similarities of interests and attitudes, and smoking may be one of these. So it may be more appropriate to see smoking as an aspect of a group lifestyle than to assume it to be a necessary badge of group membership.

On the basis of what has been learned from this review, prevention of health risk behaviours in young people needs to take the following three aspects into account: context, transitions, and identity.

Context

Influence is exerted on individuals from the social contexts themselves. The ecology of these environments, where drinking and smoking are prevalent among throngs of people of the same age, establishes these activities as normative pursuits. Within the environments, each person is located within overlapping peer systems where one's best friends are surrounded by other friends and acquaintances. The non-drinker or non-smoker may be with her best friends, but the clique is immersed in a wider social crowd, where importance is given to drinking as a means of acquiring adult status and as a marker of social sophistication, and where their norms are pervasive. Moreover, we need to understand the social costs for a young person of giving up smoking or drug use. A doctor recounted the case of 'Paula', who took the decision to give up dope, and the difficulties that she encountered, such as anxiety and panic attacks. She found that to keep her commitment it was necessary to make a break from her boyfriend and her old group: 'It was too hard to stay off drugs while being with them' (Klinbail, 2005, p. 33).

Transitions

A further aspect for health education is dealing with the link between health risk behaviours and social transitions, including those that affect youth and emerging adults as they move into higher education and the workplace. In these new contexts, where affiliation with peers is an engine for identity growth, drinking and smoking operate as social lubricants for group attachment. Binge drinking and the use of illicit drugs are problematic behaviours associated with university transition. Weitzman *et al.* (2003) describe a 'comprehensive prevention approach' to binge drinking in college, but admit that such an approach is rare. This would include 'delaying drinking onset and discouraging high school consumption' (p. 33) before students enter college, along with college interventions that adopt 'environmentally oriented approaches to maximize substance-free housing and reduce access to cheap alcohol'. Weitzman *et al.* report that the implementation of these environmental changes on college campuses did reduce alcohol consumption and its related harms.

Identity

A challenge awaiting health educators is how to blunt the influence of social crowds in creating identities around smoking, drinking and the use of illegal drugs. The key component of the smoker identity is the partying lifestyle and appeal to the opposite sex. Lloyd *et al.* (1997) see that the challenge for prevention and intervention programs is to find ways of making the non-smoker identity more attractive to regular and occasional smokers. They point out that the identities of smoker and non-smoker contain different components, so that appeals to health (such as 'smoking shortens your life') or being mature (when maturity has different meaning for smokers and non-smokers) make no impact on smokers, although they may be successful with non-smokers. La Greca *et al.* (2001) alert us to the way that 'lifestyle clusters in health risk behaviour' are associated with particular crowd identities, and how these lifestyle clusters pose real difficulty for health education programs aimed at single risk behaviours such as smoking or binge drinking.

Whither health education?

Researchers have become sceptical that health education can arrest the trend of adolescent initiation into smoking, particularly among adolescent girls, whose rate of smoking has exceeded that for males for more than a decade. Indeed, Plumridge *et al.* (2002) comment that health authorities in New Zealand 'appear to be losing the battle to prevent smoking among the young' (p. 167), despite widespread knowledge of health risk. Governments are complicit in supporting the tobacco industry while wringing their hands at the rising general health costs that confront them.[3] One may question the commitment of governments to health education when, for example, Britain's revenues from tobacco were over £8000 million in the 2003–2004 financial year, but government expenditures on anti-smoking education and on assistance to quit smoking were £30 million and £41 million respectively.

Alcohol and drug education programs in Australia have been based on the principle of harm minimization – an overarching strategy that aims at reducing the many harms associated with drug and alcohol abuse by adopting a stance of reasonableness towards use rather than outright prohibition. Supporters of zero tolerance are opposed to harm minimization; they see it as going soft on drugs and 'sending the wrong message'. The Australian Drug Foundation said in their submission to the National Drug Strategic Framework in 2003 that never was such an approach 'so maligned, misrepresented and ill-defined'; but they added that when it is explained properly, it is 'understood and accepted by almost the whole community'. Harm minimization recognizes that young people have a right to make up their own minds about alcohol use, and that the majority do want to learn how to avoid the harms from alcohol, such as losing self-control, being sick, having motor vehicle accidents, encountering violence, and getting into trouble with parents or police. Programs in harm minimization contain activities where young people have opportunities to identify for themselves the situations that constitute the greatest potential harm and learn ways that these can be avoided. By recognizing that young people are capable of adopting a responsible course of action in relation to health risk behaviour, and of building their own protection strategy, this approach seeks to establish the appropriate basis of trust and respect that will encourage them to want to do so.

Part IV

Social support

9   Social support in schools

The fundamental task of schools is to create a community where students feel they belong and that their contribution is valued. Schools are communities whose very nature is based upon collaboration, cooperation and mutual support, and every day they perform minor miracles in shaping the lives of young people. In fulfilment of their role in fostering youth development, and buffering their students from the disturbances of outside events and social conditions, they are continually engaged in support work. Teachers are frequently required to reassure students who are adjusting to a new school environment, as well as respond to students who are upset by peer victimization. Sometimes the events are so distressing that students require counselling intervention. It would be wrong, however, to assume that providing emotional support or counselling is the only way to respond to students needing help. Support of an informational kind is also vitally important, even if these forms of support go unremarked in most writings on the subject. Support is wide-ranging in form, and the task of this chapter is to examine the nature of school support and trace the actions taken by schools to provide support to adolescent students.

Schools are engaged in the business of creating 'developmentally instigative environments' through support systems that connect students to other students, teachers, and the wider community. The disconnection that some young people experience in society challenges the school to find ways of connecting them so that they form attachments and gain a sense of belonging. The support structures that are put in place in schools, and the actions performed by school personnel, help young people build attachments to society. Among the questions that the chapter seeks to answer are these: What are the characteristics of a school that create a sense of community? What elements are therapeutic in the school environment? How is support enacted in schools and in the classroom? To what extent can peers contribute as helpers and supports?

Schools as supportive communities

The most obvious point of entry to the topic of support in school is how the school presents itself to the outsider, and the impression it makes on a new student. I begin with the most basic questions that a new student can ask about a school. What is the school like? Is it a friendly place? Do the teachers care about their students? Will I be happy here? Schools are much more than bricks, mortar, and panelled classrooms; they have traditions, memories, history, and procedures. These features underpin the atmosphere, climate, or ethos of a particular school and provide a frame for assessing its supportive qualities. Pace (1971) was one of the originators of the study of environmental quality in universities, and he captures the vibrant social nature of a university in these words:

> A university is a habitat, a society, a community, an environment, an ecosystem. It should be judged by the quality of life that it fosters, the opportunities for experiences and exploration it provides, the concern for growth, for enrichment and for culture that it exemplifies.
>
> (Pace, 1971, p. 14)

There is sunlight in this statement. It looks beyond the corporate face of a university to its social face, in a message of interdependency, life, growth, opportunity, and adventure. Pace's words prompt us to think of a university as a social system that is sustained by goals, purposes and traditions, directed at providing benefits to its inhabitants.

It is the social and communal aspects of colleges and schools, rather than their institutional features, which are emphasized in this chapter. The measure of their strength in promoting growth, enrichment and culture (both of individuals and of the society) resides in their collective, communal and interconnected structures, resources, programs and philosophy. People are their concern; and their goals extend beyond building up intellectual assets to include developing social assets and the accumulation of social capital.

Focus on the social setting of school

Recent years have seen calls from leading researchers in education for efforts to be directed at the social influences affecting student motivation, learning and achievement. For example, a major review of research by Wang *et al.* (1997) identified the major influences on learning, and noted that eight of the top eleven were 'social-emotional' in type – for example, parental support, classroom management, classroom climate, peer relations, teacher–student interactions. What is significant is that these calls for a shift in focus towards the whole school environment are also being made by researchers involved in school-based intervention research. There is a confluence of several previously separate streams of educational research – on school effectiveness, on the management of antisocial and risk behaviour, and on social belonging – each with separate empirical and theoretical traditions, and written for different audiences, which reinforces the earlier social climate tradition that is represented by Pace's statement.

A powerful driver of the change in emphasis towards regarding the school as a community comes from prevention and intervention programs. Their perspective has been variously termed prevention science (Albee, 1996), prevention programming (Greenberg *et al.*, 2003), and moving 'from risk to resilience' (G. Miller *et al.*, 1998, p. 365). Instead of earlier concerns with identifying the individual characteristics that contribute to risk, in accordance with a philosophy of social inoculation, emerging themes are a broad approach to prevention, a focus on the environment of school, and attention to the social-emotional climate of schools and classrooms. Intervention programs have come to recognize that the school itself is a crucial factor, and that comprehensive improvements must be made to the social environment before individual behaviour changes will become sustainable. The title of a review article by Reinke and Herman (2002) expresses the current emphasis: 'Creating school environments that deter antisocial behaviours in youth'. Educators seek to engage in 'social asset building' not only to increase student skills, but to enhance their connection to school. Thus they link the challenges of risk prevention among youth with the broader issue of school improvement and reform (see Greenberg *et al.*, 2003). Schaps and Solomon (2003) reviewed a selection of well-known comprehensive school-wide drug prevention programs in the United States, and listed the major factors emphasized by the programs: school supportiveness, sense of community, and student attachment to school. The programs first seek to establish a supportive environment so that students will gain the confidence to develop self-protective attitudes and behaviours. The authors comment that:

> Virtually every project that aims to change the school environment is trying to make it more supportive ... and thereby increase student attachment to school. Thus, the development of a sense of community is a central concern.
>
> (Schaps and Solomon, 2003, pp. 317–318)

In the discussions in these reviews on schools as supportive environments, frequent reference is made to social bonding, attachment, and sense of connectedness (McNeely and Falci, 2004; McNeely *et al.*, 2002; Townsend and

McWhirter, 2005). These terms are derived not from the literature on social networks, but chiefly from Hirschi's (1969) theory of the link between social bonds and delinquency. The significance and the continuing appeal of Hirschi's work lie in the importance placed on the adolescent's social bond with the school as a key protection against delinquency. Research on delinquency has confirmed the claims made by Hirschi that attachment to school – expressed as concern for their teachers' opinions of them, commitment to educational goals, and involvement in school activities – is a reliable protection against antisocial tendencies. However, the relation between school communal organization and student bonding has generally been assumed rather than demonstrated empirically. A recent nationwide survey by Payne *et al.* (2003) addressed this question of how schools operate to generate in their students a sense of attachment to school. The researchers speculated that the adults in the school create the school community through organization and collaboration, and express this sense of community in several ways: for example, in the daily transactions of school tasks and procedures, and in promoting a warm, inclusive and participatory climate for the students, so that students experience feelings of attachment and belonging. Importantly, they are careful to distinguish between the communal features of school social organization (which are 'external to the individual' (p. 754) and reflected in supportive interpersonal relations, collaborative practices, and a shared set of goals and norms) and bonding as an 'internal' process, resulting from personal attachment and commitment to the school. Their research findings provided some confirmation for these claims: schools that were more communally organized had significantly lower levels of delinquency and teacher victimization, and the students in these schools were more bonded to the school.

School as a small world

Let us return to the saying 'it's a small world' and how it may be applied to our understanding of the social environments of schools and colleges. An appreciation of the small-world structure of the school may be particularly valuable for examining and reviewing the flow of various kinds of information, including support as information that its members are valued. Previous chapters have shown that people are linked to others in a structured social world consisting of clusters of friends, relatives and acquaintances that are weakly linked to other clusters. To consider the school as a small world, we first need to discard the ideas attached to personal social networks. A school may contain a large number of these, but what is relevant here is to consider how the school as a whole functions as a social network. If we were then to map the social ties of school inhabitants, including students, teachers and administrative and support staff, using the relations 'knows', 'likes', or 'interacts with', the resulting network graph would show a pattern based on acquaintanceship ties rather than organizational frameworks such as staff and students, classes, year levels, or curriculum areas. This means that the school network would reflect other relations that link the actors in the clusters, some of which would be affiliation ties associated with membership in the same class or sports team.

Within the clusters, students, teachers, administrators and ancillary staff would be connected to one another by various exchange processes, many of which are maintained by regular face-to-face interaction. These ties cut across age and gender boundaries. Between clusters, the links may be of a different kind, based on formal organizational roles or specific acquaint-anceship ties. While the small-world structure of the school merits some degree of reflection in itself, the significance of this structure for promoting the development of its inhabitants deserves further elaboration. In contrast to a tight-knit family or community, where members are bound together by strong ties which can sometimes restrict individual development, the small-world structure is more permeable and more open to diverse sources of information, and thus capable of adapting to the changing needs of its inhabitants. This means that attachment security is balanced with exploration and adventure, and that the bonds of attachment to the school can enhance rather than impede the development of autonomy.

Developing a supportive school

Through these general practices of communicating a welcoming atmosphere and valuing both students and staff, a school builds the foundation that underpins its educational programs, as well as its actions at times of crisis support for specific groups of students. What is argued here is that a support philosophy should pervade the whole school rather than be an activity performed by selected members of the school staff. It is reflected in the concept of a *supportive school environment*. The essential nature of a supportive environment is 'care for the present and future well-being of all students' (Tasmania, 1988, p. 48), and is captured by McMillan and Chavis (1986) in the concept of 'sense of community'. They wrote that:

> Strong communities are those that offer their members positive ways to interact, important events to share and ways to resolve them positively, opportunities to honour members, opportunities to invest in the community, and opportunities to experience a spiritual bond among members.
>
> (McMillan and Chavis, 1986, p. 14)

Based on their original work, we can distinguish four features of a supportive environment:

A *supportive environment creates a sense of community*

Schools are most effective when they are equally concerned with the morale of teachers and the well-being of students. The notion of shared ownership and mutual support is captured in the concept of community. Initially a school is a collectivity of individuals. Through the application of order and routine, it becomes an organization. But it takes personalization of roles, conduct that is respectful of others, and a corporate identity for it to be transformed into a community.

A *supportive environment establishes a sense of membership*

Membership refers to the sense of shared belonging and personal relatedness to the school. Through membership each person is associated with others, identifies with the larger group, and gains emotional security from that knowledge. When people value their membership and that of others, the very act of valuing reinforces their status and place as part of the school, thus integrating them into the institution.

A *supportive environment is sustained by shared emotional connection*

Shared emotional connection is based on a shared history. The greater the commitment to this history, through investment of energy and involvement with other community members, the greater is the emotional connection. Schools use activities and rituals to build traditions that link students together. Sharing in common events assists in making all members of a school conscious of their roots, helps them to feel a sense of honour and pride, and increases their awareness of the values they hold in common.

A *supportive environment promotes healthy interpersonal relationships*

The school community is comprised of the networked relations of its members. By sustaining open communication and positive interpersonal relationships, members strengthen their connections to one another and seek to act for the common good of all. The community as a whole is alert to the concerns of individuals, responsive to changes in their well-being, and able to respond early to signs of emotional disturbance or distress.

Providing support

The quality of the school as a supportive environment is detectable in how it responds to newcomers, how it manages crisis events, and how it cares for students and teachers in the ups and downs of daily school life. We examine each of these aspects in turn.

Transition support

New situations contain elements of uncertainty. For young adolescents, moving into a new middle school or secondary school remains an adjustment problem despite the fact that it was identified as a problem in Britain and North America more than fifty years ago. 'It was scary and no one seemed to know anything. We all stood around in bunches like wet rats' (Power and Cotterell, 1981, p. 10). These words capture the misery and uncertainty in young adolescents not yet assigned a classroom and thus not yet part of their new school, huddled lumps of humanity standing in the rain. Like refugees and victims of a natural disaster, they wait patiently for someone to take charge and tell them what is happening. The school newcomer is unsure what to do and where to go; s/he is apprehensive and fearful of doing something wrong. S/he comes to the new school with a feeling of dread, expecting the worst. One diarist wrote, 'I stayed way from the gym because I thought something fatal might happen.' When the expected calamity failed to materialize, they were relieved, and reported in their diaries that 'Nothing much happened to me today, and I felt alright.'

Adelman (1988) says that when a person is uncertain, 'A sense-making strategy is to seek feedback and assistance from others' (p. 185). In school transition, an important element is information about how things are organized so that newcomers can be part of the system and not outside it. The simple kinds of support from teachers that relieve student anxiety are shown in Box 9.1. Barber and Olsen (2004) found that connection with a teacher

---

Box 9.1 Experiences of teacher support in school transition

- I started worrying about when to get my books, and then the teacher told me what to do.
- The teacher was just as nice today as she had been (yesterday).
- The work we did today – I thought it would be hard, but it wasn't. It was fun.
- When we started English, the teacher was really friendly. He even made a joke, and I enjoyed English for the first time.

---

was the most salient factor in alleviating anxiety during school transitions, but unfortunately student perceptions of support from teachers 'decreased at every transition' (p. 22) through the education system. Evidence from longitudinal research such as that of Reddy *et al.* (2003) also shows that not only does teacher support as perceived by young adolescents 'wane significantly', but the effects of declining teacher support were traceable as well, in lower student self-esteem and in greater levels of depression across the years of middle school.

The format of some school responses to student uncertainty is through counselling and special support programs, but the format of other responses utilizes organizational structures, curriculum resources and teaching strategies. For example, schools often create school-within-a-school structures as supportive environments for young adolescents who are newcomers to secondary school, and these have had dramatic effects on improving teacher–student relations and in strengthening attachments of young adolescents to the school. The mini-schools are described in the STEP project devised by Felner and his co-workers (e.g. Felner *et al.*, 2001). This work underlines the importance of creating a bounded environment where the people and the procedures are familiar, so that students feel safe and that they belong.

Crisis support

Schools are not immune to traumatic events. The images that come to mind are the *Time Magazine* photographs of grief-stricken adolescents clinging to one another in the wake of the shootings at Columbine High School which left thirteen people dead. How does a school deal with fatalities among its students from shootings or terror attacks? The trauma can engulf not only the students but teachers and administrators as well. When a school mourns, what support is available to the many people who are grieving?

The impact of a traumatic school incident, such as a shooting or an explosion or a school bus crash, on members of the school is likely to be considerable. Estimates of the proportion of students, teachers and administrators who will experience post-traumatic stress range from 65 to 85 per cent. People are left numb with disbelief. Their emotions are drained while they grapple with trying to understand how and why the catastrophe has occurred. In discussing the impact of violent traumatic events on young people and the implications for crisis support provision, Jordan (2003) has proposed a trauma and recovery model that distinguishes between primary victims and secondary victims, who show different responses to the catastrophic event. Primary victims comprise those who are injured or who were directly involved in the event as witnesses or as persons who reacted to the threat by hiding or protecting themselves. Secondary victims are those who hear about the event and are 'empathically engaged' with the victims. Jordan's model of coping with a catastrophic school shooting suggests four stages from trauma to recovery for these victims: experiencing the traumatic event, displacement or separation, loss of a loved one, and recovery. For each stage, she describes behavioural responses, cognitive responses, and psychological needs. Her article provides a framework for understanding the trauma associated with catastrophic violence which can assist psychologists, counsellors and mental health professionals in their support work with victims and their families.

Schonfeld (2002) described the reactions of adolescents to the traumatic events of September 11, and discussed the roles that health care providers can take in order to help them. He drew attention to the fact that although a terrorist attack is a shared experience on one level, it is also 'fundamentally a very personal experience' (p. 302) which each person reacts to differently. He lists some potential symptoms of adjustment reactions to terrorism as including sleep problems, anxiety, difficulties with concentration, and pessimism about life. As adolescents move through the reaction to the trauma, and struggle with disturbing images, feelings, thoughts, and recurring traumatic memories, they may also regress, so as to become 'more demanding or more selfish, or have more difficulty getting along with peers and other family members' (p. 306).

Schonfeld points out that the post-traumatic stress reaction that causes the greatest difficulty for receiving help and support is an avoidance of any thoughts or feelings associated with the traumatic event, in what he calls 'psychological numbing'. This reaction to events that are emotionally overwhelming has been reported before: people insulate themselves from their feelings and interpretations of the details by displays of disinterest and a lack of emotion about the present or the future, and submerge themselves in the matters of everyday existence, which they perform in a perfunctory manner. When someone shows interest in them or expresses care or concern, their retort is 'Whatever'. In recognition of these kinds of reaction, Schonfeld puts an emphasis on informational support, helping adolescents to understand what has happened and to express their emotions, arguing that 'children and adolescents are better able to deal with a situation if they feel they understand it' (2002, p. 305). An interesting point he makes is that a question may sound as if the adolescent is seeking information when the real question is whether or not they are safe; that is, whether the world still operates according to the same old rules.

With regard to terrorism, Miller (2004) reminds his readers of the limited impact of therapies for the victims. He warns that we should not expect families to 'totally work through' the trauma of their loved one's murder and that we should avoid using phrases like 'You'll get over it'. He says, 'They won't'; and adds that, 'The intended effect of terrorism is, after all, a psychological one' (p. 13), which means that the increased fear, anxiety and hyper-vigilance that people experience in the aftermath of a terror attack are not easily dispelled. In these circumstances, trained mental health professionals will be 'vital resources' (p. 13).

A trauma and grief psychotherapy devised at the University of California, Los Angeles (see Layne *et al.*, 2001; Saltzman *et al.*, 2001) is being used in schools both in America and overseas, where children and adolescents have been victims of traumatic violence through school shootings or war. Its school-based group approach, and the fact that it is evaluated, justify its inclusion in this chapter. The aim of the program is to reduce post-traumatic stress. Therapy consists of five foci: the traumatic experiences and individual stress reactions; reminders of trauma and loss; post-traumatic adversities; the interplay between trauma and grief; and recovery and developmental progression. Therapy is conducted in schools but not in class time, generally before or after the day's classes, and consists of twenty sessions in four modules. These contain handouts, group exercises, and discussion topics, and are conducted by two therapists. Group activities include therapeutic exposure to the trauma, cognitive restructuring, stress-management and relaxation exercises, and practical problem-solving. The program was implemented in Bosnia and Herzegovina in twelve schools in 1997–1998 and in a further thirty-two schools the following year, and has continued since, sponsored by UNICEF. The effects of therapy were evaluated in a Bosnian population of eighty-seven adolescents and youth, 15–20 years of age. Researchers found that approximately half the students showed clear improvements in reduced stress and grief symptoms, and that these reductions in distress were accompanied by higher levels of positive adaptation, such as greater compliance to school rules and increased interest in school. Similar reductions in complicated grief symptoms and improvements in school performance were reported in young American adolescents who had been exposed to community violence and then participated in group psychotherapy (Saltzman *et al.*, 2001).

Because there are formidable barriers to refugee families obtaining counselling support from mental health professionals in countries like Britain and Australia, schools may be the only place where help is available. In Britain, a manual has been devised by Patrick Smith and his colleagues that equips members of the school who are not mental health professionals with the knowledge and procedures necessary for using the program with students who have been traumatized by war. It adopts a 'psycho-social-educational' approach, and includes cognitive behavioural techniques. Although it has already been employed in various countries, it had not been formally evaluated until Ehntholt *et al.* (2005) conducted a counselling intervention among adolescents in a London school. The adolescents were refugees from war-affected countries where they had been exposed to high levels of war-related trauma. The authors reported a 'statistically significant but psychologically modest' effect of the program. The severity and intrusiveness of post-traumatic stress symptoms were diminished in their adolescent participants and there was an overall improvement in their behaviour. Two months after the conclusion of therapy, the benefits had faded, which is not surprising, given that the news is full of bombings and destruction, and given that many adolescents still had relatives in their home countries who remained exposed to violent conflict. The merit of the approach lies in demonstrating the benefits that arise from the collaboration of health professionals and teachers. It shows, according to its authors, that 'a population of children that does not readily access mental health facilities can receive such help through a school-based service' (p. 247).

Support services in crisis events are always going to be insufficient. A side effect of the terrorist attacks of September 11 was the trauma of students in schools in downtown New York. The total population of these schools was 3400 students. The response of mental health professionals was to devise support programs for the schools in the form of psycho-educational services. Brown and Bobrow (2004) discussed the problems encountered by mental health professionals who were not part of the school when implementing these kinds of school-based support in a crisis situation. The four main goals of their psycho-educational program were to provide information that would increase the knowledge of trauma reactions among students, school personnel and parents; enable normalization of these reactions to trauma; connect students to professional social support; and promote healthy forms of coping. Following on from the information phase, they expected to work in the schools assessing and counselling those students who had identifiable levels of distress. However, only about 200 students received assessment and treatment from the intervention team. The conclusion made by Brown and Bobrow was that psycho-education was an effective means of reaching a broad population of children and adolescents in a short period, but that there were flaws in the strategy of rapidly mobilizing a team of professionals to work with schools. For example, some mental health professionals were uncomfortable with the concept of school-based interventions, while schools for their part were resistant to the assessment and treatment program. The authors admit that school personnel and parents might have been more accepting of the intervention phase if the psycho-educational program had begun with the teachers and parents, and got them on side before the materials were distributed to the students.

Everyday support

How do schools create a community in their everyday practices? Secondary schools are complex structures with many of the features of corporations: they are comprised of specialist and ancillary staff, and led by a management group which has oversight of the school's varied resources and assists communication across its sectors and departments. The individual can easily become lost in its buildings and departments. But most schools adopt practices to humanize their environment, and try to cultivate an atmosphere that is open, friendly, and welcoming. They conduct their work with the minimum of fuss and formality so students can move around the school relaxed and comfortable in its many settings. Principals are not locked in their offices but mingle with the students. One in my acquaintance would sit down with his students and even share their lunch, while another was out of her office and interacting with students to such an extent that younger adolescents were unaware that she was actually their principal!

The philosophy of openness and accessibility is endorsed by the teaching and administrative staff as part of their meeting routine. It can be detected at the staff morning tea, which is held at least once a week in Australian schools. Some private schools with a boarding school system hold catered morning teas on a daily basis. While the informal gatherings have social (and gastronomic) attractions, they serve to oil the wheels of school communication and maintain the sense of community among school staff. Indeed, the school morning tea is the place where news is disseminated, small meetings arranged, and opinions canvassed on policy matters.

Extra-curricular programs

An important means of integrating young people into the school and into the community is through participation in extra-curricular activities. The benefits for students are that they feel more connected to their school and more identified with it. Generally speaking, the level of adolescent involvement in extra-curricular activities is high. For example, Mahoney *et al.* (2002) report that 75 per cent of 14-year-olds participate in structured activities outside the classroom, and Feldman and Matjasko (2005) give a figure of 70 per cent. The benefits of participation have been confirmed by several major reviews over a period of almost twenty years (including Gilman *et al.*, 2004; Holland and Andre, 1987; Jordan and Nettles, 2000; Mahoney *et al.*, 2003; and Marsh and Kleitman, 2002). In the most recent of these reviews, Feldman and Matjasko (2005) list the benefits of student participation in school-based structured extra-curricular activities as follows: positive attitudes to school and higher academic performance; reduced rates of school dropout; lower substance abuse (but this is qualified); lower delinquency; less sexual activity (among girls); and better psychological adjustment. Marsh and Kleitman (2002) take a different approach. Given that there is a great diversity of extra-curricular activities, they identify differences in effects according to the types of activities. They found consistently positive effects from participation in academic clubs and school journalism, and mostly positive effects from participation in sports and in performing arts.

What accounts for these benefits? Feldman and Matjasko (2005) reason that the benefits of extra-curricular activities arise from several features. First, the settings themselves provide opportunities for youth 'to act out developmental tasks' in ways that classrooms do not provide (p. 161). Second, youth have the chance to build new social ties with adults and other peers. And third, involvement strengthens adolescent connections to the school and their identification with it. Mahoney (2000) has shown that for antisocial youth, participation in extra-curricular activities has the potential of introducing them to peers who are outside their antisocial network, and this factor adds to the positive impact. However, the benefits need to be qualified, as they depend on changes occurring in the individual's network. Where the young person remained in their network of antisocial peers, extra-curricular participation had negative effects, which suggests that network composition influences the nature of peer support, either to resist change (where the network is a delinquent one) or to sustain it (where the new network contains prosocial peers).

One of the justifications for holding a school camp for the students entering the middle school, or for the incoming seniors in the high school, is to break down barriers between different peer networks. Batiuk *et al.* (2004) report the case of a middle school that has employed camps as a regular strategy for reducing conflict among cliques and thus improving the climate of the school. The program is simple. It withdraws students on a weekend retreat and assigns them to teams of six to eight members, each monitored by a teacher. The teams are the basic units for cooperative activities conducted over the weekend, during which adolescents participate in exercises in conflict resolution. Evaluation of the program found that there was a distinct reduction in intergroup conflict when students returned to school.

The camp strategy is also advocated by Salmivalli (1999) as a means of resolving the problem of group bullying. We have seen in earlier chapters that her research has highlighted how peers other than the bullies contribute to school bullying. For example, the reinforcers or urgers do not participate directly in the act of bullying but they maintain and support it by their interest and curiosity in watching the bully activity. Another group is the outsiders who refrain from involvement but 'allow bullying to go on by silently approving it' (p. 454). Camps allow for the dispersal of cliques that foment bullying by assigning them to different groups that are then required to work together. Salmivalli calls this intervention 're-networking the class', because the intervention creates the chance for new ties to form.

Schools offer opportunities for stimulating activity for those students who are not interested in sport, through music and performing arts. Many of the community arts programs are unreported by researchers because they are local and so commonplace (like the annual Gilbert and Sullivan concerts in schools, the class plays, and local drama festivals) that their value is taken for granted. A community arts program in West Melbourne (Stokes, 2003) links young emerging artists with other youth to create drama and dance forms. The artistic and dramatic activities provide a medium for young people to develop a confident voice through which they can express their feelings and concerns.

More widely known is the rock eisteddfod, which emerged in Australia in the late 1970s as a way of promoting healthy lifestyles for adolescents 12–15 years of age. Thus a 'soft-sell' approach to drug and alcohol prevention soon grew into an Australia-wide competition known as the Rock Eisteddfod Challenge, and has since become an international movement variously known as the Smokefree Stage Challenge in New Zealand, the Rock Challenge in Britain, and Rocka in the United States. It provides young people with a great deal of enjoyment, creates group attachment and strengthens the sense of community in a school. Participants say, 'you have the time of your life'. They have the chance of 'having fun with your friends, getting stage experience, and supporting my school'. Because parents are involved as helpers in making costumes and stage props, the rock concert activity links the school and its students to its local community.

Schools have also included performing arts in their curriculum in response to student demand arising from the rock eisteddfods. The health prevention benefits of participation and social integration are convincing, and justify its continued sponsorship by major corporations; but the engine of change lies at the interactional level: in fostering peer relationships and adolescent connections to adults, and affirming adolescents' energy, initiative and imagination.

Sources of support

Support from peers

Peers are a valuable educational resource for helping their fellow students deal with a variety of learning and adjustment issues. Adolescents often prefer to discuss personal concerns with peers rather than school personnel.

The positive social benefits that accrue from peers as helpers only gained recognition from studies that investigated peers tutoring each other in structured learning environments. Once this information became available, a plethora of studies emerged on how to enlist peers as helpers to deal with many issues that confront students in schools today.

Peers provide support in different forms that range from peer mediation and peer counselling to peer-assisted learning. I have deliberately grouped the instructional forms with social support forms to emphasize the valuable role that peers can play in natural helping systems, and not just as crisis supports. In a special issue on peer support in the *Journal of Adolescence*, Cowie (1999) comments on 'the enormous potential that peer-led interventions have for deepening our awareness of interpersonal relationships and [for] illuminating controversial aspects of our life in contemporary society' (p. 436).

Peer support groups

Concerns that are common to young adolescents in the transition from primary to secondary school (or middle school) are about bullying, lack of friends, difficulties with schoolwork, and bossy and unfriendly teachers. What can peer support do to alleviate these concerns? Naylor and Cowie (1999) describe an anti-bullying system; Rainey *et al.* (1997) explain how to set up peer support groups; and Logan (1997) reports on facilitating a peer consultation group. Naylor and Cowie found that in schools with a peer support program to reduce bullying, creating a 'caring school' was mentioned by 87 per cent of teachers, 75 per cent of peer supporters and by at least 40 per cent of the potential users of these systems. They also note that many of the student victims reported that the existence of a support system had given them strength to overcome the bullying problem. This illustrates how peer supporters can act as a buffer against bullying.

Despite consistent evidence that peer helpers can benefit other students across the domains of learning, interpersonal development and social adjustment, teachers have often been reluctant to employ students in instructional and counselling roles. It seems surprising that teachers would devalue peer contributions to the classroom when small-group work has frequently been advocated as an effective form of learning. Cooperative group work is considered difficult to set up, with training needed in interpersonal and small-group skills if the group is to work effectively. But peers cooperate naturally in other cultures and in non-school settings, so the problem may be one of our own making, in that we place such emphasis on competition and individualism that peer groups are regarded as structures that exist for us to manipulate.

Turner (1999) discusses ways of training young people in listening and basic counselling, as well as mentoring them so that they can function effectively as supports, without being overwhelmed or isolated. She warns us not to see peer support systems as a cost-cutting exercise or regard it as a replacement for formal support. It is a support process in its own right. She writes:

> A peer support project is not quick or easy to establish and is not a cheap alternative to professional services. Peer support requires skilled and committed adult support and supervision to function effectively and, crucially, to prevent young peer supporters handling complex psychosocial and emotional problems inappropriately on their own. Peer support is not automatically self-sustaining and organization, planning and persistence are needed for an effective initiative in the long-term.
>
> (G. Turner, 1999, p. 570)

Peer counselling

Peer counselling, helping, and mentoring are support systems that operate as protective processes, where students learn how to help and counsel their peers. Ehly and Vasquez (1998) see peer counselling as a valuable form of support that can complement the counselling work in schools, and argue that students should be actively involved in establishing a support system in the school. Students 'commit to a coherent agenda of activities that bring them into contact with fellow students [who are] requesting the assistance of a peer' (p. 219). Recognition of peers as support resources, encouraging them to provide support to fellow students, and valuing their capabilities as helpers are marks of a supportive school.

A major source of practical wisdom on peer counselling is the work of Tindall (Tindall, 1995; Tindall and Gray, 1989), who recruited peers as counsellors when she found herself inundated by student concerns in her role as a school counsellor in a middle school. Realizing that she would never reach all the students needing help, and that counselling resources would always be inadequate, she built on the tendencies of young people to rely on their peers as helpers. Her peer counselling program is based on 'strategies that give away counselling skills and attitudes' (Tindall and Gray, 1989, p. 1), and takes the advice of Miller[1] that was given twenty years previously. Tindall's philosophy is counter-intuitive to the traditional view of expertise, where only the qualified expert is allowed to provide counselling and support, but she regards that view as privileged and exclusive.

Characteristics of peer helpers

How we spontaneously react to other people, without preparing ourselves to respond to a problem, determines our impact on those needing our help. Brammer and MacDonald (1999) state that, 'Our personalities are the principal tools of the helping process' (p. 36), and we would do well to use them to advantage. What personal characteristics are important if peers are to be effective in providing support? Attitudes and behaviours such as giving careful attention to what the other person is saying, knowing something about their circumstances, and responding to their concerns by getting quickly to the heart of the problem, all convey a sense of expertise that translates into benefits to the other person as well.

Listening is the foundation for effective communication. When someone is described as 'a good communicator', we think that such a person is skilful with words, and able to find a way of expressing ideas, feelings, or points of disagreement that enable disputing parties to find common ground. But they may be skilful with silences. Through the silences of good listening they find the right words.

Silence can be an effective tool, but adolescents often lack the patience to be silent until they find the right words. For example, when a young person is seriously ill and his mates pay him a visit, what store of experience can they draw upon in order to say the right thing? In one such case that I am familiar with, a 13-year-old who had been treated for leukaemia was recovering at home after chemotherapy, and his schoolmates called to see him. The conversation turned away from the nature of his illness and how he was coping with it, to what he was going to do about his surfboard and skateboard, and which of the group might expect to inherit them! Adolescents need practice in the skills of communicating concern.

When a listener is focused on the other person, s/he is alert to what emotions the person is showing as well as to what the person is saying. The listener indicates their attention in subtle ways – through eye contact, body posture, 'pacing' their listening signals to the rhythm of the speaker's story, nodding, shifting their gaze, and making various murmurs and sounds that confirm that they are following. The other person picks up on these cues, relaxes and becomes more willing to express feelings and seek help. Genuineness is important in communication with young people. Drury *et al.* (1998) warn that adolescents who are being helped are not fussy about particular communication skills, but instead value 'shared meaning and understanding, and negotiation between different points of view' (p. 178). In short, adolescents are not conned by fake listening. The implications for training peer helpers are that we should emphasize their personal qualities and genuine willingness to help as a precondition to learning such skills as attending, reflexive listening, and paraphrasing.

Support from teachers

What is meant by teacher support? Educational psychologists have fallen into the trap of thinking of teacher support in warm fuzzy tones. Phrases like teacher nurturance and caring carry a notion of support as soft, but support can be expressed in hard ways as well. Teachers can communicate that they care for their students in instrumental ways. Reassurance is communicable by giving direction and guidance, rather than only by smiles. One can be caring but uncompromising, strict but fair, thorough but unsentimental. Teacher support is not one-dimensional. Of course, teachers may at times adopt roles as counsellors, parents, and even friends to adolescents. But the teaching role is the one for which they were trained, and it is a complex and demanding one. At times teaching requires the performance skills of an orchestra conductor, the decisiveness of a drill sergeant, the encyclopaedic knowledge of a quizmaster, the logistics grasp of a battle commander, the passion for discovery of an explorer, and the sense of humour of Billy Connolly.

Insights about adult–adolescent relations outside the classroom (see Chapter 10) suggest that what is important for young people is the opportunity to learn for themselves, where they can be assisted to develop their competence and sense of agency. Young people of various ages have said for decades that classroom structures limit their agency and autonomy, and that there is a sameness and predictability to their classroom experience that is sometimes only relieved by mucking up. What is missing is novelty and challenge, either through hands-on discovery or through work that is highly demanding, even if in performing it they are likely to make mistakes. Young people shouldn't have to wait until they undertake postgraduate research or until they join the Peace Corps to have opportunities for authentic learning.

What has failed with young adolescents is instruction that is skill-focused, but content-free. The secondary school's emphasis on teaching the basics of literacy and numeracy 'because they didn't learn them well enough in primary school', thus delaying students' exposure to complex and challenging material until the skills are established, does little for students' interest in classroom activities. Learning becomes a chore. On the other hand, when learning is contextualized, students employ the skills of expression and calculation as they seek solutions to problems that have relevance to their lives, and find that they are 'doing' maths without difficulty. Students respond positively to the opportunity to apply knowledge, to generate and construct meaning, and they work harder.

The instructional support exercised most commonly in effective classrooms has been called 'instructional conversations' by Tharp and Gallimore (1988). In these formats teachers prod students to think further and more deeply by listening, asking, reviewing and discussing. Teachers are involved as joint participants with students in the learning journey rather than as voices shouting instructions from the sidelines. The conversations follow the progress of learning in the individual student or in the group, with the teacher supplying feedback through affirming nods and murmurs, as well as by alerting and follow-up questions, in ways that link students' actions and decisions to reasoning and understanding. In the classrooms where I have observed this 'joint productive activity' (Bradford, 1999) – and I have witnessed it across a wide spectrum of the curriculum – the participants seem to be pulled along by the intrinsic challenge of the enquiry itself. Meaning is derived from the application of knowledge and skills in such a way that participants have a 'eureka' experience of deep learning, somewhat like the 'flow' that is produced by intense concentration in challenging outdoor activities.

Classroom support

If motivation is central to the problem of schooling for adolescents, as I argued in Chapter 7, what are the implications for teachers? Teaching is essentially the creation of environments. Through interacting with the students, a teacher establishes a task structure and creates a social climate that fosters student involvement and learning. Seifert (2004) analysed the major psychological theories of motivation so as to translate them into general principles that make sense to teachers, and concluded that 'ultimately the critical factor may be how the teacher and students interact' (p. 148). I would add, with the concept of attachment in mind, that an important aspect is how the teacher and students *relate*. Research by Patrick *et al.* (2004) highlights the importance of how teachers relate to their students, from the very beginning of the year, for establishing the foundations of a supportive classroom environment. They observed nine Grade 6 teachers, and found evidence that teachers who established harmonious supportive relations at the beginning of the school year, using humour, respect, empathy, and a positive view of the year ahead, encouraged respect and thoughtfulness among their students. Moreover, there was less evidence of disruptive behaviour and of self-handicapping avoidance strategies among their students.

A substantial body of research exists on classroom goals and motivation. For example, Deci and his co-workers (e.g. Deci and Ryan, 1987; Ryan and Deci, 2000) have conceptualized instruction in terms of support for the satisfaction of the needs for autonomy, relatedness, and competence. Autonomy is seen to be fostered by teachers who allow students room to show initiative and take responsibility (e.g. Reeve, 1998); relatedness is promoted by a style of teaching that shows care and acceptance (e.g. Wentzel, 1997); and competence is fostered by challenge and instructional feedback. An observational study of teachers by Reeve *et al.* (1999) contrasted autonomy-controlling and autonomy-supportive teachers, noting that while the teachers were similar in style in many respects, they differed in the amount of initiative they encouraged from their students. The controlling teachers sought student compliance, whereas the autonomy-supportive teachers displayed the following qualities: they listened more, gave fewer directives, asked more questions, resisted giving the solutions, responded more to student-generated questions, and offered more 'perspective-taking' statements. Wentzel (1997) focused on teacher support from the viewpoint of 'pedagogical caring'. She found that young adolescent students made a distinction between teachers who care and teachers who did not care along two major dimensions: the extent of their 'democratic interactions' in the classroom, and the emphasis they placed on students as individuals. For example, the caring teachers communicated in an open manner that listened to the students and paid attention to their views, in contrast to an uncaring style where students were told what to do, yelled at, interrupted or ignored. The caring teachers also treated their students as persons. They spoke to them by name, noticed when they were struggling with the schoolwork, and asked them if something was wrong. They were ready to offer help with an academic problem and took time to make sure the student understood the work.

Belonging

An associated concept is that of classroom belonging, which Goodenow (1993) defined as 'the sense of being accepted, valued, included and encouraged by others ... and of feeling oneself to be an important part of the life and activity of the class' (p. 25). She investigated the role of classroom belonging as an influence on classroom motivation, and found that belonging related strongly to student expectancies for success across four school academic subjects. Peer relationships contribute to adolescents' sense of classroom belonging, and it appears that establishing a cohesive class and a sense of attachment early in the year has positive benefits. Hamm and Faircloth (2005) found that students who begin the year with the sense that they belong are more likely to have a positive view of the classroom climate at the end of the year. In another study, Faircloth and Hamm (2005) found that networks within the classroom contribute to students' sense of belonging across the school year. However, the peer networks became more differentiated in the course of the year so that the sense of belonging within networks became more similar, but between networks it became more dissimilar. This finding suggests that belonging relates to the kind of network that students are affiliated with. Students whose peer network felt a strong attachment to the class were themselves likely to feel they belonged, whereas for students whose network did not feel attached to the teacher or to the class, their sense of belonging deteriorated. Faircloth and Hamm recommend that:

> The strategies adopted by school personnel to tap into belonging to animate student motivation and achievement should capitalize on the multiple avenues through which students can be connected to schools, while remaining sensitive to potential variability across the ethnic groups represented within the school.
>
> (2005, p. 306)

What are the implications of these aspects of support for preventing school truancy and early dropout from school? The accepted argument is that adolescents truant and drop out of school because they do not feel they belong, and the alternatives to school are more attractive. Research suggests that the early adolescent years are a crucial period for preventing student disengagement from school, and that effective prevention requires change in the nature of schools themselves. It is generally agreed that changes in the school environment, such as greater teacher vigilance and monitoring of student absence, a pastoral approach to students, a concerted attempt to make the school a welcoming place, and a more responsive curriculum, are essential if student absenteeism and truancy are to be reduced. Where schools have adopted such strategies, the results are impressive in improving the overall attendance rate and in reducing truancy.

In reality, supportive environments occur at different levels of the ecological environment – peer to peer, classroom, and school – and efforts to promote supportive relationships can profitably be undertaken at any of these levels. The consequences are highly important for enhancing student academic motivation and achievement through these efforts at fostering student attachment. Faircloth and Hamm (2005) make the point that belonging is 'the underlying factor in the relationship between motivation and achievement' (p. 305) rather than 'a correlate of achievement'; in short, when teachers create a classroom (and school) where students feel attached to their teacher and integrated into the classroom networks, students are able to direct their energies to academic matters, and become more engaged in classroom tasks and more ready to interact confidently with others.

Underlying this discussion of community and supportive environment in schools and within classrooms is an ecological or contextual understanding of social environments, and central players in establishing and maintaining these environments are the teachers. Few people would dispute their importance as support providers in relation to school achievement, but the message from this chapter is their centrality as supports for students across the wide range of school experiences. Their influence as significant others in providing support to adolescent students was explored by Rosenfeld *et al.* (2000). Instead of comparing the relative importance of different support sources (parents, friends, teachers), they viewed these different significant others as members of the adolescent's support network, each supporting the adolescent student in different ways. They found that the greatest benefit to the student occurred when teacher support was *complemented by* parent and peer support. They wrote, 'Although teacher support appears to be a necessary condition for positive school behaviour, affect, and outcomes, it is not a sufficient condition' (p. 219), and is most effective when combined with support from parents or friends. Moreover, the support that seemed most valuable was informational, insofar as it reduced students' uncertainty about specific school matters, and enabled them to be more in control of their circumstances. It provided students 'with the insight to recognize alternatives to their stressful situations, the skills to make their school experiences more positive, and the awareness to recognize the help available from teachers, family and friends' (p. 220). What is of crucial importance is teachers who build trust, establish a classroom climate of mutual respect, and relate to their students as real people. CBS television host Dan Rather once said, 'The dream begins with a teacher who believes in you, who tugs and pushes and leads you to the next plateau, sometimes poking with a sharp stick called "truth".'

Conclusion: creating a supportive ethos

At various points in this chapter, I have referred to the ethos of the school as a place where students feel welcome and where they feel valued for themselves. What actions can be taken in school administration and in curriculum in order to create a supportive school? I conclude with six suggested actions.

1   *De-institutionalize the school.* This means establishing an environment that emphasizes the human aspects of the organization, where institutional protocols are made as invisible as possible in order to serve its student clients. Schools should manage time and space in order to enrich student experience. At present, many schools have impoverished spaces for students to meet and socialize; some are so crowded that students compete for a few metres of turf, and they are so noisy that you can't relax. Students are allowed use of the spaces not claimed by buildings or other structures, suggesting that little thought has been

given to adolescent social spaces in schools, including where students hang out when they are not in class. There should also be periods of uncluttered time; liberal management of time recalls the practice at Rugby school where the academic curriculum was limited to the mornings, and the afternoon was opened up to sport and leisure.

2   *Humanize the curriculum.* Provide diverse pathways to adolescent accomplishment. This means that student initiative and endeavour are valued across many domains, and not merely in academic and sporting areas. Schools should promote diversity and a rich educational experience through art and craft, technical activities and cultural events. Invite community organizations like the bonsai society, the chamber music group, or the vintage car club to stage a fair. Establish a program of regular talks by speakers with interesting lives or achievements, for example an Olympic rower, a local historian, a biochemist, an Antarctic explorer, a hospice chaplain. Arrange that some of the speakers are invited because of their stories and others because of their collections (of photographs, rocks, gadgets) which could be displayed at the school.

3   *Start upstream, before the problems have become wide and deep.* This means giving attention to students' needs for acceptance, recognition, and mastery and being alert to student disengagement and distress as early signs of school dysfunction. There is now more than fifty years of research identifying the negative impacts of school transition on adolescents' motivation and achievement. Leading researchers in the field have continually recommended that schools create environments that are more appropriate to young adolescents, and they have produced evidence that these environments produce positive benefits. Moreover, school practices should enable students to have a voice on issues of personal concern. This means establishing a pattern of regular but informal discussions on a slate of topics that are posted in advance, conducted by the school counsellor or chaplain with input from a guest. The purpose of these sessions is, first, to provide an agenda for normalizing the discussion of delicate topics in science, mental health, ethics or religion, to help students talk about matters of personal concern (e.g. my mother is dying of breast cancer) without being 'counselled' about them. A second purpose is to make access to support as easy and informal as possible through establishing a habit of school meetings, so that anyone can turn up to a discussion without people assuming that they have a problem.

4   *Maintain connections between the school and its constituency.* This means establishing regular and direct contact between school personnel and members of the business community, to focus on the

mutual benefits of the connection for education, student employment and business prosperity. Openness to the community includes regular contact with parents on the kinds of subjects covered in this book, in informal meetings and newsletters, which goes beyond supplying parents and members of the community with a school newsletter as the basis for 'communication'. It also means that members of staff are encouraged to maintain their professional expertise as musicians, geographers or linguists by active participation in their fields as well as through involvement in professional associations, so that their own lives are richer and the school benefits.

5   *Ensure that school staff are accessible to students and to fellow members of staff.* This means managing time as well as space. Design physical settings and plan social events within the school to increase the opportunity for informal contact among teachers, as well as between students and teachers.[2] Locate teacher common rooms near to the students. Remove as many institutional barriers as possible between the teachers and their students so that students can approach any teacher without fear, confident that the teacher has their best interests in mind.

6   *Value the students for themselves, not for what they achieve, and make the message known.* This means implementing many of the support principles discussed in this chapter. Make the climate welcoming, so that students know that they are important and that the school wants to form an attachment with them rather than expecting that the student should show allegiance to the school. It also means fostering contact with past students (alumni) out of real interest in their lives after graduation, rather than for fund-raising purposes. Strategic contact with them and publishing news concerning their activities and achievements are some of the ways of valuing students after they have completed their schooling.

10 Youth and community organizations

This chapter reviews the opportunities for social support provided through network ties to youth and community organizations. It examines how youth encounter adults through these organizations and form attachments that integrate them into the society. The kinds of questions it seeks to answer are these: What contribution do adults make in connecting youth to society? What are the characteristics of productive relationships between young people and adults? How important are youth and community organizations for building attachment in youth, and for creating their sense of place in the community?

From a networks perspective, youth and community organizations provide a means for young people to widen their network range by forming relationships with adults outside their family, as well as with other youth. Becoming a member of a youth club is a social experience. While the individual is taking part in recreational activities, s/he also has opportunities to make new social contacts, form new friendships, and acquire different values. These settings also allow relations to form between adults and youth, and for the adult leader to communicate that the young person matters as an individual. More broadly, these relations generate a sense of connection and belonging. Over time, interaction with club members and participation in the activities and rituals lead to the formation of attachments between the young person and the club, and an investment in its culture.

The focus of the chapter is youth capabilities rather than youth problems. Such a stance reflects my own interest and experience, but sits easily with emerging themes in the youth literature like positive psychology (e.g. Rich, 2003), youth assets (e.g. Scales *et al.*, 2000), and positive youth development (e.g. Roth and Brooks-Gunn, 1998). For too long, young people have been 'problematized' by researchers and policy-makers, as if the only justification to study youth or spend government money on them was to 'sort them out'. Overlooked in youth problem research is the obvious fact that most young people lead perfectly normal and untroubled lives. Our goal should be to enlist youth knowledge and idealism for the benefit of society, rather than shut them up from contributing to the community. Positive youth development is concerned not with placing limits on young people but with providing opportunities, challenges, and exposure to new experiences. Roth and Brooks-Gunn (1998) expressed the view that 'Young people need access to safe places, challenging experiences, and caring people in their daily lives' (p. 427).

Youth work and youth organizations

Youth organizations are often located within a discourse on the productive use of leisure space, to allay public fears of disruptive youth roaming the streets unsupervised. The very word often attached to such youth work – organized – conveys a message of adult supervision or control, and suggests that a sense of purpose and direction attaches to these public endeavours. In contrast to the historical concerns with socialization and control, new voices (e.g. Hirsch *et al.*, 2000) are more concerned with providing environments suitable for young people's personal development. The viewpoint taken in this chapter recognizes the value to youth of adult direction, but agrees with Hirsch in valuing the agency and capabilities of young people themselves. Community contexts and youth organizations are examined in terms of their potential to provide challenges, create fun, and promote skills, as well as offer access to supportive adults.

Contested public spaces

We are interested in youth organizations as ways of structuring the social environment for young people, mindful that the clubs and programs created by previous generations may no longer be acceptable to or appropriate for the youth of today. Young people have different leisure interests from their parents, and it is not surprising that they prefer to spend their leisure time with those of their own age. The preference for socializing with one's own age group and with people having similar interests is accepted for the seniors in our community, but it has long been considered a problem where young people are concerned. When young people are seen massing with their friends in public areas, there are calls for greater supervision and control. For example, Panelli *et al.* (2002) analysed media constructions of youth in newspaper articles and letters to the editor in Dunedin (New Zealand) across a period of nine months. Several negative youth themes were prominent: youth as troublemakers, youth as victims, and youth as irresponsible. Public space featured in about 11 per cent of the stories. Concerns were expressed about unsupervised youth hanging about without good reason, which suggest that some adults think that young people have no rights to public space. In contrast to the largely negative articles in the newspapers, young people themselves provided much more balanced reports of their use of public space, including suggestions for overcoming the negatives in their experiences.

Public spaces have long been favoured by youth as places for hanging out and for meeting their friends. Past generations congregated on street corners, and some youth still do; but suburban shopping malls have replaced street corners as meeting places for many urban young people. Lewis (1989) described these places as 'social magnets' and estimated that adolescents visit these places every day, for hours on end. For some young people, he notes, 'their social life revolves around the mall' (p. 885) because this is the only place where they can escape from the difficulties of home and school. Indeed, young people may claim these spaces as their own; Gill (1991) noted that teenagers who met regularly in Chadstone mall, in suburban Melbourne, regarded it as 'not only the civic space but their space'.

Plazas and open spaces in the city centre and adjacent to suburban shopping malls often serve as assembly points and marshalling arenas for young people on Friday and Saturday nights, where friends can meet and organize themselves into crowds for a later entertainment activity. They are also zones of high social stimulation, in a general hubbub with lots of people just standing around, seeing and being seen, and just being part of the action. Clark and Uzzell (2002) identified the affordances of public spaces like the town centre at Guildford, near London, for 11- to 15-year-old adolescents. They found that the town centre afforded the leisure opportunity for youth to be active, free to be themselves, free from parent pressures, in their own space with similar people, and able to meet up with friends. Clearly, public spaces are associated with meeting people like oneself where there is an absence of restraint. Woolley and Johns (2001) described how skateboarders used spaces in the town centre to establish territories so they could engage in an active form of hanging out. The factors in choice of location that were important for young skateboarders were 'accessibility, "trickability", sociability and compatibility' (p. 228).

The increasing restrictions placed on youth access to public and quasi-public space have the effect of creating barriers between adults and young people. Planning of town spaces by authorities is seldom youth-friendly. Crane and Dee (2001) remarked on the 'exclusionary potential of new urbanism' for restricting youth access to public space. For example, development in urban design such as the gentrification of older areas into high-rise residential precincts, the creation of walled suburban residential developments, and the renewal of urban brownfield spaces have similar effects in excluding young people from areas of the city that were previously accessible. Woolley and Johns (2001) found examples of surfaces in town squares being altered to make them unsuitable for skateboarders to use, without providing alternatives for young people's use. Within the quasi-public (but privately policed) shopping malls, spaces are designed for traffic flow, not for loitering or for casual socializing in groups. Thus, by design, gatherings of young people in shopping malls are social anomalies that must be 'moved on' by zealous security guards. Concerns over the use of public space by young people need resolution, through better urban planning as well as through new forms of youth organization, because the future of our cities depends on integrating young people into society, including respecting their use of leisure space.

Origins of youth organizations

Youth work has its origins in the activities of churches and voluntary organizations in the eighteenth and nineteenth centuries. These bodies were concerned with providing structures through which adults could reach youth and connect them to the orderly world of adult responsibility and citizenship. They were committed to youth socialization, to mould character and develop citizens, so that young people would acquire habits of diligence and self-control, rather than congregate in groups, separate from adult society, aimlessly whiling away their time. Over the ensuing years, the meanings associated with youth work have widened beyond the religious and moral focus of organizations such as the Sunday school (begun in the 1780s) and the YMCA (begun in 1844). The emphasis on promoting moral behaviour and character development has enlarged to recognize the educational validity of leisure and recreation; and the focus has shifted away from 'muscular Christianity' towards social relaxation and personal development so that individuals can obtain greater enjoyment from non-work time. For example, the YMCA began as a Bible class and Christian education program, but soon widened its activities to include physical education in the gymnasium and cultural activities. Its invention of basketball promoted skill development in team games.

There have been major shifts in program emphasis in the YMCA over the last eighty years. Putney (1997) notes that they mirror changes within the larger society, from concern with character-building in the early twentieth century, to emphases on skills and self-reliance in the 1960s, and the 'narcissism of personal wellness' in the 1980s. As the 'Y' has moved 'upscale' to supply facilities for corporate fitness, the previous emphasis on clubs has diminished and the old gyms and meeting rooms for young men have been replaced by fitness studios. Putney regretfully comments that the three sides of the YMCA triangle – body, mind, and spirit – have blurred into one: the body. An observation made by the editors of the same book is that the religious underpinning of the YMCA clubs has now 'all but disappeared' (Mjagkii and Spratt, 1997, p. xi) in cities around the world, along with the original concern to provide city youth with a social space.

The Scouts movement began in 1907, and remains the world's largest voluntary organization. The number of young men who had been Boy Scouts exceeded 66 million by 1981, and the number of girl members had reached 25 million in 1991. Scouting, like the YMCA, was structured for group socialization. Its programs were designed to appeal to the assumed gang-like characteristics of adolescent boys – with activities like exploring, climbing, collecting, outdoor camping and lighting campfires. The bushcraft that was integral to scouting derived from Baden-Powell's experiences in guerrilla warfare from Afghanistan to Zululand; and the importance of leadership and group cooperation that was fostered in the army transferred well into the scouting formula. The Scouts movement grew rapidly, fuelled by an enthusiasm from its founder that never diminished. In some ways the creators of the uniformed groups that emerged in the early part of the twentieth century were like Peter Pan, forever adolescent. Notably, Baden-Powell, Seton, and Beard Robinson all married late, if they married at all. For example, Baden-Powell married when he was 55 years old. In his history of scouting, MacLeod (1983) suggests that their own bachelor experiences may explain their policy of encouraging boys to make a partial break from their families, join boys' groups and stay in these, rather than 'become involved with girls' (p. 142).

The clubs and societies were designed not only to structure the time of young people but to bring them within the reach and surveillance of adults. For example, each troop in the Scouts and the Boys Brigade was overseen by adults, although they had a leadership structure that placed older adolescents in charge of younger ones. In this respect, the youth organizations sought to arrest the 'drift' away from adult contact into unsupervised peer company, and prevent the presumed antisocial consequences of peer association. This concern with structuring youth leisure time has been roundly criticized by some radical sociologists as being reformist and welfarist, but they miss the point. There are well-documented developmental benefits that flow to young people from the community provision of structured recreational activities, as Mahoney (2000), Mahoney and Cairns (1997), Marsh (1992) and Marsh and Kleitman (2002) have demonstrated, and there are further advantages for youth from having access through youth organizations to competent and caring adults.

The value of structured recreation

Compared with unstructured leisure time, structured forms of recreation provide shape and direction to enhance individual enjoyment. Activities conducted within an organized framework allow youth to develop skills, and much skill learning involves adults as teachers or mentors. Most modern youth organizations provide some opportunity for the learning and mastery of skills, as they always have; these may range from learning bushcraft and first aid in the Scouts or Guides, to using light effectively in a photography club, or playing goalie in a sports team. Surfing would be regarded as about as free and unstructured a form of sport as one could imagine, yet surfing and board-riding competitions that arise at local levels and extend to international levels depend on the contribution of adults and older youth for their organization. The organized forms of the sport of surfing exist because they provide benefits to participants – such as challenge and assessing one's skills against those of others – that are unable to be achieved in any other way. Moreover, the adult organizers often obtain sponsorship from local businesses, which helps provide equipment and facilities during a competition, and they recruit local helpers at the surf carnivals for the essential tasks of serving barbecue steaks and cold refreshments!

The research has shown that structured forms of recreation, ranging from sports to hobbies, yield greater satisfaction than unstructured leisure (e.g. Delle-Fave and Bassi, 2003; Dworkin *et al.*, 2003; McGee *et al.*, 2005). For example, Delle-Fave and Bassi cite 17-year-olds who saw the value of team sports in demanding their concentration, their best effort and self-control, as well as the enjoyment of meeting their team-mates and sharing the fun of the sport. Structured youth activities also divert adolescents from association with older and deviant peers (Mahoney and Stattin, 2000), and connect them to caring adults in their community who are available when they need advice or support. Adolescents are not corralled in youth organizations and brainwashed by adults, as the critics may suppose. They remain agents of their own development. The distinction is nicely made in the Dworkin *et al.* (2003) study. They quote a young woman whose previous experience had taught her caution and not to believe what coaches told her, but the opportunity to interact regularly with her coach through the club structure led her to newfound respect. As a consequence, she said, 'I chose to take what he [her coach] was telling me and apply it to my life.'

Further evidence of the impact of participation in sports clubs and youth groups comes from the Dunedin longitudinal study, where McGee *et al.* (2005) draw on data from early adolescence to young adulthood to conclude that club participation is associated with growth in youth personality and sociability, and the strengthening of youth attachments to parents and peers, and also to their school or workplace.

From a networks perspective, voluntary organizations can be appreciated as social structures comprised of ties between members. Not only do social networks link actors to other actors: they also link actors to groups. Thus joining an organization confers social benefits in the form of ties to a whole new pool of potential friends. In addition there are the benefits from links to unrelated adults, and the coping resources conferred on youth from adults' supportive influence in their lives. Membership of a youth organization not only exposes youth to the activities provided but introduces them into 'the productive social network' of the organization (Gilman *et al.*, 2004), where adult and peer members function as informal sources of support and education, and assistants to young people in interpreting their own biographies. McGee *et al.* (2005, p. 1) state that the effect of participation is 'to widen the social convoy to which young people are exposed', and they conclude that 'from a youth development perspective, the support and promotion of different organized groups in the community is critical' (p. 15).

Overlooked in much of this research is the role of church youth groups as sources of support and as agents providing young people with direction in their lives. Little is known about participation in church youth groups. A national survey in the USA in 2001 found that one in three adolescents attend Sunday schools and youth groups and 60 per cent attend services of worship. The same source noted that young adults in America are 'significantly less likely' than other age groups to attend church services or act as volunteers in church programs.[1]

The importance of churches, mosques and temples as community centres and resources for youth needs to be recognized. Indeed, the key role played by black churches in the community life of African-Americans dates back to the American Civil War, yet the black church has been termed 'the invisible institution' because so little is known about it. Where studies on church groups do exist, they tend to focus on the protective and buffering effects of youth participation in reducing their involvement in serious crime (e.g. Johnson *et al.*, 2000) or in rescuing youth from the dangers of street culture (e.g. Cook, 2000). Nevertheless, the studies also quote individual young people talking of themes central to this chapter, such as their sense of belonging (feeling 'at home'), their adoption of standards of behaviour consistent with church values, and their access to a social network that contains caring and competent adults. Cook also found that youth group membership provided the Boston adolescents with gainful activities – something to do – which diverted them from risky street crimes and violence.

Team sports

Evidence of the benefits of team sports for youth development is found in the research. Sport channels youth energy in creative and productive directions. Participation in team sports connects the participants to the broader community of the school or the town or district that the team represents.

Morris *et al.* (2004) conducted a study on sport sponsored by the Australian Sports Commission and concluded that team sports had a positive effect
on young people's social skills. No direct relation was established between
participation in sport and a reduction in antisocial behaviour, but Morris
commented that the consensus view is that sport and physical activity have
a positive influence on the conditions that generate antisocial behaviour,
both through reducing boredom and by instilling positive attitudes.

Sport contains rules not only about the game but about player behaviour
as well. This is the reason that cricket has become an attractive sport in
Compton, Los Angeles, where youth workers have applied it as a form of
youth programming. According to Ted and Theo Hayes, the promoters, the
appeal of cricket is its 'etiquette', which accepts the umpire's decision without dissent, in contrast with the spoil-sport behaviour found in baseball. Ted
Hayes said: 'If it is baseball and the umpire calls you out, you kick sand on
the umpire, spit on him, call his mother names, carry on and cause a fight.
But in cricket, you fold your bat, hold your shoulder up, your head up, your
chin up, and walk off the field in dignity because you played your best and
the umpire's the last word' (ABC Radio National, 10 September 2004). The
Compton program of 'cross-generational mentoring' through cricket has
grown in popularity to the extent that a team travelled to England in 2004 to
play a competition match. On the tour, the etiquette paid off when the team
was entertained by Prince Edward at Buckingham Palace. Hayes recounted
that, 'here was Prince Edward hanging out with these Mexican dudes, man,
and these homeless guys, black dudes; and he was very relaxed, and they
were very relaxed with him'.

Team sports, unlike individual sports and non-sport encounters, direct
the attention of players beyond the events of winning or losing an individual game, to cement them into the club traditions. A significant feature
of bonding the members of a sporting team together is what Fine (1988)
describes as 'the creation of collective meaning'. The emphasis on the lad-
der of progress links each game in the season to the whole, so that players are not only focused on winning a particular game but are also aware
of their part in the team's (and the club's) 'evolving history'. Team bonds
are strengthened as members collectively act to make meaning from each
game that is played. Team members will recall games where they narrowly
defeated a strong team, or where they won against the odds; and particular
team members will acquire legendary stature from some feat of skill (or
luck). Fine dryly remarked that these heroic moments 'have lengthy referential afterlives' (1988, p. 311). The custom of social anchoring to the group
through tale-telling is observed at any reunion. It is as old as time, and can
be traced back to the celebrations in the Norse sagas and in the dances of
the corroboree.

Wilderness adventure

Youth and the outdoors go together. Baden-Powell knew this; and Australian schools have long exploited this through special outdoor centres (like Timbertop, where the young Prince Charles was enrolled) or camping programs. Reddrop (1997) writes, 'Outdoor programs vary in format, context, and content, but they share one important element: they are all designed to challenge young people, either in an emotional, social or physical way' (p. 3). There is something special when you take forty 17-year-olds on an outback safari. They learn to share the duties of making camp, cooking, and cleaning; they tramp through the canyons to discover a magical wall of weeping rock, draped in luminescent moss; they stumble along a pitch-dark trail to reach a lookout just as the sun rises; at night they lie in their sleeping bags looking up at the brilliant stars; and they sleep like logs. At these moments the emotional and social benefits are memorable; and knowledge that they shared in special experiences provides a strong bond of friendship.

A feature of wilderness adventures is the group context. The nature of adventure pursuits means that people who begin the adventure as relative strangers must live in close proximity for days on end, encounter unpredictable natural elements together, and learn group cooperation in order to achieve their objectives. The group has an interest in each person's success because the group reaps the benefits of each individual's achievement. Ewert and Heywood (1991) comment that, 'the use of the natural environment as a place to promote and develop groups ... has become a popular education and management-training technique' (p. 593). Youth have to partner one another, or at least depend on each other's strengths. This relationship is in contrast to street situations which seek to probe the weaknesses of the other in order to enhance one's ego. The building of trust through partnership has a reinforcing effect on adult instructors too; at some of the outdoor education sites in Australia, instructors have volunteered to work for reduced salaries or just for their keep in order to remain involved when an outdoor centre was facing funding cuts.

Individual development

Wilderness also has a psychological impact at the individual level. An interesting characteristic of adventure challenges is what Ewert (1989) calls 'the aloneness inherent in the activities' (p. 56). On a rock climb, or kayaking over rapids, the individual is on their own in a contest with nature. Despite the presence and encouragement of others, the challenge is for the individual to perform, and it requires total concentration. There is no use complaining about the difficulties of the rapids or the discomfort of the cold, because nature does not listen to your complaints. You learn to put up with these discomforts and to persist with the task that you set yourself, knowing that each decision and action has an irrevocable personal consequence. Once you begin the rope descent, or enter the rapids, there is no turning back: you have to 'go through with it', and commit total effort, strength, and concentration. The outcomes of outdoor challenge include increased confidence with being able to cope individually in unpredictable situations.

To illustrate, I refer to three wilderness adventures that I observed, led by Rob Simson. These trips took 17-year-olds into remote sandstone gorge country in central Queensland. Group cooperation as well as individual initiative and endurance were tested. Their experiences included extensive hiking to reach the gorge campsite, exploration forays into side gorges where Aboriginal rock art was discovered, rafting journeys into the canyon sections, and even the butchering of a trapped calf, which we cooked. The meat was the toughest I have ever chewed. There was also the aesthetics of camping by a stream where the cream-coloured sandstone bluffs rose sheer, as backdrop to the bright flowers of golden wattles, purple hakeas, crimson bottlebrush, and soaring smooth-barked eucalypts, and where the only sounds were the birdcalls from flocks of parrots, wrens and honeyeaters. The culmination of the week's adventure was a compass trek through uninhabited bush. Each person had to carry food and water for three days and find their way through the dense bush to the pickup point some forty kilometres away in an adjoining valley. These adventures provided intense physical challenges unique to the adolescent participants. They alone experienced the tiredness of the hiking and the fear of becoming lost or injured; they had to make the decisions themselves and accept the consequences; and at journey's end they knew the joy of winning through.

Therapeutic adventure programs

The largest wilderness adventure project in Australia is Project Hahn in Tasmania, which has been running since 1993. It provides a variety of wilderness challenges for adults and young people, exploiting Tasmania's large areas of diverse wilderness close to its major cities. There are four- to six-day courses in caving, wild-river kayaking, mountain hiking and abseiling, as well as snow hiking and camping. Project Hahn excels in its comprehensive programming and has a well-developed educational rationale for its 'bush counselling' work with troubled young people. For example, it sets out five principles: giving and accepting constructive feedback, no put-downs, respecting physical and emotional safety, goal-setting at appropriate levels of challenge, and abstinence in relation to use of substances and sexual activity. It also has a low-fee policy, made possible through government subsidy, in order to make the programs affordable to a wide range of the community and to encourage attendance. Youth may be sponsored by agencies, or may elect individually to enrol in a course. Leaders follow a client-centred and non-interventionist approach, so that young people are encouraged to solve problems themselves and accept responsibility for their actions. This means that problems encountered on a hike are discussed between the adolescent and the counsellor in an open fashion, so that the adolescent is encouraged to explain what the problem is, aware that the decision is theirs to make and that the adult is not going to take over. The effect is to promote youth confidence and trust through reasoning rather than complaint, and foster growth in personal responsibility.

Some delinquent youth can benefit from adventure programs, but the nature of their problems should be taken into account before an assignment is made. When delinquent youth are enrolled in outdoor programs, the courses should include support from adults and not be offered with the purpose of 'toughening them up' through a punishing 'boot camp' type of experience. There are several reasons for this: first, many troubled youth are unused to the wilderness and become scared and unhappy; second, many are just not fit or skilled enough to profit from the outdoor challenges; and third, when youth are struggling just to survive each new test, they become angry, resentful, and uncooperative.

Australian television in 2004 featured a misguided attempt to 'sort out' five troubled adolescents by sending them on an eight-day trek across the Kokoda Track in Papua New Guinea, a tough challenge for the fittest walker. 'The experience of 14-hour-a-day treks was less than transformative', was Horin's wry comment (*Sydney Morning Herald*, 6 November 2004). Opinions were canvassed from experienced outdoor leaders on the merits of the trek. They all said that the physically demanding approach of Kokoda or the Tallong wilderness challenge (described in the previous edition of this book, and since discontinued) is destined to fail with troubled young people because the programs are too intense.

Survival treks seem to be more about adults punishing young people than caring about them. An 18-year-old described his gruelling experience of a three-day canoe trip in this way: 'Only one of us enjoyed it; the rest wanted to get back. It felt as if we were trapped.' There is a fine line, then, between wilderness adventure and wilderness torture. The guiding principle of youth outdoor programs has to be educational, where the focus is on building individual competencies and fostering self-development, not on making individual youth struggle to survive.

Youth and community service

At a period when democratic values are being extolled by political leaders, the role of schools and community organizations in contributing to civic engagement and responsible citizenship is attracting increased attention. The renewed interest in citizenship and volunteerism coincides with a time when character has regained a foothold in the literature on youth development. Citizenship is concerned with the individual's place in the wider community, whereas character focuses on personal qualities. Community service has long been regarded as a pathway to youth citizenship, and has been invoked over the years as a solution to public perceptions that young people are self-absorbed, disrespectful, and disconnected from adults in society. Service and volunteer work are widely valued as:

- a means of connecting youth to key institutions and the values of morality and selfless work for the good of others that these institutions uphold;
- a source of social capital through interactions with civic-minded adults and exposure to the norms and values of the adult world;
- an avenue for civic engagement, including participation in political activities;
- an opportunity to gain a sense of direction in life and moral anchoring and commitment to society.

School sponsorship of community service has grown rapidly in North America in recent years, as schools make a requirement that all students perform some community service. Almost half the American public high schools now offer service learning programs, and approximately 90 per cent of students attend schools where they have access to 'service opportunities' (McLellan and Youniss, 2003). The level of youth volunteering has traditionally been very high in the USA, compared with other countries, where the rate of youth participation varies from about 22 to 35 per cent. For example, the level of community involvement among adolescents in northern Europe and in Australia is low, although collecting for charities in these countries may be quite high. Da Silva *et al.* (2004) found that 'only a small proportion' of Australian adolescents aged 16–17 were actively engaged in the kinds of activity that indicate civic responsibility: political activities, community activities, or volunteer work; and furthermore, they displayed a low level of political awareness. It is difficult to say what proportion of youth participate in volunteer activities, given the definitions of participation, which may range from once in a year to once a week, and the different kinds of activities that are included, which range from helping in the annual Cleanup Australia to working regularly as an aide caring for disabled people. Roker *et al.* (1999) found that in Britain the range of youth volunteer activities was considerably wider than that portrayed in research, and that males were just as likely as females to volunteer. What they noted was that the students in their study, who were aged 14–16 years, were opposed to any form of school compulsion on them to become involved in community work; they regarded volunteering as an exercise of choice, an activity that was qualitatively different from school subjects.

Some authorities have noted that there is a general lack of involvement in politics and the community among youth and young adults. Andolina *et al.* (2002) undertook to strip away the meanings that modern 'Dot-comers' aged 18–24 give to terms like volunteering, citizenship, and community. They report that young people found the term 'citizen' largely irrelevant to them, expressed little trust in politicians and political institutions, and limited the concept of community to local concerns. Whereas experts had advised the research team that the 'Dot-comers' were concerned with issues of social justice and the environment, and were interested in working together to achieve change, the responses obtained in the focus groups from 'Dot-comers' themselves did not substantiate these claims. The 'Dot-comers' were interested instead in more present-day matters: their work, their friends and their families. They adopted a personal view of life, which placed a value on living honestly and respecting others' rights, rather than trying to change the world. They were not involved in group efforts on behalf of others, expressed little interest in consumer and political action, and had no desire to stay informed about the wider world. Andolina *et al.* (2002) found that they 'held very few illusions that their volunteer work would "solve" any problems' (p. 193) beyond those in their immediate situation. This stance is consistent with Stoneman's view. She writes:

> In comparison to their engagement in service, young people are not involved in politics in large numbers, either as voters or in campaigns, because on the one hand they do not perceive that they can make a difference; on the other hand, nobody has organized, persuaded, funded, and led them to be involved.
>
> (Stoneman, 2002, p. 221)

Developmental outcomes

Traditional views of community service have emphasized its protective and compensatory functions in youth development; that is, directing youth away from idle or unsavoury pursuits towards productive activities and fostering civic values, concern for others, and leadership skills. In this respect, its goals are very similar to the socialization objectives of youth organizations. Adults are comfortable with the notion of transmitting adult-approved social values and norms to the next generation through involvement in community service, oblivious of the contribution that young people can make to renewing society and energizing the adults around them. Indeed, youth participation in community programs is sometimes justified as a means of tapping into the idealism and energy of young people and increasing the number of helpers at the coalface, with no intention that their actions might serve a larger agenda, such as adults' own development and as an engine for societal change. What are the benefits of community service and volunteer work for young people themselves?

Volunteer work and community service are justified as fostering altruism, a necessary feature of many professions. Exposure to people in need through community service can shape an adolescent's future goals and lifepath, by bringing into sharp relief aspects of that individual's career plans and the competencies relevant to that career. Like Charlie Brown, who declared 'I love mankind. It's people I can't stand', the discovery that working with needy or dysfunctional individuals is 'not my thing' is better made early rather than late. One of the Pancer and Pratt (1999) informants explained that the experience of volunteer work 'helped me decide what I want to do with my life'. Having been a volunteer does not mean that one decides to build a career around working with homeless people or caring for the disabled, even if the experience was a positive one; rather, the concreteness of the experience continues to shape one's outlook and priorities, and gives focus to one's lifepath.

Researchers have noted that there is consistency in people's social or community orientation across extensive periods of their lives. It is evident in civic engagement by people who had been involved in civil rights activities twenty-five years earlier; and in the community leadership of persons who were members of 4-H and similar organizations in their youth. The consistency in these patterns of involvement suggested to Youniss *et al.* (1999) that participation in these youth organizations at a 'developmentally opportune' period was significant enough to shape their identity in ways that remained central to their adult lives. We can interpret this consistency in terms of the theory frames discussed in this book: social identity theory suggests that group identification with members in the organization and self-categorization as a member of the organization establish the kind of identity and values that become fundamental to the person's self-concept. Moreover, the ties established with people in the organization grow over time into bonds of affiliation and obligation. Metz *et al.* (2003) illustrate the operation of these social and psychological processes. They found that adolescents who participated in 'social cause' forms of community service (such as helping disabled or homeless people) were more committed to future voluntary service than were adolescents who performed standard kinds of community service such as tutoring, mowing lawns or office work. It is likely that working with voluntary groups as volunteers supplied richer meaning to the activity.

A theme favoured by Youniss is that identity development occurs through service learning: 'Participation in organizations and movements provides experience with normative civic practices and ideologies, and shapes youth's emerging identities in a long-lasting form' (Youniss *et al.*, 1997, p. 630). Participation works like an apprenticeship, where the young person engages in the day-to-day activities of work as a helper and is exposed at the same time to the workings and philosophy of the organization. Through 'participatory action' the young person is also engaged in identity work, as civic involvement in the organization generates a new social category membership which becomes incorporated into their identity.

Youniss and Yates (1997) studied the effects of community service on high school students who worked as volunteers in a soup kitchen catering for 300–400 homeless people of all ages. In this case, their continuing participation as volunteers was linked to the school curriculum through class discussions. What the investigators noticed were changes in attitudes and understanding across the year, as participants had opportunity to interact with homeless people on a daily basis, as well as with adult volunteers, and to reflect on their experiences through diaries and class discussion. As volunteers they encountered rudeness and hostility, which forced them to interpret the situation and their own role as helpers. They came to understand the daily stresses on the people they worked with, learning that such behaviour was not unexpected; and they gained an insight that their volunteer work was not dependent on receiving thanks and appreciation from those they helped. Their emotional reactions ranged from sympathy for the homeless people and guilt about their own initial prejudices, to anger that society and governments allowed the plight of these people to continue with no appreciable change in their circumstances. One student linked the rewards from his volunteer work to the Phil Collins song 'Another Day for you and me in Paradise'. Another admitted that the homeless people 'didn't need my pity. They needed my actions, and I didn't know what to do.'

Their development appeared to proceed along a course from concrete experience to awareness, to emotional commitment, to appraisal. At the appraisal stage, their own identity work appeared to produce at least three valid options: persistence (continued service), social activism, or withdrawal. Faced with complex and ongoing human problems – and the television world news reminds us of their immensity almost every day – denial and withdrawal are understandable responses. The invitation offered through volunteer work in the community is to begin. My own resolve was steeled by a comment I recall being made some forty years ago by the Anglican Bishop of Zambia at the time. In response to the individual feeling of powerlessness when faced with starvation in Africa, he said, 'All that the individual is asked to do is to take hold of the edge of a great problem, and work at some cost to oneself.'

Connections to significant adults

How does a young person learn to be socially responsible? What supplies a mature perspective that takes others into account? The long-held view is that the developing person benefits from exposure to authentic lives. The primary sources of authenticity are parents, but they include other family members as well as unrelated adults, whose characteristics are captured in the phrase 'significant others'. The discussion in this chapter is limited to the unrelated adults who are significant in young people's lives. We have already located some of these adults in youth and community organizations. Our next task is to examine the characteristics of these adults that make them significant supports. Is their encouragement a valued feature of the relationship? Or are they important because they take an interest in the young person's concerns?

Our understanding of support suggests that adults who are significant to young people are not restricted to providing advice or guidance. Attachment is also involved, and the attachment source supplies a sense of security and reassurance. The support functions are widespread and not directed at problem youth; indeed, this analysis of adults as significant others is directed at their role as informal or natural mentors who relate with normal young people rather than engage with at-risk youth. Natural mentoring occurs in communities and organizations where adults are visible and accessible, and where their personal biographies are known. In contrast to mentors who are recruited to help needy adolescents and who are trained for the task, most of the mentoring of youth that occurs in real life is 'enacted informally by ordinary people, often in response to exigent circumstances for short periods of time', say Stanton-Salazar *et al.* (2003, p. 238). That includes all of us.

Hendry *et al.* (1992) asked adolescents at Scottish secondary schools to describe the relationship functions of significant others using a method that encouraged them to describe actual persons known to them. The adolescents were in their first year (ages 11–12) or in their fourth year (ages 15–16) of high school, and were asked to nominate one family member and one unrelated person who were significant to them. Adults (mostly teachers and group leaders) were chosen as a significant non-family member by 34 per cent of the respondents, the remainder choosing predominantly same-sex friends. The prominent roles of the unrelated adults who were significant others for young people were believer, enabler, and teacher. The supporter function was endorsed only for friends. The teachers who were nominated were described as challenging, while the youth group leaders nominated were distinctively seen as role models. When younger adolescents were compared with older ones, only the believer characteristic maintained its importance across the age groups.

Tatar (1998) asked Israeli adolescents and adults to identify the people who were significant others for them during their own adolescence, currently (for the 360 adolescent respondents), or retrospectively (for the 395 adults). He defined a significant individual as one who the respondent perceived as having an important influence on her/him. Family members were identified separately from non-family members. Tatar found a remarkably high level of agreement between the two reporting groups concerning the importance of parents as sources of support (72 and 70 per cent for the adolescents and adults respectively), whereas siblings were important for 20 per cent. Differences emerged in the designations of significant others among persons outside the family. Whereas 71 per cent of the adolescents nominated same-sex friends, the adults gave less importance to peers (48 per cent) and instead nominated teachers (23 per cent) and other adults (13 per cent) as important to them as adolescents. These figures compared with much smaller nominations among the current adolescents. The marked differences in relative importance given to teachers and others by the adults in Tatar's study may reflect the breadth that a retrospective view brings to such perceptions.

The coach relationship with young people

In sport, the coach can occupy a formative role in a person's development. The coach's significance was evident at testimonial dinners held in Sydney in the mid-1990s, where former star Rugby League players took the opportunity to say how their lives were influenced by particular coaches. Players from Sydney's Eastern Suburbs premiership team of 1974 recalled how Jack Gibson, the legendary Rugby League coach, was available to players whenever they needed help. One quipped that in the interests of the players, he was 'out at all hours, never home, and sending his wife insane'. Because the club attracted 'young blokes from the country' who were naive about city ways, these young men needed direction. They benefited from being taught by the coach about the importance of training and self-discipline: 'Work hard, persevere, and you'll do alright; otherwise, get back on the bus and go home.'

Another legendary Australian coach is Wayne Bennett, who has been the Brisbane Broncos coach for eighteen years in the tough Australian Rugby League competition and has coached them to a record six premierships. In April 2005, Bennett was inducted into the modern-day coaching Hall of Fame after becoming the first Australian Rugby League coach to record 300 career wins. The simple approach taken by the former policeman to coaching and to his relationships with players is to emphasize the importance of character. A measure of his influence is the tribute from star five-eighth and Australian captain Darren Lockyer, who testified that Bennett 'not only has made me a better player, but a better man'.

Staging of the world gymnastic championships in Brisbane in 1994 prompted news stories about the mentor role of Frank Vig, the Hungarian gymnast known as the 'father' of the sport in Queensland because he helped hundreds of young people to develop their skills, several becoming Olympians. One gymnast recalled how he was 'always there at the "Y" [the YMCA] – he was a minder for us all. I could never have gone as far as I did in the sport without his help.' Such influences are notable when the statement is by an outstanding achiever: we can only speculate whether the testimonies of elite sportspersons are indicative of the experiences of lesser players. Perhaps elite players had greater opportunity to develop a special relationship with their coach. Now in his nineties, Frank Vig still has contact with some of his former Olympians. As I was writing this, he phoned to ask me to visit him, and we talked about his life. He told how he escaped the German army by less than an hour by rowing in the fog across a lake into safe territory. He later came to Australia as a refugee, and sought a job with the Brisbane YMCA as a part-time instructor, citing his past membership in the Hungarian Olympic team ('I wasn't near being the best gymnast, however'). The work grew and he became full-time director of the gymnastics program. At the recent dedication of a suburban YMCA in his honour, he made a speech in which he emphasized how important the 'Y' was to him by saying 'it saved my life'. While his words can be interpreted as meaning that the 'Y' gave a refugee a new start and shaped the direction of his life, Frank Vig explained to me that he deliberately chose that phrase to describe the deeper social impact that the 'Y' had made on his life, in giving him purpose, friendship, and a second home.

Teachers as significant others

Between 6 and 13 per cent of adolescents mention teachers as significant others, but Galbo (1989) believes that the impact of teachers is greater than the surveys suggest. He reasoned that adolescents 'do not perceive themselves in the same way that teachers perceive adolescents' (p. 551), so that the helping and guidance functions performed by teachers are masked by the teacher's formal roles. Galbo has a point. Sometimes it is only much later that the significance of the teacher at a critical point in a person's life is appreciated. Discovery of my own role as a significant other was uncovered in a reunion with former students whom I had taught nearly twenty-five years earlier. One man recalled the advice I had given him as a 17-year-old about being less introverted; another spoke of visiting my home with a group of students to plan a field trip (my house was close to the school) and what that invitation meant to him. Although they were important to these young men, I have no recollection of these actions.

Sometimes teacher influence is more dramatic, as Dorothy Rowe, the eminent psychologist who was recently voted one of the fifty wisest living people in Britain, described in an interview. An encounter with her history teacher on a railway platform changed the direction of her life. Rowe had been offered a university scholarship to be a teacher, but her family opposed her accepting it because she would be bonded to the state for five years. She recalled:

> I decided that I couldn't cope with the degree of unpleasantness I was getting at home and that I'd go down to Sydney and turn down the chance to go to university and instead go to teachers college ... and I was standing at the ticket office buying my ticket. That done, I turned around and there was my history teacher, Miss Wishart, and she asked me what I was going to do, and I told her what the problems were and she said, 'Don't worry about the bond. You go to university.' So I took her wicked advice.
>
> (Dorothy Rowe interview, ABC Radio National, 3 January 2005)

These examples of teacher actions stand out because they demonstrate genuine interest in students as persons in their own right. Most of the time, acts of this kind go unrecorded because they occur in a stream of general contact that from the young person's perspective seems unremarkable.

Recent years have seen a growing interest in the importance of teachers as agents for building adolescent resilience. For example, Debold *et al.* (1999) chose the term 'cultivating hardiness' in the title of their book about adolescent girls and their relations with adults. This book, like the writings of others, takes into account the perspective of young people themselves and their wish for closer and more equal relations with their teachers, sometimes denied by the formal structures of schools which create ambivalence in teachers about becoming friends with their students. Debold *et al.* cite instances where adolescents encountered teachers behaving naturally, 'like a person', including examples where teachers said or did something that showed they personally cared about the student, and 'know how I'm feeling'. Psychologists have extolled the importance of being authentic as a basis for healthy relationships; these writings point out that young people value authentic relations with their teachers. What is noteworthy is that these relations seem to emerge outside the classroom, where the settings are more informal and personalized so that both the teacher and the adolescent students seem more relaxed about interacting with one another. There is a possibility then that in extra-curricular settings and in organized youth groups adults have more opportunities to be significant others for some young people.

Youth–adult partnerships

A contributor to development as a citizen is adolescents' association with civic-minded adults. But outside the structure of organized youth clubs, how can such productive associations be fostered? Camino (2000) points out that 'adolescents operate on the fringes of adult community life' (p. 11), and previous chapters have charted the negative consequences of youth marginalization for health risk and antisocial behaviour. Clearly, if young people are to make productive contact with adults, the initiative must come from adult society. Recent research by Zeldin (2002) and Camino and Zeldin (2002) suggests that association with youth in community activities has benefits for the adults as well. The direct benefits for adults include positive beliefs about young people and greater understandings of themselves; and the indirect benefits are a greater sense of belonging and community cohesion. Zeldin (2002) admits that there are limits to these benefits. 'Adult confidence appears to diminish as the community-building activity requires adolescents to take on roles that have been typically assumed by adults' (p. 663).

The problem in youth–adult contact is that adults find it particularly difficult to relinquish their power in order to work alongside youth as equal partners. Camino (2000) explores the risks and rewards for adults that flow from establishing youth–adult partnerships in building community. Her subject matter is youth/adult partnerships (Y/APs), which adopt the goal of working with, rather than for, youth. She notes that moving beyond the principles of working together and mutual respect was 'not a smooth undertaking' (p. 14). The participants struggled to accept that being equal does not necessarily mean being the same, and that not interfering can also result in not providing the support and direction that young people may need at a crucial point in the project. The adults made mistakes of taking over, out of frustration that deadlines would not be met, and made other mistakes of hanging back when they should have been more proactive. Through these discoveries, youth came to learn ways of signalling when they wanted help, and the adults came to learn how to employ constructive feedback as a means of direction. In the process, important principles were learned about the nature of youth–adult partnerships. Adults learned to trust and rely on youth, and young people learned to accept their limitations in skill and knowledge, and to utilize the feedback to remedy these.

A source of wisdom for adults working with youth is Stoneman (2002). Her involvement began in the late 1970s, working with small groups of adolescents in East Harlem on projects to rebuild their dilapidated surroundings. This work has grown into a national organization called Youth-Build USA. Stoneman's article opens out the zones for adult involvement with young people while emphasizing the scope for youth leadership. She shows that as youth take more responsibility, the scope for adults to continue to support them does not disappear, but grows. Two themes are particularly noteworthy in her paper: the 'enormous energy' possessed by youth, and the point that youth civic engagement does not come easily. She writes, 'It takes a deliberate consistent effort to organize any group of people into any form of civic activity' (2002, p. 221). Instead of civic engagement, Stoneman prefers to speak of leadership development, where youth are taught that they can make a difference. Rather than direct, control, or entertain young people, her approach is to listen to them, learn from them, and give them access to the resources they need in order to implement their vision. Her emphasis is on the 'facilitative, respectful, liberating role' of adults, which she admits is contrary to the typical adult role where youth are concerned. She admits that the adult role that she adopts and recommends is 'one that takes concentration, practice, and oftentimes training' (p. 223).

Adults who are concerned about getting the job done 'properly' and efficiently will see these ideas as crazy because they value the process above the product; indeed for Stoneman the process is in many ways the really important outcome. But adults may not be aware just how authoritarian their leadership style appears to adolescents. A balance is needed between adult guidance and youth leadership; Stoneman (2002) argues that, 'Adults must take the initiative both to change the institutions and to activate and train the young people' (p. 224), and in many cases, adults themselves will need training in the necessary skills.

Developing close trusting relationships

How does a relationship develop to become significant? What are the attributes of such a relationship? They include trust, respect, open acceptance of the other (Carl Rogers's 'unconditional positive regard'), and genuineness in normal social interaction. Some suggest that a relationship between an adolescent and an adult person becomes significant when the adult communicates the idea that the adolescent matters as a person. This is evident in the testimonies of sportspeople already mentioned.

Beam *et al.* (2002) investigated the role of nonparental adults as very important persons (VIPs). They reported that 82 per cent of the Grade 11 adolescents they surveyed reported having at least one nonparental adult who played an important part in their lives. Half of these were relatives. The majority of the relationships had developed naturally and gradually, rather than as a sudden response to special circumstances. The relationship grew because the adult took an interest in the adolescent as an individual. There was very little conflict in the relationship, which was valued not only by the adolescent but by the VIP as well. One respondent said that her VIP 'gives me correct advice as an adult'. Others valued the opportunity to talk about anything personal without being set new rules or restrictions, safe in the knowledge that the VIP would not be shocked or judgemental, and confident that the adult would maintain faith in them. They commented that the relationship was unique in that it contained both parent-like and peer-like qualities, providing support that was beyond the capability of peers and an open-minded type of advice that was difficult for parents.

From the adult's perspective, there may be no conscious enlistment of the adolescent into an 'admiration society'. Often it is through a chance remark that the adult comes to realize that her/his relationship with a particular young person is significant, and that her/his actions and attention have made a difference to that young person's life. These relations are characterized by equality and depend, according to Gottlieb (1991), on the successful pairing of an attentive adult with a young person who needs to be recognized, within a freely chosen relationship. These adult–youth relations are free of social category memberships, so that the exchanges draw on different conversational routines, where the agenda is not concerned with image and self-display. Gottlieb and Sylvestre (1994) describe the qualities of the relationships between youth and their significant adults as 'marked by informality, spontaneity, acceptance, and sustained interaction' (p. 72). The qualities that appeal to youth were pointed out to Philip and Hendry (1996) by 15-year-old adolescents, who described two youth workers as a composite of adult wisdom together with peer-like informality. 'They go out with you' and 'they are alright to us'; 'they listen'; 'they give an honest opinion' (p. 195).

An additional dimension in my view is adult reserve, the practice of acting circumspectly at all times out of respect for the young person's own development. By exercising reserve, the adult puts a brake on their own ego, as a caution against becoming emotionally too close or intrusive. In my

---

Box 10.1 Principles for building relationships in youth work

Belief and respect	Have a realistic belief in what the person is now, and respect for that, without judgement or condemnation.
Integrity	Be what you claim and do what you promise.
Confidentiality	Be a person who can be trusted with other people's information and not disclose any of it.
Realistic limits	Know what you know and the limits of your knowledge and ability, and don't assume more.
Source of support	Provide back-up, advice, and a reality check.

(adapted from Martin, 2002, pp. 125–128)

---

experience as an adolescent, this reserve was characteristic of the support and understanding expressed by elderly unrelated adults. Like a bird on the window ledge, I was made welcome, but I remained free to come and go at my own choosing. I was accepted on my own terms. Where adult reserve is not exercised, there is a risk of psychological harm, either to the adolescent, through denying them opportunities for emotional development with people of their own age, or to the adult, through psychological investment in the younger person that becomes obsessive (the Pygmalion syndrome). Martin (2002) captures the essence of quality relations between adults and youth in his remarkably instructive and insightful book on youth work, which I have summarized in Box 10.1.

Case histories of natural mentoring among minority youth explore the zone where caring adults 'lie just outside the personal network of needy adolescents' (Stanton-Salazar *et al.*, 2003, p. 242). The authors illustrate how this gap may be bridged so that the young person gains access to the resources of the adult world. One case story is that of Enrique, who was struggling with school and confused about his future. A friend persuaded him to attend a three-day church-sponsored retreat, and he returned to his home with 'a new sense of tranquillity' (p. 240). He began attending the youth group of the local Catholic church, and there he met the group coordinator, who became a 'father figure' to the fatherless young man. They would sit up late into the night, 'talking about so many things', and the youth saw himself in a new light, as he moved 'into another world'. He explained that the priest 'is a very important person in my life, right?' The account given of the relationship that formed between the priest and the street youth shows that although it was transitory (the priest moved to another parish), such mentor relationships can still be psychologically important. The authors' message is that because contact between an adolescent and a caring adult is often happenstance, the 'art' is for the adult to act with integrity and to be constant, so that the possibility remains that an attachment may develop from an established basis of respect.

Making the connection

Much territory has been covered in this chapter. A wide range of different organizations and formats have been described whose major purpose is connecting young people to adults. The question of how to reach youth still hangs in the air. How does one drop a trailing line in the water so that they might bite on it? Clearly, this notion of 'reaching youth' is more complex than merely providing facilities for young people, and it requires patience. One can never be sure that the facilities provided by local government will attract young people, because many youth are not club-oriented and prefer to hang around with their friends, mucking about and not doing much. Government-funded sports and leisure complexes are unlike the places favoured by these young people for leisure purposes: what they prefer are amusement arcades, cafés, and pubs, multi-purpose halls, and the parks with 'kick-about areas'. It is also clear that places that lack organization and supervision are less effective than ones that contain activities that are structured in some way.

Reaching youth implies that an emotional connection is established which is supportive and beneficial to the young person's development. Successful youth work is not about the activity but about the nature of the connection between adults and youth. Young (1999) in her valuable book on youth work stresses the centrality of relationships, and how a connection is made when the youth worker remembers details about the young person, such as dates, events, concerns, names of pets, or personal achievements. The message that a young person hears is 'I matter' and the judgement made of the youth worker is 'S/he noticed me; s/he is tuned in to where I am'. In the school context, these principles are demonstrated in the practice of a school principal of my acquaintance who was Canada's teacher of the year in 1998. She has a rule of ensuring that in every lesson that she teaches she will find time to speak individually to each student in her class. She accepts that this is sometimes difficult, and that she has to work at it, but the payoff makes the effort worthwhile. Another entry point into forming relationships and highlighted by Young is activities, including activities where the youth worker is a novice and has to rely on a young person for help or instruction. Examples may range from computing to outdoor activities like fishing, rafting, ropes, or sailing. Grandparents know this principle and exploit it in building a relationship with a young grandchild, but its utility for connecting to youth is often overlooked.

Secrets of successful youth work

What makes some youth programs successful where others struggle and wither away? How important is leadership in these? How important is the program of activities? Four principles of successful youth work can be extracted from the writings encountered in this chapter.

1 Effective youth work creates a sense of place attachment that young people describe as home (e.g. Cook, 2000; Hirsch *et al.*, 2000), and confers a sense of belonging and identity; for example, being a member of the 'Y' is a characteristic one shares with the champions, the Olympians, the great coaches. Club membership makes these champions accessible and potential influences as models and as mentors.

2 Successful youth organizations display the capacity to let young people express their views, determine their priorities, and make their own decisions. The BGCA club meeting (Hirsch *et al.*, 2000) provided a safe environment for adolescent girls to express their opinions, knowing their opinions were valued and their suggestions heard.

3 Effective youth work is marked by a quality of relating to young people that is 'like a friend yet not like a friend'. This phrase underlines that honesty, trust, acceptance, and reciprocity are important in the youth worker's relations with young people, just as they are in friendship. However, attentiveness to adolescent concerns is tempered by the realization by both parties that there is a boundary that separates the youth worker from the youth, to protect youth from unnecessary intrusion by adults into their lives.

4 A further factor for successful youth work is ensuring youth participation in the decisions and management of the youth organization. Stoneman's experience stamps her advice with authority. She writes,

> Every aspect of society that affects young people directly is experienced very differently by the young people compared with the adults. If this is so, then the decisions guiding those aspects of society would be much better informed if young people participated in making them.
>
> (Stoneman, 2002, p. 226)

We would be wise to take her advice.

Conclusion

11 Networked youth futures

Traditional organizational structures are being blown apart. We are moving
to a world of networked organizations that dynamically link workers,
knowledge, and customers.

(McEachern and O'Keefe, 1998, p. 9)

The topics discussed in this book have covered an extensive territory. In
traversing the rangelands where young people are found, I have encountered some steep terrain and have cut through the wire on a few fences that
separated different discipline fields. On the journey, I have sought vantage
points to gain a broader view as well as to check my bearings. In this brief
final chapter, I want to describe to you the broad sweep of the landscape
traversed, point out some of the landmarks, celebrate my discoveries, and
propose a few suggestions for the stakeholders involved in the education,
training, guidance and care of young people. First, I describe the networked
nature of modern society and the nature of knowledge in the internet age.
Second, I discuss social capital and the application of network knowledge to
the role of schools. Finally, I revisit the transition of young people into their
mid-twenties and apply knowledge about social networks to youth futures.

Knowledge in the networked society

Communications and information technology are transforming our world,
and networks are frequently invoked to explain the changing structure of
human society. We have moved beyond the computer age and the information age to Castells's network society and to new notions of knowledge. The
fastest growing part of my university's reference library is the section on
the internet and the future of knowledge, where one encounters the topics
of knowledge management and organizational knowledge. The internet has
prompted companies to look beyond information to rethink the way they

deal with knowledge, and place more importance on the systems within an organization that generate knowledge. These are human rather than technical. Thus knowledge management is linked to organizational knowledge and 'establishing an environment in which knowledge can evolve' (Callaghan, 2002, p. 35).

A common feature of some of the most recent writings on knowledge management is the emphasis on human networks, reflected in the book titles themselves; for example, *Communities of Practice* (Wenger, 1998), *In Good Company* (Cohen and Prusak, 2001), and *The Social Life of Information* (Seely Brown and Duguid, 2000). Allee (2003) states in her recent book *The Future of Knowledge* that, 'the basic pattern of all living systems, including organizations, is the network' (p. 51). Her books focus on modelling business corporations into 'a networked pattern of living systems' and on 'learning to work with network principles' (p. xiv). Instead of hierarchically structured companies, she encourages people to think in terms of flat management structures, where what is important is not their centre but the pieces and parts at the edge.

Human groups are valuable as knowledge creators. From their work at Xerox Corporation, Seely Brown and Duguid (2000) identify 'social amalgams' (p. 77) for problem-solving in technology, which occur when different people in an organization, through 'collaboration, narration and improvisation' (p. 104), form 'networks of practice' (p. 141). An illustration is their story of the Xerox photocopier repairmen. The men found that the faults they encountered in the field did not respond to documentation of the repair as described in the manual written by the designers and engineers, either because the error code did not match the problem or because the solution did not fit. They were forced into finding a solution themselves. They adopted a practice whereby when they met a difficulty in the field they would contact one another or meet on the road to share their problem and use their pooled knowledge to solve the problem. In parallel with the information in the manuals, there grew a body of practical knowledge from the field. The success of the repairmen's knowledge was sufficient for Xerox to accept that revising the manuals was inefficient and that it was better to support the field reps with two-way radios. Eventually the repairmen's practical knowledge about the photocopier problems was linked with the technical knowledge of the designers and engineers and assembled into a database known as the *Eureka* system. The repairmen refused to accept any financial reward for creating the *Eureka* database, seeing this as knowledge that they had created. Allee (2003) sees this story as an illustration of a breakthrough in knowledge production that occurs from 'supporting people in the natural ways they weave the living web of knowledge' (p. 107).

When people are recognized as important knowledge producers, astute managements look for ways of designing the environment to foster social exchange. Cohen and Prusak (2001) tell the story of the supervisor at a large corporation who intentionally delayed the start of staff meetings so that people had time to fraternize. From that event, they extract this principle:

> If you want people to connect, to talk, to begin to understand and depend on one another, give them places and occasions for meeting, and enough time to develop networks and communities.
>
> (Cohen and Prusak, 2001, p. 99)

Management in a networked school environment

Technology-supported management systems can enhance the effectiveness of schools to develop appropriate supports and guidance processes. The goal of a networked school is to improve knowledge management and communication within the school and enhance the school's ability to respond to the social and emotional problems that adversely affect students' learning. Information technology makes it possible to design an intelligent decision support system that represents through a networked knowledge base the range of information about students, including their backgrounds, goals and achievements, together with the complexity of school practices and procedures, in a format that is accessible to school personnel. Intranets can reduce the time taken for schools to gather data on students who may be at risk, improve communication and data exchange, and in addition link the school to external advisory systems to design prevention and intervention procedures. Teachers are able to converse through local communication webs which make the implicit knowledge of expert practitioners accessible to fellow teachers in ways that mirror the informal collegial networks that are found in good schools. In addition, the decision paths can be traced and recorded as a documentation of procedures for later review and evaluation, as well as for legal purposes.

The message from leading writers about the future of knowledge is that 'the network is the most natural and powerful vehicle for creating and sharing knowledge' (Allee, 2003, p. 114). For a school to understand knowledge management, Petrides and Guiney (2002) argue 'It must understand and appreciate the human element that adds value to the information' (p. 1704). They refer to the knowledge not found in documents, but which constitutes the knowledge that underpins the history, procedures and traditions of the school. This knowledge resides in people, not in the regulations; and they warn that a management system founders when people are left out, or when an organization is restructured so that its workforce is downsized and its cultural memory lost.

Wise administrators intent on creating a supportive school environment will apply a network approach to knowledge management in their school or college. They will trace the information flow through the school, and determine its network structure. Further, they will examine the school's 'informational politics' including who provides information, who receives the information, who are the information brokers, and who are the people not included in the initial flow of information. Knowledge of the social network structures within the school will alert them to possible social clusters of teacher resistance to an organizational change, which may operate as a type of social contagion to block reform programs that are aimed at changing people's attitudes or work habits (see Bovasso, 1996). In school–community partnerships, administrators will establish 'boundary spanning' roles in their schools (Bradshaw, 1999), and strengthen both the internal links among staff as well as the external links with community agencies and stakeholder groups, so that those who are boundary spanners, working on the edge of the boundaries of the school and community networks, are effective in their role. These examples suggest that when schools see themselves as networked organizations concerned with knowledge management, they manage not only information differently, but also their staff and student relations. 'The way we model the world influences the way we affect the world' (Coiera, 1997, p. 11).

Social capital

The Academy Award winning film *The Pianist* tells the true story of a Polish young man who before the outbreak of war played piano recitals on the radio. He escapes being herded onto the train for Auschwitz through the intervention of a collaborator, and is then hidden from the Nazis in safe houses by friends. As I watched this movie I was struck by the fact that he is saved from the death camps by weak tie links in his social network. His protection is none of his own doing: he does not seek help from network contacts, but is given help without any effort on his part; in fact, he is compliant as others provide for his safety. This story illustrates the power of social capital, 'the stock of active connections among people' (Cohen and Prusak, 2001). The pianist's stock has accumulated over time, through his pursuit of excellence in his craft, leading to his recognition and respect as a concert performer on public radio, and probably assisted by family ties and his connections to music-lovers in the community.

A large literature has grown around social capital, a concept that is related to cultural capital and one that, according to Horvat *et al.* (2003), has been 'plagued by "conceptual murkiness"' (p. 321), which they attribute to the vagueness of the statements describing the concept that were made by its separate originators, Coleman and Bourdieu, and which led to variations in its interpretation and application by subsequent researchers. While networked relations are seen as central to the aggregation of social resources into social capital, these relations have been studied among individuals, groups, and whole communities. For Coleman (1988), social capital is embedded in social structures that are comprised of dense, overlapping social networks whose membership is characterized by common standards, trust, and reciprocity. Putnam (1993) adopts a similar view of social capital as 'features of social organisation, such as trust, norms, and networks that can improve the efficiency of society by facilitating coordinated actions' (p. 167). In their examination of parent links with schools, Horvat *et al.* (2003) define social capital as 'the material and immaterial resources that individuals and families are able to access through their social ties' (p. 323). Kogut and Walker (2001) distinguish between Coleman's 'old-world' view of social capital as located in dense cohesive networks, and Burt's 'new-world' understanding of social capital as brokering positions that enable the flow of resources and information across structural holes in a network, and they conclude that, 'The concept of networks as small worlds integrates these two views of social capital' (p. 328). What can be seen from these statements from a varied body of research studies is that networks continue to feature prominently in discussions of the concept of social capital. Indeed, Cohen and Prusak (2001) comment that, 'Almost all the theorists who write about social capital make networks central to their analysis. Some even define social capital solely in terms of networks' (p. 55).

Network theorists (e.g. Kadushin, 2004; Lin, 1999) regard social capital as equivalent to social network resources. In his critical examination of the concept of social capital, Lin asks, 'Is it a fad or does it have enduring qualities that will herald a new intellectual enterprise?' (p. 28). He explains why social capital works 'in instrumental and expressive actions' by analysing four elements: information, influence, social credentials, and reinforcement, and concludes that social networks scholarship is crucial to the future of social capital discussions. He writes:

> Social networks scholarship has much to say and to do about the development and future of social capital. Without anchoring the concept in social networks and embedded resources, chances are that social capital [will] fade away as an intellectual enterprise.
>
> (Lin, 1999, p. 48)

Kadushin (2004) provides a perceptive and at times amusing critique of social capital in his review of four recent books on the subject. He shows that the authors acknowledge the central value of social networks, but they view social network resources as investments. The analogy to investment in real capital is in his opinion the weakest aspect of social capital theorizing, leaving him sceptical about the general usefulness of the term. Kadushin points to the negatives of 'cultivating' social network ties as 'investments', where one's reason for seeking people out as friends is what they can do for you, rather than how interesting they are in their own right. It is this 'scheming' and somewhat unsavoury aspect of cultivating and building one's contacts that adds a note of caution to the application of social capital at the individual level.

Cohen and Prusak (2001) sketch out a more positive view of social capital at the group level. For them, social capital is basically predicated on trust, the foundation for which lies in densely networked social relations. They illustrate the importance of trust by describing the operations of the Boston diamond market, where paper records of transactions are minimal, and where contracts are concluded with a handshake. Trust runs deep through the network of traders who are linked through multiplex ties of kinship, religion and commerce. However, trust decays as network span increases; that is, you can trust a good friend to provide material help, but you are less confident that the friend of a friend of your friend is just as dependable. In the shift from what some call *thick trust* (based on strong ties) to *thin trust* (based on weak ties) the contact person's reputation rather than the personal relationship you have with them becomes all that you can rely on; and the basis of their reputation is word-of-mouth, obtained through indirect social ties.

Network knowledge

Network knowledge[1] is the accumulation of knowledge on the interlinked nature of persons, groups and organizations. It is knowledge about the patterned nature of people's relations to others and to groups, which lies right under our nose. Network knowledge extends beyond awareness of a friend of a friend of a friend to providing an orientation to the social world 'in terms of sets, patterns and linkages' (Trevillion, 2000, p. 514). It is knowledge of how people are tied to one another and how they influence one another, and of how through these human contact nets knowledge is shared and shaped in communities of practice. Moreover, such knowledge is not distanced from people and locked away by research practices as the exclusive property of researchers. Instead, as Trevillion argues, 'it is owned by all those taking part in the research network' (p. 514) and is as accessible and meaningful to them as to the researcher. It is the kind of knowledge that Miller (1969) discussed in his famous presidential address about 'giving psychology away', where he argued that:

Our responsibility is less to assume the role of experts and try to supply psychology ourselves than to give it away to the people who really need it – and that includes everyone. The practice of valid psychology by non-psychologists will inevitably change people's conceptions of themselves and what they can do. When we have accomplished that, we will really have caused a psychological revolution.

(Miller, 1969, p. 1074)

Network knowledge is more than the intuitive grasp of social networks that is reflected in the cry made on meeting a stranger and discovering that we have common friends: 'What a small world!' – a response that was mentioned at the very beginning of this book. In that form of knowing, experience is sensed, or apprehended. We are surprised that a relation exists where none was expected, and we acknowledge its existence without being able to fathom why, or perhaps without even wanting to understand. That is, the person senses the pattern, rule, principle, and marvels at its intricacy – like admiring the fine filigree of the spider's web laden with dew and resplendent in the early morning sunlight. But another form of knowing involves us in analysis and interpretation; this is comprehension of experience, and it is this kind of knowledge that Miller's words refer to, because it changes not only people's understandings of themselves, but also 'what they can do'. According to the experiential learning theory proposed by Kolb (1984), these forms of grasping at experience occur together, but the merit of knowing by comprehension lies in the framework it provides for interpreting and understanding our experience. Where apprehension yields a personal kind of knowledge, comprehension requires concepts in order to understand and communicate our experience, and it produces social knowledge. Young people are intuitively aware of network relations; but in order to apply their network knowledge, objective frames are needed. I believe that they will benefit from an ordered understanding of how networks function, and that such knowledge about networks is to their advantage.

How is network knowledge acquired? Most people have an intuitive grasp of social relations; they notice how their lives are embedded in networked relationships, and are aware of the small worlds they inhabit. The chapters in this book have extended these understandings, by showing the operation of social networks in the establishment and maintenance of social ties within families, friendships, schools, work groups and community organizations. They have also provided abstract and systematized forms of knowledge about networks, to enable readers not only to refine their intuitive grasp (or apprehension) of network patterns but also to develop a conceptual grasp (or comprehension) of network relations and structures.

Social networks are more complex than they first appear to be, and they exert influences on behaviour at many levels of society.

In his theory of experiential learning, Kolb (1984) refers to a second dimension, applicable to both the above forms of knowledge: transformation of the knowledge acquired either by *intention* through reflection and integrative enquiry, or by *extension* through dispersive enquiry and experimentation. Suffice it to say that the transformation process is concerned with applying knowledge in various ways, to improve relationships or to gain some advantage. Indeed, the purpose of all forms of teaching is in Kolb's view to 'introduce order into what would otherwise be a seamless unpredictable flow of apprehended sensations' (1984, p. 43). The *extension* function is an active form of enquiry, and has benefits not only for young people themselves but also for those who work professionally with them.

Youth futures

How can network knowledge empower youth futures? Some answers have been suggested in the previous chapter, which described how youth and community organizations connect young people to adults who act as models and mentors. But relationships are important in other ways than for social support. In terms of social capital, Stanton-Salazar (1997, p. 5) describes social networks as 'conduits for transmitting the effects of socio-economic background, race, and gender' and also as 'lifelines to resources that permit low-status individuals to overcome social structural barriers to experience healthy social development, school achievement, and social mobility'. The relationships forged between young people and adults also function as bridges to 'the previously opaque worlds of adulthood' (Jarrett *et al.*, 2005, p. 51). As trust is developed, adults reveal their own world, fleshing out their lifepath through story-telling. Frank Vig's story and Stanton-Salazar *et al.*'s account of the priest befriending the boy are examples (see Chapter 10). Jarrett *et al.* (2005) supply testimonies of what youth learned from 'guided forays into adult worlds' of bankers, actors, and animators. For example, Dean learned from his banker contact 'how money works'; Tien found out 'how it is being an animator'; and Juan learned from his actor contact 'about some stuff he did before'. Jarrett *et al.* commented that:

> The community adults whom the youth met became sources of social capital. They provided the youth with information, assistance, exposure to adult worlds, support, and encouragement. The youth described this social capital as helping them achieve current goals and prepare for transitional steps into adulthood. These resource-rich adults provided the youth with information about colleges and inside knowledge

about career worlds that influenced the youth thinking about career paths.

(2005, p. 53)

Network knowledge in practice

Lin's idea of social capital is that network knowledge leads to investment in social networks. If any proof for this assertion were required, one has only to observe a politician or business leader at a cocktail party, or an academic researcher at a conference, and watch them 'work the room'. Compare their skills at networking with those of many leading scientists, who are ineffective at promoting their discoveries and getting the rewards and recognition they deserve. The conclusion to be drawn is that network knowledge has special value as applied knowledge. The point has been well made by de Sola Pool and Kochen (1978) who wrote, 'A friend of a friend is useful only if one is aware of the connection. Also a channel is useful only if one knows how to use it' (p. 7). To illustrate the application of network knowledge in charting one's lifepath, I provide a case study of my own son 'D', used with his permission. My instructions were as follows:

> What I would like is for you to sketch out in a set of boxes along a time-line your job choices and career plans, and show the people who were influences via your network, including the indirect links – friend of a friend type.

The resulting map (Figure 11.1) displays three associated aspects on a timeline spanning ten years: 'D's' roles, the institutional/corporate environments he was linked to, and the relevant people in his social network. The nature of the influence of particular network members is described in the accompanying notes (Box 11.1).

This case study of a partial network of significant others shows the long-term influence of selected network members on a young person's lifepath, both directly in supplying crucial information, and indirectly, by connecting that person to corporations containing resources and career opportunities. The case example further shows how an individual person's lifepath is intertwined with the life trajectories of friends and work colleagues. The accompanying notes to Figure 11.1 (see Box 11.1) provide evidence of the active nature of information search that was conducted by one young person through his evolving personal network, and reveal his sophisticated understanding of network ties and how they function. The information obtained through network contacts allowed him to weigh various options about his future, in some cases some years before the decision point was

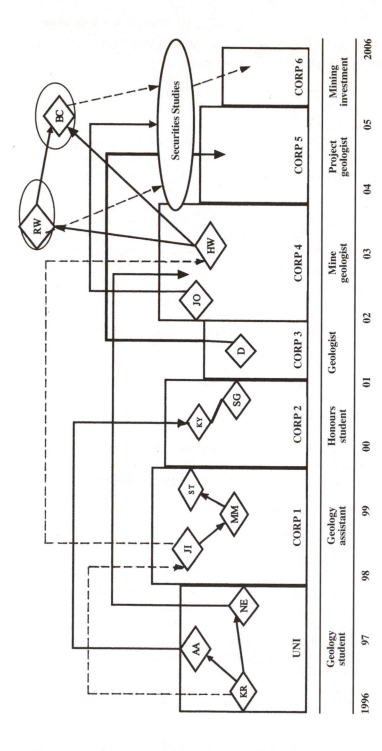

Figure 11.1 Chart of social network influences on biography – a case study

Box 11.1 Explanatory notes to the chart (Figure 11.1)

1 Influences from UNI Friends on path 1 – to Geological assistant at CORP 1
AA and KR: both students in geology, had both taken a year off study to work with a mining company (under the Cooperative Education Program with industry). Their experience awoke my interest. I won a position as Geological assistant at CORP 1 (where KR had also worked).

2 Influences from UNI Friends and work contacts on path 2 – to Honours student
Both AA and KR also planned to study Honours, and their reasons (better job prospects) sounded convincing. During my year at CORP 1, I explored this idea by asking the geologists on staff. I decided to take this path, and argued with my parents about its benefits. Because the Honours required fieldwork employment with a mining company, I benefited from AA's contacts with two geologists at CORP 2, (KY and SG). One of these people was affiliated with the university Honours program.

3 Work contacts at CORP 1 influence path 3 – to CORP 3, and path 4 – to CORP 4
Jobs were difficult to find after my graduation, as there was a slow-down in the mining industry. I got a job with CORP 3, based on my experience at CORP 1, not my degree. When CORP 3 experienced financial difficulties, I sought a change and was again able to benefit from contacts JI and ST (made at CORP 1) to move to CORP 4.

4 Influence of work contacts at CORP 3 on path 5 – to CORP 5
Desire for greater job challenges led me to apply for the position of Project geologist at CORP 5, a very large gold mine. I was able to find out about the company and the project from D who worked with me at CORP 3.

5 Influence of work contacts at CORP 4 on path 6 – to CORP 6
The move to CORP 6 represented a major change in direction, away from mines, and depended on two influences: one was a workmate who was studying in a course on securities investment, and the other was in-direct contact with two senior people in the investment world (RW and BC). These people together gave me the information and encourage-ment to do the studies to make me qualified to seek a career change.

reached. Worth noting is that none of these network members were connected to 'D's' family or dependent on family influence; all were recruited in the course of 'D's' transition from a youth at college to becoming a qualified geologist. The pathways seemed erratic at the time, although they look much more definite in retrospect, and flow out of friendships formed and mentors found along the way. They illustrate the point made by Stanton-Salazar that:

> Personal access to many valued resources and opportunities in society – by way of social networks – occurs through the messy business of commanding, negotiating, and managing many diverse (and sometimes conflicting) social relationships and personalities.
>
> (Stanton-Salazar, 1997, p. 4)

We may conclude from the case study that, despite Kadushin's troubled feelings concerning 'the "investment" analogue to economic capital theory' (2004, p. 86), network knowledge need not be exploitative. It may be practical good sense. People have for ages applied their network knowledge to improve their social prospects as well as their fortunes, through going to the 'right' schools, mixing in the 'right' circles, and marrying into the 'right' social stratum. In a wider sense, knowing how a society or an organization is structured is as important for a person's social advancement, and possibly their social survival, as formal knowledge about history, engineering, or zoology. It is also important for doing one's job in a complex society. Network knowledge is consciously applied every day by lawyers, doctors, and university professors in the pursuit of their profession, as they refer a client or a patient to a specialist consultant, or consult a colleague about a technicality. Yesterday's headline in the business pages of a national newspaper drew attention to a report which found that most major corporations in Australia are headed by people with a sales or marketing background; the article implied that corporations view knowledge about social systems as more important in their leaders than expert knowledge about technical processes. Indeed the business world places such value on the network knowledge of politicians that it is not uncommon to find that a politician on retirement from government is offered a seat on the board of a large corporation.

Network thinking is the application of network knowledge to understanding how modern society operates. We employ this kind of thinking when we look for the people who fulfil brokering and gatekeeper roles in a community or business organization. It is the thinking that occurs in community organizations when its members plan a project and are gathering the human resources needed for the project to succeed. It is the kind of thinking that arises from the application of network knowledge, looking at social relations within organizations and the structures that comprise them. Network thinking not only takes into account who is linked to whom but also considers how they are linked. It requires an appreciation of the importance of strong tie links, where actors are densely interconnected, as well as the role of weak tie links, where a key actor may be weakly linked to one or two members of the organization. Trevillion (2000) characterized the professional knowledge used by social workers as network knowledge. What he sees as distinctive about the social worker's orientation to the world is its relational emphasis; the social worker attempts to understand the individual's relations to others 'in terms of sets, patterns and linkages' (p. 514), and applies this knowledge concerning the networked nature of families, communities and organizations in their thinking.

The benefits for teachers of network knowledge include being able to detect the networks that exist in particular classrooms. At the most basic level, this means knowing who are Paul and Paula's friends, and who are definitely not their friends. When teachers employ network thinking to analyse their classroom, they become sensitive to a range of other features of adolescent networks, such as indirect ties linking students, as well as the multiplexity of ties. Rather than dismiss this knowledge as of no consequence, they come to appreciate its value for understanding the emotional significance of particular relationships and how influences are exerted among students. It is also important that teachers are tuned in and take the peers seriously when they bring disturbing information about one of their friends who is showing signs of psychological trauma. This is a cry by the peers for help from school personnel. One school in my experience ignored for some months peer attempts to get help when they noticed that their friend had cut herself across the wrists. Several months passed with no action taken by the school authorities until the friends again called on staff for help, stating that she had been cutting herself again. This time the student was sent to the school counsellor, but, even at that stage, the seriousness of the situation was not fully understood until the girl cut herself in the counsellor's office. The school then sought urgent help from mental health professionals.

Policy-makers can also benefit from the application of network knowledge when confronted by 'wicked problems' – those that are often found 'at the boundaries of natural and social systems' (van Bueren *et al.*, 2003, p. 193). Van Bueren *et al.* suggest that a reason for impasse in resolving wicked problems is the absence of network knowledge that would inform the participants about the sources of blockage. This knowledge, which may pertain to inaction in committee meetings of the kinds they describe, would make participants aware that 'their actions influence other actors' interests and [that] solving the problem usually requires the joint action of various actors' (p. 211). Van Bueren *et al.* illustrate the use of a network framework to analyse an ongoing zinc industry debate in the Netherlands between industrialists, architects, water managers, policy-makers and researchers and consultants. The purpose of including their study here is to suggest the wider use of network knowledge in management.

Network knowledge is a protection against rash decisions. In our social life we are continually exposed to the risk of network revision, recklessly selling off some of our 'investments' in social capital. We discover that a person lets us down or is disloyal; we are introduced to someone who is unfriendly or unpleasant; we are given glowing accounts of someone in a government agency but find them decidedly unhelpful. In a fit of pique, we 'cross them off our list': we revise our network. However, the tendency to personalize our weak tie relations is detrimental to a wise application of network knowledge. Borgatti and Cross (2003) propose that the relational aspects of social networks can be detrimental to people's information-seeking. That is, people take account of the relationship between themselves and others who may be a source of information before deciding whether to seek their help. For example, adolescents often equate liking a subject in school with their feelings about the teacher, so they are dismissive of teachers they don't like and see them as people they would never ask for advice. They may be so blinded by a stereotype (he's a Nerd!) that they don't attempt to utilize the Nerd's expertise, and in these kinds of ways 'lock into a limited set of people [who may] yield suboptimal information' (Borgatti and Cross, 2003, p. 442). This kind of quick judgement of others occurs at all ages, but it may have more serious consequences for young people who are seeking information through weak tie links, but who are not fully confident in their network knowledge.

Youth in the networked society

Whither youth?

The notion of transition was introduced early in this book as a general framework for young people's development. A series of transitions, whether associated with environmental change or status change, can be flagged from early adolescence to young adulthood. It is noticeable that over time the transitions become more complex and less standardized, from the transition into middle school/junior high school, to the transition into high school, and then to college or into the workforce. They become less predictable as the pathways become more diverse, and as the developmental tasks become more demanding. Where the young adolescent experiences the move to middle school/junior high school as part of a cohort of peers, the pathways progressively become less structured and more individualized after that, as each person enters the period of emerging adulthood.

Social commentators argue that the transition to adulthood for today's youth has possibly become 'less predictable and more precarious' (Shanahan, 2000, p. 685). They see that the forces for social change have 'pushed to the limit the old notion of youth as a transition to adulthood' (Wyn and Dwyer, 2000, p. 153) and undermined the concept of a linear transition, replacing it with multiple erratic paths, like wallaby tracks through the bush, lacking any reassuring signposts about the direction to take. The state has retreated as a partner in fostering young people's development, so that the onus is now on individuals themselves to organize the requirements for being a citizen. Young people must identify the opportunity structures themselves and coordinate their lives on their own. The individual writes the script for their own lifecourse 'in response to contextual discontinuities and multiple options' (Heinz, 2002, p. 42), and each determines the timing of their own adult markers.

The individualization of the lifecourse suggests that young people neglect to maintain an association with older adults in order to cut their own path, and that they isolate themselves from adult advice and influence in the belief that older generations are out of touch and unable to relate to the unique circumstances that they are faced with. While it is true that one never steps into the same stream twice, previous generations also had to struggle with the freedoms and uncertainties brought about by social change. The poet T. S. Eliot wrote about the generation between the world wars who engaged in a search for meaning which took them far afield, but returned them to their starting point, so that they knew it for the first time. The generation that followed them was portrayed as overwhelmed by the pace of change: in Arthur Miller's *Death of a Salesman*, the adolescent son is paralysed into inaction derived from the mid-life crisis of his salesman father, who is struggling to 'take hold of some kind of life'. In Samuel Beckett's *Waiting for Godot*, the tramps wait for someone to arrive who will sort out their situation for them, but no one ever comes. The lack of certainty, the diminishing sense of control over one's future, the restless exploration of alternatives, and the reluctance to settle into an adult life pattern are characteristics ascribed to modern youth and young adults, but they were known to their parents and grandparents as well. What has changed is that in the twenty-first century a greater emphasis is given to individual choice, coping, and adaptability, and a reduced role is assigned to society and the welfare state. Technology is heralded as ushering in new potentials for personal fulfilment. Heinz (2000) refers to deregulation, decentralization, and de-welfarization. Seely Brown and Duguid (2000) ironically comment on 'the 6-D future' offered by CIT (communications and information technology), and add other features: the workplace will be disaggregated, and even the state will be denationed.

On agency and biography

The individualization of the lifecourse draws attention to agency, which is understood as the active process of choosing appropriate institutional involvements, organizational memberships, and interpersonal relationships. Agency thus translates into the capacity of a person to shape her/his own biography. Agency is not hostile to dependence: it is a matter of balance. Ahier and Moore (1999) write that dependence has to be seen as 'a process continually managed and negotiated within and with reference to a network of others' (p. 519).

To speak of young people as agents of their own development is a bold idea. In a sense it is true that each of us writes our own biography, makes our own choices, and charts out our own lifepath. But it is my view that people have far less control over their futures than the agency theorists would claim; instead, youth are at best opportunistic, making the most of the life chances that come their way. The key attributes of this kind of agency are the capacity to recognize the chance that is offered, and the flexibility to be able to respond in a timely and appropriate manner when opportunity comes knocking. In short, the notion of an individualized biography exaggerates the degree of agency and diminishes the extent to which a person relies on others, both for guidance and encouragement, and also as models to emulate.

How does a person assemble and construct their biography? Few people can create a personal biography without recourse to existing prototypes, schematics like the conscientious student, the loyal friend, the dutiful son/ daughter, the responsible worker. I suggest that biographies emerge from the storehouse of social capital generated by communities and made accessible through social networks. The community maintains the storehouse of prototypic social identities, but not all existing prototypes are congruent with community values. For example, one does not find a pasta dish on the menu in a Thai restaurant. Particular versions of these prototype identities are generated within communities and consensually validated by them to the extent that their component traits are an agreed basis of the social reputation that individuals then 'work up' for themselves. The individual reworks the finer details of traits that comprise that identity, assisted by the guiding and affirming help of significant others in their social network, in a similar way to the actor in a play, filling out the character part so that it is stamped with her/his own personality. However, without the encouragement, advice, and guidance of significant others, the individual young person would have difficulty in fleshing out the role into a personalized identity that can become incorporated into their biography. Personal biographies are not individual constructions but are the products of engagement in a social environment. They are life threads connected to social and historical events.

Indeed, this chapter has shown that it is possible to describe an individual biography in social network terms, by tracking social network ties and their links to organizations and workplaces, and to the opportunity structures that these contain. Thus social networks are important for young people's development, not only as convoys of social support but as conduits to social capital. Twenge and Baumeister (2005, p. 42) emphasize their importance for youth development in these words: 'To find a fully functioning human being, it may be generally necessary to look in the middle of a rich, supportive social network.' To conclude this book, Verna Allee's advice to organizations can well be applied to professional endeavours in enhancing youth futures: 'If you have a dollar to spend on technology, spend it connecting, not collecting' (Allee, 2003, pp. 81–82).

Notes

1 Young people and development

1 James Côté provides a sociological analysis of modern American youth in his book *Arrested Adulthood*, published in 2000.
2 In their review, they refer to studies of time perspective (p. 517) and the work of Novotny, who identifies the characteristics of *acceleration* and *fragmentation* as producing for modern youth a sense of constant busyness in a present time that seems to have expanded.

2 The science of social networks

1 For the reader who seeks technical information, books by D. M. Kirke (2006), J. Scott (2001), and S. Wasserman and K. Faust (1994), among others, should be consulted.
2 The term 'cluster' appears in the research without a precise definition being supplied, but its use seems generally consistent with that described by Barnes (1969, p. 64) as 'a relatively dense area of the network', and in this context suggests that it is a component of the wider social network.
3 A large selection of computer programs for the analysis of social network data can be found at http://www.insna.org/INSNA/soft_inf.html. 3D displays are located at the Kinemage website at http:kinemage.biochem.duke.edu/ (both sites were accessed 4 October 2006). Also consult the 2004 book by Linton Freeman: *The Development of Social Network Analysis: A Study in the Sociology of Science*. It traces the history of network displays in more detail.

3 Networks and groups

1 UCINET, GRADAP and NEGOPY are network analysis packages commonly used in research. Information about the nature and capabilities of these programs is found on the INSNA website at http://www.insna.org/INSNA/soft_inf.html
2 Crowd is used in the literature on young people to describe different sociality structures. To avoid confusion in the understandings of what is meant by crowds in different chapters, my practice is to distinguish the various uses of the term 'crowd' by a qualifying term. Thus Dunphy's concept of adolescent crowds is designated as the 'peer crowd'; Brown's concept of crowds is labelled 'social crowds' or 'crowd types'; and the crowd as described in studies of mobs and crowd disorder is termed the 'mass crowd' or the 'large crowd'.

3 Researchers who have employed self-report methods (e.g. Kiesner *et al.*, 2002; Tarrant, 2002) have found that less then 5 per cent of adolescents claim not to belong to any friendship group.

4 See another application of this approach in Chapter 11.

5 To follow the changes in the plays, visit http://www.jibble.org/shakespeare/ and for details on how to view the videos, visit http://library.kent.ac.uk/mirrors/ jibble.org/ (both accessed 4 October 2006). The videos of the networks in Shakespeare's plays run in sequence by scene in .avi format (which is several years old), so I found that it was necessary to convert the videos from .avi format, with advice about the appropriate Codec, obtained from http://msmvps.com/ blogs/chrisl/articles/10453.aspx and then going to another site at http://www. fourcc.org/ to download the Codec to play the videos. A bit messy, but you can get some idea of the network decay from the first site listed.

4 Friends and mates

1 In this section, social cluster is used, instead of network, but it should be clear by now that all interlinked relations may be regarded as types of social networks.

5 Loners and outsiders

1 For a modern analysis of attitudes to immigrants in Europe, read *The Outsider: Prejudice and Politics in Italy*, by P. M. Sniderman, P. Peri, R. J. P. de Figueiredo and T. Piazza, Princeton, NJ: Princeton University Press, 2002.

2 The adult who works with youth is necessarily isolated from them, even while they are working in their midst. The consequence of separateness is that teaching, and, for that matter, youth work, can be a lonely occupation, as Knobloch and Goldstein (1971) explained. They introduced their book with the Beatles song 'Eleanor Rigby', which carries the refrain 'All the lonely people – where do they all come from?', and suggest that 'many of them must be in classrooms with children' (p. 5). They add that the very nature of a teacher's work makes them not only physically separate from other adults but psychologically separate as well.

3 This assumes that the teacher or youth worker has healthy relations with the groups of young people they lead or instruct, and that they are not treated as outsiders by the groups. The art of professional practice is to be sufficiently an outsider to be effective in seeing the relationships within the groups in an objective manner, and not being vulnerable to the group's manipulation of one's own need to be accepted and belong.

8 Smoking, drinking and drug use

1 This has now been expanded into a book, published in 2006 by Pan Macmillan (Kirke, 2006).

2 Among Norwegian young men, the appeal of smoking in cultivating a tough masculine image has seen a renewed popularity of the 'Marlboro man' (see Krange and Pedersen, 2001).

3 For example, in June 2005, a newspaper report in Australia revealed that a plan to increase the size of health warnings on cigarette packs, which had been four years in the making, had been dumped by the Federal Government, after tobacco companies had lobbied for such a result.

9 Social support in schools

1 For details on Miller's argument to 'give psychology away', see Chapter 11.
2 This comment is not meant as a proposal for work intensification. Teachers are our most valuable public asset, and their well-being is an important matter to consider when establishing a supportive school.

10 Youth and community organizations

1 See Barna updates: http://www.barna.org (accessed 4 October 2006).

11 Networked youth futures

1 I coined this term to capture the higher-order level of knowledge about network relations and processes, comparable to higher cognitive systems in cognitive theories of knowledge. However, the term had been previously employed in a similar way by Steve Trevillion, and I wish to acknowledge this fact.

References

Abel, G. and Plumridge, E. W. (2004). Network 'norms' or 'styles' of 'drunken comportment'? *Health Education Research, 19*, 492–500.

Abel, G., Plumridge, L., and Graham, P. (2002). Peers, networks or relationships: strategies for understanding social dynamics as determinants of smoking behaviour. *Drugs Education, Prevention and Policy, 9*, 325–338.

Adelman, M. (1988). Cross-cultural adjustment: a theoretical perspective on social support. *International Journal of Intercultural Relations, 12*, 183–204.

Ahier, J., and Moore, R. (1999). Post-16 education, semi-dependent youth and the privatisation of inter-age transfers: re-theorising youth transition. *British Journal of Sociology of Education, 20*, 515–530.

Ahmed, T. (2004). Identity and Islam. 10 February. www.zmag.org (accessed 23 September 2006).

Albee, G. W. (1996). Revolutions and counterrevolutions in prevention. *American Psychologist, 51*, 1130–1133.

Allee, V. (2003). *The future of knowledge: increasing prosperity through value networks*. London: Butterworth-Heinemann.

Alschuler, A. J. (1980). *School discipline: a socially literate solution*. New York: McGraw-Hill.

Al-Sharideh, K. A., and Goe, W. R. (1998). Ethnic communities within the university: an examination of factors influencing the personal adjustment of international students. *Research in Higher Education, 39*, 699–725.

American Psychiatric Association (2000). *Diagnostic and statistical manual of mental disorders: DSM-IV*. Washington, DC: American Psychiatric Association.

Andersson, B.-E., and Strader, K. (2004). Perceptions of school and future adjustment to life: a longitudinal study between the ages of 18 and 25. *Scandinavian Journal of Educational Research, 48*, 459–470.

Andolina, M. W., Jenkins, K., Keeter, S., and Zukin, C. (2002). Searching for the meaning of youth civic engagement: notes from the field. *Applied Developmental Science, 6*, 189–195.

Arnett, J. J. (1998). Risk behavior and family role transitions during the twenties. *Journal of Youth and Adolescence, 27*, 301–320.

Arnett, J. J. (2000). Emerging adulthood: a theory of development from the late teens through the twenties. *American Psychologist, 55*, 469–480.

Asendorpf, J. B., and Wilpers, S. (1998). Personality effects on social relationships. *Journal of Personality and Social Psychology, 74*, 1531–1544.

Asher, S. R., and Dodge, K. A. (1986). Identifying children who are rejected by their peers. *Developmental Psychology, 22*, 444–449.

Australia (1996). *Truancy and exclusion from school: report of the inquiry into truancy and exclusion of children and young people from school.* Canberra: House of Representatives Standing Committee on Employment, Education and Training.

Baerveldt, C., Van Duijn, M. A. J., Vermeij, L., and Van Hemert, D. A. (2004). Ethnic boundaries and personal choice. Assessing the influence of individual inclinations to choose intra-ethnic relationships on pupils' networks. *Social Networks, 26*, 55–74.

Barber, B. K., and Olsen, J. A. (2004). Assessing the transitions to middle and high school. *Journal of Adolescent Research, 19*, 3–30.

Barnes, G. M., Welte, J. W., and Dintcheff, B. (1992). Alcohol misuse among college students and other young adults: findings from a general population study in New York state. *International Journal of Addiction, 27*, 917–934.

Barnes, J. A. (1954). Class and committee in a Norwegian island parish. *Human Relations, 7*, 39–58.

Barnes, J. A. (1969). Networks and political process. In J. C. Mitchell (ed.), *Social networks in urban situations* (pp. 51–76). Manchester: Manchester University Press.

Barnes, J. A., and Harary, F. (1983). Graph theory in network analysis. *Social Networks, 5*, 235–244.

Baron, S. W., and Tindall, D. B. (1993). Network structure and delinquent attitudes within a juvenile gang. *Social Networks, 15*, 255–273.

Batiuk, M. E., Boland, J. A., and Wilcox, N. (2004). Project trust: breaking down barriers between middle school children. *Adolescence, 39*, 531–538.

Baumeister, R. F., and Leary, M. R. (1995). The need to belong: desire for interpersonal attachments as a fundamental human motivation. *Psychological Bulletin, 117*, 497–529.

Baxter, L. A., Mazanec, M., Nicholson, J., Pittman, G., Smith, K., and West, L. (1997). Everyday loyalties and betrayals in personal relationships. *Journal of Social and Personal Relationships, 14*, 655–678.

Baxter, L. A., Dun, T., and Sahlstein, E. (2001). Rules for relating communicated among social network members. *Journal of Social and Personal Relationships, 18*, 173–199.

Beam, M. R., Chen, C., and Greenberger, E. (2002). The nature of adolescents' relationships with their 'Very important' nonparental adults. *American Journal of Community Psychology, 30*, 305–325.

Bearman, P. S., Moody, J., and Stovel, K. (2004). Chains of affection: the structure of adolescent romantic and sexual networks. *American Journal of Sociology, 110*, 44–91.

Bian, Y. (1997). Bringing strong ties back in: indirect ties, network bridges and job searches in China. *American Sociological Review, 62*, 366–385.

Blase, J. (ed.). (1991). *The politics of life in schools: power, conflict, and cooperation.* Newbury Park, CA: Sage.

Blishen, E. (ed.). (1969). *The school that I'd like.* Harmondsworth: Penguin.

Bo, I. (1989). The significant people in the social networks of adolescents. In K. Hurrelmann and U. Engel (eds), *The social world of adolescents* (pp. 141–165). Berlin: Walter de Gruyter.

Boissevain, J. (1974). *Friends of friends: networks, manipulators and coalitions.* Oxford: Blackwell.

Boissevain, J., and Mitchell, J. C. (eds) (1973). *Network analysis: studies in human interaction.* The Hague: Mouton.

Bonacich, P. (2004). Book review: The invasion of the physicists. *Social Networks, 26*, 285–288.

Borgatti, S. P., and Cross, R. (2003). A relational view of information seeking and learning in social networks. *Management Science, 49*, 432–445.

Bovasso, G. (1996). A network analysis of social contagion processes in an organizational intervention. *Human Relations, 49*, 1419–1435.

Bowlby, J. (1969). *Attachment and loss: Attachment* (Vol. 1). Harmondsworth: Penguin.

Bradford, D. J. (1999). Exemplary urban middle school teachers' use of five standards of effective teaching. *Teaching and Change, 7*, 53–58.

Bradley, G., and Wildman, K. (2002). Psychosocial predictors of emerging adults' risk and reckless behaviors. *Journal of Youth and Adolescence, 31*, 253–265.

Bradshaw, L. K. (1999). Principals as boundary spanners: working collaboratively to solve problems. *NASSP Bulletin, 83* (December), 38–47.

Brammer, L., and MacDonald, G. (1999). *The helping relationship: process and skills* (7th edn). Boston: Allyn and Bacon.

Brannen, J., and Nilsen, A. (2002). Young people's time perspectives: from youth to adulthood. *Sociology, 36*, 513–537.

Brewer, D. D. (2000). Forgetting in the recall-based elicitation of personal and social networks. *Social Networks, 22*, 29–43.

Broadbent, R. (1994). Young people's perceptions of their use and abuse of alcohol. *Youth Studies Australia, 13*(3), 32–35.

Brown, B. B., and Klute, C. (2003). Friendships, cliques, and crowds. In G. R. Adams and M. D. Berzonsky (eds), *Blackwell handbook of adolescence* (pp. 330–348). Malden, MA: Blackwell Publishers.

Brown, B. B., Mory, M., and Kinney, A. (1994). Casting adolescent crowds in relational perspective: caricature, channel, and context. In R. Montemayor, G. R. Adams and T. P. Gullotta (eds), *Advances in adolescent development: Vol. 6. Personal relationships during adolescence* (pp. 123–167). Newbury Park, CA: Sage.

Brown, E. J., and Bobrow, A. L. (2004). School entry after a community-wide trauma: challenges and lessons learned from September 11th, 2001. *Clinical Child and Family Psychology Review, 7*, 211–221.

Buchanan, M. (2002). *Nexus – small worlds and the groundbreaking science of networks.* London: Norton.

Bucholtz, M. (1999). Why be normal? Language and identity practices in a community of nerd girls. *Language in Society, 28*, 203–223.

Buddie, A. M., and Parks, K. A. (2003). The role of the bar context and social behaviors on women's risk for aggression. *Journal of Interpersonal Violence, 18*, 1378–1393.

Buford, B. (1991). *Among the thugs.* London: Secker and Warburg.

Bukowski, W., and Sippola, L. K. (2001). Groups, individuals and victimization. A view of the peer system. In J. Juvonen and S. Graham (eds), *Peer harassment in school* (pp. 355–377). London: Guilford.

Burt, R. S. (2001). Attachment, decay, and social network. *Journal of Organizational Behavior, 22*, 619–643.

Burt, R. S. (2002). Bridge decay. *Social Networks, 24*, 333–363.

Button, L. (1974). *Developmental group work with adolescents.* London: University of London Press.

Cairns, R. B., Perrin, J. E., and Cairns, B. D. (1985). Social structure and social cognition in early adolescence: affiliative patterns. *Journal of Early Adolescence, 5*, 339–355.

Cairns, R. B., Cairns, B., Neckerman, H., Gest, S. D. *et al.* (1988). Social networks and aggressive behavior: peer support or peer rejection? *Developmental Psychology, 24*, 815–823.

Cairns, R. B., Leung, M.-C., Buchanan, L., and Cairns, B. D. (1995). Friendships and social networks in childhood and adolescence: fluidity, reliability, and interrelations. *Child Development, 66*, 1330–1345.

Cairns, R. B., Xie, H., and Leung, M. (1998). The popularity of friendship and the neglect of social networks: toward a new balance. In W. M. Bukowski and A. H. N. Cillessen (eds), *Sociometry then and now: building on six decades of measuring children's experiences with the peer group* (Vol. 80: New directions for child development, pp. 25–53). San Francisco: Jossey-Bass.

Callaghan, J. (2002). *Inside intranets and extranets: knowledge management and the struggle for power.* Basingstoke: Palgrave.

Camino, L. (2000). Youth–adult partnerships: entering new territory in community work and research. *Applied Developmental Science, 4*(Suppl. 1), 11–20.

Camino, L., and Zeldin, S. (2002). From periphery to centre: pathways for youth civic engagement in the day-to-day life of communities. *Applied Developmental Science, 6*, 213–220.

Cantin, S., and Boivin, M. (2004). Change and stability in children's social network and self-perceptions during transition from elementary to junior high school. *International Journal of Behavioral Development, 28*, 561–570.

Carberry, J., and Buhrmester, D. (1998). Friendship and need fulfilment during three phases of young adulthood. *Journal of Social and Personal Relationships, 15*, 393–409.

Carlson, E. A., Sroufe, L. A., and Byron, E. (2004). The construction of experience: a longitudinal study of representation and behavior. *Child Development, 75*, 66–83.

Carter, D. S. G., Bennetts, C., and Carter, S. M. (2003). We're not sheep: illuminating the nature of the adolescent peer group in effecting lifestyle choice. *British Journal of Sociology of Education, 24*, 225–241.

Casswell, S., Pledger, M., and Pratap, S. (2002). Trajectories of drinking from 18 to

26 years: identification and prediction. *Addiction, 97*, 1427–1437.

Chipuer, H. M., and Pretty, G. H. (2000). Facets of adolescents' loneliness: a study of rural and urban Australian youth. *Australian Psychologist, 35*, 233–237.

Chisholm, L., and Du Bois-Reymond, M. (1993). Youth transitions, gender and social change. *Sociology, 27*, 259–279.

Clark, C., and Uzzell, D. L. (2002). The affordances of the home, neighbourhood, school and town centre for adolescents. *Journal of Environmental Psychology, 22*, 95–108.

Cobb, S. (1976). Social support as a moderator of life stress. *Psychosomatic Medicine, 38*, 300–314.

Cohen, D., and Prusak, L. (2001). *In good company. How social capital makes organizations work*. Boston: Harvard Business School.

Coiera, E. (1997). *Guide to medical informatics, the Internet, and telemedicine*. London: Chapman and Hall Medical.

Coleman, J. S. (1961). *The adolescent society*. New York: Free Press.

Coleman, J. S. (1988). Social capital in the creation of human capital. *American Journal of Sociology, 94*(Suppl.), S95–S120.

Collins, W. A. (2003). More than myth: the developmental significance of romantic relationships during adolescence. *Journal of Research on Adolescence, 13*, 1–24.

Connolly, J., Furman, W., and Konarski, R. (2000). The role of peers in the emergence of heterosexual romantic relationships in adolescence. *Child Development, 71*, 1395–1408.

Cook, K. (2000). You have to have somebody watching your back, and if that's God, then that's mighty big: the church's role in the resilience of inner-city youth. *Adolescence, 35*, 717–730.

Côté, J. E. (2000). *Arrested adulthood: the changing nature of maturity and identity*. New York: New York University Press.

Cotterell, J. L. (1991). The emergence of adolescent territories in a large urban leisure environment. *Journal of Environmental Psychology, 11*, 25–41.

Cotterell, J. L. (1994). Analyzing the strength of supportive ties in adolescent social supports. In F. Nestmann and K. Hurrelmann (eds), *Social networks and social support in childhood and adolescence* (pp. 257–267). Berlin: Walter de Gruyter.

Covington, M. V., and Omelich, C. L. (1988). I can resist anything but temptation: adolescent expectations for smoking cigarettes. *Journal of Applied Social Psychology, 18*, 203–227.

Cowie, H. (1999). Peers helping peers: interventions, initiatives and insights. *Journal of Adolescence, 22*, 433–436.

Crane, P., and Dee, M. (2001). Young people, public space and new urbanism. *Youth Studies Australia, 20*(1), 11–18.

Crossley, N. (2005). The new social physics and the science of small world networks. *Sociological Review, 53*, 352–359.

Cullingford, C. (1999). The relationship between delinquency and non-attendance at school. In E. Blyth and J. Milner (eds), *Improving school attendance* (pp. 55–72). London: Routledge.

Curry, G. D., Decker, S., and Egley, A. J. (2002). Gang involvement and delinquency in a middle school population. *Justice Quarterly, 19*, 275–292.

Cutrona, C. E. (1982). Transition to college: loneliness and the process of social adjustment. In L. A. Peplau and D. Perlman (eds), *Loneliness: a sourcebook of current theory, research and therapy* (pp. 291–309). New York: Wiley.

Damico, S. B. (1976). Clique membership and its relationship to academic achievement and attitude toward school. *Journal of Research and Development in Education, 9*, 29–35.

da Silva, L., Sanson, A., Smart, D., and Toumbourou, J. (2004). Civic responsibility among Australian adolescents: testing two competing models. *Journal of Community Psychology, 32*, 229–255.

Davey, J., Davey, T., and Obst, P. (2002). Alcohol consumption and drug use in a sample of Australian university students. *Youth Studies Australia, 21*(3), 25–32.

Davies, S. (1999). Subcultural explanations and interpretations of school deviance. *Aggression and Violent Behavior, 4*, 191–202.

Debold, E., Brown, L. M., Weseen, S., and Brookins, G. (1999). Cultivating hardiness zones for adolescent girls: a reconceptualization of resilience in relations with caring adults. In N. Johnson, M. Roberts and J. Worell (eds), *Beyond appearance: a new look at adolescent girls* (pp. 181–204). Washington, DC: American Psychological Association.

Deci, E. L., and Ryan, R. M. (1987). The support of autonomy and the control of behavior. *Journal of Personality and Social Psychology, 53*, 1024–1037.

Degenne, A., and Lebeaux, M.-O. (2005). The dynamics of personal networks at the time of entry into adult life. *Social Networks, 27*, 337–358.

Delle-Fave, A., and Bassi, M. (2003). Italian adolescents and leisure: the role of engagement and optimal experience. *New Directions for Child and Adolescent Development, 99*, 79–93.

Delorme, D. E., Kreshel, P. J., and Reid, L. N. (2003). Lighting up: young adults' autobiographical accounts of their first smoking experiences. *Youth and Society, 34*, 468–496.

Demuth, S. (2004). Understanding the delinquency and social relationships of loners. *Youth and Society, 35*, 366–392.

Denscombe, M. (1985). *Classroom control: a sociological perspective*. London: Allen and Unwin.

de Sola Pool, I., and Kochen, M. (1978). Contacts and influence. *Social Networks, 1*, 5–51.

Dishion, T. J., MCord, J., and Poulin, F. (1999). When interventions harm: peer groups and problem behavior. *American Psychologist, 54*, 755–764.

Dornyei, Z. (2000). Motivation in action: towards a process-oriented conceptualisation of student motivation. *British Journal of Educational Psychology, 70*, 519–538.

Dovidio, J. F., Validzic, A., and Gaertner, S. L. (1998). Intergroup bias: status, differentiation, and a common ingroup identity. *Journal of Personality and Social Psychology, 75*, 109–120.

Drury, J., and Reicher, S. (2000). Collective action and psychological change: the emergence of new social identities. *British Journal of Social Psychology, 39*, 579–604.

Drury, J., Catan, L., Dennison, C., and Brody, R. (1998). Exploring teenagers' accounts of bad communication: a new basis for intervention. *Journal of Adolescence, 21,* 177–196.

Du Bois-Reymond, M. (1998). 'I don't want to commit myself yet': young people's life concepts. *Journal of Youth Studies, 1,* 63–79.

Dunphy, D. (1963). The social structure of urban adolescent peer groups. *Sociometry, 26,* 230–246.

Dworkin, J. B., Larson, R., and Hansen, D. (2003). Adolescents' accounts of growth experiences in youth activities. *Journal of Youth and Adolescence, 32,* 17–26.

Eder, D. (1988). Building cohesion through collaborative narration. *Social Psychology Quarterly, 51,* 225–235.

Ehly, S., and Vasquez, E. (1998). Peer counselling. In R. Topping and S. Ehly (eds), *Peer assisted learning* (pp. 219–233). Marwah, NJ: LEA.

Ehntholt, K. A., Smith, P. A., and Yule, W. (2005). School-based cognitive-behavioural therapy group intervention for refugee children who have experienced war-related trauma. *Clinical Child Psychology and Psychiatry, 10,* 235–250.

Eiser, J. R., Morgan, M., Gammage, P., Brooks, N., and Kirby, R. (1991). Adolescent health behaviour and similarity-attraction: friends share smoking habits (really), but much else besides. *British Journal of Social Psychology, 30,* 339–348.

Elder, G. H. (1998). The life course as developmental theory. *Child Development, 69,* 1–12.

Elliot, A. J., and Church, M. (2003). A motivational analysis of defensive pessimism and self-handicapping. *Journal of Personality, 71,* 369–396.

Emler, N., and Reicher, S. (1995). *Adolescence and delinquency: the collective management of reputation.* Oxford: Blackwell.

Engel, U., Nordlohne, E., Hurrelmann, K., and Holler, B. (1987). Educational career and substance use in adolescence. *European Journal of Psychology of Education, 2,* 365–374.

Ennett, S. T., and Bauman, K. E. (1993). Peer group structure and adolescent cigarette smoking: a social network analysis. *Journal of Health and Social Behavior, 34,* 226–236.

Ennett, S. T., and Bauman, K. E. (1994). The contribution of influence and selection to adolescent peer group homogeneity: The case of adolescent cigarette smoking. *Journal of Personality and Social Psychology, 67,* 653–663.

Ennett, S. T., and Bauman, K. E. (1996). Adolescent social networks: school, demographic and longitudinal considerations. *Journal of Adolescent Research, 11,* 194–215.

Esbensen, F.-A., Deschenes, E. P., and Winfree, L. T., Jr (1999). Differences between gang girls and gang boys: results from a multisite survey. *Youth and Society, 31,* 27–53.

Estrada, F. (2001). Juvenile violence as a social problem. *British Journal of Criminology, 41,* 639–655.

Everhart, R. B. (1982). The nature of 'goofing off' among junior high school adolescents. *Adolescence, 17,* 177–187.

Ewert, A. W. (1989). *Outdoor adventure pursuits: foundations, models, and theories.* Columbus, OH: Publishing Horizons.

Ewert, A. W., and Heywood, J. (1991). Group development in the natural environment: expectations, outcomes, and techniques. *Environment and Behavior, 23,* 592–615.

Faircloth, B. S., and Hamm, J. V. (2005). Sense of belonging among high school students representing 4 ethnic groups. *Journal of Youth and Adolescence, 34,* 293–309.

Fallis, R. K., and Opotow, S. (2003). Are students failing school or are schools failing students? Class cutting in high school. *Journal of Social Issues, 59,* 103–119.

Falzon, L. (2000). Determining groups from the clique structure in large social networks. *Social Networks, 22,* 159–172.

Fang, X., Li, X., Stanton, B., and Dong, Q. (2003). Social network positions and smoking experimentation among Chinese adolescents. *American Journal of Health Behavior, 27,* 257–267.

Feld, S. L. (1981). The focused organization of social ties. *American Journal of Sociology, 86,* 1015–1035.

Feldman, A. F., and Matjasko, J. L. (2005). The role of school-based extracurricular activities in adolescent development: a comprehensive review and future directions. *Review of Educational Research, 75,* 159–210.

Felner, R. D., Favazza, A., Shim, M., Brand, S., Gu, K., and Noonan, N. (2001). Whole school improvement and restructuring as prevention and promotion – lessons from STEP and the project on high performance learning communities. *Journal of School Psychology, 39,* 177–202.

Fergusson, D. M., Lynskey, M. T., and Horwood, L. J. (1996). Factors associated with continuity and changes in disruptive behavior patterns between childhood and adolescence. *Journal of Abnormal Child Psychology, 24,* 533–553.

Fine, G. A. (1988). Team sports, seasonal histories, significant events: little league baseball and the creation of collective meaning. *Sociology of Sport Journal, 2,* 299–313.

Finn, J. D. (1989). Withdrawing from school. *Review of Educational Research, 59,* 117–142.

Fischer, C. S. (1982). *To dwell among friends: personal networks in town and city.* Chicago: University of Chicago Press.

Fischer, C. S., Jackson, R. M., Stueve, C. A., Gerson, K., Jones, L. M., and Baldessare, M. (1977). *Networks and places: social relations in the urban setting.* New York: Free Press.

Fraley, R. C., and Davis, K. E. (1997). Attachment formation and transfer in young adults' close friendships and romantic relationships. *Personal Relationships, 4,* 131–144.

Fraley, R. C., and Shaver, P. R. (1998). Airport separations: a naturalistic study of adult attachment dynamics in separating couples. *Journal of Personality and Social Psychology, 75,* 1198–1212.

Frances, P. (1975). *Beyond control? A study of discipline in the comprehensive school.* London: Allen and Unwin.

Francis, B. (1999). Lads, lasses and (new) labour: 14–16 yr old students' responses to the 'laddish behaviour of boys' underachievement' debate. *British Journal of Sociology of Education, 20,* 355–371.

Frank, K. A. (1995). Identifying cohesive subgroups. *Social Networks, 17,* 27–56.

Freeman, L. C. (1992). The sociological concept of group – an empirical-test of 2 models. *American Journal of Sociology, 98*, 152–166.

Freeman, L. C. (1996). Cliques, Galois lattices, and the structure of human social groups. *Social Networks, 18*, 173–187.

Freeman, L. C. (2000). Visualizing social networks. *Journal of Social Structure, 1*(1), http://www.cmu.edu/joss/.

Freeman, L. C. (2004). *The development of social network analysis: a study in the sociology of science.* North Charleston, SC: BookSurge.

Friedkin, N. E. (1981). The development of structure in random networks: an analysis of the effects of increasing network density on five measures of structure. *Social Networks, 3*, 41–52.

Furlong, A. (2000). Introduction: Youth in a changing world. *International Social Science Journal* 164, 129–134.

Furman, W., and Buhrmester, D. (1992). Age and sex differences in perceptions of networks of personal relationships. *Child Development, 63*, 103–115.

Furstenberg, F. F. (2000). The sociology of adolescence and youth in the 1990s: a critical commentary. *Journal of Marriage and the Family, 62*, 896–910.

Galbo, J. J. (1989). The teacher as significant adult: a review of the literature, *Adolescence, 24*, 549–556.

Galliher, R., Welsh, D., Rostosky, S., and Kawaguchi, M. (2004). Interaction and relationship quality in late adolescent romantic couples. *Journal of Social and Personal Relationships, 21*, 203–216.

Gerber, R. W., and Newman, I. M. (1989). Predicting future smoking of adolescent experimental smokers. *Journal of Youth and Adolescence, 18*, 191–201.

Gill, R. (1991). Scenes from a mall. *Sunday Age*, 2 June.

Gilman, R., Meyers, J., and Perez, L. (2004). Structured extracurricular activities among adolescents: findings and implications for school psychologists. *Psychology in the Schools, 41*, 31–41.

Giordano, P. C. (2003). Relationships in adolescence. *Annual Review of Sociology, 29*, 257–281.

Giordano, P. C., Cernkovich, S., and Pugh, M. (1986). Friendship and delinquency. *American Journal of Sociology, 91*, 1170–1201.

Glover, D., Gough, G., Johnson, M., and Cartwright, N. (2000). Bullying in 25 secondary schools: incidence, impact and intervention. *Educational Research, 42*, 141–156.

Goodenow, C. (1993). Classroom belonging among early adolescent students: relationships to motivation and achievement. *Journal of Early Adolescence, 13*, 21–43.

Gordon, R. A., Lahey, B. B., Kawai, E., Loeber, R., Stouthamer-Loeber, M., and Farrington, D. P. (2004). Antisocial behaviour and youth gang membership: selection and socialisation. *Criminology, 42*, 55–87.

Gottlieb, B. H. (1991). Social supports in adolescence. In M. E. Colten and S. Gore (eds), *Adolescent stress: causes and consequences* (pp. 281–306). New York: McGraw-Hill.

Gottlieb, B. H., and Sylvestre, J. C. (1994). Social support in the relationships between older adolescents and adults. In F. Nestmann and K. Hurrelmann (eds),

Social networks and social support in childhood and adolescence (pp. 53–73). Berlin: Walter de Gruyter.

Graber, J. A., and Brooks-Gunn, J. (1996). Transitions and turning points: navigating the passage from childhood through adolescence. *Developmental Psychology, 32*, 768–776.

Graff, J. (2005). Streets of fire. *Time Magazine*, 14 November.

Graham, K., and Wells, S. (2001). Aggression among young adults in the social context of the bar. *Addiction Research and Theory, 9*, 193–219.

Graham, K., and Wells, S. (2003). Somebody's gonna get their head kicked in tonight! Aggression among young males in bars – a question of values? *British Journal of Criminology, 43*, 546–566.

Graham, S., and Juvonen, J. (2002). Ethnicity, peer harassment, and adjustment in middle school: an exploratory study. *Journal of Early Adolescence, 22*, 173–199.

Grahame, P. R., and Jardine, D. W. (1990). Deviance, resistance, and play: a study in the communicative organization of trouble in class. *Curriculum Inquiry, 20*, 284–304.

Granovetter, M. (1973). The strength of weak ties. *American Journal of Sociology, 78*, 1360–1380.

Granovetter, M. (1983). The strength of weak ties: a network theory revisited. *Sociological Theory, 1*, 201–233.

Greenberg, M. T., Weissberg, R. P., O'Brien, U., Zins, J. E., Fredericks, L., Resnick, H. *et al.* (2003). Enhancing school-based prevention and youth development through coordinated social, emotional, and academic learning. *American Psychologist, 58*, 466–474.

Griffiths, V. (1995). *Adolescent girls and their friends: feminist ethnography.* Aldershot: Avebury.

Grossman, L. (2005). Grow up? Not so fast. *Time*, 24 January, pp. 38–46.

Guerrero, L. K. (1997). Interactions with same-sex friends, opposite-sex friends and romantic partners: consistency or change? *Journal of Social and Personal Relationships, 14*, 31–58.

Hallinan, M. T., and Kubitschek, W. N. (1999). Conceptualizing and measuring school social networks: comment on Morgan and Sorensen. *American Sociological Review, 64*, 687–693.

Hallinan, M. T., and Smith, S. (1989). Classroom characteristics and student friendship cliques. *Social Forces, 67*, 898–919.

Hamm, J. V., and Faircloth, B. S. (2005). Peer context of mathematics classroom belonging in early adolescence. *Journal of Early Adolescence, 25*, 345–366.

Hansen, K. (2003). Education and the crime-age profile. *British Journal of Criminology, 43*, 141–168.

Harford, T., and Grant, B. (1987). Psychosocial factors in adolescent drinking contexts. *Journal of Studies on Alcohol, 48*, 551–557.

Hartup, W. W. (1999). Constraints on peer socialization: let me count the ways. *Merrill-Palmer Quarterly, 45*, 172–183.

Havighurst, R. J. (1972). *Developmental tasks and education* (3rd edn). New York: McKay.

Hawker, D. S. J., and Boulton, M. J. (2000). Twenty years' research on peer victimization and psychosocial maladjustment: a meta-analytic review of cross-sectional studies. *Journal of Child Psychology and Psychiatry and Allied Disciplines, 41*, 441–455.

Hawkins, J. D., Graham, J. W., Maguin, E., Abbott, R., Hill, K. G., and Catalano, R. F. (1997). Exploring the effects of age of alcohol use initiation and psychosocial risk factors on subsequent alcohol misuse. *Journal of Studies on Alcohol, 58*, 280–290.

Haynie, D. L. (2001). Delinquent peers revisited: does network structure matter? *American Journal of Sociology, 106*, 1013–1057.

Heinz, W. R. (2000). Youth transitions and employment in Germany. *International Social Science Journal*, 164, 161–170.

Heinz, W. R. (2002). Self-socialization and post-traditional society. In R. A. J. Setterstein and T. J. Owens (eds), *Advances in life course research (vol. 7): New frontiers in socialization* (pp. 41–64). Chicago: JAI Press.

Hendry, L. B. (1989). The influence of adults and peers on adolescents' lifestyles and leisure-styles. In K. Hurrelmann and U. Engel (eds), *The social world of adolescents* (pp. 245–263). Berlin: Walter de Gruyter.

Hendry, L. B., and Kloep, M. (2002). *Lifespan development: resources, challenges and risks*. London: Thomson Learning.

Hendry, L. B., Roberts, W., Glendinning, A. G., and Coleman, J. C. (1992). Adolescents' perceptions of significant others in their lives. *Journal of Adolescence, 15*, 255–270.

Hendry, L. B., Kloep, M., and Wood, S. (2002). Young people talking about adolescent rural crowds and social settings. *Journal of Youth Studies, 5*, 357–374.

Hirsch, B. J., Roffman, J., Deutsch, N. L., Flynn, C., Loder, T., and Pagano, M. (2000). Inner-city youth development organizations: strengthening programs for adolescent girls. *Journal of Early Adolescence, 20*, 210–230.

Hirschi, T. (1969). *Causes of delinquency*. Berkeley, CA: University of California Press.

Hobfoll, S. E., and Stokes, J. P. (1988). The process and management of support. In S. W. Duck (ed.), *Handbook of personal relationships* (pp. 497–517). New York: Wiley.

Hogg, M. A., and Abrams, D. (1988). *Social identifications*. London: Routledge.

Hogg, M. A. (1996). Intragroup processes, group structure and social identity. In W. P. Robinson (Ed.), *Social groups and identities: Developing the legacy of Henri Tajfel* (pp. 65–93). Oxford: Butterworth-Heineman.

Holland, A., and Andre, T. (1987). Participation in extracurricular activities in secondary school: what is known, what needs to be known? *Review of Educational Research, 57*, 437–466.

Horvat, E. M., Weininger, E. B., and Lareau, A. (2003). From social ties to social capital: class differences in the relations between schools and parent networks. *American Educational Research Journal, 40*, 319–351.

Hufton, N. R., Elliott, J. G., and Illushin, L. (2002). Educational motivation and engagement: qualitative accounts from three countries. *British Educational Research Journal, 28*, 265–289.

Hussong, A. M. (2002). Differentiating peer contexts and risk for adolescent substance use. *Journal of Youth and Adolescence, 31*, 207–220.

Iannotti, R. J., and Bush, P. J. (1992). Perceived vs actual friends' use of alcohol, cigarettes, marijuana, and cocaine: which has the most influence? *Journal of Youth and Adolescence, 21*, 375–389.

Jackson, C. (2003). Motives for 'laddishness' at school: fear of failure and fear of the feminine. *British Educational Research Journal, 29*, 581–598.

Jackson, S., Jacob, M., Landman-Peeters, K., and Lanting, A. (2001). Cognitive strategies employed in trying to arrange a first date. *Journal of Adolescence, 24*, 267–279.

Jarrett, R. L., Sullivan, P. J., and Watkins, N. D. (2005). Developing social capital through participation in organized youth programs: qualitative insights from three programs. *Journal of Community Psychology, 33*, 41–55.

Johnson, B. R., Jang, S. J., De Li, S., and Larson, D. (2000). The 'invisible institution' and black youth crime: the church as an agency of local social control. *Journal of Youth and Adolescence, 29*, 479–498.

Johnson, F., and Aries, E. (1983). Conversational patterns among same-sex pairs of late-adolescent close friends. *Journal of Genetic Psychology, 142*, 225–238.

Johnson, M. K. (2002). Social origins, adolescent experiences, and work value trajectories during the transition to adulthood. *Social Forces, 80*, 1307–1341.

Johnston, K. L., and White, K. M. (2004). Binge drinking in female university students. *Youth Studies Australia, 23*(2), 22–30.

Jones, D. C. (1991). Friendship satisfaction and gender: an examination of sex differences in contributors to friendship satisfaction. *Journal of Social and Personal Relationships, 8*, 167–185.

Jones, W. H., Freemon, J. E., and Goswick, R. A. (1981). The persistence of loneliness: self and other determinants. *Journal of Personality, 49*, 27–48.

Jordan, K. (2003). A trauma and recovery model for victims and their families after a catastrophic school shooting: focusing on behavioral, cognitive, and psychological effects and needs. *Brief Treatment and Crisis Intervention, 3*, 397–411.

Jordan, W. J., and Nettles, S. M. (2000). How students invest their time outside of school: effects on school-related outcomes. *School Psychology of Education, 3*, 217–243.

Juvonen, J. (1991). Deviance, perceived responsibility, and negative peer reactions. *Developmental Psychology, 27*, 672–681.

Juvonen, J. (1992). Negative peer reactions from the perspective of the reactor. *Journal of Educational Psychology, 84*, 314–321.

Kadushin, C. (2004). Review: Too much investment in social capital? *Social Networks, 26*, 75–90.

Kafetsios, K., and Nezlek, J. B. (2002). Attachment styles in everyday social interaction. *European Journal of Social Psychology, 32*, 719–735.

Kandel, D. B., and Davies, M. (1991). Friendship networks, intimacy, and illicit drug use in young adulthood: a comparison of two competing theories. *Criminology, 29*, 441–468.

Kanevsky, L., and Keighley, T. (2003). To produce or not to produce? Understanding boredom and the honor in underachievement. *Roeper Review, 26*(1), 20–28.

Kenford, S. L., Wetter, D. W., Welsch, S. K., Smith, S. S., Fiore, M. C., and Baker, T. B. (2005). Progression of college-age cigarette samplers: what influences outcome. *Addictive Behaviors, 30*, 285–294.

Kenway, J., Kraack, A., and Hickey-Moody, A. (2006). *Masculinity beyond the metropolis*. New York: Palgrave Macmillan.

Kiesner, J., Cadinu, M., Poulin, F., and Bucci, M. (2002). Group identification in early adolescence: its relation with peer adjustment and its moderator effect on peer influence. *Child Development, 73*, 196–208.

Kinney, D. A. (1993). From nerds to normals: the recovery of identity among adolescents from middle school to high school. *Sociology of Education, 66*, 21–40.

Kirke, D. M. (1996). Collecting peer data and delineating peer networks in a complete network. *Social Networks, 18*, 333–346.

Kirke, D. M. (2004). Chain reactions in adolescents' cigarette, alcohol and drug use: similarity through peer influence or the patterning of ties in peer networks? *Social Networks, 26*, 3–28.

Kirke, D. M. (2006). *Teenagers and substance use: social networks and peer influence*. London: Pan Macmillan.

Klein, M. W., Kerner, H. J., Maxson, C. L., and Weitekamp, E. G. M. (eds) (2001). *The Eurogang paradox: street gangs and youth groups in the US and Europe*. London: Kluwer.

Klerks, P. (2001). The network paradigm applied to criminal organisations: theoretical nitpicking or a relevant doctrine for investigators? Recent developments in the Netherlands. *Connections, 24*(3), 53–65.

Klinbail, R. (2005). Real cases: Changing ill-conceived beliefs. *Medical Observer,* 27 May, p. 33.

Klingman, A., and Zeidner, M. (1993). School-related anger in Israeli adolescent students: major determinants and coping strategies. *School Psychology International, 14*, 339–353.

Klovdahl, A. S. (1981). A note on images of networks. *Social Networks, 3*, 197–214.

Klovdahl, A. S., Potterat, J. J., Woodhouse, D. E., Muth, J. B., Muth, S. Q., and Darrow, W. W. (1994). Social networks and infectious disease – the Colorado Springs study. *Social Science and Medicine, 38*(1), 79–88.

Knobloch, P., and Goldstein, A. P. (1971). *The lonely teacher*. Boston: Allyn and Bacon.

Kobus, K. (2003). Peers and adolescent smoking. *Addiction. Special Issue: Contexts and adolescent tobacco use trajectories, 98*(Suppl. 1), 37–55.

Kogut, B., and Walker, G. (2001). The small world of Germany and the durability of national networks. *American Sociological Review, 66*, 317–335.

Kolb, D. (1984). *Experiential learning*. Englewood-Cliffs, NJ: Prentice Hall.

Krange, O., and Pedersen, W. (2001). Return of the Marlboro man? Recreational smoking among young Norwegian adults. *Journal of Youth Studies, 4*, 155–174.

Kreager, D. A. (2004). Strangers in the halls: isolation and delinquency in school networks. *Social Forces, 83*, 351–390.

Krohn, M. D. (1986). The web of conformity: a network approach to the explanation of delinquent behavior. *Social Problems, 33*, S81–S93.

Krohn, M. D., Massey, J. L., and Zielinski, M. A. (1988). Role overlap, network multiplexity, and adolescent deviant behavior. *Social Psychology Quarterly, 51*, 346–356.

Kuntsche, E. N., and Kuendig, H. (2005). Do school surroundings matter? Alcohol outlet density, perception of adolescent drinking in public, and adolescent alcohol use. *Addictive Behaviors, 30*, 151–158.

Kuo, M., Wechsler, H., Greenberg, P., and Lee, H. (2003). The marketing of alcohol to college students: the role of low prices and special promotions. *American Journal of Preventative Medicine, 25*, 204–211.

Kuttler, A. F., and La Greca, A. M. (2004). Linkages among adolescent girls' romantic relationships, best friendships, and peer networks. *Journal of Adolescence, 27*, 395–414.

Kuttler, A. F., La Greca, A., and Prinstein, M. (1999). Friendship qualities and social-emotional functioning of adolescents with close, cross-sex friendships. *Journal of Research on Adolescence, 9*, 339–366.

La Greca, A. M., Prinstein, M. J., and Fetter, M. D. (2001). Adolescent peer crowd affiliation: linkages with health-risk behaviors and close friendships. *Journal of Pediatric Psychology, 26*, 131–143.

Lahey, B. B., Gordon, R. A., Loeber, R., Stouthamer-Loeber, M., and Farrington, D. P. (1999). Boys who join gangs: a prospective study of predictors of first gang entry. *Journal of Abnormal Child Psychology, 27*, 261–276.

Layne, C. M., Pynoos, R. S., Saltzman, W. R., Arslanagić, B., Savjak, N., Popović, T. *et al.* (2001). Trauma/grief-focused group psychotherapy: school-based postwar intervention with traumatized Bosnian adolescents. *Group Dynamics: Theory, Research, and Practice, 5*, 277–290.

Leary, M. R., Kowalski, R. M., Smith, L., and Phillips, S. (2003). Teasing, rejection, and violence: case studies of the school shootings. *Aggressive Behavior, 29*, 202–214.

Lease, A. M., McFall, R. M., and Viken, R. J. (2003). Distance from peers in the group's perceived organizational structure: relation to individual characteristics. *Journal of Early Adolescence, 23*, 194–217.

Le Bon, G. (1896/1947). *The crowd: a study of the popular mind*. London: Ernest Benn.

Lei, J. L. (2003). (Un)necessary toughness: those 'loud black girls' and those 'quiet Asian boys'. *Anthropology and Education Quarterly, 34*, 158–181.

Leonard, K. E., Quigley, B. M., and Collins, R. L. (2002). Physical aggression in the lives of young adults: prevalence, location, and severity among college and community samples. *Journal of Interpersonal Violence, 17*, 533–550.

Levin, I., and Stokes, J. P. (1986). An examination of the relation of individual difference variables to loneliness. *Journal of Personality, 54*, 717–733.

Levitt, M. J. (2005). Social relations in childhood and adolescence: the convoy model perspective. *Human Development, 48*, 28–47.

Lewis, G. H. (1989). Rats and bunnies: core kids in an American mall. *Adolescence, 24*, 881–889.

Liebow, E., McGrady, G., Branch, K., Vera, M., Klovdahl, A., Lovely, R. *et al.* (1995). Eliciting social network data and ecological model-building: focus on choice of name generators and administration of random-walk study procedures. *Social Networks, 17,* 257–272.

Lin, N. (1999). Building a network theory of social capital. *Connections, 22*(1), 28–51.

Lindsay, J. (2001). Sex, drugs and drinking: health risks in the social lives of young workers. *Youth Studies Australia, 20*(4), 11–18.

Lindsay, W. (1987). Social skills training with adolescents. In J. C. Coleman (ed.), *Working with troubled adolescents* (pp. 107–122). London: Academic Press.

Lintonen, T. P., and Konu, A. I. (2004). The misperceived social norm of drunkenness among early adolescents in Finland. *Health Education Research, 19,* 64–70.

Liu, M., and Chen, X. (2003). Friendship networks and social, school and psychological adjustment in Chinese junior high school students. *Psychology in the Schools, 40,* 5–17.

Lloyd, B., Lucas, K., and Fernbach, M. (1997). Adolescent girls' constructions of smoking identities: implications for health promotion. *Journal of Adolescence, 20,* 43–56.

Logan, W. L. (1997). Peer consultation group: doing what works for counselors. *Professional School Counseling, 1*(2), 4–9.

McCarty, C. (2002). Structure in personal networks. *Journal of Social Structure, 3*(1). http://www.cmu.edu/joss/index.html

McEachern, T., and O'Keefe, B. (1998). *Re-wiring business: uniting management and the Web.* New York: Wiley.

McEvoy, A., and Weller, R. (2000). Antisocial behaviour, academic failure and school climate: a critical review. *Journal of Emotional and Behavioral Disorders, 8,* 130–140.

McFarland, D. A. (2001). Student resistance: how the formal and informal organization of classrooms facilitate everyday forms of student defiance. *American Journal of Sociology, 107,* 612–678.

McGee, R., Williams, S., Howden-Chapman, P., Martin, J., and Kawachi, I. (2005). Participation in clubs and groups from childhood to adolescence and its effects on attachment and self-esteem. *Journal of Adolescence, 29,* 1–17.

McGrady, G. A., Marrow, C., Myers, G., Daniels, M., Vera, M., Mueller, C. *et al.* (1995). A note on implementation of a random-walk design to study adolescent social networks. *Social Networks, 17,* 251–255.

McLellan, J. A., and Youniss, J. (2003). Two systems of youth service: determinants of voluntary and required youth community service. *Journal of Youth and Adolescence, 32,* 47–58.

MacLeod, D. I. (1983). *Building character in the American boy.* Madison, WI: University of Wisconsin Press.

McMillan, D. W., and Chavis, D. M. (1986). Sense of community: a definition and theory. *Journal of Community Psychology, 14,* 6–23.

McNeely, C., and Falci, C. (2004). School connectedness and the transition into and out of health-risk behaviour among adolescents: a comparison of social belonging and teacher support. *Journal of School Health, 74,* 284–292.

McNeely, C., Nonnemaker, J. M., and Blum, R. W. (2002). Promoting school connectedness: evidence from the national longitudinal study of adolescent health. *Journal of School Health, 72*, 138–146.

Maehr, M. L. (1976). Continuing motivation – analysis of a seldom considered educational outcome. *Review of Educational Research, 46*, 443–462.

Mahoney, J. L. (2000). School extracurricular activity participation as a moderator in the development of antisocial patterns. *Child Development, 71*, 502–516.

Mahoney, J. L., and Cairns, R. B. (1997). Do extracurricular activities protect against early school dropout? *Developmental Psychology, 33*, 241–253.

Mahoney, J. L., and Stattin, H. (2000). Leisure activities and adolescent antisocial behavior: the role of structure and social context. *Journal of Adolescence, 23*, 113–127.

Mahoney, J. L., Schweder, A. E., and Stattin, H. (2002). Structured after-school activities as a moderator of depressed mood for adolescents with detached relations to their parents. *Journal of Community Psychology, 30*, 69–86.

Mahoney, J. L., Cairns, B. D., and Farmer, T. W. (2003). Promoting interpersonal competence and educational success through extracurricular activity participation. *Journal of Educational Psychology, 95*, 409–418.

Margulies, R., Kessler, R., and Kandel, D. B. (1977). A longitudinal study of onset of drinking among high-school students. *Journal of Studies on Alcohol, 38*, 879–912.

Marsh, H. W. (1992). Extracurricular activities: beneficial extension of the traditional curriculum or subversion of academic goals? *Journal of Educational Psychology, 84*, 553–562.

Marsh, H. W., and Kleitman, S. (2002). Extracurricular school activities: the good, the bad, and the non-linear. *Harvard Educational Review, 72*, 464–511.

Martin, A., Marsh, H. W., Williamson, A., and Debus, R. L. (2003). Self-handicapping, defensive pessimism, and goal orientation: a qualitative study of university students. *Journal of Educational Psychology, 95*, 617–628.

Martin, L. (2002). *The invisible table: perspectives on youth and youthwork in New Zealand*. Palmerston North: Dunedin Press.

Martino, W. (1999). Cool boys, party animals, squids and poofters. Interrogating the dynamics and politics of adolescent masculinities in school. *British Journal of Sociology of Education, 20*, 238–263.

Maxwell, K. A. (2002). Friends: the role of peer influence across adolescent risk behaviors. *Journal of Youth and Adolescence, 31*, 267–277.

Mendelson, M. J., and Aboud, F. E. (1999). Measuring friendship quality in late adolescents and young adults: McGill friendship questionnaires. *Canadian Journal of Behavioural Science, 31*, 130–132.

Merten, D. E. (1996a). Visibility and vulnerability: responses to rejection by nonaggressive junior high school boys. *Journal of Early Adolescence, 16*, 5–26.

Merten, D. E. (1996b). Information versus meaning: toward a further understanding of early adolescent rejection. *Journal of Early Adolescence, 16*, 37–45.

Metz, E., McLellan, J., and Youniss, J. (2003). Types of voluntary service and adolescents' civic development. *Journal of Adolescent Research, 18*, 188–203.

Michell, L., and Amos, A. (1997). Girls, pecking order and smoking. *Social Science and Medicine, 44*, 1861–1869.

Milgram, S., and Toch, H. (1969). Collective behaviour: crowds and social movements. In G. Lindzey and E. Aronson (eds), *The handbook of social psychology* (2nd edn, Vol. 4, pp. 507–610). Reading, MA: Addison-Wesley.

Miller, G. (1969). Psychology as a means of promoting human welfare. *American Psychologist, 24*, 1063–1075.

Miller, G., Brehm, K., and Whitehouse, S. (1998). Reconceptualizing school-based prevention for antisocial behaviour within a resiliency framework. *School Psychology Review, 27*, 364–379.

Miller, L. (2004). Psychotherapeutic interventions for survivors of terrorism. *American Journal of Psychotherapy, 58*, 1–16.

Mitchell, J. C. (1973). Networks, norms and institutions. In J. Boissevain and J. C. Mitchell (eds), *Network analysis: studies in human interaction* (pp. 15–35). The Hague: Mouton.

Mitchell, J. J. (1998). *The natural limitations of youth: the predispositions that shape the adolescent character.* Stamford, CN: Ablex.

Mjagkii, N., and Spratt, M. (eds) (1997). *Men and women adrift.* New York: New York University Press.

Moffitt, T. E. (1993). Adolescence-limited and life-course-persistent antisocial behavior: a developmental taxonomy. *Psychological Review, 100*, 674–701.

Montemayor, R., and van Komen, R. (1985). The development of sex differences in friendship patterns and peer group structure during adolescence. *Journal of Early Adolescence, 5*, 285–294.

Moody, E. J. (2001). Internet use and its relationship to loneliness. *Cyber-Psychology and Behavior, 4*, 393–401.

Moody, J. (2001). Peer influence groups: identifying dense clusters in large networks. *Social Networks, 23*, 261–283.

Moody, J., and White, D. R. (2003). Structural cohesion and embeddedness: a hierarchical concept of social groups. *American Sociological Review, 68*, 103–127.

Moore, M. M. (1995). Courtship signaling and adolescents: 'Girls just wanna have fun'? *Journal of Sex Research, 32*, 319–328.

Morahan-Martin, J., and Schumacher, P. (2003). Loneliness and social uses of the Internet. *Computers in Human Behavior, 19*, 659–671.

Moreno, J. L. (1934). *Who shall survive? A new approach to the problem of human interrelations.* Washington, DC: Nervous and Mental Disease Publishing Company.

Morgan, M., and Grube, J. W. (1991). Closeness and peergroup influence. *British Journal of Social Psychology, 30*, 159–169.

Morris, L., Sallybanks, J., Willis, K., and Makkai, T. (2004). Sport, physical activity and antisocial behaviour in youth. *Youth Studies Australia, 23*(1), 47–52.

Mosbach, P., and Leventhal, H. (1988). Peer group identification and smoking: implications for intervention. *Journal of Abnormal Psychology, 97*, 238–245.

Moss, H. B., Lynch, K. G. and Hardie, T. L. (2003). Affiliation with deviant peers among children of substance dependent fathers from pre-adolescence into adolescence: associations with problem behaviors. *Drug and Alcohol*

Dependence, 71, 117–125.

Mouton, S., Hawkins, J., McPherson, R., and Copley, J. (1996). School attachment: perspectives of low-attached high school students. *Educational Psychology, 16*, 297–304.

Naylor, P., and Cowie, H. (1999). The effectiveness of peer support systems in challenging school bullying: the perspectives and experiences of teachers and pupils. *Journal of Adolescence, 22*, 467–479.

Nichols, J. D., and White, J. (2001). Impact of peer networks on achievement of high school algebra students. *Journal of Educational Research, 94*, 267–273.

Nickerson, A. B., and Nagle, R. J. (2005). Parent and peer attachment in late childhood and early adolescence. *Journal of Early Adolescence, 25*, 223–249.

Nurmi, J.-E., Toivonen, S., Salmela-Aro, K., and Eronen, S. (1997). Social strategies and loneliness. *Journal of Social Psychology, 137*, 764–777.

Oetting, E. R., and Beauvais, F. (1987a). Common elements in youth drug abuse: peer clusters and other psychosocial factors. *Journal of Drug Issues, 17*, 133–151.

Oetting, E. R., and Beauvais, F. (1987b). Peer cluster theory, socialisation characteristics, and adolescent drug use: a path analysis. *Journal of Counselling Psychology, 34*, 205–213.

O'Keeffe, D. J. (1994). *Truancy in English secondary schools*. London: HMSO.

Olweus, D. (1978). *Aggression in the schools: bullies and whipping boys*. Washington, DC: Hemisphere.

Osgood, D. W., Wilson, J. K., O'Malley, P. M., Bachman, J. G., and Johnston, L. D. (1996). Routine activities and individual deviant behavior. *American Sociological Review, 61*, 635–655.

Owens, L., Shute, R., and Slee, P. T. (2000). 'Guess what I just heard!' Indirect aggression among teenage girls in Australia. *Aggressive Behavior, 26*, 67–83.

Pace, C. R. (1971). *Thoughts on evaluation of higher education*. Iowa City: The American College Testing Program.

Pancer, S. M., and Pratt, M. W. (1999). Social and family determinants of community service involvement in Canadian youth. In M. Yates and J. Youniss (eds), *Roots of civic identity: international perspectives on community service and activism in youth* (pp. 32–55). Cambridge: Cambridge University Press.

Panelli, R., Nairn, K., Atwool, N., and McCormack, J. (2002). Hanging out: print media constructions of young people in 'public space'. *Youth Studies Australia, 21*(4), 38–48.

Parkhurst, J. T., and Asher, S. R. (1992). Peer rejection in middle school: subgroup differences in behavior, loneliness, and interpersonal concerns. *Developmental Psychology, 28*, 231–241.

Parks, M., and Floyd, K. (1996). Meanings for closeness and intimacy in friendship. *Journal of Social and Personal Relationships, 13*, 85–107.

Patrick, H., Turner, J. C., Meyer, D. K., and Midgley, C. (2004). How teachers establish psychological environments during the first days of school: associations with avoidance in mathematics. *Teachers College Record, 105*, 1521–1558.

Patten, S. B., and Arboleda-Flórez, J. A. (2004). Epidemic theory and group violence. *Social Psychiatry and Psychiatric Epidemiology, 39*, 853–856.

Payne, A., Gottfredson, D. C., and Gottfredson, G. D. (2003). Schools as communities. *Criminology, 41,* 749–777.

Pearson, M., and Michell, L. (2000). Smoke rings: social network analysis of friendship groups, smoking and drug-taking. *Drugs Education, Prevention and Policy, 7,* 21–37.

Peplau, L. A., Micelli, M., and Morasch, B. (1982). Loneliness and self evaluation. In L. A. Peplau and D. Perlman (eds), *Loneliness: a sourcebook of current theory, research, and therapy* (pp. 135–151). New York: Wiley.

Petersen, A. C. (2004). Honouring the Thornburgs: pursuing policy-relevant research. *Journal of Early Adolescence, 24,* 12–28.

Petrides, L. A., and Guiney, S. Z. (2002). Knowledge management for school leaders: an ecological framework for thinking schools. *Teachers College Record, 104,* 1702–1717.

Pettigrew, T. E. (1998). Reactions toward the new minorities of Western Europe. *Annual Review of Sociology, 24,* 77–103.

Philip, K., and Hendry, L. B. (1996). Young people and mentoring – towards a typology? *Journal of Adolescence, 19,* 189–201.

Planalp, S., and Benson, A. (1992). Friends' and acquaintances' conversations I: perceived differences. *Journal of Social and Personal Relationships, 9,* 483–506.

Pleydon, A. P., and Schner, J. G. (2001). Female adolescent friendship and delinquent behavior. *Adolescence, 36,* 189–205.

Plumridge, E. W., Fitzgerald, L. J., and Abel, G. M. (2002). Performing coolness: smoking refusal and adolescent identities. *Health Education Research, 17,* 167–179.

Poulin, F., Dishion, T. J., and Haas, E. (1999). The peer influence paradox: friendship quality and deviancy training within male adolescent friendships. *Merrill-Palmer Quarterly, 45,* 42–61.

Power, C. N., and Cotterell, J. L. (1979). *Students in transition.* Adelaide: School of Education, Flinders University.

Power, C. N., and Cotterell, J. L. (1981). *Changes in students in the transition from primary to secondary school.* Canberra: Australian Government Publishing Service.

Pulkkinen, L., and Narusk, A. (1987). Functions of adolescent drinking in Finland and the Soviet Union. *European Journal of Psychology of Education, 11,* 311–326.

Putnam, R. D. (1993). *Making democracy work: civic traditions in modern Italy.* Princeton, NJ: Princeton University Press.

Putney, C. (1997). From character to body-building? The YMCA and the suburban metropolis 1950–1980. In N. Mjagkii and M. Spratt (eds), *Men and women adrift* (pp. 231–249). New York: New York University Press.

Radmacher, K., and Azmitia, M. (2006). Are there gendered pathways to intimacy in early adolescents' and emerging adults' friendships? *Journal of Adolescent Research, 21,* 415–448.

Rainey, L. M., Hensley, F. A., and Crutchfield, L. B. (1997). Implementation of support groups in elementary and middle school student assistance programs. *Professional School Counseling, 1*(2), 36–44.

Raven, J. (1994). *Managing education for effective schooling: the most important problem is to come to terms with values.* Unionville, NY: Trillum Press.

Reddrop, S. (1997). *Outdoor programs for young offenders in detention: an overview.* Hobart: National Clearinghouse for Youth Studies.

Reddy, R., Rhodes, J. E., and Mulhall, P. (2003). The influence of teacher support on student adjustment in the middle school years: a latent growth curve study. *Development and Psychopathology, 15,* 119–138.

Reeve, J. (1998). Autonomy support as an interpersonal motivating style: is it teachable? *Contemporary Educational Psychology, 23,* 312–330.

Reeve, J., Bolt, E., and Cai, Y. (1999). Autonomy-supportive teachers: how they teach and motivate students. *Journal of Educational Psychology, 91,* 537–548.

Reicher, S. (1987). Crowd behaviour as social action. In J. Turner (ed.), *Rediscovering the social group: a self-categorization theory* (pp. 171–203). Oxford: Blackwell.

Reicher, S., Stott, C., Cronin, P., and Adang, O. (2004). An integrated approach to crowd psychology and public order policing. *Policing, 27,* 558–572.

Reinke, W. M., and Herman, K. C. (2002). Creating school environments that deter antisocial behaviors in youth. *Psychology in the Schools, 39,* 549–559.

Reis, H. T., Sheldon, K. M., Gable, S. L., Roscoe, J., and Ryan, R. M. (2000). Daily well-being: the role of autonomy, competence, and relatedness. *Personality and Social Psychology Bulletin, 26,* 419–435.

Rheingold, H. (2002). *Smart mobs.* Cambridge: Perseus Publishing.

Rice, R. E., Donohew, L., and Clayton, R. R. (2003). Peer network, sensation seeking, and drug use among junior and senior high school students. *Connections, 25*(2), 32–58.

Rich, G. J. (2003). The positive psychology of youth and adolescence. *Journal of Youth and Adolescence, 32,* 1–3.

Richards, W. D., and Rice, R. E. (1981). The NEGOPY network analysis program. *Social Networks, 3,* 215–223.

Roberts, K. (1997). Prolonged transitions to uncertain destinations: the implications for careers guidance. *British Journal of Guidance and Counselling, 25,* 345–360.

Robins, G., Pattison, P., and Woolcock, J. (2005). Small and other worlds: global network structures from local processes. *American Journal of Sociology, 110,* 894–936.

Robinson, N. S. (1995). Evaluating the nature of perceived support and its relation to perceived self-worth in adolescents. *Journal of Research on Adolescence, 5,* 253–280.

Roker, D., Player, K., and Coleman, J. C. (1999). Exploring adolescent altruism: British young people's involvement in voluntary work and campaigning. In M. Yates and J. Youniss (eds), *Roots of civic identity: international perspectives on community service and activism in youth* (pp. 56–72). Cambridge: Cambridge University Press.

Rook, K. S. (1984). Promoting social bonding: strategies for helping the lonely and socially isolated. *American Psychologist, 39,* 1389–1407.

Rook, K. S. (1987). Social support versus companionship: effects on life stress, loneliness, and evaluations by others. *Journal of Personality and Social Psychology, 52*, 1132–1147.

Roscoe, B., and Skomski, G. (1989). Loneliness among late adolescents. *Adolescence, 24*, 947–955.

Rosenfeld, L. B., Richman, J. M., and Bowen, G. L. (2000). Social support networks and school outcomes: the centrality of the teacher. *Child and Adolescent Social Work Journal, 17*, 205–226.

Roth, J., and Brooks-Gunn, J. (1998). Promoting healthy adolescents: synthesis of youth development program evaluations. *Journal of Research on Adolescence, 8*, 423–459.

Roth, M. A., and Parker, J. G. (2001). Affective and behavioral responses to friends who neglect their friends for dating partners: influences of gender, jealousy and perspective. *Journal of Adolescence, 24*, 281–296.

Rutter, M., Giller, H., and Hagell, A. (1998). *Antisocial behaviour by young people.* Cambridge: Cambridge University Press.

Ryan, A. M. (2001). The peer group as a context for the development of young adolescent motivation and achievement. *Child Development, 72*, 1135–1150.

Ryan, R. M., and Deci, E. L. (2000). Self-determination theory and the facilitation of intrinsic motivation, social development, and well-being. *American Psychologist, 55*, 68–78.

Ryan, R. M., and Powelson, C. L. (1991). Autonomy and relatedness as fundamental to motivation and education. *Journal of Experimental Education, 60*, 49–66.

Salmivalli, C. (1999). Participant role approach to school bullying: implications for interventions. *Journal of Adolescence, 22*, 453–459.

Salmivalli, C., Huttunen, A., and Lagerspetz, K. M. J. (1997). Peer networks and bullying in schools. *Scandinavian Journal of Psychology, 38*, 305–312.

Saltzman, W. R., Pynoos, R. S., Steinberg, A. M., and Aisenberg, E. (2001). Trauma- and grief-focused intervention for adolescents exposed to community violence: results of a school-based screening and group treatment protocol. *Group Dynamics: Theory, Research, and Practice, 5*, 291–303.

Salzinger, L. L. (1982). The ties that bind – the effect of clustering on dyadic relationships. *Social Networks, 4*, 117–145.

Sanford, S., and Eder, D. (1985). Adolescent humor during peer interaction. *Social Psychology Quarterly, 47*, 235–243.

Sarkar, S., and Andreas, M. (2004). Acceptance of and engagement in risky driving behaviors by teenagers. *Adolescence, 39*, 687–700.

Sarnecki, J. (1990). Delinquent networks in Sweden. *Journal of Quantitative Criminology, 6*, 31–50.

Scales, P. C., Benson, P. L., Leffert, N., and Blyth, D. (2000). Contribution of developmental assets to the prediction of thriving among adolescents. *Applied Developmental Science, 4*, 27–46.

Schafer, M., Korn, S., Smith, P. K., Hunter, S. C., Mora-Merchan, J. A., Singer, M. M. *et al.* (2004). Lonely in the crowd: recollections of bullying. *British Journal of Developmental Psychology, 22*, 379–394.

Schaps, E., and Solomon, D. (2003). The role of the school's social environment in preventing student drug use. *Journal of Primary Prevention, 23*, 299–328.

Schmitt, M. T., Spears, R., and Branscombe, N. R. (2003). Constructing a minority group identity out of shared rejection: the case of International students. *European Journal of Social Psychology, 33*, 1–12.

Scholte, R. H. J., Van Aken, M. A. G., and Van Lieshout, C. F. M. (1997). Adolescent personality factors in self-ratings and peer nominations and their prediction of peer acceptance and peer rejection. *Journal of Personality Assessment, 69*, 534–554.

Schonfeld, D. J. (2002). Supporting adolescents in times of national crisis: potential roles for adolescent health care providers. *Journal of Adolescent Health, 30*, 302–307.

Schreck, C. J., Miller, J. M., and Gibson, C. L. (2003). Trouble in the school yard: a study of the risk factors of victimization at school. *Crime and Delinquency, 49*, 460–484.

Schreck, C. J., Fisher, B. S., and Miller, J. M. (2004). The social context of violent victimization: a study of the delinquent peer effect. *Justice Quarterly, 21*, 23–47.

Schulenberg, J. E., Maggs, J. L., Dielman, T. E., Leech, S. L., Kloska, D. D., Shope, J. T. *et al.* (1999). On peer influences to get drunk: a panel study of young adolescents. *Merrill-Palmer Quarterly, 45*, 108–142.

Schuster, B. (1999). Outsiders at school: the prevalence of bullying and its relation with social status. *Group Processes and Intergroup Relations, 2*, 175–190.

Scott, D., and Paxton, K. (1997). Joy-riding among British youth. *Psychological Reports, 81*, 297–298.

Scott, J. (2001). *Social network analysis: a handbook* (2nd edn). London: Sage.

Seely Brown, J., and Duguid, P. (2000). *The social life of information*. Boston: Harvard Business School.

Seidman, S. B. (1983). Network structure and minimum degree. *Social Networks, 5*, 269–287.

Seifert, T. L. (2004). Understanding student motivation. *Educational Research, 46*, 137–149.

Seiffge-Krenke, I. (2000). Diversity in romantic relations of adolescents with varying health status: links to intimacy in close friendships. *Journal of Adolescent Research, 15*, 611–636.

Selzer, V. C. (1989). *Psychosocial worlds of the adolescent*. New York: Wiley.

Sennett, R. (1998). *The corrosion of character: the personal consequences of work in the new capitalism*. New York: Norton.

Shanahan, M. J. (2000). Pathways to adulthood in changing societies: variability and mechanisms in life course perspective. *Annual Review of Sociology, 26*, 667–692.

Sheehan, M., and Ridge, D. (2001). 'You become really close. You talk about the silly things you did, and we laugh': the role of binge drinking in female secondary students' lives. *Substance Use and Misuse, 26*, 347–372.

Sherif, M., and Sherif, C. (1964). *Reference groups*. New York: Harper and Row.

Shrum, W., and Cheek, N. H. (1987). Social structure during the school years: onset of the degrouping process. *American Sociological Review, 52*, 218–223.

Shulman, S., Laursen, B., Kalman, Z., and Karpovsky, S. (1997). Adolescent intimacy revisited. *Journal of Youth and Adolescence, 26*, 597–617.

Sidanius, J., Van Laar, C., Levin, S., and Sinclair, S. (2004). Ethnic enclaves and the dynamics of social identity on the college campus: the good, the bad, and the ugly. *Journal of Personality and Social Psychology, 87*, 96–110.

Sieving, R. E., Perry, C. L., and Williams, C. L. (2000). Do friendships change behaviors, or do behaviors change friendships? Examining paths of influence in young adolescents' alcohol use. *Journal of Adolescent Health, 26*, 27–35.

Simmel, G. (1908/1955). *The web of group-affiliations*, trans. Reinhard Bendix. Glencoe, IL: Free Post.

Simon, B. (2004). *Identity in modern society: a social psychological perspective.* Oxford: Blackwell.

Smart, D., Vassallo, S., Sanson, A., and Dussuyer, I. (2004). *Report 290: Patterns of antisocial behaviour from early to late adolescence.* Canberra: Australian Institute of Criminology.

Smith, E. R., Murphy, J., and Coats, S. (1999). Attachment to groups: theory and management. *Journal of Personality and Social Psychology, 77*, 94–110.

Smith, H., and Thomas, S. P. (2000). Violent and non-violent girls: contrasting perceptions of anger experiences, school, and relationships. *Issues in Mental Health Nursing, 21*, 547–575.

Smith, J., and Baltes, P. B. (1999). Lifespan perspectives on development. In M. H. Bornstein and M. E. Lamb (eds), *Developmental psychology* (pp. 47–72). Hillsdale, NJ: Lawrence Erlbaum Associates.

Smith, P. K., Singer, M. M., Hoel, H., and Cooper, C. L. (2003). Victimization in the school and the workplace: are there any links? *British Journal of Psychology, 94*, 175–188.

Snijders, T. A. B., and Baerveldt, C. (2003). A multilevel network study of the effects of delinquent behaviour on friendship evolution. *Journal of Mathematical Sociology, 27*, 123–151.

Spears, R., Postmes, T., Lea, M., and Watt, S. E. (2001). A SIDE view of social influence. In J. P. Forgas and K. D. Williams (eds), *Social influence: direct and indirect processes* (pp. 331–350). Sydney: Psychology Press.

Spencer-Rodgers, J., and McGovern, T. (2002). Attitudes toward the culturally different: The role of intercultural communication barriers, affective responses, consensual stereotypes, and perceived threat. *International Journal of Intercultural Relations, 26*, 609–631.

Sperling, M. B., and Berman, W. H. (eds) (1994). *Attachment in adults.* London: Guilford.

Sprecher, S., Felmee, D., Metts, S., Fehr, B., and Vanni, D. (1998). Factors associated with distress following the breakup of a close relationship. *Journal of Social and Personal Relationships, 15*, 791–809.

Sroufe, L. A., and Waters, E. (1977). Attachment as an organizational construct. *Child Development, 48*, 1184–1199.

Stanton-Salazar, R. D. (1997). A social capital framework for understanding the socialization of racial minority children and youths. *Harvard Educational Review, 67*, 1–40.

Stanton-Salazar, R. D., Spina, S. U., and Yuki, M. (2003). Informal mentors and role models in the lives of urban Mexican-origin adolescents. Intergroup comparison versus intragroup relationships: a cross-cultural examination of social identity theory in North American and East Asian cultural contexts. *Anthropology and Education Quarterly, 34*, 231–254.

Stattin, H., Gustafson, S. B., and Magnusson, D. (1989). Peer influences on adolescent drinking: a social transition perspective. *Journal of Early Adolescence, 9*, 227–246.

Stephen, D. E., and Squires, P. A. (2003). Adults don't realize how sheltered they are. A contribution to the debate on youth transitions from some voices on the margins. *Journal of Youth Studies, 6*, 145–164.

Stiller, J., and Hudson, M. (2005). Weak links and scene cliques within the small world of Shakespeare. *Journal of Cultural and Evolutionary Psychology, 3*, 57–73.

Stokes, H. (2003). *Engaging young people in school through the arts* (Working Paper No. 24). Melbourne: Australian Youth Research Centre.

Stoneman, D. (2002). The role of youth programming in the development of civic engagement. *Applied Developmental Science, 6*, 221–226.

Stott, C., and Reicher, S. (1998). Crowd action as intergroup process: introducing the police perspective. *European Journal of Social Psychology, 28*, 509–529.

Sunwolf, and Leets, L. (2003). Communication paralysis during peer-group exclusion: social dynamics that prevent children and adolescents from expressing disagreement. *Journal of Language and Social Psychology, 22*, 355–384.

Sunwolf, and Leets, L. (2004). Being left out: rejecting outsiders and communicating group boundaries in childhood and adolescent peer groups. *Journal of Applied Communication Research, 32*, 195–223.

Tajfel, H. (1978). Social categorisation, social identity, and social comparison. In H. Tajfel (ed.), *Differentiation between social groups* (pp. 61–76). London: Academic Press.

Tajfel, H. (1981). *Human groups and social categories*. Cambridge: Cambridge University Press.

Tannen, D. (1990). Gender differences in topical coherence: creating involvement in best friends' talk. *Discourse Processes, 13*, 73–90.

Tarrant, M. (2002). Adolescent peer groups and social identity. *Social Development, 11*, 110–123.

Tasmania (1988). Supportive school environments. *The Tasmanian Education Gazette, 22*(April), 46–50.

Tatar, M. (1998). Significant individuals in adolescence: adolescent and adult perspectives. *Journal of Adolescence, 21*, 691–702.

Tharp, R., and Gallimore, R. (1988). *Rousing minds to life: teaching, learning, and schooling in social context*. Cambridge: Cambridge University Press.

Thompson, R. A. (2005). Multiple relationships multiply considered. *Human Development, 48*, 102–107.

Thornberry, T., Krohn, M. D., Lizotte, A., and Chard-Wierschem, D. (1993). The role of juvenile gangs in facilitating delinquent behaviour. *Journal of Research in Crime and Delinquency, 30*, 55–87.

Thornberry, T. P., Krohn, M. D., Lizotte, A. J., and Smith, C. A. (2003). *Gangs and delinquency in developmental perspective*. Cambridge: Cambridge University Press.

Thurlow, C. (2001). Naming the 'outsider within': homophobic pejoratives and the verbal abuse of lesbian, gay and bisexual high-school pupils. *Journal of Adolescence, 24,* 25–38.

Thurlow, C. (2002). Teenagers *in* communication, teenagers *on* communication. *Journal of Language and Social Psychology, 22,* 50–57.

Tindall, J. A. (1995). *Peer programs: an in-depth look at peer helping: planning, implementation, and administration.* St Charles, MO: Accelerated Development.

Tindall, J. A., and Gray, H. D. (1989). *Peer counselling.* Philadelphia: Research Press.

Tolson, J. M., and Urberg, K. A. (1993). Similarity between adolescent best friends. *Journal of Adolescent Research, 8,* 274–288.

Townsend, K. C., and McWhirter, B. T. (2005). Connectedness: a review of the literature with implications for counseling, assessment, and research. *Journal of Counseling and Development, 83,* 191–201.

Trevillion, S. (2000). Reform through school networks: a new kind of authority and accountability. *British Journal of Social Work, 30,* 505–517.

Turner, G. (1999). Peer support and young people's health. *Journal of Adolescence, 22,* 567–572.

Turner, J. C. (1991). *Social influence.* Milton Keynes: Open University Press.

Turner, J. C. (1999). Some current issues in research on social identity and self-categorization theories. In N. Ellemers, R. Spears and B. Doosje (eds), *Social identity: context, commitment, content* (pp. 6–34). Oxford: Blackwell.

Turner, J. C., Hogg, M. A., Oakes, P. J., Reicher, S. D., and Wetherell, M. S. (1987). *Rediscovering the social group: a self-categorization theory.* Oxford: Blackwell.

Twenge, J. M., and Baumeister, R. F. (2005). Social exclusion increases aggression and self-defeating behavior while reducing intelligent thought and prosocial behavior. In D. Abrams, M. A. Hogg and J. M. Marques (eds), *The social psychology of inclusion and exclusion* (pp. 27–46). New York: Psychology Press.

Unger, J. B., Rohrbach, L. A., Howard-Pitney, B., Ritt-Olson, A., and Mouttapa, M. (2001). Peer influences and susceptibility to smoking among California adolescents. *Substance Use and Misuse, 36,* 551–571.

Urberg, K. A., Degirmencioglu, S. M., Tolson, J. M., and Halliday-Scher, K. (1995). The structure of adolescent peer networks. *Developmental Psychology, 31,* 540–547.

Urberg, K. A., Degirmencioglu, S. M., and Pilgrim, C. (1997). Close friend and group influence on adolescent cigarette smoking and alcohol use. *Developmental Psychology, 33,* 834–844.

Urberg, K. A., Degirmencioglu, S. M., and Tolson, J. M. (1998). Adolescent friendship selection and termination: the role of similarity. *Journal of Social and Personal Relationships, 15,* 703–710.

Urberg, K. A., Shyu, S., and Liang, J. (1990). Peer influence in adolescent cigarette smoking. *Addictive Behaviors, 15,* 247–255.

Urdan, T. C., Midgley, C., and Anderman, E. M. (1998). The role of classroom goal structures in students' use of self-handicapping strategies. *American Educational Research Journal, 35*, 101–122.

van Bueren, E. M., Klijn, E.-H., and Koppenjan, J. F. M. (2003). Dealing with wicked problems in networks: analyzing an environmental debate from a network perspective. *Journal of Public Administration Research and Theory, 13*, 193–212.

Van den Bree, M. B., Whitmer, M. A., and Pickworth, W. B. (2003). Predictors of smoking development in a population-based sample of adolescents: a prospective study. *Journal of Adolescent Health, 35*, 172–181.

van Duijn, M. A. J., Zeggelink, E. P. H., Huisman, M., Stokman, F. N., and Wasseur, F. S. (2003). Evolution of sociology freshmen into a friendship network. *Journal of Mathematical Sociology, 27*, 153–191.

van Ijzendoorn, M. H. (2005). Attachment in social networks: toward an evolutionary social network model. *Human Development, 48*, 85–88.

Van Roosmalen, E. H., and McDaniel, S. A. (1989). Peer group influence as a factor in smoking behavior of adolescents. *Adolescence, 24*, 801–816.

Verkuyten, M., and Brug, P. (2003). Educational performance and psychological disengagement among ethnic minority and Dutch adolescents. *Journal of Genetic Psychology, 164*, 189–200.

Verlinden, S., Hersen, M., and Thomas, J. (2000). Risk factors in school shootings. *Clinical Psychology Review, 20*, 3–56.

Vider, S. (2004). Rethinking crowd violence: self-categorisation theory and the Woodstock 1999 riot. *Journal for the Theory of Social Behaviour, 34*, 141–165.

Walker, H. M., Ramsey, E., and Gresham, F. M. (2004). *Antisocial behavior in school: evidenced-based practices* (2nd edn). Belmont, CA: Thomson/ Wadsworth.

Wang, M. C., Haertel, G. D., and Walberg, H. J. (1997). Learning influences. In H. J. Walberg and G. D. Haertel (eds), *Psychology and educational practice* (pp. 199–211). Berkeley, CA: McCutchan.

Ward, B. (1982). Changes in student participation in different instructional settings. *Journal of Early Adolescence, 2*, 363–387.

Warrington, M., Younger, M. J., and Williams, J. (2000). Student attitudes, image, and the gender gap. *British Educational Research Journal, 26*, 393–407.

Wasserman, S., and Faust, K. (1994). *Social network analysis: methods and applications*. Cambridge: Cambridge University Press.

Watts, D. J. (1999). Networks, dynamics, and the small-world phenomenon. *American Journal of Sociology, 105*, 493–527.

Weeks, M. R., Clair, S., Borgatti, S. P., Radda, K., and Schensul, J. J. (2002). Social networks of drug users in high-risk sites: finding the connections. *AIDS and Behavior, 6*, 193–206.

Weimann, G. (1983). The strength of weak conversational ties in the flow of information and influence. *Social Networks, 5*, 245–267.

Weiss, R. S. (1974). The provisions of social relationships. In Z. Rubin (ed.), *Support systems and mutual help* (pp. 17–26). Englewood Cliffs, NJ: Prentice Hall.

Weiss, R. S. (1982). Attachment in adult life. In C. M. Parkes and J. Hinde (eds), *The place of attachment in human behaviour* (pp. 171–184). London: Tavistock.

Weitzman, E. R., Nelson, T. F., and Wechsler, H. (2003). Taking up binge drinking in college: the influences of person, social group, and environment. *Journal of Adolescent Health, 32,* 26–35.

Weitzman, E. R., Nelson, T. F., Lee, H., and Wechsler, H. (2004). Reducing drinking and related harms in college evaluation of the 'a matter of degree' program. *American Journal of Preventative Medicine, 27,* 187–196.

Wellman, B. (1988). Structural analysis: from method and metaphor to theory and substance. In B. Wellman and S. D. Berkowitz (eds), *Social structures: a network approach* (pp. 19–61). Cambridge: Cambridge University Press.

Wenger, E. (1998). *Communities of practice: learning, meaning, and identity.* Cambridge: Cambridge University Press.

Wentzel, K. R. (1997). Student motivation in middle school: the role of perceived pedagogical caring. *Journal of Educational Psychology, 89,* 411–419.

Whitney, I., and Smith, P. K. (1993). A survey of the nature and extent of bullying in junior/middle and secondary schools. *Educational Research, 35,* 3–25.

Williams, K. D., and Govan, C. L. (2005). Reacting to ostracism: retaliation or reconciliation? In D. Abrams, M. A. Hogg and J. M. Marques (eds), *The social psychology of inclusion and exclusion* (pp. 47–64). New York: Psychology Press.

Williams, P. (2001). Alcohol-related social disorder and rural youth: victims and perpetrators. *Youth Studies Australia, 20*(3), 11–19.

Willis, P. (1977). *Learning to labour: how working class kids get working class jobs.* New York: Columbia University Press.

Wiltshire, S., Amos, A., Haw, S., and McNeill, A. (2005). Image, context and transition: smoking in mid-to-late adolescence. *Journal of Adolescence, 28,* 603–617.

Wittenberg, M. T., and Reis, H. T. (1986). Loneliness, social skills, and social perception. *Personality and Social Psychology Bulletin, 12,* 121–130.

Wolff, S. (1995). *Loners: the life path of unusual children.* London: Routledge.

Woolley, H., and Johns, R. (2001). Skateboarding: the city as a playground. *Journal of Urban Design, 6*(2), 211–230.

World Health Organization (1992). *The ICD-10 classification of mental and behavioural disorders. Clinical descriptions and diagnostic guidelines.* Geneva: World Health Organization.

Wyn, J., and Dwyer, P. (1999). New directions in research on youth in transition. *Journal of Youth Studies, 2,* 5–21.

Wyn, J., and Dwyer, P. (2000). New patterns of youth transition in education. *International Social Science Journal, 2*(164), 147–159.

Xu, Y. Y., Farver, J. A. M., Schwartz, D., and Chang, L. (2004). Social networks and aggressive behaviour in Chinese children. *International Journal of Behavioral Development, 28,* 401–410.

Yoneyama, S., and Naito, A. (2003). Problems with the paradigm: the school as a factor in understanding bullying (with special reference to Japan). *British Journal of Sociology of Education, 24,* 315–330.

Young, K. (1999). *The art of youth work.* Lyme Regis: Russell House.

Youniss, J., and Yates, M. (1997). *Community service and social responsibility in youth*. Chicago: Chicago University Press.

Youniss, J., McLellan, J. A., and Yates, M. (1997). What we know about engendering civic identity. *American Behavioral Scientist, 40*, 620–631.

Youniss, J., McLellan, J. A., Su, Y., and Yates, M. (1999). The role of community service in identity development: normative, unconventional, and deviant orientations. *Journal of Adolescent Research, 14*, 248–261.

Zeldin, S., and Topitzes, D. (2002). Neighborhood experiences, community connection, and positive beliefs about adolescents among urban adults and youth. *Journal of Community Psychology, 30*, 647–669.

Zisman, P., and Wilson, V. (1992). Table hopping in the cafeteria: an exploration of 'racial' integration in early adolescent social groups. *Anthropology and Education Quarterly, 23*, 199–220.

Author index

Subject index

X